D1544879

WITHDRAWN

ROUSSEAU
JUDGE OF JEAN-JACQUES:
DIALOGUES

Dess par Dessin.

J. J. Rousseau.

ROUSSEAU
JUDGE OF JEAN-JACQUES:
DIALOGUES

THE COLLECTED WRITINGS OF ROUSSEAU

Vol. I

EDITED BY

ROGER D. MASTERS AND CHRISTOPHER KELLY

TRANSLATED BY

JUDITH R. BUSH, CHRISTOPHER KELLY

AND ROGER D. MASTERS

PUBLISHED FOR DARTMOUTH COLLEGE
BY
UNIVERSITY PRESS OF NEW ENGLAND
HANOVER AND LONDON

UNIVERSITY PRESS OF NEW ENGLAND

Printed in the United States of America

∞

Library of Congress Cataloging in Publication Data
Rousseau, Jean-Jacques, 1712–1778.
[Rousseau juge de Jean-Jaques. English]
Rousseau, judge of Jean-Jacques, Dialogues / Jean-Jacques Rousseau ;
edited by Roger D. Masters and Christopher Kelly ; translated by
Judith R. Bush, Christopher Kelly, and Roger D. Masters.
p.   cm. — (The Collected writings of Jean-Jacques Rousseau ;
vol. 1)
Translation of: Rousseau juge de Jean-Jaques.
Includes bibliographical references.
ISBN 0–87451–495–9
1. Rousseau, Jean-Jacques, 1712–1778—Authorship. 2. Dialogues,
French—Translations into English. 3. Dialogues, English—
Translations from French. I. Masters, Roger D. II. Kelly,
Christopher, 1950–   . III. Bush, Judith R. IV. Title. V. Series:
Rousseau, Jean-Jacques, 1712–1778. Works. English. 1989 ; vol. 1.
PQ2034.A3   1989 vol. 1
[PQ2040.R8]
848'.509 s—dc20   89–40234
[848'.509]   CIP

5 4 3 2 1

This project has been supported by the National Endowment for the Humanities, a federal agency that supports the study of such fields as history, philosophy, literature, and the languages. Support has also been provided by the French Ministry of Culture—Direction du Livre et de la Lecture, Pro Helvetia, and the National Endowment for the Humanities Translation Fund.

CONTENTS

PREFACE

Although Jean-Jacques Rousseau is a significant figure in the Western tradition, there is no standard edition of his major writings available in English. Unlike those of other thinkers of comparable stature, moreover, many of Rousseau's important works either have never been translated or have become unavailable. The present edition of the *Collected Writings of Rousseau* is intended to meet this need.

Our goal is to produce a series that can provide a standard reference for scholarship that is accessible to all those wishing to read broadly in the corpus of Rousseau's work. To this end, the translations seek to combine care and faithfulness to the original French text with readability in English. Although, as every translator knows, there are often passages where it is impossible to meet this criterion, readers of a thinker and writer of Rousseau's stature deserve texts that have not been deformed by the interpretive bias of the translators or editors.

Wherever possible, existing translations of high quality have been used, although in some cases the editors have felt minor revisions were necessary to maintain the accuracy and consistency of the English versions. Where there was no English translation (or none of sufficient quality), a new translation has been prepared.

Each text is supplemented by editorial notes that clarify Rousseau's references and citations or passages otherwise not intelligible. Although these notes do not provide as much detail as is found in the critical apparatus of Pléiade edition of the *Oeuvres complètes* (which has become the standard for the original French texts), the English-speaking reader should nevertheless have in hand the basis for a more careful and comprehensive understanding of Rousseau than has hitherto been possible.

Each volume is preceded by an introduction situating its contents in the broader context of the thought and career of Jean-Jacques Rousseau. Given the number of Rosseau's works and variety of topics they cover, volumes will be organized by theme and subject rather than in chronological order.

August, 1989   R.D.M.
                                                                       C.K.

CHRONOLOGY
OF ROUSSEAU'S LIFE

1712
Jean-Jacques Rousseau born in Geneva on June 28. His mother dies as a result of complications from childbirth; he is brought up by his aunt, then by his father, Isaac.

1722
Rousseau's father flees Geneva after a quarrel; Rousseau lives with relatives and later becomes an apprentice to an engraver.

1728
Rousseau leaves Geneva, running away from his apprenticeship. He converts to Catholicism, thereby losing his Genevan citizenship.

1742
After years of an unsettled life and self-education, including several periods of study at Les Charmettes in Chambéry (where he was the lover of Mme de Warens), Rousseau arrives in Paris to present his "Project Concerning New Signs for Music" to the Académie des Sciences.

1743–44
Rousseau serves as secretary to the French ambassador to Venice.

1745
Rousseau finishes his opera *The Gallant Muses* and is accused of plagiarism by Rameau. Liaison with Thérèse Levasseur begins. Relations with Diderot, Condillac, Voltaire.

1746
Birth of the first of Rousseau's five illegitimate children, each of whom is sent to the Hospice des Enfants-Trouvés. First stay at Chateau of Chenonceau as secretary to the Dupin family.

1747?
Rousseau writes the *Engagement téméraire*, probably to be performed for the entertainment of the Dupins.

Abridged and modified from "Chronologie de J.-J. Rousseau," *Oeuvres complètes* (Paris: Bibliothèque de la Pléiade), vol I, ci–cxviii. All references to this edition will be to "Pléiade" followed by volume number and page (see p. 259).

1749

Rousseau writes articles on music for the *Encyclopédie*. In October, while on his way to visit Diderot in the Prison of Vincennes, he reads the question proposed by the Academy of Dijon: "Whether the re-establishment of the sciences and the arts has contributed to purifying morals" and forms his "system" of thought (Rousseau's so-called Illumination of Vincennes).

1750

The *Discourse on the Sciences and Arts* (or *First Discourse*) is awarded the prize by the Academy of Dijon and is published at the beginning of the following year.

1751

Rousseau begins his career as a music copyist, an occupation he will practice until the end of his life.

1752

Rousseau composes *The Village Soothsayer*, which is performed before the king at the Chateau of Fontainebleau with great success.

1753

Rousseau writes the *Letter on French Music*, his contribution to the controversy concerning the relative merits of French and Italian music (the "querrelle des Bouffons"). The *Letter* draws sharp reactions, and Rousseau is hanged in effigy by the orchestra of the Paris Opera.

1754

Rousseau reconverts to Protestantism and reacquires his status as a citizen of Geneva.

1755

Publication of the *Discourse on Inequality (Second Discourse)*.

1756

Against the advice of his friends Diderot and Grimm, Rousseau moves to a house in the country (l'Ermitage) offered to him by Mme d'Epinay. He works on manuscripts of the Abbé de Saint-Pierre.

1757

Rousseau quarrels with Diderot over the latter's play *The Natural Son* (in which Diderot used the line "only the bad man lives alone"). Subsequently, he quarrels with Grimm and Mme d'Epinay and leaves his house for another one (Montlouis in Montmorency).

1758

After reading d'Alembert's proposal that Geneva build a theater,

Rousseau writes the *Letter to d'Alembert*. Completion of Rousseau's novel *Julie, or the New Heloise*.

1760–61
Publication of *Julie* in London, then Paris. Completion of *The Social Contract* and *Emile*.

1762
Publication of *Emile* and *The Social Contract*. After *Emile* is condemned and its author's arrest ordered by the Parlement of Paris (June 9), Rousseau flees France. He seeks asylum in the territory of Berne. Geneva burns both *Emile* and *The Social Contract* and decrees Rousseau's arrest (June 19). Bernese government expels Rousseau, who goes to Môtiers (in the territory of Neuchâtel, which is ruled by Frederick II of Prussia). Rousseau writes *Letter to Beaumont*, answering censure of *Emile* by Christophe de Beaumont, the archbishop of Paris.

1763
Completion of the *Dictionary of Music*. *Letter to Beaumont* published; Rousseau renounces his Genevan citizenship.

1764
Rousseau writes *Letters Written from the Mountain*, replying to the criticism of *The Social Contract* published by Tronchin, Procureur Générale of Geneva. Voltaire anonymously publishes the *Sentiment des Citoyens*, announcing Rousseau's abandonment of his children.

1765
After a sermon directed against him and the stoning of his house, Rousseau leaves Môtiers for the Isle of Saint-Pierre on the Lake of Bienne. Expelled by the government of Berne, Rousseau decides to take refuge in England at the invitation of David Hume.

1766
Rousseau goes to England with Hume and de Luze, settling first in Chiswick and then at Wootton, where Rousseau starts writing the *Confessions*. Rousseau soon quarrels with Hume. At the urging of Rousseau's enemies, Hume publishes his version of the quarrel.

1767
Rousseau returns to France under the pseudonym Jean-Joseph Renou, visiting first the Marquis de Mirabeau and then the Prince de Conti at Trye. The *Dictionary of Music* is published.

1768
Rousseau settles in Bourgoin (in the Dauphiné), where he formally marries Thérèse Levasseur.

1770

Rousseau returns to live in Paris and gives first private readings from the *Confessions*, which he had begun in England and recently finished.

1771

After further readings from the *Confessions*, Mme d'Epinay asks the police to forbid Rousseau to give them.

1772

Rousseau finishes *Considerations on the Government of Poland* and begins *Rousseau, Judge of Jean-Jacques* (the *Dialogues*).

1776

Rousseau attempts to deposit the manuscript of the *Dialogues* on the great altar of Notre Dame Cathedral. He gives a copy of the manuscript to Condillac and a copy of the first dialogue to Brooke Boothby.

1776–78

Rousseau writes the *Reveries of the Solitary Walker*.

1778

At the invitation of Girardin, Rousseau moves to Ermenonville, where he dies on July 2.

INTRODUCTION
by Christopher Kelly
and Roger D. Masters

Most students of Rousseau's political thought have tended to ignore his autobiographical writings, or at most to cite passages in which he explains the circumstances in which his obviously theoretical works were written. Those who make greater use of the autobiographical works usually do so in order to interpret Rousseau's thought in the light of his personality. As a rule this approach entails discrediting the theoretical works by exposing Rousseau's personal derangement. Such students follow Burke, who denounced Rousseau's "mad confessions of his mad faults" as part of an attack on the principles of the French Revolution.[1] Only a few scholars have attempted any systematic treatment of the theoretical significance of the autobiographical works.[2]

If this characterization is true for the autobiographical works in general, it is all the more true of *Rousseau, Judge of Jean-Jacques* (more familiarly known as the *Dialogues*). This book has surely been the least read of Rousseau's important works; until recently, most of those who read it seemed primarily interested in the *Dialogues* as evidence of the depth of Rousseau's paranoia. Even a critic who attempts to be sympathetic describes the work by saying, "The terrible paranoid nightmare is frequently illuminated by flashes of extraordinary lucidity and insight."[3] Virtually all of Rousseau's other major works were translated almost immediately upon their publication in French. The present translation of the *Dialogues* is the first to appear in English.

One of the reasons for this long period of neglect is very easy to see. At first or at any subsequent glance, the *Dialogues* is a very peculiar book. It consists of three dialogues between a character named "Rousseau" and an interlocutor identified only as a "Frenchman." The two discuss the bad reputation of a famous author, his true character, a virtually universal conspiracy being conducted against him, and the substance of his books. The "Rousseau" of the *Dialogues* both is and is not Rousseau himself; that is, he is Rousseau as he would be if he had read but not written his books and had only recently arrived in France. The author of the books is "Jean-Jacques," the character to be judged by "Rousseau" and the "Frenchman." This preliminary splitting of Rousseau into two is complicated by further divisions that take place within the discussion. The major additional division is between the author, "Jean-Jacques" as he really is, and his public image as a "monster." This disproportion leads to the suggestion that there are two different people: one of them, "Jean-Jacques," is a monster; the other, the real author of the books, is not. The dizzying quality of these divisions reaches its height when "Rousseau" reports after a visit to "Jean-Jacques" that the latter is composing a series of dialogues about his false public reputation. In effect, the character meets his author at the very moment the author is writing about him (p. 136–137).

Both Rousseau's claim about the existence of a universal conspiracy against him and the procedure of splitting himself into numerous characters, images, and counterimages are cited as major pieces of evidence by those who wish to assert Rousseau's insanity. Nevertheless, it should be recognized that such a procedure is not entirely unique to Rousseau or to presumed madmen. The trilogy of Platonic dialogues formed by the *Theaetetus, Sophist,* and *Statesman* consists of conversations among a cast of characters including Socrates; a boy named Theaetetus, who looks exactly like Socrates; a young friend of Theaetetus who is named Socrates; and a somewhat mysterious Eleatic stranger who questions his interlocutors in a manner that partially (though not completely) resembles that of Socrates himself. One of the major themes of the trilogy is the question of the relationship between images and their originals. Furthermore, the trilogy is partially framed by another dialogue about how Socratic dialogues came to be written and preserved. Thus, Plato apparently thought that a sort of splitting of characters would be dramatically appropriate in the illustration of an important philosophic issue as well as a demonstration of the problematic relationship between a written text and the people or subject matter about which it is written.

The issues involved in the communication or transmission of written philosophic doctrines, which are of immense importance throughout the Platonic corpus, are Rousseau's overriding concern in the *Dialogues.* This work is not overtly concerned with the general issue of the relationship between original and image. It is, however, concerned with a narrow version of this issue: the relationships among Rousseau as he is, as he appears in his books, and as he is perceived by others. It is, above all, the work in which Rousseau undertakes his most comprehensive reflection on the relationships among himself as an author, his books, and his audience. Rousseau's reflections on the misjudgments of his books and the proper way to judge them links the theme of the *Dialogues* to another Platonic dialogue, the *Apology,* in which Socrates both judges and is judged by an audience that does not understand him.

The parallels between the *Apology* and the *Dialogues* are worth noting. In both cases, a philosopher is accused of violating society's legal, ethical, and religious standards; in both, the defense entails presenting the thinker's life and works in a manner that addresses the difference between popular and philosophic judgment; in both, the claim of the philosopher's moral concern for the city is combined with an implicit condemnation of the political life. Despite the autobiographical nature of the *Dialogues,* it—like the *Apology*—is written by an author who is absent from the action of the dialogue. As these parallels suggest, the treatment of these issues within the *Dialogues* makes it worthy of the attention of anyone who hopes to understand the most serious themes within Rousseau's thought.

The Place of the *Dialogues* within Rousseau's "System"

The *Dialogues* has an important place within what Rousseau calls his "system" in part because it is one of the most important contexts in which he claims that he *has* a system. Rousseau first announced the existence of a system in the Preface to *Narcisse,* a defense of the *First Discourse,* which was written in 1753–54 (Pléiade, II, 964).* In the *Dialogues,* he has the "Frenchman" declare that the content of Jean-Jacques's books "were things that were profoundly thought out, forming a coherent system which might not be true, but which offered nothing contradictory" (p. 209). This insight could almost be said to be the culminating moment of the *Dialogues.* Thus, at the end of his literary career, Rousseau reaffirms what he had asserted at the beginning, that his thought is consistent and has been explained consistently in all of his works.

That the *Dialogues* is meant to bring Rousseau's literary enterprise to a sort of completion by stressing the connection of his first and last works is also indicated by Rousseau's choice of epigraph, *"Barbarus hic ego sum quia non intelligor illis"* (Here I am the barbarian because no one understands me). This line from Ovid is also the epigraph of the *First Discourse.* Some reflection on the significance of the shared epigraph can indicate the similarities and differences between the two works. In fact, in the *Dialogues* "Rousseau" insists on the importance of epigraphs for indicating the character of a book (p. 218).

Some scholars have noted that in the *Discourse* the epigraph points to certain complications in the argument that are not immediately apparent.[4]

---

* All references to the definitive French edition of Rousseau's *Oeuvres complètes* (Paris: Bibliothèque de la Pléiade) cite volume and page in this form.

In the first place, it indicates that Rousseau anticipates that his argument will be misunderstood. Second, the epigraph identifies Rousseau himself with one of the very poets he condemns in the text of the *Discourse*. As Rousseau was obliged to point out to his critics time and again, his attack on the arts and sciences is not a blanket condemnation. As he announces in the same title page that contains the epigraph, Rousseau most openly adopts the perspective of the "Citizen of Geneva" when writing the *Discourse*. His epigraph calls attention to his exile from Geneva (and his loss of citizenship) and his less open adoption of the perspective of the poet. Along with its attack on the effect of the arts on healthy communities, the *Discourse* contains a complaint against the degradation of contemporary taste that compels an artist like Voltaire to "lower his genius to the level of his time" (Pléiade, III, 21). In sum, even in his first work, Rousseau was capable of splitting himself into a number of personae in his effort to present the complexities of an argument. He can be both the citizen who objects to the "crowd of obscene authors," including Ovid, and also a spokesman for Ovid himself. He can address himself to citizens, common people, and philosophers in the same work.

The first of these implications of the epigraph is also reflected in the *Dialogues;* although rather than simply predicting a lack of understanding, the citation of Ovid now complains about an existing one. In spite of his efforts to expound his system, Rousseau's thought continues to be misunderstood. This theme of misunderstanding predominates over all others in the *Dialogues*. Here the focus on Rousseau's position as a writer is not subordinated to his position as a citizen. He no longer identifies himself as the "Citizen of Geneva." Rousseau's analysis of Geneva in the *Letters Written from the Mountain* indicates that he came to believe that the Genevans shared the corruption of the French. Accordingly, in the *Dialogues,* his two personae are "Jean-Jacques" the writer and "Rousseau" the reader. "Rousseau" is Genevan, but he only very occasionally shows ardor for his homeland (cf. p. 84).

If the epigraph of the *Dialogues* is not entirely novel for Rousseau, neither is its form. Aside from the dialogue contained in his plays and operas, Rousseau wrote one other dialogue with himself as a character—the second preface to *Julie*. To his interlocutor, who is a man of letters, Rousseau explains why he does not identify himself as a citizen on the title page of this work. Once again he is concerned with misinterpretation of his intentions. Also, some of his responses to the critics of the *First Discourse* resort to a sort of dialogue form as Rousseau quotes individual objections and his responses. He adopts a similar procedure in the *Letter to Beaumont*. Thus, he regularly uses something approaching a dialogue form when he seeks to answer critics or to prevent misunderstanding.

The themes of misunderstanding and self-explanation clearly link the *Dialogues* to its immediate predecessor, the *Confessions*. In his introduction to the *Dialogues*, "On the Subject and Form of This Writing," Rousseau explains the relationship between these two works quite clearly.[5] He indicates that he wrote the *Dialogues* in recognition of a failure of the *Confessions*. He warns:

> As for those who want only some agreeable rapid reading, who sought and found only that in my *Confessions*, and who cannot tolerate a little fatigue or maintain their attention in the interest of justice and truth, they will do well to spare themselves the boredom of reading this. It is not to them I wished to speak, and far from seeking to please them, I will at least avoid the ultimate indignity of seeing that the picture of the miseries of my life is an object of amusement for anyone. (p. 7).

This statement points to the great difference in form between these two autobiographical works and provides some justification for Michel Foucault's characterization of the *Dialogues* as the "anti-*Confessions*."[6] It should be kept in mind, however, that Rousseau's statement is less a criticism of the substance of the *Confessions* than it is a description of the failure of some of that work's readers.

Rousseau claims that those who read the *Confessions* only for pleasure have missed its point. To the extent that this is a criticism of the *Confessions* itself, it implies only that Rousseau made it too easy for his readers to seek pleasure rather than understanding. The *Dialogues*, then, is based on an acknowledgment of the unreliable character of readers. The change in focus from the title *Confessions* to *Rousseau, Judge of Jean-Jacques* indicates this acknowledgment. By confessing to his readers, Rousseau made them his judges as well as his confessors. In the *Dialogues* he has removed the readers from their office: not they but he himself will be the judge of Jean-Jacques.

This acknowledgment of a failure of the *Confessions* and its audience is not a criticism of the substance of the *Confessions*. By showing the proper way to judge Jean-Jacques, the *Dialogues* can be regarded as a sort of training manual for readers of the *Confessions* or indeed for any of Rousseau's other works. Once they have learned from Rousseau how to judge, they can then turn back to the other works and read them properly. Rather than being simply the anti-*Confessions*, the *Dialogues* is the cure for its defects. Whatever defect the *Confessions* may have by being too agreeable a book can be overcome by the more fatiguing *Dialogues*. It is not until his *Reveries of the Solitary Walker*, if even then, that Rousseau decides that his audience is simply uneducable.

This brief sketch of the relationship between the *Dialogues* and several of Rousseau's other works has revealed two different aspects of this baffling work. First, the *Dialogues* brings Rousseau's philosophic system to a sort of completion. Rousseau's reuse of his first epigraph and his device of splitting himself into different characters affirm that his entire body of work is internally consistent and guided by a single purpose. Second, the *Dialogues* focuses special attention on judgments made about Jean-Jacques himself. Rousseau insists on the goodness of his own character and on its being misunderstood. Perhaps the key to understanding the *Dialogues* is to see why these two themes, one theoretical and the other personal, should be contained in the same work. What is the relationship between Rousseau's system and the character of Jean-Jacques?

The Author and His System

A preliminary description of the relationship between Rousseau's system and the character of Jean-Jacques can come from a rephrasing of the question. Whereas the central part of the *Dialogues* is a description of "Jean-Jacques" 's character, the necessity for this description is provided by the false descriptions of "Jean-Jacques" circulating in public opinion. From the beginning of the work, the "real Jean-Jacques" is placed in opposition to his reputation as "an abominable man" or even a "monster" (pp. 8, 12). Furthermore, the character of the monster is opposed to the character of the books, such as *Julie* and *Emile*. "Rousseau" has read the books but as a recent arrival from abroad is unacquainted with the bad reputation of the supposed author. The "Frenchman" knows the reputation, but because of it he has not read the books. The mystery to be solved by these interlocutors is the mystery of the disproportion between the books and the reputation of the author. Are the books exemplars of virtue or of hypocrisy? Are they filled with a subtle and corrupting poison, or have their influential interpreters injected them with venom where there was none before? If the books are filled with virtue, how could they have been written by "soul of mire" (p. 8)? Is the monster "Jean-Jacques" a plagiarist, and if so, who is the real author of these books?

Contained in this series of questions is a Rousseauian account of the importance of the relationships among an author, his books, and his readers. Unlike some of today's critics, he insists that books do or can contain intelligible teachings about matters such as virtue or nature that are in the world outside the texts. On such matters, in principle, the books need no support beyond the force of their arguments and their correspondence to experiences accessible to the readers. In spite of his insistence on the truth of his reasoning, or perhaps because of it, Rousseau is also acutely aware of the difficulties involved in the accurate interpretation of his books. The character "Rousseau" read these books without any prejudices about their author. His position as a recently arrived foreigner gives him a privileged status as a reader.[7] This was a necessary, although not a sufficient, condition for his ability to detect the meaning of the books.

"Rousseau" explains the need to approach the books with an open mind: "Don't even think of the Author as you read, and without any bias either in favor or against, let your soul experience the impressions it will receive. You will thus assure yourself of the intention behind the writing of these books" (p. 31). For readers not in "Rousseau's" fortunate position of ignorance, successful understanding is a profound problem. For this unlucky majority, Rousseau presents the interpretation of the books as dependent in decisive ways on a prior interpretation of the author. Within the *Dialogues,* the first dialogue sets out the issues to be discussed, and the second investigates "Jean-Jacques" 's true character. It is only after this investigation that the third dialogue can describe the content of the books and the proper method for reading them. Thus, at first, the *Dialogues* is less concerned with the status of the author's system than it is with the way that system will be approached by readers. Far from being concerned with a matter of purely personal interest to Rousseau (or of professional interest to students of abnormal psychology), the *Dialogues* is concerned with the effective communication of a philosophic teaching and its dependence on the author's name or reputation.

The issue at the center of the *Dialogues* has both a narrow scholarly importance and a broader political significance. This introduction began by referring to a tradition of Rousseau scholarship that focuses on Rousseau's personality and regards his books purely as expressions of that personality. In effect, the *Dialogues* predicts and attempts to preempt such a critical response. To be sure, modern scholars are more likely to characterize Rousseau as a madman (or as someone suffering from mental illness) than as a monster. As a result, they adopt a condescending tone rather than outright hostility to his works. Like the "Frenchman" of the *Dialogues,* these critics are distracted from the substance of Rousseau's writings because their view of the author's personality makes it inconceivable to them that his works could be profound or true. In Rousseau's account, his works and their system can be rescued from such interpretations only by a defense of his character (unless there are other interpreters who, like the "Rousseau" of the *Dialogues,* come to the works in ignorance of the claims made about Jean-Jacques's character or at least with openness to alternative claims). The *Dialogues* is Rousseau's attempt to avoid depending on such an occurrence.

One explanation of the political aspect of Rousseau's project of forcing his readers to focus on his personality can be seen in his account of the importance of nonrational persuasion in politics. Although one can debate Rousseau's revolutionary intentions and his prudential conservatism, it cannot be denied that Rousseau wished his books to have an influence outside the academy or scholarly conference. From the beginning of his career Rousseau distinguished between what is necessary to win "the approval of a few wise men" and "the approval of the public" (*First Discourse,* Pléiade, III, 3). Although he expresses a preference for the former, he is by no means indifferent to the latter. The importance of this distinction led Rousseau to write in popular forms, such as novels, plays, and autobiography, normally shunned by philosophers and to adopt a decidedly unacademic tone even in his most philosophic works. Although the *Dialogues* must be understood in part as an attempt to defend Rousseau's character before the public, his choice of a less popular form indicates that his true audience is "good minds" rather than seekers of pleasure (p. 7). In sum, the *Dialogues* is a philosophic or unpopular dramatization of the need to influence unphilosophic readers.

In the *Dialogues* the distinction between the philosophic audience and the popular audience is embodied in two characters, "Rousseau" and the "Frenchman," as they begin the discussion. From the beginning "Rousseau" declares: "About things I can judge by myself, I will never take the public's judgments as rule for my own" (p. 19). He resolves to be guided neither by "the secret desires" of his heart nor by "the interpretations of others." In short he insists on being an independent "judge" of "Jean-Jacques" (p. 85). The "Frenchman," on the contrary, is completely dependent on public opinion. His knowledge of "Jean-Jacques" and his books is the product of hearsay. He consistently responds to "Rousseau's" arguments by making appeals to the number of people who are on the other side and to the good character of their authorities. In the end, the "Frenchman" reads and understands the books, but he does so only after he hears the defense of "Jean-Jacques" 's character given in the second dialogue. He may end as a philosophic reader, but he begins as an unphilosophic one. Unlike "Rousseau," his openness to the book is dependent on his opinion of the character of the author. He is the picture of someone enslaved to public opinion because of his trust in the authority of those who direct it.

This connection between trust in the character of the author of a teaching and acceptance of the teaching has an important place in Rousseau's understanding of political life. Frequently he emphasizes the near impotence of reason alone to have an effect on more than a few people (see, for example, Pléiade, IV, 1142–1144 and III, 955). Others can be influenced only by a variety of nonrational methods of persuasion. One might even say that, for Rousseau, the very possibility of social life is constituted by the susceptibility of humans to this nonrational persuasion, a susceptibility that they lack in the isolation of the pure state of nature. Perhaps Rousseau's clearest example of the importance of the authority given by character (although far from his only one) appears in the *Letters Written from the Mountain*, in which he defends *The Social Contract*. In the course of this defense, he explains the success of Christianity. There he distinguishes three different "proofs" of Christian doctrine. The least significant are miracles, which can inspire only those people who are "incapable of coherent reasoning, of slow and sure observation, and slave of the senses in everything" (Pléiade, III, 729). Most certain is the doctrine itself, but this "proof" is understood only by a few. The most important "proof" for the widespread acceptance of the doctrine is the character of those who preach it. Rousseau says that "their sanctity, their veracity, their justice, their morals pure and without stain, their virtues inaccessible to human passions are, along with the qualities of understanding, reason, mind, knowledge, prudence, as many respectable indices, the combination of which, if nothing belies them, form a complete proof in their favor, and say that they are more than men" (Pléiade, III, 728). As this passage makes clear, Rousseau was convinced that the truth of a teaching was insufficient to give it a practical efficacy in the public arena, even, or especially, among good and just people. Thus, the defense of "Jean-Jacques" 's character is indispensable if his system is to have any practical effect. Even fundamentally just people will simply not give a hearing to those who have a bad reputation.[8]

Some who have opposed Rousseau's popular influence have agreed with his analysis of the connection between opinions about his character and that influence. Burke's treatment of Rousseau in his "Letter to a Member of the National Assembly" was mentioned above. There Burke attacks Rousseau on personal grounds much more than on the basis of an analysis of his thought. He justifies this approach by saying, "Your assembly, knowing how much more powerful example is found than precept, has chosen this man (by his own account without a single virtue) for a model."[9] Burke's remark is in complete accord with Rousseau's analysis.

The Place of Rousseau's System within the *Dialogues*

To this point the *Dialogues* can appear as a necessary prelude to Rousseau's system that, if it is successful, predisposes the reader to approach the system with an open mind. As such the *Dialogues* is external to the system; as the precondition of—or even advertisement for—the system, it would not be not a part of the system itself. There are, however, two respects in which the *Dialogues* represents the system. First, there is the description of the system that is given in the third dialogue; second, there is what could be called the drama of the *Dialogues,* which embodies or portrays crucial aspects of the system.

The description of the system given in the third dialogue is a very simple one. Having been convinced of the necessity of reading "Jean-Jacques" 's books by "Rousseau's" account of the author's character in the second dialogue, the "Frenchman" has undertaken the task of deciphering the system. He claims that, among the books of this age, "Jean-Jacques" 's are uniquely difficult to read. They are filled with very paradoxical ideas and maxims (p. 211) as well as apparent contradictions. These real paradoxes and apparent contradictions can be clarified only by a sustained effort of study. At the end of this effort, however, one will discover a clear system, which is based on one main principle and a number of secondary principles, of which the "Frenchman" mentions only one.

The main principle of the system could be called a revolutionary theodicy. The "Frenchman" says, "I saw throughout [the books] the development of his great principle that nature made man happy and good, but that society depraves him and makes him miserable" (p. 213). In its insistence on natural happiness, this principle is a rejection of the Hobbesian, or liberal, understanding of human life outside society as miserable. In its insistence on untainted natural goodness and the social origin of depravity, it is a rejection of the Christian understanding of original sin.[10] The second principle cited by the "Frenchman" limits the revolutionary consequences that might be drawn from the first principle. "But human nature does not go backward, and it is never possible to return to the time of innocence and equality once they have been left behind" (p. 213). It is this secondary principle that accounts for "Jean-Jacques" 's prudential conservatism. Because he has no hopes for the reinstitution of natural goodness, he restricts himself to recommending measures that will mitigate or retard the inevitable corruption. In a work devoted to his public reputation, Rousseau is silent about the possibility of a radical change of society that would cure corruption without a return to nature.

The account of the basic principles of the author's system is useful, but it by no means claims to be a complete exposition. One would like to see a list of the other secondary principles, for example. One should also keep in mind that this characterization of the system is given by the "Frenchman." "Rousseau" warns earlier that one should be careful about attributing to "Jean-Jacques" opinions expressed by characters in his works (pp. 69–70).

The "Frenchman's" account of his reading is an extremely important one, and so is Rousseau's presentation of the results of this reading. The "Frenchman" does not experience the immediate communication of the ideal world portrayed in the first dialogue. He understands "Jean-Jacques" 's books only after he has read them numerous times with particular care. Furthermore, he grasps the basic principles of the writings more obviously than he does their implications and details. Finally, even when he transcribes texts, he makes many small errors, some of which could be attributed to carelessness and others to rewriting passages. He appears to be unable to see exactly what is before his eyes when he reads. Thus, Rousseau reveals or suggests the practical impossibility of a perfect reading even from the most sympathetic and painstaking reader. Even though suggesting that both immediate transparent communication and the lesser goal of a perfect reading of a text are impossible, Rousseau indicates that the "Frenchman" does achieve an essentially correct understanding of both the books and their author. Perfect transparency is impossible, but genuine understanding is merely difficult. Nevertheless, this account can orient the potential reader, who can begin to judge any one of Rousseau's books by seeing how the work in question applies these principles to a particular problem, such as an education that can preserve natural goodness or the options available within particular corrupt societies.

Within the *Dialogues,* the account of the system has an additional function, that of explaining "Jean-Jacques" himself and his relationships with the conspirators. After all, if this system is a true account of human nature, it should be able to explain those most unusual individuals, the discoverer of the system and those who conspire to make him miserable. In fact, the "Frenchman" admits that "his system may be false" (p. 212) but insists that the one thing it unquestionably describes accurately is "Jean-Jacques." "Jean-Jacques" 's account of natural human goodness and happiness depends on his ability to reject the social distortions of human nature. To some extent, or in some sense, he must have moved backward so that he could rediscover nature. "A man had to portray himself to show us primitive man like this" (p. 214). This assertion of "Jean-Jacques" 's own naturalness is only the echo of what "Rousseau" has already asserted about him: "He is what nature made him. Education changed him only a little" (p. 107; see also p. 159). In making this claim of an intimate relationship between the author's personality and his system, "Rousseau" and the "Frenchman" seem to be defending the personality at the expense of the system. The claim that the system is simply a reflection of its author's character is a claim that one would be likely to make to attack any author of a systematic explanation of nature. "Rousseau" and the "Frenchman" are not attacking the system, however. Instead, they are pointing out that "Jean-Jacques" was able to discover the true principles of human nature only because he is the virtually unique example of someone who has "removed the rust" (p. 214) from his own nature. "Jean-Jacques" 's discovery of his system depends on his having acquired some access to primitive nature. For his books to be true, he must be, in some sense, the man of his books.

If "Jean-Jacques" is the incarnation of the great principle of his system, he appears to be the refutation of the second principle; that is, if he is a natural man, he seems to demonstrate that nature can go backward at least in some individuals. To some extent, this is precisely what Rousseau intends to teach. Emile's education, for example, is meant to show how it might be possible for some individual to escape the corruption of a social upbringing.

Although all of this is true, it must also be said that the "Jean-Jacques" of the *Dialogues* bears only a very limited resemblance to the natural humans described in the first part of the *Second Discourse* or to the young Emile. Like these natural humans, he is good, but not virtuous (p. 127), and like them he is free from the distinctive social passion of amour propre. Unlike them, however, he is a knower, a discoverer of a philo-sophic system that is beyond their comprehension. In addition, he pos-sesses the most important natural attribute only in a very qualified sense. Purely natural humans live completely in themselves (Pléiade, IV, 249). Especially, they lack imagination that could take their thoughts from themselves (Pléiade, III, 144). As for "Jean-Jacques," it is true that "he can truly say, in contrast to those people in the Gospel and those in our day, that where his heart is, there too is his treasure" (p. 122),[11] but this means only that he is free from the torment of foresight that plagues the Christian who hopes for salvation or the bourgeois who hopes for wealth. "Jean-Jacques" 's "heart" exercises itself in constantly renewed flights of the imagination; one such flight allowed him to rediscover nature, but others led him to purely imaginary worlds. In the latter flights, even his perception of nature, his "physical sensitivity," is radically altered by his imaginative "moral sensitivity" (pp. 113–130). He sees nature very differently from those natural humans who seek only food and rest. Thus, rather than being a natural human, "Jean-Jacques" is a civilized human who has preserved some natural characteristics along with some radically civilized ones. The manner of being represented by "Jean-Jacques" is one of developed civilized imagination liberated from the corruption of amour propre and foresight. Instead of being a natural human, he is an example of what social humans could be. Even in "Jean-Jacques," nature has not quite gone backward; the irreversible departure from nature has been given a direction that is both salutary and somewhat consistent with nature.

This picture of a quasi-natural civilized human must be understood in contrast to the opposite picture of the conspirators. However implausible one might find Rousseau's presentation of the plot (as as we shall see, the plan is complicated), one must also acknowledge that the conspirators are extreme versions of the corruption Rousseau attributes to social humans in his theoretical works. Whereas "Jean-Jacques" represents civilized imagination liberated from foresight and amour–propre, the conspirators represent civilized imagination enslaved to foresight and amour–propre. The conspirators are the victims of the most extreme departure from nature just as much as they are the vicious perpetrators of a crime against an innocent man. They are immensely powerful, exercising complete control over the government of France and the public opinion of Europe (pp. 76–77). Nevertheless, the direction of this power into a conspiracy against "Jean-Jacques" is a sign of their enslavement. They are obsessed with the future when they take endless precautions to control "Jean-Jacques" 's present and future reputation. Furthermore, they live outside themselves in a much more radical sense than "Jean-Jacques" does, even though they exercise power in the real world and he flees to imaginary worlds. "While he is occupied with himself, they are occupied with him too. He loves himself and they hate him. That is the occupation of both. He is everything to himself; his is also everything to them. As for them, they mean nothing either to him or to themselves" (p. 154–155). Thus, the *Dialogues* presents two different pictures of the extreme possibilities open to civilized humans: seeking one's happiness in flights of imaginative reverie and withdrawal from public life or seeking one's happiness in the distant future and the exercise of power over one's fellows. These are the opposing poles around which civilized humans, unable to go back to the forest and live with the bears and unfortunate not to live in the healthy communities of antiquity, must orient their lives.

The *Dialogues* reveals much about Rousseau's obsession with a conspiracy directed against him by his former friends Diderot and Grimm with the active complicity of both philosophes like Voltaire and d'Alembert and the French government. Surely, a part of this obsession must be attributed (and is attributed by Rousseau himself) to his peculiar personality. For two reasons, however, it would be a mistake to connect the conspiracy solely to Jean-Jacques's psychological condition. First, Rousseau did in fact experience persecution from the French government, the Genevan government (which apparently acted against Rousseau because of pressure from the French government), and other governments. Public demonstrations were, in fact, stirred up against him. Finally, his former friends and his associates actually did make concerted efforts to damage his reputation and financial position. Examples abound to illustrate the ill will of many of Rousseau's contemporaries and of their efforts to act on that ill will.[12]

The second reason for paying attention to Rousseau's discussion of the conspiracy has less to do with Jean-Jacques's personality or mental state. In the *Dialogues,* he claims that he is only incidentally the object of the conspiracy. Its true object is to destroy the current foundation of society and to provide a new one that would solidify the influence of a faction or sect of intellectuals sharing the opinions of Grimm, Diderot, and the others. This charge warrants serious attention because it so precisely mirrors these men's understanding of themselves. Who would want to deny that around the project of Diderot's *Encyclopedia* was united a party or sect linked by both generally shared opinions and interests, that these men and women hoped to modify the traditional basis of public opinion, which they regarded as infamous prejudices; that they hoped to gain influence over the public; and that to do so, they had to act in a more or less conspiratorial way.[13] Rousseau's claim is that the Enlightenment's "party of humanity" is in fact essentially indistinguishable from other parties and that its effects will be pernicious. Thus, the *Dialogues* present in a more radical form arguments against the Enlightenment project that Rousseau had already made in the *First Discourse,* the *Letter to d'Alembert,* and elsewhere. He claims that it is his opposition to this project that causes him to be treated as a traitor.

Conclusion

One would hardly wish to deny that the *Dialogues* contains expressions of Rousseau's mental anguish at the time of its composition. Nevertheless, to be read properly, this work must also be seen as a dramatization of the fundamental principles of Rousseau's systematic thought and his deepest reflections on the problem of making this systematic thought accessible to an audience. By attempting to teach his reader how to judge Jean-Jacques, Rousseau hopes not only to secure his own reputation but also to open the way to an accurate understanding of his thought.

The conclusion of the *Dialogues* and, still more, the postscript called "History of the Preceding Writing" indicate that Rousseau was not optimistic about prospects for the success of his work. In the latter, Rousseau seems to abandon hope of finding the sort of readers who can understand his work. Even in the *Dialogues* itself, the converted "Frenchman" and "Rousseau" conclude only that they will offer consolation to "Jean-

Jacques" and work unobtrusively to preserve his works for the day they can be appreciated as they deserve. Rousseau's principle that nature never goes backward and that, at best, corruption can only be retarded implies that proper judgments about Jean-Jacques and his system will be rare indeed: his readers will all be more or less denatured and corrupt. If it is true that the denaturing undergone by civilized humans removes them so far from primitive nature that they cannot recognize it (p. 147), it is hard to see how Rousseau could expect any readers to understand either him or his system. In fact, near the conclusion of the *Dialogues*, "Rousseau" suggests that people will recover "those innate feelings that nature has engraved on all hearts" only after the depth of corruption has been reached (p. 242). It will only be at this point that a general appreciation of "Jean-Jacques" and his system could occur. In other words, the complete, popular success of the *Dialogues* depends on changes in human nature that Rousseau considers himself powerless to bring about. If the principles of Rousseau's system are true, he is constantly faced with the paradoxical relationship between the author and his readers that is the theme of the *Dialogues*.

The *Dialogues* itself can overcome that paradox for only a few readers who have avoided the general corruption. Only these few can join "Rousseau" in judging "Jean-Jacques."

NOTE ON THE TEXT
AND ITS TITLE

Rousseau tells the story of the composition of *Rousseau juge de Jean-Jaques—Dialogues* in the "History of the Preceding Writing" appended to the work (see pp. 246–257 below). There are no apparent reasons for doubting the details of his account. He wrote the work over a period of four years, beginning sometime in 1772 and concluding by the beginning of 1776, at which time he tried and failed to deposit a copy of the work on the great altar of Notre Dame.

Rousseau returned to France in 1767 after an exile that began shortly after the publication and condemnation of *Emile* in 1762. For almost three years he lived under the pseudonym Jean-Joseph Renou to avoid prosecution, but in 1770 he resumed the use of his own name and moved openly to Paris. In the years immediately following his return to France, he completed the *Confessions* and wrote the *Considerations on the Government of Poland*. Aside from the composition of the *Dialogues*, the period 1772 to 1776 represents a lull in Rousseau's literary career after the astonishing productivity of the preceding twenty years. In addition to his daily fifteen minutes of work on the *Dialogues*, Rousseau restricted himself to his profession of copying music (around 11,200 pages in seven years), his hobby of botany, and a little composing.

There are three (or perhaps four) complete manuscripts of the *Dialogues* and an additional manuscript of the First Dialogue. The complete manuscripts include the one that Rousseau brought to Notre Dame and then gave to Condillac (see pp. 249–250 below). Rousseau gave a second copy to the Count d'Angevilliers. This manuscript has either disappeared or is the same as one in the library of the Palais Bourbon, the origin of which is otherwise unclear. Rousseau gave a third manuscript to the Genevan minister Paul Moultou in 1778. The additional manuscript of the First Dialogue was given to the Englishman Brooke Boothby in 1776.[1]

Boothby published the First Dialogue in London in 1780, not long after Rousseau's death, in spite of the intense opposition of some of Rousseau's friends. The three dialogues were published in 1782 with numerous cuts. The first complete publication of the text occurred in Volume 1 of the *Oeuvres complètes* published by the Bibliothèque de la

Pléiade in 1958. This translation is based on the Pléiade edition, which relies on the latest manuscript, the one given to Moultou in 1778.

In the Geneva manuscript there is no title given for the work as a whole, although the title *Rousseau juge de Jean-Jaques* appears at the head of the First Dialogue. In the London manuscript this title appears at the head of the entire work and is followed by a subtitle, *Dialogues*, and the epigraph *Barbarus hic ego sum, quia non intelligor illis*. This manuscript also gives titles to the three dialogues: "On the system of conduct with respect to J. J. adopted by the administration with the approbation of the public," "On the nature of J. J. and his habits," and "On the spirit of his books and conclusions."

As a rule scholars refer to *Rousseau juge de Jean-Jaques—Dialogues* by the short title *Dialogues*. In so doing they link it with the other so-called autobiographical works, the *Confessions* and the *Reveries* (which is also shortened from its complete title, *Les Rêveries du promeneur solitaire*). The short title is convenient, but its absence from some of the manuscripts suggests that the longer title has the better claim to be Rousseau's own choice.

The translation of the long title into English poses some difficulties because the word *juge* can be either a noun or a verb in French. This ambiguity cannot be preserved in English. The few scholars who have translated this title are divided between *Rousseau Judges Jean-Jacques* and *Rousseau, Judge of Jean-Jacques*.[2] We have elected the latter for a number of reasons, none of which could be said to exclude the alternative. The reader should attempt to keep the ambiguity in mind.

Rousseau's use of the noun and the verb does not decisively indicate one translation over the other. The expression "the judges of Jean-Jaques" (*les juges de Jean-Jaques*) occurs once in the work (p. 76; Pléiade, I, 761). In this context it refers to those who judge "Jean-Jacques" incorrectly. Rousseau, the character in the *Dialogues*, can be understood as the proper judge of "Jean-Jacques." The expression to "judge about him" (*juge de lui*) occurs three times (pp. 125, 194, 222; Pléiade, I, 821, 910, 947) and in each case "him" refers to "Jean-Jacques." It is also worth noting that Rousseau characteristically uses the verb form *juger de* to refer to judging in a broad sense. For the strict legal sense he usually employs simply *juger*.

Our choice of title, *Rousseau, Judge of Jean-Jacques*, should not be read as suggesting that the character "Rousseau" is the subject of the *Dialogues*, because "Jean-Jacques" is in fact the center of attention. The titles of the individual dialogues referred to above indicate that the attention paid to "Jean-Jacques" follows a course of development. Whereas the First Dialogue begins by placing special emphasis on the need for a proper legal verdict concerning the alleged crimes of "Jean-Jacques" (see p. 57–65; Pléiade, I, 733–743), the later dialogues turn into a wider investigation of his character and his books as "Rousseau" learns about the character of "Jean-Jacques" and as the other interlocutor, the Frenchman, learns to judge his books. Both characters demonstrate how to judge, and by doing so they invite the reader first to learn and then to share their activity.

Special thanks are due to Peter Stillman for helpful comments on the manuscript.

ROUSSEAU
JUDGE OF JEAN-JACQUES:
DIALOGUES

Barbarus hic ego sum, quia non intelligor illis.
Ovid. *Tristia*[1]

If I dared address a prayer to those into whose hands this writing will fall, it would be to read all of it before making use of it and even before talking about it with anyone. But very certain beforehand that this favor will not be granted to me, I keep silent and give over everything to providence.

ON THE SUBJECT AND FORM
OF THIS WRITING[2]

I have often said that if someone had given me ideas about another man like those my contemporaries have been given about me, I would not have behaved toward him as they do toward me. This assertion has left everyone utterly indifferent, and I have not seen in anyone the least curiosity about how my behavior would have differed from that of others, and what my reasons would have been. I have concluded from this that the public—perfectly sure of the impossibility of acting more justly or more honestly than it does with respect to me—was consequently sure that in my assumption I would have been wrong not to imitate it. In the public's self-confidence, I have even believed I noticed a haughty disdain that could come only from a high opinion of its own virtue and that of its guides in this matter. All that being concealed from me by an impenetrable mystery which cannot be reconciled with my reasons, I have been prompted to state my reasons in order to submit them to anyone who would be kind enough to correct me. For if my error exists, it is not without consequence. It forces me to think ill of everyone around me; and since nothing is further from my wishes than to be unjust and ungrateful toward them, those who would disabuse me by bringing me back to better judgments would substitute gratitude for indignation in my heart, and would make me appreciative[3] and thankful by showing me my duty to be so. That is not, however, the only motive that has prompted me to take pen in hand. Another that is stronger and no less legitimate will make itself felt in this writing. But I declare that in these motives there is no longer the hope or even the desire to get at last, from those who have judged me, the justice they deny me and are very determined to deny me forever.[4]

In wishing to complete this task, I found myself in a most unusual quandary! The problem was not to find reasons in favor of my feeling, but to imagine any opposing ones, to establish a semblance of equity for actions where I saw none whatsoever. Yet seeing all Paris, all France, all Europe behave toward me with the greatest confidence on the basis of maxims that are so new and so inconceivable to me, I could not assume that this unanimous agreement was without any reasonable or at least apparent foundation, and that a whole generation would agree to suppress wantonly all natural enlightenment, to violate all the laws of justice, all the rules of good sense, without purpose, without profit, without pretext, uniquely to gratify a whim whose goal and cause I could not even glimpse. The profound, universal silence—no less inconceivable than the mystery it veils, a mystery that has been hidden from me for fifteen years with a care that I refrain from characterizing and with a success that appears extraordinary—this terrifying and terrible silence has kept me from grasping the least idea that could clarify these strange attitudes for me. Left to my conjectures for all enlightenment, I have not been able to formulate any explanation of what is happening to me such that I could believe I had unraveled the truth. Sometimes when strong clues have led me to think I had discovered the purpose and authors of the intrigue along with its foundation, the numberless absurdities I saw arising from these assumptions soon forced me to abandon them; and all those which my imagination has troubled itself to put in their place have not stood up any better to the slightest scrutiny.

Yet in order not to fight a chimera, not to slander a whole generation, it was necessary to assume some reasons on the side approved and followed by everyone. I spared nothing in seeking them, in imagining those likely to seduce the multitude; and if I found none that could have produced that effect, Heaven is my witness that it is not for lack of will or efforts, and that I carefully collected all the ideas my understanding could supply for that purpose. When all my efforts led to nothing that could satisfy me, I made the only choice left to reach an explanation: being unable to argue on the basis of private motives that were unknown and incomprehensible to me, I would reason on the basis of a general hypothesis that could combine them all. This was to choose, from among all possible assumptions, the one that was worst for me, best for my adversaries, and from that vantage point—as well adapted as possible to the maneuvers of which I have seen myself to be the target, the demeanors I have glimpsed, the mysterious comments I have overheard here and there—to examine what would have been the most reasonable and most just behavior on their part. Exhausting everything that could be said in their favor was the only means I had to discover what they say in fact; and this is what I have tried to do, attributing to them all plausible motives and specious arguments, and collecting all imaginable charges against myself. Despite all that, I admit I often blushed at the reasons I was forced to ascribe to them. If I had found better ones, I would have used them with all my heart and strength, and all the more easily in that I am certain none would have held up against my replies, because these are derived immediately from the first principles of justice and first elements of good sense, and are applicable to all possible cases of a situation like mine.

As the dialogue form appeared to me best suited to discuss the pros and cons, I chose it for that reason. In these conversations I took the liberty of resuming my family name, which the public judged it appropriate to take from me, and following its example, I refer to myself as a third party, using my Christian name to which the public chose to reduce me. By making my other interlocutor a Frenchman, I did nothing that was not obliging and decent for the name he bears, since I refrained from making him an accomplice in the behavior I disapprove, and I would have done nothing unjust in portraying him here with the traits that his whole nation eagerly displays toward me. I even took the trouble to bring him back to more reasonable feelings than those I have found in any of his compatriots, and the person I placed on stage is such that it would be as fortunate for me as it would be honorable to his country if he were imitated by many there. If I sometimes engage him in absurd reasoning, I state most sincerely at the outset that it is always despite myself, and I believe I can challenge all France to find more solid reasoning to justify the singular practices focused on me, in which that country appears to glorify itself so much.

What I had to say was so clear and I felt it so deeply that I am amazed by the tediousness, repetitiousness, verbiage, and disorder of this writing. What would have made it lively and vehement coming from another's pen is precisely what has made it dull and slack coming from mine. The subject was myself, and I no longer found on my own interest that zeal and vigor of courage which can exalt a generous soul only for another person's cause. The humiliating role of my own defense is too much beneath me, too unworthy of the feelings that inspire me for me to enjoy undertaking it. Nor, as it will soon be felt, is that the role I wanted to assume here. But I could not examine the public's behavior regarding me without viewing myself in the most deplorable and cruel position in the world. I had to focus on sad and harrowing ideas, bitter and revolting memories, feelings that are least suited to my heart. And it was to that state of sorrow and distress that I had to return every time some new outrage, countering my repugnance, made me renew the effort to continue this frequently abandoned writing. Unable to endure such a sorrowful occupation continuously, I engaged in it for brief moments only, writing each idea as it came to me and then stopping, writing the same thing ten times if it came to me ten times, without ever recalling what I wrote previously, and becoming aware of it only when reading the whole thing, too late to make corrections, as I shall explain shortly. Anger sometimes stimulates talent, but disgust and heartbreak stifle it. And after reading this, it will be felt that those had to be the constant dispositions in which I found myself during this painful labor.

Another difficulty made it tiring for me: it was, forced to speak ceaselessly about myself, to speak with justice and truth, without praise and without deprecation. That is not hard for a man who is honored as he deserves by the public. He is thereby dispensed from taking the trouble to do so himself. He can equally well be silent without demeaning himself, or frankly attribute to himself the qualities that everyone sees in him. But how will the person who feels worthy of honor and esteem, yet whom the public freely disfigures and defames, adopt a tone that does himself justice? Should he speak of himself with praise that is merited but generally denied? Should he boast of the qualities he feels he has but which everyone refuses to see? There would be less pride than baseness in thus prostituting the truth. Praising oneself in these circumstances, even with the most rigorous justice, would be degrading oneself rather than doing oneself honor, and it would show little understanding of men to believe that such protestation can dissuade them about an error in which they choose to believe. A proud, disdainful silence is more appropriate in such a case, and would have been more to my taste. But it would not have fulfilled my purpose, and to do so I had necessarily to say how, if I were someone else, I would view a man such as myself. I have tried to discharge such a difficult duty equitably and impartially—without insulting the incredible blindness of the public, without proudly boasting about those virtues it refuses to see in me, yet without accusing myself of vices I do not have, with which it takes pleasure in charging me—by explaining simply what I would deduce about a constitution like mine carefully studied in another man. If restraint and moderation are found in my descriptions, let me not be given credit for that. I declare that if I only had a little more modesty, I would have spoken much more honorably about myself.

Seeing the excessive length of these dialogues, I tried several times to prune them, eliminate the frequent repetitions, and introduce some order and continuity. I could never bear this new torment. The lively feeling of my misfortunes revived by this reading stifles all the attention it requires. It is impossible for me to retain anything, collate two sentences, and compare two ideas. As I force my eyes to follow the lines, my oppressed heart moans and sighs. After frequent and futile attempts, I renounce this labor of which I feel incapable, and for want of being able to do better, I confine myself to transcribing these formless essays which I am in no condition to correct. Even as they are, if the work were still to be done, I would not do it for anything in the universe. I am even forced to abandon multitudes of ideas that are better or better expressed than those which are here, ideas I had scribbled on scraps of paper hoping I could easily incorporate them. But despondency has overcome me to the point where even this little bit of work is impossible. After all, I have said just about everything I had to say. It is drowned in a chaos of disorder and repetitions, but it is there. Good minds will be able to find it. As for those who want only some agreeable rapid reading, who sought and found only that in my *Confessions,* and who cannot tolerate a little fatigue or maintain their attention in the interest of justice and truth, they will do well to spare themselves the boredom of reading this. It is not to them I wished to speak, and far from seeking to please them, I will at least avoid the ultimate indignity of seeing that the picture of the miseries of my life is an object of amusement for anyone.

What will become of this writing? What use could I make of it? I do not know, and this uncertainty has added greatly to the discouragement that never left me while I worked on it. Those who dispose of me knew about it as soon as it was begun, and given my situation, I see no possible way to keep it from falling into their hands sooner or later.* Thus, following the natural course of events, all the trouble I have taken is a total waste. I do not know what choice Heaven will suggest to me, but I shall hope until the end that it will not abandon the just cause. Into whatever hands Heaven makes these pages fall, if there may still be a human heart among those who read them, that is enough for me, and I will never despise the human species so much that I will not find in that idea some reason for confidence and hope.

* The unhappy history of this work found at the end of these dialogues tells how this prediction proved true.[5]

FIRST DIALOGUE

Rousseau

What incredible things I have just learned! I can't get over it. No, I will never get over it. Just heaven, what an abominable man! How he has hurt me! How I am going to detest him!

A Frenchman

And take note that this is the same man whose pompous productions charmed you so, carried you away with the beautiful precepts of virtue he displays in them with such ostentation.

Rousseau

Say with such strength. Let's be just, even with the wicked. At most, ostentation elicits cold, sterile admiration, and will surely never charm me. Writings that elevate the soul and enflame the heart deserve another word.

The Frenchman

Ostentation or strength, what does the word matter if the idea is the same, and if this sublime jargon, drawn out of an impassioned head by hypocrisy, is no less dictated by a soul of mire?

Rousseau

This choice of a word seems less indifferent to me than to you. For me it greatly changes the ideas, and if there were only ostentation and jargon in the writings of the Author you portrayed, he would horrify me less. A perverse man, whose heart hardens listening to dry sermons and preachings, might examine himself and become a decent man if one knew how to seek and revive in his heart those feelings of rectitude and humanity which nature places there in reserve and which the passions stifle. But someone who can coldly contemplate virtue in all its beauty, who can portray its most touching charms without being moved by them, without feeling struck by any love of virtue, such a being, if he can exist, is hopelessly wicked; he is a moral cadaver.

The Frenchman

What do you mean, if he can exist? Given the effect this wretch's writings have had on you, what do you mean by this doubt after the discussion we have just had? Explain yourself.

Rousseau

I'll explain what I mean, but it will be either the most useless or most superfluous of efforts, since everything I will say to you can be understood only by those to whom there is no need to say it.

Picture an ideal world similar to ours, yet altogether different.[6] Nature is the same there as on our earth, but its economy is more easily felt, its order more marked, its aspect more admirable. Forms are more elegant, colors more vivid, odors sweeter, all objects more interesting. All nature is so beautiful there that its contemplation, inflaming souls with love for such a touching tableau, inspires in them both the desire to contribute to this beautiful system and the fear of troubling its harmony; and from this comes an exquisite sensitivity which gives those endowed with it immediate enjoyment unknown to hearts that the same contemplations have not aroused.

There as here, passions are the motive of all action, but they are livelier, more ardent, or merely simpler and purer, thereby assuming a totally different character. All the first movements of nature are good and right. They aim as directly as possible toward our preservation and our happiness, but soon lacking strength to maintain their original direction through so much resistance, they let themselves be deflected by a thousand obstacles which, turning them away from their true goal, make them take oblique paths where man forgets his original destination. Erroneous judgment and the strength of prejudices contribute a great deal to our being thus misled. But this effect comes mainly from weakness of the soul, which—effortlessly following nature's impulse—is deflected on colliding with an obstacle, just as a ball takes the angle of reflection, whereas something that pursues its course with more vigor is not deflected, but like a cannonball pushes the obstacle away or is destroyed and falls on contact.[7]

The inhabitants of the ideal world I am talking about have the good fortune to be maintained by nature, to which they are more attached, in that happy perspective in which nature placed us all, and because of this alone their soul forever maintains its original character. The primitive passions, which all tend directly toward our happiness, focus us only on objects that relate to it, and having only the love of self as a principle, are all loving and gentle in their essence. But when they are deflected from their object by obstacles, they are focused on removing the obstacle rather than reaching the object; then they change nature and become irascible and hateful. And that is how the love of self, which is a good and absolute feeling, becomes amour-propre, which is to say a relative feeling by which one makes comparisons; the latter feeling demands preferences, whose enjoyment is purely negative, and it no longer seeks satisfaction in our own benefit but solely in the harm of another.[8]

In human society, as soon as the host of passions and prejudices it engenders has misled man, and the obstacles it amasses have deflected him away from the true goal of our life, the only recourse of the wise man—battered by the constant collision of others' passions and of his own, and no longer able to discern among the many directions that lead him astray the one that would direct him correctly—is to withdraw from the crowd as much as possible and remain patiently wherever he chances to be, with the certainty that by not acting, he at least avoids rushing to his destruction and committing new errors. Since he sees in the agitation of men only the madness he wishes to avoid, he pities their blindness even more than he hates their malice, he does not fret about returning evil for evil, insult for insult; and while he sometimes seeks to parry his enemies' thrusts, he does so without trying to retaliate, without arousing his passion against them, without leaving either his place or the calm he wishes to maintain.

Our inhabitants, following less profound views, reach almost the same goal by the opposite route, and it is their very ardor that maintains their inaction. The heavenly state to which they aspire, and which becomes their prime need through the strength with which it appeals to their hearts, makes them ceaselessly concentrate and direct all the powers of their soul to attain it. The obstacles that hold them back cannot occupy them to the point of making them forget for a moment. And this is what causes their extreme disgust for everything else and their total inaction when they despair of attaining the sole object of all their wishes.

This difference comes not only from the kind of passions but also from their strength, for strong passions cannot be led astray as others can. Two lovers, one very infatuated, the other rather indifferent, will nonetheless be equally irritated by a rival, the one because of his love, the other because of his amour-propre. But it may very well happen that the latter's hatred, having become his principal passion, will outlive his love and even grow after that love is dead; whereas the former, who hates only because he loves, stops hating his rival as soon as he no longer fears him. Now if weak and indifferent souls are more subject to passions of hatred, which are only secondary and deflected passions; and if great and strong souls, maintaining their original direction, better preserve the gentle, primitive passions born directly from the love of self, you can see how, in the inhabitants of that other world, passions very different from those which tear apart unhappy human beings here are derived from greater energy of the faculties and from an original relationship which is better felt. Perhaps people in those regions are not more virtuous than those around us, but they know how to love virtue better there. Nature's true inclinations being all good, in surrendering to them, people there are themselves good, whereas virtue among us often requires fighting and conquering nature, and they are rarely capable of such efforts. Long unfamiliarity with resisting can even weaken their souls to the point of doing evil through weakness, fear, or necessity. They are not exempt from either faults or vices. Even crime is not foreign to them, for there are deplorable situations in which the highest virtue is scarcely enough to guard against it and which force a weak man to do evil despite his heart. But the express will to harm, venomous hatred, envy, baseness, betrayal, deceit are unknown. Too often, guilty people are seen there; a wicked one has never been seen. Finally, if they are not more virtuous than people are here, they are at least less ill-disposed toward others if only because they know better how to love themselves.

They are also less active, or to state it better, less restless. Their efforts to get the object they contemplate consist in vigorous thrusts, but as soon as they feel their impotence, they stop without looking within reach for equivalents of that unique object which is the only thing that can tempt them.

Since they do not seek their happiness in appearances but rather in intimate feelings, they expend little energy trying to move from the rank in which fortune has placed them. They hardly seek to rise and would move down without repugnance to relationships more to their taste, since they know very well that the happiest status is not that which the crowd honors most but rather that which makes the heart most content. Prejudices have very little hold on them, opinion does not lead them, and when they feel its effect, it isn't they who are subjugated, but those who influence their fate.

Although sensuous and voluptuous, they make light of opulence, and do nothing to acquire it, knowing the art of enjoyment too well to be ignorant of the fact that true pleasure cannot be bought for money. And as for the good a rich man can do, they also know it is not the man but his wealth which does it; that the wealth would do better still without the man if it were divided among many or rather eliminated by this distribution; and that all the good a rich man thinks he does through his wealth rarely equals the real evil that must be done to acquire it. Besides, as they love their freedom even more than their comforts, they would fear having to buy these with wealth, if only because of the dependency and complications connected with the care of preserving it. The inseparable retinue of opulence would burden them a hundred times more than they enjoy the sweetness of whatever good they would derive from it. The torment of possession would poison for them all the pleasure of its enjoyment.

Thus bounded on all sides by nature and reason, they stop and spend life enjoying it, doing each day whatever seems good for themselves and beneficial for others, without regard to the estimation of men and the caprices of opinion.[9]

The Frenchman

I'm racking my brain unsuccessfully to see what these fantastic beings you describe have in common with the monster we were just talking about.

Rousseau

Nothing, without a doubt, and I believe that to be the case. But let me finish.

Beings who are so uniquely constituted must necessarily express themselves in other ways than ordinary men. It is impossible that with souls so differently modified, they should not carry over into the expression of their feelings and ideas the stamp of those modifications. If this stamp is not noticed by those who have no notion of that manner of being, it cannot escape the notice of those who know it and are themselves affected by it. It is a characteristic sign, by which initiates recognize one another; and what gives great value to a sign so little known and even less used is that it cannot be counterfeit, it can never act except at the level of its source, and when it does not come from the heart of those who imitate it, it does not reach those hearts capable of distinguishing it. But as soon as it reaches them, it cannot be mistaken; it is true as soon as it is felt. It manifests itself most surely in the entire conduct of life, rather than in a few scattered actions. But in lively situations where the soul is involuntarily exalted, the initiate quickly distinguishes between his brother and the person who without being so wants only to adopt its accent; and this distinction makes itself felt equally in writings.[10] The inhabitants of the enchanted world write few books in general, and do not arrange to write them; it is never a profession for them. When they do write, they have to be forced to do so by a stimulus stronger than interest and even glory. This stimulus—difficult to contain, impossible to counterfeit—makes itself felt in everything it produces. A felicitous discovery to publicize, a beautiful and great truth to share, a general and pernicious error to combat, or some matter of public utility to establish: these are the only motives that can bring them to take up the pen. And even then the ideas must be new enough, beautiful enough, striking enough to put their zeal in effervescence[11] and force it to express itself. In their world there is no proper time or age for this. Since writing is not a profession for them, they will begin or end early or late, depending upon the stimulus that provokes them. When someone has said what he has to say, he will remain tranquil as before, without leaping into the literary fray, without feeling that ridiculous urge to repeat himself over and over, and scribble endlessly on paper, an urge which is said to be part of the profession of Author.

And one who may have been born with genius will never suspect it himself and will die without being known by anyone if no object activates his zeal to the point of forcing it to show itself.

The Frenchman

My dear M. Rousseau. You certainly look to me like one of the inhabitants of that world.

Rousseau

I recognize one at least, without any doubt, in the Author of *Emile* and *Heloise*.

The Frenchman

I saw that conclusion coming. But to grant you all these obscure fictions, you must first be consistent: having appeared convinced of that man's abominations, here you are praising him to the skies because he has written novels. As for me, I understand nothing of these enigmas. I beg you to tell me, for once, your true feeling about him.

Rousseau

I have told you without mystery and I will repeat it for you without evasion. The strength of your proofs leaves me with no doubt whatever about the crimes they attest, and about that I think exactly as you do. But you combine things that I separate. The Author of the Books and of the crimes appears to you to be the same person. I believe I am correct to see them as two. That, Sir, is the key to the enigma.

The Frenchman

How can that be, I ask you. This strikes me as something entirely new.

Rousseau

Incorrectly, I think. Didn't you tell me that he is not the Author of *The Village Soothsayer*?

The Frenchman

I did, and it is a fact no one doubts any longer. But as for his other works, I have not yet heard anyone doubt his authorship.

Rousseau

Yet the second account seems to me a consequence quite related to the first. But to judge their relationship better, it is necessary to know what proof they have that he is not the Author of the *Soothsayer*.[12]

The Frenchman

The proof! There are a hundred of them, all authoritative.

Rousseau

That's a lot. I will be satisfied with one. But for good reason, I want it to be independent of another person's testimony.

The Frenchman

Very willingly! Therefore without talking to you about the well-attested plagiarisms of which this piece has been shown to be composed, without even stressing the question of whether he knows how to versify and therefore whether he could have written the verses of *The Village Soothsayer*, I will rely on something more positive and certain. He does not know music. From this one can conclude with certainty, in my opinion, that he did not write the music of that Opera.

Rousseau

He does not know music! Now there is another discovery I never would have suspected.

The Frenchman

Don't take it on faith from me or from anyone else, but verify it yourself.

Rousseau

If I had to overcome my horror of approaching the person you just depicted, it surely would not be to prove whether he knows Music. The question is not of sufficient interest in relation to such a scoundrel.

The Frenchman

It must have appeared less indifferent to our Gentlemen than to you. Because the incredible trouble they took and still take daily to establish this proof more solidly among the public exceeds all they did to uncover proof of his crimes.

Rousseau

That strikes me as rather bizarre, because once the larger issue has been well proved, one does not usually get so excited about proving the smaller.

The Frenchman

Oh, with respect to such a man, nothing large or small should be overlooked. The love of truth joins together with the horror of vice to destroy an usurped reputation in all its ramifications; and those who were eager to show that he is a detestable monster must be no less eager now to show that he is a little plagiarist without talent.

Rousseau

You must admit that this man's destiny has some striking peculiarities. His life is divided into two parts that seem to belong to two different individuals, with the period that separates them—meaning the time when he published books—marking the death of one and the birth of the other.[13]

The first, a peaceful, gentle man, was well liked by all who knew him, and his friends remained faithful to him. Little suited to large social groups by his timidity and his tranquil nature, he liked seclusion not in order to live alone, but to bring together the sweetness of study and the charms of intimacy. He consecrated his youth to the cultivation of beautiful knowledge and pleasing talents, and when he needed to draw on these acquisitions to subsist, he did this so discreetly and unostentatiously that the people who were closest to him did not even imagine he had enough wit to write books. His heart, made for attachments, was given without reservation. Obliging toward his friends to the point of weakness, he allowed himself to be subjugated by them in such a way that he could no longer remove that yoke with impunity.

The second—a hard, fierce, gloomy man—earns the loathing of everyone he flees, and in his awful misanthropy takes pleasure only in displaying his hatred of the human race. The first—alone, without study, and without a teacher—conquered all difficulties by means of zeal, and consecrated his leisure not to idleness or even less to harmful works, but to filling his head with charming ideas, his heart with delightful feelings, and to formulating projects—chimerical, perhaps, because they were useful— whose execution, had it been possible, would have brought happiness to the human race.[14] The second—all caught up in his odious schemes— was unable to give any of his time or his mind to pleasant occupations, let alone to useful viewpoints. Throwing himself into the most brutal debauchery, he spent his life in taverns and houses of ill-repute, burdened with all the vices one brings or contracts, having nurtured only the dissolute and base tastes that are inseparable from such places. His ignoble inclinations are in ridiculous contrast to the lofty products he has the audacity to claim. He appeared in vain to leaf through books and attend to philosophic research. He understood nothing, conceived of nothing but his horrible systems; and after supposed attempts whose only goals were to impose on the human race, he ended as he had begun, by knowing only how to do evil.

Finally, without drawing this comparison out to all its ramifications, and to end with the one that led me to it, the first—timid to the point of stupidity—scarcely dared to show his friends the works of his leisure time. The second—with an even more stupid impudence—proudly and publicly attributed to himself the works of others about the things he understood least. The first was passionately fond of music, made it his principal occupation, and was successful enough to make discoveries, find flaws, suggest corrections. He spent a large part of his life among performers and music lovers, at times composing music of all types on various occasions, at times writing about this art, proposing new viewpoints, giving composition lessons, verifying through tests the advantages of the methods he proposed, and always proving himself more knowledgeable in all aspects of this art than most of his contemporaries, of whom several in truth were better versed in some aspect than he, but none of whom better understood the whole and followed its relationships.[15] The second—so inept that he was involved with music for forty years without ever being able to learn it—was reduced to the occupation of copying music for want of being able to compose it. Even though he does not find himself learned enough for his chosen trade, that does not stop him from claiming with stupid shamelessness that he is the Author of things he cannot perform. You will admit that such contradictions are hard to reconcile.

The Frenchman

Less so than you believe, and if your other enigmas were no more obscure than that, you would have me less in suspense.

Rousseau

Enlighten me about this one, then, whenever you choose, because as for me I profess I don't understand it at all.

The Frenchman

Willingly and with ease; but begin by clarifying your question for me.

Rousseau

There is no longer any question about the fact you have just revealed. In that respect we are in perfect agreement and I fully espouse your conclusion, but I would carry it further. You say that a man who can write neither music nor verse did not write *The Village Soothsayer*, and that is incontestable. I would add that the person who falsely pretends to be the Author of that Opera is not even the Author of the other works that bear his name, and this is scarcely less evident. For if he did not write the words of the *Soothsayer* since he does not write verse, he did not write the *Allée de Sylvie*, which can hardly be the work of a scoundrel. And if he did not write the music for it since he does not know music, he did not write the *Letter on French Music* either, nor still less the *Dictionary of Music*, which can only be the work of a man versed in that art and knowing composition.[16]

The Frenchman

I don't share your feeling about that, nor does the public, and we have in addition the opinion of a great foreign Composer who has recently come to this country.[17]

Rousseau

And I ask you, do you know this foreign composer well? Do you know why and by whom he was called to France, what motives prompt him suddenly to write only French music and to come settle in Paris?

The Frenchman

I am a bit suspicious about all that, but it is nonetheless true that J.J., as his greatest admirer, gives his judgment more weight.

Rousseau

An admirer of his talent, well and good; I am too. But as for his judgment, one would first have to be knowledgeable about many things before knowing how much authority he should be given.

The Frenchman

Since you are suspicious of him, I am willing not to support his authority here or even that of any other composer. But speaking for myself, I would still say that one doubtless has to know Music in order to compose it, whereas one can ramble on about that art without knowing a thing about it, and many a person who writes in a very learned way about music would have a hard time making up a good continuo for a minuet or even notating it.

Rousseau

I suspect that is so. But is it your intention to apply that idea to the *Dictionary* and its Author?

The Frenchman

I admit I was thinking about that.

Rousseau

You were thinking about that! Since that is the case, allow me, please, to ask one more question. Have you read that book?

The Frenchman

I would be very sorry ever to have read a single line of it, or of any books bearing that odious name.

Rousseau

In that case, I am less surprised that you and I think so differently about everything that relates to them. Here, for example, you would not confuse this book with those you speak of, which—being based only on general principles—contain only vague ideas or elementary notions drawn perhaps from other writings and familiar to all who know a little music. In contrast, the *Dictionary* goes into detail about rules, showing their basis, application, exceptions, and everything that should guide the composer in their use. The Author even makes a point of elucidating certain parts that have previously been unclear to composers and almost unintelligible in their writings. The article, *Enharmonic*, for example, explains that category with such clarity one is amazed to think of the obscure way it was discussed by all others who had previously written about that subject. I will never be persuaded that this article and those on *Expression, Fugue, Harmony, License, Mode, Modulation, Preparation, Recitative, Trio** and a

---

* All the articles on Music that I had promised to do for the *Enclyclopedia* were written by the year 1749 and submitted by M. Diderot to M. d'Alembert the following year for inclusion in the section *Mathematics,* for which he was responsible. Shortly after, his *Elements of Music* appeared, which he had little difficulty producing. In 1768 my *Dictionary* was published, and soon after a new edition of his *Elements* with additions. Between the two publications, a *Dictionary of Fine Arts* also appeared in which I recognized several of the articles I had done for the *Encyclopedia*. M. d'Alembert was so well disposed toward my *Dictionary* still in manuscript form that he generously volunteered to M. Guy to read the proofs, a favor which, on the the latter's notice, I begged him not to accept.

great number of others scattered through the *Dictionary* and surely not plagiarized from anyone, are the work of someone who knows nothing about Music, who is talking about things he does not understand; nor that a book from which one can learn composition is the work of someone who did not know it.

It is true that several other equally important articles remained only listed to avoid leaving the vocabulary incomplete, as he points out in his preface. But would it be reasonable to judge him on the basis of articles he did not have the time to write rather than on those he completed and that surely required as much knowledge as the others? The Author concurs, he even announces what is missing in his book and gives the reason for this flaw. But just as it stands, it would still be a hundred times easier to believe that a man who does not know music had written the *Soothsayer* than the *Dictionary*. Look at all the people, especially in Switzerland and Germany, who do not know a note of music yet, guided solely by their ear and their taste, compose very pleasant and correct pieces, although they have no knowledge of the rules and can store their compositions only in their memory. But it is absurd to think that a man can teach and even elucidate in a book a science he does not understand, and that is even more true of an art whose language alone requires several years of study before one can understand and speak it. I therefore conclude that a man who could not write *The Village Soothsayer* because he did not know music, could not, for all the more reason, write the *Dictionary*, which required much more knowledge.

The Frenchman

Knowing neither of these works, I cannot judge your reasoning by myself. I only know that the assessment of the public about this is totally different; that the *Dictionary* is thought to be a heap of sonorous, unintelligible phrases, and that the article *Genius* is cited, which everyone extols and which says nothing about music. As for your article *Enharmonic* and the others which, according to you, deal in a relevant way with the art, I have never heard anyone talk about them, except perhaps for a few musicians or foreign music lovers who appeared to take them seriously before they were better instructed. But our people say and have always said that they understand nothing of the book's jargon.

As for the *Soothsayer*, you saw the transports of admiration generated by its last revival. The public's enthusiasm, reaching delirium, bears witness to the sublimity of this work. J.J. was divine, he was a modern Orpheus; this opera was a masterpiece of art and of the human mind. And this enthusiasm was never greater than when it was learned that the divine J.J. did not know music. Now whatever you may say, from the fact that a man who does not know music could not write a prodigy of the art that is universally admired, it doesn't follow according to me that he could not write a book that is little read, little understood, and even less appreciated.

Rousseau

About things I can judge by myself, I will never take the public's judgments as rules for my own, and especially when it is as infatuated as it has become for the *Village Soothsayer* after having heard it with a more moderate pleasure for twenty years. This sudden infatuation—whatever caused it at a time when the supposed Author was an object of public derision—was sufficiently unnatural that it lacked authority among sensible people. I have told you what I thought of the *Dictionary*, not on the basis of public opinion or of the famous article *Genius*—which, having no particular relevance to the art, is there only as a joke—but after an attentive reading of the whole work, most of the articles of which will help produce better music when artists are able to benefit from them.

As for the *Soothsayer*, although I am certain no one feels the true beauties of that work better than I, I am far from finding these beauties in the same places as the infatuated public does. They are not the products of study and knowledge, but rather are inspired by taste and sensitivity. And it would be easier to prove that a learned composer did not write the piece if he lacked bel canto and ingenuity than to prove that an ignorant man could not have written it because he lacks the knowledge that compensates for genius and does nothing without hard work. As for the scientific part, there is nothing in the *Village Soothsayer* that goes beyond elementary principles of composition; and not only is there no music student who would not be prepared in this respect to do as well after three months, but it is doubtful that a learned composer could resign himself to be so simple. It is true that the Author of this work followed a hidden principle in it which is felt without being noticed, and which gives his songs an effect not felt in any other French music. But this principle—unknown by all our composers, disdained by those who have heard of it, proposed only by the Author of the *Letter on French Music*, who later made it into an article in the *Dictionary*, and followed only by the Author of the *Soothsayer*—is an important additional proof that these two Authors are one and the same. But all that demonstrates the inventiveness of an amateur who has thought about art rather than the routine of a professor who possesses it in a superior manner. What does honor to the musician in this work is the recitative: it is as well modulated, punctuated, accented as French recitative can be. Its form was new, at least it was then to such a degree that no one wanted to risk presenting this recitative at Court, although it was better adapted to the language than any other. I have difficulty seeing how recitative can be plagiarized, unless the words are plagiarized as well, and if only that were the work of the author, I myself would have preferred to write the recitative without the airs than the Airs without the recitative. But I have too great a sense of the same hand in everything to be able to divide it among different authors. The very thing that makes this opera valuable for people with taste is the perfect accord between the words and the music, the close relationship of the parts that compose it, the precise fit of everything that makes it the most unified work I know of its type. The Musician thought, felt, and spoke like the poet throughout; what is expressed by one always corresponds so faithfully to what is expressed by the other that they are seen to be moved by the same spirit always. And I am told that such a perfect and rare unity results from a randomly joined pile of plagiarisms? Sir, there would be a hundred times more art in composing such a piece from scattered, disconnected bits than in creating it oneself from start to finish.

The Frenchman

Your objection is not new to me. It even appears so solid to many people that changing their minds about partial thefts—although those are all well proved—they are now persuaded that the entire piece, both words and music, is the work of another hand, and that the charlatan was skillful enough to get hold of it and impudent enough to claim it. That even appears so well established there is scarcely any more doubt about it. For after all, some explanation like it had to be found. This work, which he is demonstrably unable to have written, had to be written by someone. They even claim to have discovered its true Author.

Rousseau

I understand. Having first discovered and proved beyond a doubt the partial thefts from which the *Village Soothsayer* was composed, people are now proving just as triumphantly that there were no partial thefts, that this work, written by one hand, was stolen in its entirety by the person who claims its authorship. So be it, for either of these contradictory truths serves as well for my purpose. But now, what is this true author? Is he French, Swiss, Italian, Chinese?

The Frenchman

That is what I don't know, because the work can hardly be attributed to Pergolese like a *Salve Regina*. . . .

Rousseau

Yes, I know one by that Author, that was even engraved. . . .

The Frenchman

It isn't that one. Pergolesi wrote the *Salve* you are talking about when he was alive, whereas the one I am talking about is another one that he wrote twenty years after his death and that J.J. appropriated saying he had written it for Mlle. Fel, just like many other motets that the same J.J.

says or will say he wrote since then, and which, by dint of more of M. d'Alembert's miracles, are and will always be by Pergolesi, whose shade he evokes whenever it suits him.

Rousseau

Now that is truly admirable. Oh, I have suspected for a long time that this M. d'Alembert must be a miracle-making Saint, and I will wager he doesn't stop with those. But, as you say, it will still be hard for him, saint though he is, to attribute the *Village Soothsayer* to Pergolese as well, and it is important not to multiply Authors unnecessarily.

The Frenchman

Why not? Nothing in the world is more natural than for a plagiarist to take things right and left.

Rousseau

I agree. But in all this plagiarized music, one is aware of the seams and patches, yet it seems to me that the music bearing J.J.'s name does not sound like that. It does not even have a national character. It is no more Italian than French. It has its own tone and none other.

The Frenchman

Everyone agrees on that. How then did the Author of the *Soothsayer* adopt in that piece an accent so novel that he used it there alone and if it is his only work, how could he serenely stand by while someone else is covered with glory for it, without trying to claim it or at least to share it by writing a second such Opera? I was promised a clear explanation of all that, for I honestly admit that to this point it remains rather obscure to me.

Rousseau

Good! You really are at a loss. The plagiarist had to make the Author's acquaintance. Either he had the piece entrusted to him by the author or he stole it from him and then poisoned him. It is altogether simple.

The Frenchman

Truly, you have such pretty ideas!

Rousseau

Don't give me the credit you deserve! These are your ideas. They are the natural outcome of everything you told me. Furthermore, and whatever is the case about the true Author of the piece, that the person who claims to be the author cannot have been in a position to have written it due to his ignorance and his inability is enough for me to conclude even more strongly that he did not write the *Dictionary* he also claims, or the *Letter on French Music*, or any of the other books that bear his name, and that it is impossible not to feel they all come from the same hand. Besides, can you conceive that a man endowed with enough talent to produce such works would, at the peak of his effervescence, so plagiarize and claim the works of another in a genre that not only is not his own but about which he understands absolutely nothing? That a man who, according to you, had enough courage, pride, boldness, and strength to resist the urge to write that is so natural in young people who feel some talent in themselves, in order to let his brain mature in silence for twenty years, in order to give more depth and weight to his long-meditated works? That this same man, his soul filled with his great and sublime views, would interrupt their development just to use cowardly and childish maneuvers to seek a reputation that is usurped and highly inferior to one he could obtain legitimately? It is people with very small talents of their own who thus deck themselves out with the talents of others; and anyone with an active, thinking brain who has felt the delirium and appeal of the work of the mind will not go servilely on another's path, decking himself out with the works of a stranger in preference to those he can draw from his own depth. Really, Sir, he who could have been so base and foolish as to claim the *Village Soothsayer* without being its author and without even knowing music never wrote a line of the *Discourse on Inequality*, or of the *Emile*, or of the *Social Contract*. Such daring and vigor on the one hand, such ineptness and cowardice on the other, will never be joined in the same soul.

This is a proof that speaks to every sensible man. That others which are no less powerful speak only to me makes me angry for my species. These proofs should speak to every soul that is sensitive and endowed with moral instinct. You tell me that all these writings that inspire me, touch me, move me, give me the sincere will to be better are merely the productions of one whose overexcited brain is guided by a hypocritical, deceitful heart. The picture of my superlunary beings has already allowed you to understand that I do not share your opinion about this. What confirms my own opinion still more is the number and extent of these very writings, throughout which I always find the same ardor of a heart inspired by the same feelings. What! This scourge of the human race, this enemy of all rectitude, all justice, all goodness imprisoned himself for ten to twelve years in the course of writing fifteen volumes speaking the sweetest, purest, most vigorous language of virtue; pitying human miseries; showing their source in the errors and prejudices of men; showing them the route of true happiness; teaching them to return into their own hearts to rediscover the seed of the social virtues they stifle under a false semblance in the misunderstood progress of society; always to consult their conscience to redress the errors of their reason; and to heed, in the silence of the passions, that interior voice which all our philosophers have such a stake in stifling and which they treat as a chimera because it no longer speaks to them. He has been scorned by them and by his whole era for having always maintained that man is good although men are wicked, that his virtues came from within himself and his vices from outside. He devoted his greatest and best book to showing how the harmful passions enter our souls, how good education must be purely negative, that it must consist not in curing the vices of the human heart—for there are no such vices naturally—but in preventing them from being born and in keeping tightly shut the passages through which they enter. Lastly, he established all of that with such luminous clarity, such touching charm, such persuasive truth that a soul which is not depraved cannot resist the appeal of his images and the strength of his reasons. And you would have it that this long sequence of writings in which the same maxims breathe throughout, where the same language is always sustained with the same heat, is the work of an imposter who always speaks not only contrary to his thinking but also contrary to his interest, since—placing his entire happiness in filling the world with misfortunes and crimes—he should consequently seek to multiply the number of scoundrels to provide himself with helpers and accomplices for the execution of his horrible projects. Whereas he really labored only to provoke obstacles and adversaries in all the proselytes of virtue his book would make.

There are other reasons that are no less strong in my mind. This putative Author, recognized by all the proofs you have provided to be the most dissolute, vilest decadent who could exist, spent his life with trollops of the streets in the worst reputed hovels. He is besotted with debauchery, rotted with syphilis, yet you would have it that he wrote these inimitable letters full of the most passionate and purest love that never grew except in hearts that are as chaste as they are tender? Don't you know that nothing is less tender than a debauched man, that love is no better known to libertines than it is to loose women, that debauchery hardens the heart, makes those who yield to it impudent, gross, brutal, cruel; that their impoverished blood—divested of that spirit of life which carries from the heart to the brain those delightful images which give rise to the intoxication of love—gives them through habit only the bitter goading of need, without adding the sweet impressions that make sensuality as tender as it is intense. Show me the love letter of an unknown person and I am certain to know by reading it whether its author is of good morals.[18] It is only in the eyes of those who are that women shine with those moving and chaste charms which alone bring delirium to truly loving hearts. The debauched see in women merely instruments of pleasure that are as contemptible as they are necessary, like those receptacles used daily for the most basic needs. I would have challenged all who chase the women of Paris to write a single one of the letters in *Heloise*, yet you would have the entire book, a book that sends me into the most angelic ecstasy, be the work of a vile, debauched man! Be assured, Sir, that this is not so. It is not wit and jargon that discovers such things. You would have it that a shrewd hypocrite, who advances toward his goals solely by ruse and guile, would heedlessly give himself over to the impetuosity of indignation against all stations, all factions without exception, and state the harshest truths equally to all? Papists, Huguenots, Nobles, the Poor, men, women, lawyers, soldiers, Monks, Priests, the devout, Doctors, Philosophers, *Tros Rutulusve fuat*, all is portrayed, all is unmasked without a single word of bitterness or personal attack on anyone, but without special treatment for any faction. You would have it that he always followed his passion to the point of arousing everything against him, bringing together everything to crush him in his disgrace, and did all that without taking care to preserve a defender or a support, without concern even for the success of his books, without at least informing himself of the impression they were producing and of the storm they were drawing down upon his head, and without becoming the least bit worried when he began to get wind of it? Does this intrepidness, this imprudence, this carelessness fit with the false and wily man you have depicted to me? Finally, you would have it that a wretch—who was refused the name *scoundrel* because it is not abject enough and given that of *knave* because it better states the baseness and indignity of his soul— you would have it that this reptile adopted and sustained throughout fifteen volumes the intrepid and bold language of a writer who, consecrating his pen to the truth, does not seek the approbation of the public and who is placed above the judgment of men by the testimony of his heart? You would have it that among so many beautiful, modern books, the only ones that penetrate to my heart, that inspire it with love of virtue, that touch it regarding human misery, are precisely the games of a detestable imposter, who scoffs at his readers and does not believe a word of what he says to them with such heat and strength. Whereas all the others, written, you assure me, by true wise men with such pure intentions, freeze my heart, shrivel it up, and inspire in me—along with feelings of bitterness, pain, and hate—only the most intolerant partisan spirit. And so, Sir, if it is not impossible for all this to be true, it is, at least, impossible that I should ever believe it, even if it were proved a thousand times. Furthermore, I am not opposing your proofs, which fully convince me. But what I do not believe, and will never believe as long as I live, is that the *Emile*, and especially the article about taste in the fourth book, is the work of a depraved heart; that *Heloise*, and especially the letter about the death of Julie, was written by a scoundrel; that the letter to M. d'Alembert on the theater is a product of a duplicitous soul, that the summary of the

Project on Perpetual Peace is that of an enemy of the human race, that the entire collection of writings by the same Author emanated from a hypocritical soul and an evil mind and not from the pure zeal of a heart burning with love of virtue. No Sir, no Sir, mine will never yield to that absurd and false persuasion. Rather I say and will always maintain that there must be two J.J.'s and that the Author of the books and the author of the crimes are not the same man. It is a feeling so deeply rooted in my heart that nothing will ever remove it.

The Frenchman

Yet it is without any doubt an error. And another proof that he wrote books is that he is still writing them every single day.

Rousseau

I was not aware of that, and I had been told, on the contrary, that for the past several years his only occupation was copying music.

The Frenchman

Well and good, copying! He pretends that in order to look poor although he is rich, and to hide his frenzy for writing books and scribbling on paper. But no one here is fooled by that and you must have come from very far away to believe that.

Rousseau

Tell me, please, what these new books he conceals so well, so appropriately, and so successfully are all about?

The Frenchman

They are nonsense of all sorts: lessons on Atheism, eulogies of modern philosophy, funeral orations, translations, satires . . . .

Rousseau

Against his enemies, no doubt?

The Frenchman

No, against the enemies of his enemies.

Rousseau

That is something I never would have suspected.

The Frenchman

Oh, you have no idea of this rascal's ruse. He does all that in order to disguise himself better. He writes violent diatribes against the present administration (in 1772), about which he has no cause for complaint; in favor of the Parliament, which treated him so badly, and of the Author of all his miseries, whom he should detest. But at each step his vanity shines through in the most inept praises of himself. For example, he most recently wrote a very dull book entitled *The Year 2240*, in which he carefully dedicates all his writings to posterity, without even making an exception of *Narcisse* and without leaving out a single line.[19]

Rousseau

In truth, that is an astonishing blunder. In the books that bear his name, I see no such stupid pride.

The Frenchman

When he used his name, he restrained himself. Now that he thinks he is well concealed, he no longer bothers.

Rousseau

He is right, it works so well for him! But Sir, what then is the true purpose of these books that such a clever man publishes, with so much mystery, in favor of men he ought to hate and whose doctrine he appeared to oppose so much?

The Frenchman

Is there any doubt in your mind? It is to make fools of the public and to display his eloquence by proving first the pro and then the con and leading his readers around by the nose to mock their credulity.

Rousseau

By my faith! Considering his distressed state, this man is in very good numor, and considering how full of hate you make him, he is hardly concerned about his enemies! For myself, without being either vain or vindictive, I can tell you that were I in his place and if I still wanted to write books, it would not be to help my persecutors and their doctrine triumph at the expense of my reputation and my own writings. If he is really the Author of those writings he does not claim, it is a powerful and new proof that he did not write those he does claim. For surely you would have to imagine that he is very stupid and very much his own enemy to recant so inappropriately.

The Frenchman

You must admit that you are very obstinate, very tenacious in your opinions. Given the little authority that public opinion has over you, it is easy to see that you are not French. Among all our Wise men who are so virtuous, so just, so far above any partiality, among all our Ladies who are so sensitive, so favorable to an Author who depicts love so well, there is no one who has shown the least resistance to the triumphant arguments of our Gentlemen; no one who did not acknowledge eagerly, joyfully that this same Author who was so beloved, this same J.J. so celebrated, but so roguish and detestable, was the shame and disgrace of the human race. And now that everyone is attached so passionately to this idea that they would not change their minds even if it were possible to do so, you alone—more demanding than everyone—come here to suggest a new and unexpected distinction, which would not be the case if there were the least basis for it. However, I agree that within all this pathos, which I see as quite meaningless, you do open some new viewpoints which could be of some use if communicated to our Gentlemen. It is certain that if it could be proved that J.J. has not written any of the books he claims, just as it is proved that he did not write the *Soothsayer*, it would remove a difficulty that still continues to stop or at least to embarrass many people, despite the convincing proofs of the misdeeds of this wretch. But I would also be very surprised if this idea could be given the least support that it would be proposed so belatedly. I see that in their effort to heap on him all the disgrace he deserves, our Gentlemen nonetheless worry sometimes about those books they detest, that they even ridicule with all their strength, but which often elicit inconvenient objections which would be removed all at once by affirming that he did not write a single word of all that, and that he is just as incapable of writing that as of writing the *Soothsayer*. But I see we have taken the opposite route here that can hardly get us back to the other. And there is such conviction that those writings are his that our Gentlemen have busied themselves for some time picking through them to extract their poison.

Rousseau

Poison!

The Frenchman

Without doubt. These lovely books have seduced you as they have others, and I am not very surprised that through all this ostentation of fine morality you did not sense the pernicious doctrines he is spreading. But I would be most surprised if those doctrines were not there. How could such a serpent not infect everything he touches with his venom?

Rousseau

And this venom, Sir! Has much already been extracted from these books?

The Frenchman

A great deal, I am told, and he even shows himself openly in a number of horrible passages which the extreme bias that people had in favor of these books prevented them from noticing at first, but which now strike with surprise and dismay everyone who, better instructed, reads them as is suitable.

Rousseau

Horrible passages? I read these books with great care, and I swear to you I found no such things in them. You would do me a favor by showing me one of them.

The Frenchman

Not having read them, I am unable to do that. But I will ask our Gentlemen for the list of those they have collected, and I will send it to you. I can recall only that they quote a note in the *Emile* where he openly teaches murder.

Rousseau

What, Sir, he openly teaches murder and that passed unnoticed in the first reading! He must surely have had readers who were either very well disposed or very distracted. And where were the eyes of the Authors on the basis of whose wise and grave indictments he has so regularly been judged? What a discovery for them! What regret to have missed it!

The Frenchman

Ah, it is because these books were so filled with things to reprove that it was impossible to take note of them all.

Rousseau

It is true that good, judicious Joli de Fleuri,[20] filled with the horror inspired in him by *The Criminal System of Natural Religion*, could hardly stop to notice bagatelles such as lessons in murder. Or perhaps, as you say, his extreme bias in favor of the book prevented him from noticing them. But, Sir, say that your seekers of poison are more surely those who put it there, and that there is none at all in the book for those who do not seek it. I have read the note to which you refer twenty times, without seeing in it anything other than lively indignation against a gothic prejudice no less extravagant than deadly, and I would never have suspected the sense your Gentlemen give it had I not seen, by chance, an insidious letter that was written to the Author on this topic, and the reply he had the weakness to write, in which he explains the sense of this note which needed no other explanation than to be read in context by decent men.[21] An Author who writes from his heart is subject, as he gets excited, to flights of impetuosity that take him beyond the goal, and to digressions that are never pitfalls for those subtle and methodical writers who, without becoming animated about anything in the world, say only what is advantageous for them to say, and phrase it so that without committing themselves they produce the effect that is in their own interest. These are the indiscretions of a self-confident man, whose generous soul does not even suspect that he can be doubted. Be assured that a hypocrite or an imposter will never expose himself openly. Our philosophers have what they call their interior doctrine,[22] but they teach it to the public only while concealing themselves, and to their friends only in secret. By always taking everything literally, one would perhaps actually find less to reproach in most dangerous books than in those we are talking about here, and in general than in those where the Author, sure of himself and speaking from an overflowing heart, yields to all his vehemence without thinking of the foothold he may be offering to the wicked man who lies in wait for him in cold blood and who seeks in all the good and useful things he offers only the unguarded spot into which he can plunge his dagger. But read all these passages with the sense they present naturally to the mind of the reader and that they had in the mind of the author when he wrote them. Read them in context, with what precedes and what follows; consult the disposition of heart into which these readings put you. It is this disposition that will clarify their true sense for you. As sole response to these sinister interpreters and as their just punishment, I would like only to make them read aloud the whole work that they tear to shreds in order to stain them with their own venom. I doubt that when they finished this reading, there would be a single one who would be so impudent as to dare renew his accusation.

The Frenchman

I know that this way of isolating and distorting passages from an Author in order to interpret them at the whim of an unjust censor's passion is generally blamed. But applying your own principles, our Gentlemen will keep you far from what you expect, for it is even less in the scattered traits than in the entire substance of the books in question that they find the poison the Author carefully spread through them. But it is blended in with so much art that one succeeds in discovering it only by the most subtle analyses.

Rousseau

In that case, it was useless to put it in. For once again, if this venom must be sought to be felt, it is there only for those who seek it or rather who put it there. For myself, for example, who did not think of looking for it, I can very well swear that I found none.

The Frenchman

What does that matter, if it has its effect without being perceived? The effect does not come from this or that passage in particular, but from the entire reading of the book. What do you say to that?

Rousseau

Nothing, except that having read several times all of the works J.J. claims, the total effect on my soul has always been to make me more humane, more just, better than I was before. I have never turned to these books without profit for virtue.

The Frenchman

Oh, I guarantee you that is not the effect of their reading on our Gentlemen.

Rousseau

Oh, I believe it! But that is not the fault of the books. For myself, the more I put my heart into them, the less I felt what it is they find pernicious. And I am sure the effect they produced on me is the same as it will be on any decent man who reads them with the same impartiality.

The Frenchman

Say with the same bias. Because those who have felt the contrary effect and who are involved in these useful researches for the public good are all men of the most sublime virtue and great philosophers who are never wrong.

Rousseau

I have nothing to reply to that yet. But do one thing: imbued with the principles of those great philosophers who are never wrong, but sincere in the love of truth, put yourself in a condition to pronounce knowingly like them, and to decide on this matter between those on one side escorted by all their disciples who swear only by their masters, and on the other all the public before they were so thoroughly indoctrinated. To do this, read for yourself the books in question, and based on the dispositions which this reading inspires in you, judge that of the Author when he was writing them and the natural effect they must produce when nothing acts to divert it. That, I think, is the surest way to bring an equitable judgment to bear on this matter.

The Frenchman

What! You want to impose on me the torture of reading an immense compilation of precepts of virtue drafted by a knave?

Rousseau

No, Sir. I want you to read the true system of the human heart, drafted by a decent man and published under another name. I do not want you to be biased against good and useful books merely because a man unworthy of reading them has the audacity to call himself the Author.

The Frenchman

Viewed in this way, one might resolve to read these books if those who have examined them best did not all agree, with the exception of yourself alone, in finding them harmful and dangerous, which proves well enough that these books were composed not, as you say, by a decent man with praiseworthy intentions, but by a clever imposter, full of bad feelings masked by a hypocritical exterior that permits them to surprise, seduce, and deceive people.

Rousseau

So long as you continue in this manner to maintain as a fact based on the authority of others the opposite opinion to my own, we will be unable to agree. When you are willing to judge for yourself, we will then be able to compare our reasons and choose the most solid opinion. But in a question of fact such as this one, I do not see why I should believe, without any convincing reason, that others have seen better than I.

The Frenchman

Don't you give any weight to the tally of voices, when you are the only one to see things differently from everyone?

Rousseau

In order to make that calculation correctly, it would be necessary to know beforehand how many of the people involved agree with you only through the eyes of others. If from the total of these loud voices we subtract those which only echo others, and if we count those who remain silent for fear of being heard, there might perhaps be less difference than you think. By reducing this multitude to the small number of people who lead the others, one strong reason would still remain for me not to prefer their opinion to my own. Because I am perfectly sure of my good faith here and I cannot say the same with any assurance about any of those who profess to think differently than I do in this matter. In short, I am judging for myself here. We cannot therefore reason as equals, you and I, unless you put yourself in a position to judge for yourself too.

The Frenchman

To please you, I prefer to do more than what you ask of me, by adopting your opinion in preference to that of the public. For I admit that even the suspicion that these books had been written by that wretch would prevent me from easily tolerating their reading.

Rousseau

Do better still. Don't even think of the Author as you read, and without any bias either in favor or against, let your soul experience the impressions it will receive. You will thus assure yourself of the intention behind the writing of these books and of whether they can be the work of a scoundrel who was harboring evil designs.

The Frenchman

If I make this effort for you, at least don't expect it to be without a cost. In order to bring myself to read these books despite my distate, you yourself, despite yours, must promise to go and see the Author, or according to you the person who claims to be; to examine him carefully, and to discern in his hypocrisy the clever imposter it has masked for so long.

Rousseau

What do you dare propose to me? That I should seek out such a man, that I should see him, keep company with him! I who am indignant at breathing the air he breathes, I who would like to put the diameter of the earth between him and me and would still feel too close? Has Rousseau seemed to you so easygoing in relationships that he would seek to frequent the wicked? If I ever had the misfortune to find that man near me, I would console myself only by calling him by the names he deserves, by confounding his hypocritical arrogance with the cruelest reproaches, by overwhelming him with the horrible list of his misdeeds.

The Frenchman

What are you saying? How you frighten me! Have you forgotten the sacred promise you made to maintain the most profound silence with him and never to let him know that you even have any suspicion of all I have unveiled to you?

Rousseau

What? You surprise me. I thought that promise involved only the time needed to explain the horrible secrets you have revealed to me. For fear of breaking the thread, it was necessary not to interrupt before the end, and you did not want me to risk discussions with an imposter before having all the necessary instructions to confound him fully. That is how I understood your motives concerning the silence you imposed on me, and I could not have supposed that the obligation to remain silent went further than what justice and the law allow.

The Frenchman

Don't be mistaken about it any longer then. Your promise, which you cannot break without violating your faith, has no other limits than life. You can, you even must spread and publish everywhere the horrible details of his vices and his crimes, labor zealously to extend and amplify his defamation more and more, make him as odious, despicable, execrable as possible to everyone. But you must always perform this good work with an air of mystery and commiseration that heightens its effect, and far from ever giving him any explanation that would enable him to reply and defend himself, you must work in concert with everyone to keep him always in ignorance of what is known and of how it is known.

Rousseau

These are duties that I was far from understanding when you imposed them on me, and now that it pleases you to explain them to me, you cannot doubt that they take me by surprise and that I am curious to learn the principles on which you establish them. Explain yourself, I beg you, and count on my full attention.

The Frenchman

Oh my good friend! With what pleasure your heart—devastated by the dishonor to humanity done by this man who should never have been born—will open itself to those feelings that glorify the noble souls of those who have unmasked this unfortunate man. They were his friends, they declared it to be so. Seduced by a decent and simple exterior, by a temperament thought then to be easygoing and sweet, by the degree of talents needed to sense theirs without pretending to be a rival they sought him out, became attached to him, and would soon have subjugated him, for it is certain that would not have been difficult. But when they saw that this man who was so simple and so sweet was suddenly taking wing and rising rapidly to a reputation they could not reach, they who had such well founded high pretentions soon began to suspect there was something beneath it that was not quite right, that this ebullient mind had not withheld its ardor for so long without mystery; and from then on, persuaded that this apparent simplicity was only a veil hiding some dangerous project, they firmly resolved to find what they sought and spent time taking the surest means so their efforts would not be lost.

They worked together, therefore, to shed light on all his ways in such a manner that nothing could escape them. He himself had put them on the track by declaring a grave fault he had committed, the secret of which he confided to them unnecessarily, to no purpose, and not—as the hypocrite said—to hide nothing from friends and in order not to appear better in their eyes than he really was.[23] But rather, as they themselves say very sensibly, to put them off the track, attract their attention, and divert them from wanting to penetrate further into the obscure mystery of his character. This folly on his part was doubtless a stroke of Heaven, which wanted to force the imposter to unmask himself or at least to furnish them with the hold they needed to do so. Profiting skillfully from this opening to set their traps around him, they moved easily from his confidence to that of the accomplices in his fault, whom they soon converted into instruments for the execution of their project. With much skill, a little money, and big promises, they won over those around him and thus by degrees became as knowledgeable or more so than he about everything that concerned him. The fruit of all these efforts was the discovery and proof of what they had suspected as soon as his books drew attention, namely, that this great preacher of virtue was only a monster laden with hidden crimes, who for forty years masked the soul of a scoundrel beneath the exterior of a decent man.

Rousseau

Please go on. What you are telling me is truly surprising.

The Frenchman

You have seen what these discoveries were. You can judge the dilemma of those who had made them. They were not of a nature to be silenced and they had not taken so much trouble for nothing. However, had there been no other drawback to publishing them than to bring the punishments he deserved to the guilty party, it was sufficient to prevent these generous men from exposing him to that. They must, they wished to unmask him, but they did not want to lose him, and the one seemed to follow necessarily from the other. How could he be confounded without being punished? How could he be spared without their becoming responsible for the continuation of his crimes, for they well knew they should not expect repentance from him? They knew what they owed to justice, truth, and public safety, but they knew no less well what they owed themselves. After having had the misfortune to live intimately with this scoundrel, they could not deliver him over to public prosecution without exposing themselves to some blame, and their honest souls, still full of commiseration for him, wanted above all to avoid scandal and to make it appear to the eyes of the world that he owed them his well-being and his preservation. Therefore, they carefully coordinated all their moves and resolved to unfold their discoveries so gradually that the public would learn about them only as it revised the prejudices held in his favor. For his hypocrisy was then meeting with the greatest success. The new route that he had cleared and that he appeared to follow with sufficient courage to match his conduct to his principles, his daring morality that he seemed to preach by example even more than in his books, and above all his apparent selflessness, of which everyone was then dupe, all these singularities which presupposed at least a resolute soul aroused the admiration even of those who disapproved of them. People applauded his maxims without accepting them and his example without following it.[24]

As these dispositions might have prevented the public from concurring readily with what one wanted it to learn, it was necessary to begin by changing them. Placing his faults in the worst possible light began the job. His imprudence in revealing them might have looked like frankness; it had to be disguised. That appeared difficult to do, because I have been told that in the *Emile* he made an almost formal admission, with regrets that would naturally spare him the reproaches of decent people.[25] Happily, the public that was then being aroused against him and sees only what one wants it to see, perceived nothing of all that; and with sufficient information to accuse and convict him without the appearance that it was he who furnished it, there was soon the necessary handle to begin the work of defaming him. Everything was marvelously disposed for that. In his brutal declamations he had, as you yourself note, attacked all stations. Everyone was most happy to work together at this task that none dared begin for fear of appearing to heed only revenge. But by means of this first fact, well established and made to appear sufficiently grave, all the rest became easy. One could, without being suspected of animosity, become the echo of his friends, who themselves accused him only while pitying him and solely to discharge their conscience. And that is how, under the direction of persons informed of the horrible character of this monster, the public—revising little by little the favorable judgments it had held so long—began to see only ostentation where it had seen courage, baseness where it had seen simplicity, boasting where it had seen disinterestedness, and ridiculousness where it had seen singularity.

It was to this state that things had to be brought to make the dark mysteries they had to reveal believable, even with all their proofs, and to allow him to live in at least apparent freedom and in absolute impunity. For once he was well known, there was no longer any need to fear that he could either fool or seduce anyone, and no longer able to acquire accomplices, he was incapable, under surveillance as he was by his friends and by their friends, to pursue his execrable projects and to do any harm in society. In this situation, before revealing the discoveries that had been made, they agreed that they would do no harm to his person, and that in order for him to enjoy perfect safety as well, he would never be allowed to know that he had been unmasked. This pledge, contracted with all possible strength, has been maintained to the present with faithfulness that borders on the amazing. Do you want to be the first to infringe it, whereas the entire public, without distinction of rank, age, sex, character, and without any exception—filled with admiration for the generosity of those who have led this affair—has hastened to share their noble views and to espouse them through pity for this poor wretch? For you must feel that his safety depends on his ignorance, and if he were ever to believe that his crimes are known, he would undoubtedly take advantage of the indulgence with which they are concealed to scheme new ones with the same impunity; that this impunity would then be too dangerous an example; and that his crimes are of the type that must either be severely punished or left in obscurity.

Rousseau

Everything you have just said is so new to me that I must wonder for a long time in order to organize my ideas about it. There are even a few points about which I would need more explanation. You say, for example, there is no need to worry that this man, once he is well known, will seduce anyone, obtain accomplices, mount any dangerous plot. That is inconsistent with what you yourself told me about the continuation of his crimes; and I would, on the contrary, worry greatly that once labeled in that manner, he would serve as a guide to the wicked to form their criminal associations and to use his deadly talents to strengthen them. The greatest evil and the greatest shame of the social state is that crime makes more indissoluble bonds in it than virtue does. The wicked join together more solidly than the good, and their relationships are far more durable, because they cannot be broken with impunity, because the secrecy of their schemes and the impunity of their crimes depend on the duration of these relationships, and they have the greatest possible interest in always being careful of each other. Whereas good men, united only by free affections that can change without consequence, break up and separate without fear and without risk as soon as they stop suiting each other. That man, as you have described him to me—plotting, active, dangerous—must be the home of the plots of all scoundrels. His freedom, his impunity, for which you so highly praise the respectable men who preserve it, is a great public misfortune. They are responsible for all the evils that can come of it, and that do come of it daily according to your own accounts. Is it praiseworthy, then, for just men to favor the wicked at the expense of the good?

The Frenchman

Your objection would have strength if the issue here were a wicked man of an ordinary type. But always keep in mind that the issue is a monster, the horror of the human race, whom no one can trust in any way, and who is not even capable of making the pact scoundrels make among themselves. It is in this respect that, equally known to all, no one at all need fear him because of his schemes. Detested by good men for his works, he is even more detested by wicked men for his books. In just punishment for his damnable hypocrisy, the rascals he unmasks in order to maintain his own mask all feel the most invincible antipathy for him. If they seek him out, it is only to take him by surprise and betray him. But you can be sure that none of them will ever try to associate him with some evil enterprise.

Rousseau

It is really a wicked person of a most unusual kind who makes himself even more odious to the wicked than to the good, and to whom no one in the world would dare suggest an injustice.

The Frenchman

Yes, doubtless of an unusual kind, so unusual that nature has never produced one and I hope will never reproduce one like him. However, don't believe that everyone is relying with blind confidence on this universal repulsion. It is one of the principal means used by the wise men who aroused it to prevent him from abusing by pernicious practices the freedom they wished to leave him, but it is not the only one. They took precautions that are no less effective by keeping him under such surveillance he cannot say a word that is not recorded nor take a step that is not noted, nor formulate a plan that is not seen through the moment it is conceived. They have made arrangements so that while he appears to be free among men, he has no real society with them; so that he lives alone in the crowd; so that he knows nothing of what is done, nothing of what is said around him, nothing especially of what concerns and interests him most; so that he feels completely encumbered with chains of which he can neither show nor see the least vestige. They have built walls of darkness around him through which he cannot see; they have buried him alive among the living. It may be the most unusual, the most amazing enterprise ever undertaken. Its total success attests to the strength of the genius that conceived it and of those who directed its execution. And what is no less amazing still is the zeal with which the entire public goes along with it, without perceiving the grandeur and beauty of the plan it blindly and faithfully executes.

However, you must realize that a project of this kind, however well devised, could not be carried out without the cooperation of the government. But this was all the easier to obtain because it concerned a man who was odious to those at the helm, an Author whose seditious writings exuded republican austerity, and who was said to hate the Visierate, disdain Visiers, want the King to govern alone, the Princes to be just, the peoples to be free, and everyone to obey the law. So the administration lent itself to the maneuvers necessary to entrap him and keep him under surveillance. Agreeing completely with all the views of the Author of the project, it saw to the safety of the guilty man as much as to his debasement, and making his defamation more solemn with a noisy air of protection, gradually deprived him, along with every kind of credit, consideration, and esteem, of all means of misusing his pernicious talents for the misfortune of the human race.

In order to unmask him more completely, they spared neither efforts, nor time, nor expense to shed light on every moment of his life from his birth to the present day. All those whose cajoleries had lured him into their snares, all those who, having known him in his youth, furnished some new fact against him, some new deed with which to charge him, all those in short who contributed to portraying him as they wished were recompensed in one way or another, and several of them were promoted, or those close to them were, for having graciously concurred with all the views of our Gentlemen. Trusted men, supplied with good instructions and much money, were dispatched to Venice, Turin, Savoy, Switzerland, Geneva, all the places where he resided.[26] There were large rewards for those who were successful in leaving behind in those countries the ideas about him they wanted spread and who brought back from them the anecdotes they wanted to have. Many people of all stations, in order to make new discoveries and contribute to the common work, undertook long trips at their own expense and on their own initiative, to document the villainy of J.J. with a zeal . . .

Rousseau

. . . that they surely would not have had in the opposite case to establish that he is a decent man. Aversion for the wicked is so much stronger in beautiful souls than attachment to the good!

That, as you say, is a project no less admirable than it is admirably executed. It would be very intriguing, very interesting to follow in detail all the maneuvers that had to be put into practice to make it so successful.

Since this case is unique in the history of the world, and gives rise to a completely new law in the code of the human race, it would be important for all the circumstances that relate to it to be fully known. The prohibition of fire and water among the Romans involved the necessities of life; this involves all that can make life bearable and sweet: honor, justice, truth, society, attachment, esteem. The Roman prohibition led to death; this one, without bringing death, makes it desirable, and lets life continue only in order to make it an awful torture. But the Roman prohibition was applied in a legal form by which the criminal was condemned judicially. I see nothing of the kind here. I am waiting to find out why there is this omission or what has been put in its place.

The Frenchman

I admit that in ordinary forms, the formal accusation and examination of the guilty party are necessary in order to punish him. But basically what do these forms matter when the offense has been well proved? The denial of the accused (for he always denies to escape torture) is worthless against the proofs and does not prevent his condemnation. Thus this formality, often useless, is especially so in the present case, where all the torches of the evidence shed light on unheard-of transgressions.

Besides, note that even if these formalities would always be necessary in order to punish, they are surely not so to grant clemency, which is the only thing at issue here. If justice alone had been listened to and this wretch treated as he deserved, it would have been necessary only to seize him, punish him, and be done with it. The difficulties, the trouble, the immense expense, and this network of snares and artifices in which he is enveloped would have been spared. But since the generosity of those who unmasked him and their tender commiseration for him did not permit them to use any violent means, they had to secure him without infringing on his freedom, and make him the horror of the universe so that he would not be its scourge.

How do they wrong him and of what could he complain? To allow him to live among men, he had to be portrayed to them as he was. Our Gentlemen know better than you that the wicked always seek and find their fellows in order to plot their evil designs with them. But we prevent them from joining with this man by making him so odious to them that they can have no confidence in him. Don't trust him, they are told; he will betray you for the sole pleasure of doing harm. Don't hope to hold him back with some common interest. He delights in crime gratuitously; it is not his interest that he seeks in it. The only good he knows for himself is what harms others. He will always prefer greater or more prompt harm to his comrades to the lesser or more remote harm he could do with them. All of that can be proved merely by examining his life. By telling his story, one drives the greatest scoundrels away from him out of terror. The effect of this method is so great and so certain that since he has been under surveillance and all his secrets brought to light, not one mortal has had the audacity yet to try to tempt him with the lure of a bad action, and it is only through the enticement of some good work that he can be caught.

Rousseau

See how opposites sometimes meet! Who would think that an excess of villainy could thus come so close to virtue? Your Gentlemen are the only ones in the world who could discover such a fine art.

The Frenchman

What makes the execution of this plan more admirable is the mystery with which it had to be concealed. This person had to be portrayed to everyone without the portrait ever reaching his own eyes. It was necessary to instruct the universe about his crimes, but in such a way that it remained a mystery only for him. Everyone had to point the finger at him while he believed he was seen by no one. In short, it was a secret that had to be confided to the entire public without ever reaching the one who was its subject. That would have been difficult, perhaps impossible to do with anyone else. But projects founded on general principles often fail. By tailoring them in such a way to the individual that they suit him alone, their execution becomes much more certain. This is what was done with our man, as skillfully as it was successfully. It was known that as a foreigner and alone, he was without support, without family, without help, that he belonged to no faction, and that his wild disposition itself tended to isolate him. To isolate him completely one had only to follow his natural inclination, make everything mesh with it, and from then on everything was easy. In sequestering him completely from the human intercourse he flees, what harm is done to him? In extending kindness to the point of allowing him at least apparent freedom, wasn't it necessary to prevent him from being able to misuse it? In leaving him in the midst of Citizens, wasn't it necessary to take pains to acquaint them thoroughly with him? Is it possible to see a serpent slip onto the public square without shouting to every person to beware of the serpent? Wasn't it above all a particular obligation of the wise men who had the skill to push aside the mask with which he covered himself for forty years and to be the first to see him beneath his disguises such as they have since shown him to everyone? This great duty to make him abhorred, to prevent him from doing harm, combined with the tender interest he inspires in these sublime men, is the true motive of the infinite care they take, of the huge expenses they make, to surround him with so many traps, to deliver him into so many hands, to ensnare him in so many ways that in the midst of this feigned freedom, he can neither say a word, nor take a step, nor lift a finger unless they know it and want it. Basically, everything they do about him is only for his own good, to avoid the harm they would have to do to him, and from which he cannot otherwise be protected. It was necessary to begin by separating him from his old acquaintances, in order to have the time to indoctrinate them well. A warrant against him was issued in Paris. What harm did that do him? For the same reason, it was necessary to prevent him from settling in Geneva. A warrant was issued there too. What harm did that do him? He was stoned in Môtiers, but the rocks that broke his windows and doors did not strike him. So what harm did they do him? He was evicted at the beginning of winter from the solitary Island where he sought refuge, and from all of Switzerland. But it was in order to force him charitably to go to England in search of the asylum long prepared for him without his knowledge, and far better than the one he obstinately chose, although he could not do any harm to anyone from there.[27] But what harm was done to him and what does he have to complain of today? Isn't he left alone in his disgrace? He can wallow at his ease in the mud where they keep him bemired. He is overwhelmed with indignities, it is true, but what does that matter? What injuries do they do him? Isn't he made for suffering them and even if every passerby spit in his face, what harm after all would that do him? But this monster of ingratitude feels nothing, is grateful for nothing, and all of the special arrangements made for him, far from touching him only aggravate his ferocity. In taking the greatest care to deprive him of all his friends, they were especially asked always to keep up the appearance and title of friend, and to maintain the same tone in deceiving him as they had previously used to welcome him. It is his guilty suspiciousness alone that makes him unhappy. Without that, he would be a little more taken in, but he would live as happily as before. In becoming the object of public horror, he found himself the object of everyone's attention. People vied to give parties for him, invite him to dinner, offer him a place to retreat, redouble their efforts to obtain his preference. From the eagerness they displayed to attract him, one would have said that nothing was more honorable, more glorious than to have him as a guest, and this was true for all stations without excepting Nobles and Princes; and my Bear was not content!

Rousseau

He was wrong, but he must have been very surprised! Those Nobles were undoubtedly not thinking like the Spanish Nobleman whose response you know when Charles V asked him for a castle in which to house the Constable of Bourbon.*[28]

---

* The Chateau of Trye is said to have been made uninhabitable since I stayed there. If this operation relates to me, it is not consistent with the eagerness which drew me there, nor with that used to engage the Prince de Ligne to offer me, at the same time, a charming

The Frenchman

The case is very different: you forget that this is a good deed.

Rousseau

Why don't you want to see that hospitality toward the Constable was as good a deed as refuge offered to a scoundrel?

The Frenchman

Oh, you refuse to see my point! The Constable knew very well that he was a rebel against his Prince.

Rousseau

Doesn't Jean Jacques know then that he is a scoundrel?

The Frenchman

The goal of the project is to behave overtly with him as if he knew nothing of the sort or as if one did not know it oneself. In this way the danger of explanations with him is avoided, and by the pretence of taking him for a decent man, he is so thoroughly beset by what appears to be eagerness for his merit that nothing relating to him nor he himself can escape the vigilance of those who approach him. As soon as he settles somewhere, which is always known in advance, the walls, the floors, the locks, everything is organized around him for the proposed goal; and providing appropriate neighbors is not forgotten, that is to say venomous spies, clever imposters, engaging women well versed in the lesson. It is rather amusing to see the loose women of our Gentlemen put on the airs of a Virgin as they try to approach this Bear. But it is apparently not virgins he wants, because he hasn't been softened by the pathetic letters that have been dictated to them, by the plaintive stories they are taught, by all of the display of their misfortunes and their virtues, nor by that of their faded charms. This Epicurean swine has suddenly become a Xenocrates for our Gentlemen.[29]

Rousseau

Wasn't he one for your Ladies? Even if this were not the most flagrant of his misdeeds, it would surely be the most unpardonable.

The Frenchman

Ah, M. Rousseau. One must always be attentive to ladies, and however a woman deals with things, that rule must never change.

I don't need to tell you that all his letters are opened, that all those from which he could draw any information are carefully held back, and that letters of all sorts are written to him by different hands, as much to explore his dispositions through his answers as to make assumptions about him from those he rejects; and that any correspondence that can be used against him someday is kept. They have discovered the art of

---

refuge on his property in a fine letter that was even circulated with great care throughout Paris.

making a solitude for him in Paris more awful than caves or the woods, so that in the midst of men he finds neither communication, consolation, nor counsel, nor enlightenment, nor anything that could help to guide him; a vast labyrinth where he is allowed to see in the darkness only false routes that lead him further and further astray. No one approaches him who has not already learned his lesson about what he must say and the tone he must use in talking to him. A record is kept of all those who ask to see him,* and they are allowed to do so only after they have received the instructions about him that I myself was charged with giving you at your first expression of a desire to know him. If he enters a public place, he is viewed and treated like someone with the plague: everyone surrounds him and stares, but keeping a distance and not talking to him, only to present a barrier to him; and if he dares to speak himself, and they deign to answer him, it is always either with a lie or by evading his questions with such a rude and scornful tone that he loses the desire to ask any. In the public garden, great care is taken to point him out to those around him, and always to place by his side a guard or a sergeant who speaks loudly about him without saying anything. He has been pointed out, described, recommended everywhere to deliverymen, Clerks, guards, spies, Chimney-sweeps, at all the Theaters, in all the cafes, to the barbers, the merchants, the peddlers, the booksellers. If he were looking for a book, an almanac, a novel, there would be none left in all of Paris, simply showing the desire for anything whatsoever is for him the infallible method of making it disappear. When he arrived in Paris, he looked for twelve little Italian Songs he had printed there twenty years ago and that he wrote just as he wrote the *Village Soothsayer*. But the collection, the Airs, the plates, everything disappeared, everything vanished on the spot, and he has never been able to recover a single copy. By multiplying small attentions, they have successfully kept him in this immense city under the eyes of the rabble, who view him with horror. Does he want to cross the river opposite the Four Nations? They will not make a crossing for him, even if he pays the full fare. Does he want his shoes polished? The shoe blacks, especially those at the Temple and the Palais Royal, will scornfully refuse to serve him. Does he enter the Tuileries or the Luxembourg gardens? Those who distribute printed tickets at the gate are under orders to pass by him with the most insulting affectation, and even to refuse him point blank if he comes up and asks for one. And all this is done not

---

* An Art gallery has been set up for this purpose in the street just opposite my door, and a discrete message attached to my door, which is kept locked, so that all who want to enter my house are obliged to seek out the neighbors, who have their instructions and their orders.

because it is important, but to point him out, make him known and more and more abhorred.

One of their finest inventions is how they have taken advantage for their own purpose of the annual custom of ceremonially burning a Swiss man of straw in the Rue aux Ours. This popular celebration seemed so barbarous and so ridiculous in this philosophic age that, already neglected, it was to be suppressed altogether had our Gentlemen not had the idea of reviving it precisely for J.J. To this end, they put his face and his clothing on the straw man, they placed a shiny knife in his hand, and have him carried with pomp through the streets of Paris; they took pains to position him directly beneath J.J.'s windows, turning the figure this way and that to show it off well to the People, to whom charitable interpreters make the desired application and incite them to burn J.J. in effigy, while awaiting something better.* And finally, one of our Gentlemen even assured me that he had the specific pleasure of seeing beggars throw alms he gave them back in his face, and you can well understand . . .

Rousseau

That they did not lose a thing. Ah, what sweetness of soul! What charity! The zeal of your Gentlemen forgets nothing.

The Frenchman

Beyond all these precautions, they have set up a very ingenious way of discovering whether there remains by misfortune some person he trusts who does not yet have the instructions and the feelings necessary to follow the generally accepted plan with regard to him. Letters are written to him by people pretending to be in distress, who implore his help or his advice to get out of difficulty. He chats with them, he consoles them, he recommends them to people he counts on. In this way, they become known, and then it is easy to convert them. You would not believe how many people have been discovered by this maneuver who still held him in esteem and whom he continued to deceive. Once known to our Gentlemen, they are soon detached from him, and by a special, but infallible art, he becomes as odious to them as he was previously cherished. But whether because he finally sees through this ploy or whether because in fact no one is left to him, these attempts have been ineffective for some time. He constantly refuses to be helpful to people whom he does not know, and even to reply to them; and that always contributes to the proposed goal

---

* There are two great drawbacks to burning me in person, which may force these Gentlemen to deprive themselves of that pleasure. The first is that once dead and burned, I would no longer be in their power, and they would lose the greater pleasure of torturing me alive. The second, which is far more serious, is that before burning me, they would finally have to listen to me, at least for the form, and I doubt that despite twenty years of precautions and schemes they would dare run that risk yet.

by making him appear to be an insensitive, hard-hearted man. For once again, nothing works better to elude his pernicious designs than to make him so hateful to everyone that his mere desire for something is enough to ensure that he cannot obtain it, and that as soon as he takes a positive interest in someone, that person no longer finds either a patron or help.

Rousseau

Indeed, all these methods you have spelled out for me cannot fail to turn this J.J. into the laughingstock and the plaything of the human race, and to make him the most abhorred of mortals.

The Frenchman

Oh, without doubt! That is the great, the true goal of the generous attentions of our Gentlemen. And thanks to their total success, I can assure you that never since the world began has a mortal lived in such a demoralizing situation.

Rousseau

But didn't you tell me, on the contrary, that tender care for his well-being played a large part in what they do for him?

The Frenchman

Yes indeed, and that above all is what is great, generous, admirable in our Gentlemen's plan, so that in preventing him from following his wishes and accomplishing his evil designs, they still seek to obtain the sweet things of life for him, so that he finds what he needs everywhere and what he could misuse nowhere. They want him to be sated with the bread of ignominy and the cup of disgrace. They even pretend to pay mocking, scoffing attention to him,* to pay respects like those lavished on Sancho on his island,[30] which make him even more ridiculous in the eyes of the populace. Finally, since he is so fond of distinctions, he has reason to be content: they are careful that he does not lack for them, and he gets what he likes when he is pointed out everywhere. Yes Sir, they want him to live, even agreeably insofar as that is possible for a wicked man without doing harm. They want his happiness to lack only the means of troubling the happiness of others. But he is a Bear who must be chained for fear he will devour passersby. The poison of his pen is feared above all, and they spare no precaution to prevent him from emitting it. They leave him no means to defend his honor, because it would be useless to him, because on this pretext he would not fail to attack the honor of someone else, and because it is not fitting for a man at the mercy of defamation to dare defame anyone. You can be sure that among the people who have been secured, the booksellers were not left out, especially those whom he used

---

* As when they wished by any means to send me the wine of honor in Amiens; when in London the Drummer of the Guards had to come play at my door, and when at the Temple, the Prince de Conti sent his Musicians to my morning rising.

to frequent. One was even held for a long time at the Bastille on other pretexts, but in fact in order to indocrinate him at greater leisure on the subject of J.J.* They recommended that all those around him be particularly vigilant about what he may write. They even tried to take all means of writing away from him, and they managed to remove all readable ink at the retreat where he was enticed in Dauphiné, so that the only thing he could find called ink was lightly tinted water, which would lose all its color in a short time. Despite all these precautions, the fellow still managed to write his memoirs, which he calls his confessions and which we call his lies, using encre de chine, which no one had thought about. But if he cannot be prevented from scribbling on paper at his ease, they prevent him at least from getting his venom into circulation. For no scrap, little or big, no note of two lines can leave his hands without falling instantly into those of persons in place to collect them all. With respect to what he says, none of that is lost. The first concern of those around him is to make him chatter, which is not difficult, nor is making him say just about anything one wants or at least how one wants it said in order to get advantage from it, sometimes by giving him false news, sometimes by getting him excited by clever contradictions, and sometimes, on the contrary by appearing to agree with everything he says. It is then especially that an exact record is kept of the hasty remarks that escape him, and that are exaggerated and commented on in cold blood. At the same time, they take all possible precautions so he cannot draw from them any enlightenment either in relation to himself or anyone else. They never pronounce the names of his first accusers in front of him, and they speak only with the greatest reserve of those who influence his lot, so it is impossible for him to get to know either what they say or what they do, whether they are in or out of Paris or even whether they are dead or alive. They never talk to him about the news, or else they tell him only what is false or dangerous, which would be new crimes on his part if he happens to repeat it. In the provinces, it was easy to prevent him from reading any newspaper. In Paris, where there would be too much show in doing this, they prevent him at least from seeing any that can give him some information about himself, and above all those in which our Gentlemen cause him to be talked about. If he inquires about something, no one

* In the same manner, at the same time, and for the same reason, they detained one of my Genevan friends, who—embittered by old grievances against the Genevan magistrates—stirred up the Citizens against them on my behalf. I thought very differently and when writing either to them or to him, I never stopped pressing them all to abandon my cause and wait for a better time to defend their rights. This did not prevent them from publishing that the complete opposite had been found in the letters I wrote him, and that I was the firebrand. How can justice, truth, innocence henceforth be expected of powerful men once they have stooped so low?

knows a thing; if he asks about someone, no one knows the person; if he asks a bit eagerly what the weather is, no one would tell him. But in contrast, every effort is made so that he finds goods that are if not cheaper at least of better quality than those he would obtain for the same price, his benefactors generously supplying the difference from their own pockets in order to satisfy the delicate tastes they assume he has and which they even try to arouse in him with bargains and low prices, to have the pleasure of noting it. By skillfully letting the common people into their confidence in this way, they publicly offer him alms despite himself in such a way that he cannot avoid them. And this charity, which they zealously publicize, has perhaps contributed more than anything else to debasing him as much as his friends desired.

Rousseau

What do you mean, his friends?

The Frenchman

Yes, it is a name our Gentlemen always like to assume in order to express all their good will toward him, all their solicitude for his happiness, and—which is really very clever—in order to accuse him of ingratitude for showing himself so insensitive to so much goodness.

Rousseau

There is something about that I do not understand very well. Please explain it to me better.

The Frenchman

As I have told you, in order that there be no danger in allowing him to remain free, his defamation had to be universal.* It was not enough to spread it in the clubs and in polite society, which was not difficult and was quickly done. It had to be spread among the entire people, and throughout the lowest ranks as well as the highest. And this presented greater difficulty, not only because the spectacle of publicly decrying him in this way without his knowledge could scandalize the simpleminded, but especially because of the inviolable law to conceal from him everything that concerned him, to remove forever everything that would clarify, all information, all means of defense and justification, all opportunity to have someone explain, to trace back to the source of the enlightenment they have about him. And it was less safe to count on the discretion of

---

* I did not want to speak here of what is done in the theater and of what is printed daily in Holland and elsewhere, because it is beyond all belief, and seeing and continually experiencing the sad results of it, I still have trouble believing it myself. All this has been going on for fifteen years, always with public approval and the consent of the government. And thus I grow old alone among all these madmen, with no consolation from anyone, yet without losing either courage or patience and, in the ignorance in which I am maintained, raising to heaven as my entire defense a heart exempt from fraud and hands pure of any evil.

the rabble for this than on that of decent people. To obtain the interest of the rabble in this mystery, without appearing to have this goal, they have admirably taken advantage of a ridiculous arrogance on our man's part, which is that he is too proud to accept gifts and does not wish to be given alms.

Rousseau

But I believe that you and I would be capable of just such arrogance. Don't you think so?

The Frenchman

Such delicacy is allowed to decent people. But by what right does a fellow like that, who acts like a beggar although he is rich, dare reject the little charities of our Gentlemen?

Rousseau

By the same right, perhaps, as the beggars reject his. However that may be, if he begs does he then receive or ask for charity? Because that is the only thing that distinguishes the beggar from the poor man, who is no richer than he but who is satisfied with what he has and asks nothing of anyone.

The Frenchman

Oh no! He does not ask for alms directly. On the contrary, he rejects them insolently first, but gives in slowly in the end when one is persistent.

Rousseau

Then he is not as arrogant as you were saying at first, and returning your question, it is my turn to ask why they persist in giving him alms as they would to a beggar since they know so well that he is rich?

The Frenchman

I have already told you why. I agree that it would be an insult to a decent man, but such a scoundrel deserves the fate of being debased by all possible means, and this is an occasion to reveal his ingratitude more clearly through that which he shows his benefactors.

Rousseau

Do you find that the intention of debasing him deserves great thanks?

The Frenchman

No, but the charity does. For as our Gentlemen put it very well, money buys everything, and nothing buys money. Whatever the intention of him who gives, even by force, he is still a benefactor and always deserves the liveliest gratitude as such. Therefore to avoid the brutal rusticity of our man, they imagined giving him one by one, without his knowledge, many well-publicized little gifts that require the participation of many people and especially of the lower classes who are thus brought without affectation into the great secret, so that scorn for his poverty and respect for his benefactors will be added to horror for his misdeeds. They find out where he purchases the goods necessary for his subsistence, and they see to it that for the same price he is given things of better quality that are therefore more expensive. In the end, this saves him nothing, and he has no need of it since he is rich. But for the same amount of money, he is better served; his baseness and the generosity of our Gentlemen thus circulate among the people, and in this way they manage to make him abject and contemptible while appearing to think only of his well-being and of making him happy despite himself. It is hard for the wretch not to be aware of this little game, and so much the better. For if he gets angry, that is greater and greater proof of his ingratitude, and if he switches vendors the same maneuver is immediately repeated, the reputation they want him to have spreads even more rapidly. Thus the more he struggles in his bonds, the tighter he makes them.

Rousseau

That, I admit, is what I did not understand well at first. But Sir, is it possible that you, in whom I have always known such an upright heart, approve such maneuvers?

The Frenchman

I would strongly condemn them for any other man, but here I admire them for the goodness of the motive that dictates them, yet without ever wanting to be involved. I hate J.J.; our Gentlemen love him, they want to preserve him at any cost. It is natural that they and I should not agree on the conduct to maintain with such a man. Their system, unjust perhaps in itself, is justified by its intention.

Rousseau

I believe that would make it suspect to me; for one does not seek good through evil nor virtue through fraud. But since you assure me that J.J. is rich, how does the public reconcile those things? Because truly nothing can seem more bizarre and less deserving than charity given by force to a rich scoundrel.

The Frenchman

Oh, the public does not put together ideas one is shrewd enough to present to it separately. It sees him as rich in order to reproach him for acting poor or to defraud him of the fruit of his labor by saying he does not need it. It sees him as poor in order to insult his poverty and treat him like a beggar. It sees him only on whichever side shows him to be most odious or most contemptible at the moment, even though that is incompatible with the other ways in which it sees him at other times.

Rousseau

It is certain that unless he is grossly insensitive, he must be as grieved as he is surprised by this mixture of attention and insults, the effects of which he feels every moment. But when, uniquely for the pleasure of making his defamation more thorough, his crimes are ignored daily, who can be surprised if he profits from this guilty indulgence in order constantly to commit new ones. I have already raised this objection, and I raise it again because you avoided it without responding. Through everything you have told me, I see that despite all the measures taken, he still goes on as before, without being the least troubled by the observers he sees surrounding him. I see that he who took such precautions that for forty years he totally fooled everyone and was taken for a decent man, uses the freedom left him only to quench his thirst for evil without bother, to commit new misdeeds daily of which he is certain none will escape his observers and which he is quietly allowed to carry out. Is it such a meritorious virtue on the part of your Gentlemen, then, to abandon decent people in this way to the fury of a scoundrel for the sole pleasure of calmly counting up his crimes, which they could so easily prevent?

The Frenchman

They have their reasons for that.

Rousseau

I don't doubt that at all. But even those who commit crimes doubtless have their reasons too. Does that suffice to justify them? It is a singular goodness, you must agree, which refuses to prevent the crime in order to make the criminal odious and which devotes itself to coddling the scoundrel at the expense of the innocent people upon whom he preys. Allowing crimes to be committed which one could prevent is not only being a witness to them, it is being an accomplice. Besides, if they always let him do everything you say he does, what good is it to spy on him so closely, with such vigilance and activity? What good is it to have discovered his works just to allow him to continue doing them as if one knew nothing about them? What good is it to constrain his will so strongly with respect to indifferent things, only to allow him total freedom as soon as it is a question of wrongdoing? One might say that your Gentlemen only seek to deprive him of all means to do anything except crimes. Does this indulgence seem to you so reasonable, so well conceived, and worthy of such virtuous persons?

The Frenchman

In all this there are things, I must admit, that I don't understand terribly well myself. But they promised to explain everything to my complete satisfaction. Perhaps in order to make him more execrable, they believed they needed to add a bit to the roster of his crimes, without much scruple about this addition which at bottom matters rather little, because since a man guilty of one crime is capable of committing a hundred, he at least wishes to commit all those of which he is accused, and one can hardly give such accusations the name of impostures.

I see that the basis of the system they follow with regard to him is the duty they assumed to unmask him thoroughly, to make him well known to all and yet never make any explanation to him, to deprive him of any knowledge of his accusers, and of any clear enlightenment about the things of which he is accused. This double necessity is based on the nature of the crimes, whose public declaration would be too scandalous, and which does not allow that he be convicted without being punished. Now, would you have them punish him without convicting him? Our judicial formalities would not permit it, and it would directly contradict the maxims of indulgence and commiseration they wish to follow with respect to him. All that can therefore be done for public safety is first to keep him under such good surveillance that he can undertake nothing without their knowing it, that he carry out nothing of importance unless they wish it, and for the rest to alert everyone to the danger of listening to and frequenting such a scoundrel. It is clear that being thus alerted, those who expose themselves to his attacks have only themselves to blame if they succumb. It is a misfortune they themselves could have avoided, since—fleeing from men as he does—it is not he who seeks them out.

Rousseau

The same might be said to those who pass through a woods where there are known to be robbers, without creating a valid reason to leave the latter every freedom to do what they want, particularly if to capture them it suffices to want to do so. But what excuse can your Gentlemen have, who themselves provide prey for the cruelty of this barbarian in the emissaries you told me they send to surround him, who make every attempt to become familiar with him, and whom he doubtless chooses as his first victims?

The Frenchman

Not at all. However intimately they live at his home, even trying to eat and drink there without concern for the risks, no harm comes to them. The people on whom he likes to vent his fury are those for whom he has esteem and inclination, those to whom he would confide as soon as their hearts open up a little to him, old friends whom he misses and from whom he still seems to seek the consolations he lacks. It is those whom he chooses to sacrifice as a matter of preference. The bond of friendship weighs heavily on him; he sees only his enemies with pleasure.

Rousseau

Facts should not be disputed, but you agree that you depict a very singular person, who poisons only his friends, who writes books only in favor of his enemies, and who flees from men in order to harm them.

What astounds me even more in all this is that there are decent people who want to seek out and frequent such a monster, whose mere approach should fill them with horror. That the rabble sent by your Gentlemen and suited to spying should take hold of him I understand with no difficulty. I understand, furthermore, that being only too happy to find someone who will tolerate him, he—a misanthrope with decent people but a burden to himself—must not be particular about relationships, that he must see, welcome, and eagerly seek out knaves like himself, to enlist them in his damnable plots. They, in turn, in hopes of finding him to be a good and hardened comrade, can expose themselves to the risks of frequenting him despite the fear of him given to them, because of the advantage they hope to derive. But that honorable people should seek to get in with him is beyond my ken, Sir. What do they say to him? What tone can they adopt with such a person? Such a great scoundrel may very well be a vile man who will suffer all sorts of insults to obtain his ends, and who will swallow all affronts without feeling them or pretending not to, as long as he is given something to eat. But you will admit that an exchange of insults and scorn on the one hand, and baseness and lies on the other, should not be very attractive to decent people.

The Frenchman

They are all the more respectable for making such a sacrifice for the public good. Approaching this wretch is a meritorious endeavor when it leads to some new discovery about his awful character. Such a character appears extraordinary, and cannot be sufficiently documented. You understand that no one approaches him to have any real society with him, but only to try to take him by surprise, to gain some new trait for his portrait, some new fact for his history, some indiscretion that can be used to make him even more odious. Besides, do you discount the pleasure of ridiculing him, of quietly calling him the insulting names he deserves when he does not dare to or cannot respond for fear of revealing the application to himself he is forced to make. It is a pleasure that can be savored without risk, because if he gets angry, he accuses himself, and if he doesn't get angry, by thus telling him the truth indirectly, one is compensated for the constraints that must be tolerated with him in pretending to take him for a decent man.

Rousseau

I don't know whether those are terribly sweet pleasures, but I don't find them terribly noble, and I suspect you believe the same thing because you have always disdained them. But Sir, in this regard has this man accused of so many crimes therefore never been convicted of any?

The Frenchman

Actually not. It is yet another gesture of extreme kindness they adopt toward him, to spare him the shame of being confounded. Hasn't he been completely judged on many invincible proofs so there is no need to hear him? Isn't convicting the guilty party superfluous where the evidence of the misdeed is apparent? It would be only an additional punishment for him. By depriving him of the useless freedom of defending himself, one deprives him only of the freedom of lying and slandering.

Rousseau

Oh thank Heaven, I am relieved! You remove a heavy burden from my heart.

The Frenchman

What is the matter with you? Why are you suddenly so joyful after the mournful, pensive look that hasn't left you during this entire conversation, and that is so different from the jovial, gay look on the faces of our Gentlemen when they talk about J.J. and his crimes?

Rousseau

I will explain if you still have the patience to listen to me, for this will require still more digressions.

You are familiar enough with my fate to know that it has scarcely allowed me to taste the prosperities of life. I have found neither the things men prize nor those I would have prized myself. You know at what cost fate sold me this dream for which they are so eager, and which—even if it had been purer—was not the food my heart needed. As long as fortune made me only poor, I did not live unhappily. I sometimes tasted true pleasures in obscurity, but I left it only to fall into a chasm of calamities, and those who pushed me in made every effort to render unbearable the ills they pretended to pity and that I would never have known without them. Once I recovered from that sweet chimera of friendship, the vain search for which caused all the misfortunes of my life, and recovered even more from the errors of opinion of which I am the victim, no longer finding among men either rectitude or truth or any of the feelings I thought were innate in their souls because they were in mine, and without which all society is only deceit and lies, I withdrew into myself, and living between myself and nature, I tasted an infinite sweetness in the thought that I was not alone, that I was not conversing with an insensitive, dead being; that my hardships were finite, my patience was measured, and all the miseries of my life were but title to the compensations and joys of a better state. I never adopted the philosophy of the happy people of the age; it does not suit me. I sought one more appropriate for my heart, more consoling in adversity, more encouraging to virtue. I found it in the books of J.J. I drew from them feelings compatible with the ones natural to me, I felt they had so much relationship to my own dispositions, that alone among all the authors I have read, he was for me the portrayer of nature and the historian of the human heart. I recognized in his writings the man I found in myself, and meditating on them taught me to find within myself the enjoyment and happiness that all others seek so far from themselves.

His example was useful above all in nurturing my confidence in the feelings that I alone among my contemporaries had preserved. I was a believer, I have always been one, though not in the same way as people with symbols and formulas. The lofty ideas I had of the divinity made me view with disgust the institutions of men and sham religions. I saw no one who thought as I did. I found myself alone in the midst of the multitude, as much because of my ideas as because of my feelings. This solitary state was sad. J.J. rescued me from it. His books strengthened me against the derision of free-thinkers. I found his principles so compatible with my feelings, I saw them grow out of such profound meditations, I saw them supported by such powerful reasons that I stopped fearing what I heard constantly shouted at me: that they were the work of prejudices and education. I saw that in this era when philosophy does nothing but destroy, this author alone edified with something solid. In all other books, I first recognized the passion that had dictated them and the personal goal the author had in mind. Only J.J. seemed to seek the truth with rectitude and simplicity of heart. He alone seemed to me to show men the route to true happiness by teaching them to distinguish reality from appearance, and the man of nature from the factitious and chimerical man whom our institutions and our prejudices have substituted for him. In short, only he appeared in his conviction to be inspired by love of the public good alone, without a secret aim and without personal interest. Moreover, I found his life and his maxims so consistent that my own were confirmed and I gained greater confidence in them from the example of a thinker who meditated about them for so long, of a writer who— scorning partisan spirit and not wishing to form or follow any sect— could have no other interest in his research than the public interest and the interest of truth. Based on all these ideas, I made a plan of living, whose charm would be a relationship with him; and I—for whom the society of men has for a long time offered only a false appearance without reality, without truth, without appeal, without any true harmony of feelings or of ideas, and more worthy of my scorn than of my zeal—I yielded to the hope of finding again in him all I had lost, of tasting once again the sweetness of a sincere friendship and of nourishing myself once again with him on those great and ravishing contemplations that constitute the highest enjoyment of this life and the only solid consolation that can be found in adversity.

I was filled with these feelings, and you may have known that, when you came with your cruel secrets to restrain my heart and chase from it the sweet illusions to which it was again ready to open itself. No, you will never know how profoundly you have broken it. To do so, you would have to feel the many heavenly ideas to which those you have destroyed were attached. I was close to the moment of being happy despite fate and men, and you thrust me back forever into all my wretchedness. You deprive me of all the hopes that made it bearable for me. That a single man thought as I did nurtured my confidence, a single truly virtuous man made me believe in virtue, inspired me to cherish it, idolize it, place all hope in it. And by taking away this support, you leave me alone in the world, swallowed up in a chasm of evils, without the least glimmer of hope in this life and ready to lose even that of finding compensation in a better order of things for all I have suffered in this one.

Your first statements overwhelmed me. The weight of your proofs made them even more devastating to me, and you cut my soul to the quick with the deepest pain I have ever felt. Then when you began to go into detail about the systematic maneuvers of which this unhappy man is the object, you elaborated the plan of action concerning him developed by the Author of these discoveries and faithfully followed by all, my divided attention made my surprise greater and my affliction less intense. I found all these maneuvers so sly, so full of ruse and cleverness, that I was unable to adopt the high opinion you wished to convey to me about those who have made a system out of them, and when you heaped praises on them, I felt my heart protest despite myself. I admired how such noble motives could dictate such base practices, how falseness, betrayal, and lying could have become the instruments of beneficence and charity, and finally how so many indirect steps could combine with rectitude! Was I wrong? Judge for yourself, and remember all you told me. Ah, at least agree that so many shadowy envelopes are a very strange cloak for virtue!

The strength of your proofs nonetheless outweighed all the suspicions these machinations could arouse in me. I saw that after all this bizarre conduct, however shocking it appeared to me, was still a work of mercy, and that wishing to spare a scoundrel the treatment he deserved, it was necessary to take extraordinary precautions to prevent a scandal about this indulgence and place it at such a high price that others would not be tempted to desire such indulgence nor would he be tempted to take advantage of it. Seeing everyone thus eagerly hasten to give him his fill of disgraces and indignities, far from pitying him I scorned him more for so shamefully buying impunity at the price of such a destiny.

You told me all that many times, and I repeated it after you, moaning. The anguish in my heart did not prevent my reason from being subjugated, and from this assent that I was forced to give you arose the cruelest state of soul for an unfortunate, decent man, from whom one pitilessly tears all his consolations, all his resources, all the hopes that made his ills bearable.

One flash of light has brought all this back to me in an instant. When I thought, when you yourself confirmed for me that this man so ignobly treated for so many atrocious crimes had never been convicted of any, you toppled all your proofs with a single word, and even if I did not see imposture where you claim to see evidence, that evidence has at least disappeared from my sight to such a degree that in all you have demonstrated, I no longer see anything more than an insoluble problem, a frightening, impenetrable mystery, which only the conviction of the guilty person could clarify for me.

You and I think very differently on this point, Sir. According to you, the evidence of his crimes takes the place of a conviction, and according to me this evidence consists so essentially in the conviction itself that it cannot exist without it. As long as the accused has not been heard, the proofs that condemn him—however strong they might be, however convincing they might appear—lack the seal that can show them to be so, even when it has not been possible to hear the accused as is the case when there is a trial held in the memory of a dead man, for in presuming he would have had nothing to say one may be right, but it is wrong to change this presumption into a certainty in order to condemn him, and a crime can be punished only when all doubt about it has been removed. But when there is even refusal to hear the accused who is alive and present, even though it would be possible and easy, when extraordinary measures are taken to prevent him from talking, when the accusation, the accuser, the proofs are hidden from him with the greatest care, then all these proofs become suspicious and lose all their strength in my mind. Not to dare subject them to the proof that would confirm them makes me presume they would not stand up to that proof. This great principle, the basis and sanction of all justice, without which human society would crumble at its foundations, is so sacred, so inviolable in practice, that if everyone in town had seen one man murder another in the public square, the murderer would still not be punished without having a hearing first.

The Frenchman

What! Do judicial formalities that must be general and without exception in the courts, albeit often superfluous, constitute law in cases of pardon and indulgence such as this? Besides, can the omission of these formalities change the nature of things, make what has been demonstrated cease to be so, make what is evident obscure; and in the example you have just proposed, would the offense be less proven, would the accused be less guilty if they neglected to hear him; and if they had broken him on the wheel on the basis of the notoriety of the deed alone without any of the customary interrogations, would they be any less certain of having justly punished a murderer? Finally, are all the forms established to prove ordinary offenses necessary with respect to a monster whose life is nothing but a web of crimes and who is recognized by the whole world to be the shame and the disgrace of humanity? Does he who is in no way human deserve to be treated as a man?

Rousseau

You make me tremble. Is it you who speaks in this way? If I believed that, I would flee rather than respond. But no, I know you too well. Let us calmly discuss with your Gentlemen these important questions on which maintenance of the social order along with the preservation of the human race depends. Following them, you always speak about clemency and pardon, but before examining just what that pardon is, we must first see whether that is really the case here and how it can occur. The right of pardon presupposes the right to punish, and consequently the prior conviction of the guilty party. That, in the first instance, is what it is all about.

You claim that this conviction becomes superfluous where the evidence prevails. And I think, to the contrary, that in the matter of an offense, evidence can come only from the conviction of the guilty party, and that no decision can be stated about the strength of the proofs that condemn him until after he has been heard. The reason for this is that in order to bring truth out of the bosom of the passions into the view of men, these passions must collide, conflict, and he who accuses must find an equal counterweight in him who defends, so that reason alone and justice can break the equilibrium and make the scale tip to one side. When one man becomes the accuser of another, it is probable, it is almost certain that he is moved by some secret passion which he is very careful to disguise. But whatever the determining reason, and even if it is a motive of pure virtue, it is always certain that from the moment he accuses he is animated by the lively desire to demonstrate that the accused is guilty, if only in order not to be perceived as a slanderer. Moreover, since he has made all his preparations at leisure, since he has taken his time putting his machinery in place and organizing his means and his proofs, the least that can be done to prevent a surprise is to expose them to the examination and the responses of the accused, who alone has sufficient interest to examine them with all possible attention, and who alone once again can provide all the clarifications necessary to judge them well. It is for a similar reason that the deposition of the witnesses, however many there may be, carries weight only after their confrontation. From this action and reaction, and from the conflict of these opposing interests, the light of the truth must naturally emerge before the eyes of the judge; at least this is the best means he has in his power. But if one of these interests acts alone with all its strength and the counterweight of the other is lacking, how will the scale remain balanced? How will the judge—whom I wish to assume is calm, impartial, animated by love of justice alone, which commonly does not inspire great efforts in another's interest—assure himself that he has weighed the pros and the cons well, that he has seen for himself through all the artifices of the accuser, that he has sorted out well the completely true facts from those he contrives, modifies, colors according to his whim; that he has even guessed those he suppresses and that change the effect of those he exposes. What daring man, no less convinced of his penetration than of his virtue, would dare to be that judge? To fulfill such a daring duty with so much confidence, he must feel as infallible as a God.

What happens if instead of assuming here a judge of perfect integrity and without passion, I assumed he was animated by a secret desire to find the accused guilty, and to be seeking only plausible means to justify his partiality in his own eyes.

This second assumption could apply more than once in the particular case that concerns us. But let us not look further than the celebrity of an Author whose past successes wound the amour-propre of those who cannot achieve such success. A person who applauds the renown of a man whom he cannot hope to rival would quickly work to make him pay dearly for his greater renown if he saw the slightest glimmer of success. As soon as a man has had the misfortune to distinguish himself to a certain point, unless he makes himself feared or belongs to some party, he should no longer count on the equity of others toward him, and he will be fortunate if even those who are more famous than he forgive him for his small share of the attention they would like to generate all alone.

I will add nothing more. I want to speak only to your reason here. Look for a reply to what I have told you that satisfies your reason, and I will be silent. While waiting, here is my conclusion. It is always unjust and rash to judge an accused person whoever he may be without a willingness to hear him. But whoever judging a man who has made a stir in the world not only judges him without a hearing but hides from him in order to judge him, whatever the specious pretext he alleges and even if he were truly just and virtuous, even if he were an angel on earth, let him search deep within himself: though he does not know it, iniquity hides at the bottom of his heart.

A foreigner, without family, without support, alone, abandoned by all, betrayed by the majority, J.J. is in the worst position anyone can be in to be fairly judged. However, in the judgments without appeal that condemn him to infamy, who has taken up his defense and spoken for him, who has taken the trouble to examine the accusation, the accusers, the proofs with that zeal and care which can only be inspired by self-interest or interest in one's most intimate friend?

The Frenchman

But haven't you, who so much wanted to be his, been reduced to silence by the proofs with which I was armed?

Rousseau

Did I have the enlightenment necessary to appreciate them and differentiate among so many obscure schemes the false colorations they may have been given? Am I acquainted with the details that must be known? Can I guess the clarifications, the objections, the solutions the accused could give about facts of which only he is adequately informed? Perhaps with a word he might have pulled away veils impenetrable to the eyes of anyone else and shed light on maneuvers that no mortal will ever sort out. I surrendered not because I was reduced to silence, but because I thought that he himself was. I have nothing, I admit, to reply to your proofs. But if you were isolated on earth, without defense and without defender, and the prey of your enemies for twenty years as J.J. has been, one could easily prove to me in secret about you what you have proved to me about him, without my having anything to reply either. Would that be enough to judge you without appeal and without wanting to hear you?

Sir, this is the first time since the world began that the first and holiest of the social laws—that without which innocence is no longer safe among men—has been violated so openly and so publicly. Whatever may be said about it, it is false that such a criminal violation can ever have the interest of the accused as a motive. Only the interest of the accusers, and a most urgent one at that, can motivate them, and only the passion of the judges can make them disregard it despite the infraction of that law. They would never tolerate the infraction if they feared being unjust. No, there is no man of good sense, not to mention an enlightened judge, who does not feel, on the basis of measures taken with such anxiety and such care to hide the accusation, the witnesses, and the proofs from the accused, that all this cannot possibly be reasonably explained except by imposture on the part of the accuser.

You nevertheless ask what harm there would be, when the crime is evident, in putting the accused on the rack without hearing him? And in reply I ask you who is the man, who is the judge bold enough to dare condemn to death an accused man convicted in accordance with all the judicial forms, after so many disastrous examples of innocents who were well interrogated, well heard, well confronted, well judged in accordance with all the forms, and on the basis of alleged evidence put to death with the greatest confidence for crimes they never committed. You ask what harm there would be, when the crime is evident in putting the accused on the rack without hearing him. I reply that your assumption is impossible and a contradiction in terms, because the evidence of a crime consists essentially in the conviction of the accused, and that all other evidence or notoriety may be false, illusory, and cause the torture of an innocent. Must the reasons for this be confirmed by examples? Unfortunately, there is no lack of them. Here is a very recent one from the Leyden Gazette, which deserves to be cited. A man accused in an English court of a flagrant offense attested by public and unanimous testimony used a rather unusual alibi as a defense. He maintained and proved that the same day and at the same time when he was seen committing the crime, he was in person busy defending himself in another court and in another city against an identical charge. This fact, no less perfectly attested, placed the judges in a strange quandary. By dint of research and investigations which assuredly would not have been undertaken otherwise, it was finally discovered that the offenses attributed to the accused had been committed by another, less well known man, but who was so similar to the first in height, appearance, and features that the one had always been mistaken for the other. This would never have been discovered if, on the basis of that supposed evidence, they had hastened to get rid of that man without deigning to hear him; and you see how, once this is the accepted practice, it can be a matter of life and death to put on clothes of one color rather than another.

Another, even more recent, article taken from the Gazette of France of October 31, 1774. "A wretch, say the letters from London, was to suffer capital punishment and was already on the scaffold when a spectator, emerging from the crowd, shouted to suspend the execution and declared himself to be the author of the crime for which this unfortunate man had been condemned, adding that his troubled conscience" (this man was apparently not a philosopher) "did not allow him at that moment to save his own life at the expense of the innocent man. After a new hearing of the case, the condemned," continues the article, "was sent away absolved, and the King thought he should pardon the guilty man due to his generosity." I think you don't need my reflections about that new hearing of the case and about the first one, by virtue of which the innocent had been condemned to death.

No doubt you have heard of that other case in which eleven jurors, having condemned the accused on the alleged evidence of the crime, the twelfth risked starving to death with his colleagues rather than to add his vote to theirs; and this, as he admitted later, was because he himself had committed the crime of which the other person appeared evidently guilty.

These examples occur more often in England where criminal procedures are public whereas in France, where everything is shrouded in the most frightening mystery, the weak are subjected to the revenge of the powerful without scandal, and the procedures—always unknown to the public or falsified to deceive it—remain an eternal secret as do the error or iniquity of judges unless some extraordinary event makes them known.

A case of this sort reminds me of these ideas each day when I awaken. Every morning before dawn, the Mass of the Magpie I hear rung at Saint Eustache seems to me a very solemn warning for Judges and all men to have less rash confidence in their enlightenment, to oppress and despise weakness less, to believe a little more in innocence, to take a little more interest in it, to be more careful with the life and honor of their fellows, and finally to fear sometimes that too much zeal in punishing crimes may cause them to commit awful crimes themselves.[31] Whether the singularity of the cases I have cited makes each of them unique of its kind, whether one disputes them, whether in sum one denies them if one wishes, how many other cases no less unexpected, no less possible, may be as singular of their kinds? Where is the person who can determine with certainty all those cases in which men, fooled by false appearances, can take imposture as evidence and error as truth? What daring man, when the judgment involves capital punishment of a man, will go ahead and condemn him without taking all possible precautions to protect himself from the traps of lying and the illusions of error? What barbarous judge, refusing to declare his crime to the accused, divests him of the sacred right of being heard in his own defense, a right which, far from protecting him from conviction if the evidence is what it is assumed to be, very often does not even suffice to prevent the judge from seeing this evidence in imposture and from spilling innocent blood, even after the accused has been heard. Do you dare believe that the courts abound in superfluous precautions for the safekeeping of innocence? Who doesn't know, on the contrary, that far from worrying about whether an accused person is innocent and from seeking to find him so, their whole endeavor, on the contrary, consists only in trying to find him guilty at any cost, and in depriving him for his defense of all those means that are not formally accorded him by law, so that if in a particular case there is an essential circumstance for which the law makes no provision it is the prisoner, even though he is innocent, who has to pay for this oversight by his punishment. Don't you know that what gratifies judges most is to have victims to torment, that they would prefer to see a hundred innocents perish than to allow one guilty person to escape, and that if they can find a way to condemn a man following all the forms even though they were persuaded of his innocence, they would hasten to let him perish in honor of the law? They lament the vindication of an accused person as they would lament a true loss. Eager to spill blood, they regretfully see the prey they had promised themselves escape their grasp, and spare nothing they can get away with so that this misfortune does not happen to them. Grandier, Calas, Langlade and a hundred others created a stir through chance circumstances.[32] But what a mass of unfortunates there are among the victims of the error or cruelty of judges, whose innocence buried under stacks of proceedings never come to light or does so only by chance long after the death of the accused and when no one takes an interest in their fate any longer. Everything shows us or makes us feel the inadequacy of the law and the indifference of judges concerning the protection of accused persons who are innocent, who are already punished before their judgment by the hardships of the cell and irons, and from whom admissions of crimes they did not commit are often extracted by torture. And yet, as though the established and too often useless formalities were also superfluous, you ask whether there would be any harm, when the crime is evident, in putting the accused on the rack without a hearing! Come, Sir, this question needed no reply from me, and if it had been a serious question when you asked it, the protests of your heart would have been answer enough.

But if this form, so sacred and so necessary, could never be omitted with regard to some scoundrel who was always known as such and who had been judged by the public voice even before he was charged with any particular thing for which he had to defend himself, what can I think when I see it put aside with so much solicitude and vigilance from the judgment of the world when it was most indispensable, from the judgment of a man suddenly accused of being an abominable monster after having enjoyed public esteem and the benevolence of all who knew him for forty years. Is it natural, is it reasonable, is it just to choose to refuse a hearing only to him who should be heard by preference, even if such a sacred formality were allowed to to be neglected for others? I cannot hide from you that such cruel and rash security in those who indulge in it with such confidence not to say such pleasure, displeases and shocks me. If someone in 1751 had predicted this cursory and disdainful manner of judging a man who was then so universally esteemed, no one would have believed him, and if the public viewed dispassionately the road it has been made to travel to lead it gradually to this strange persuasion, it would itself be amazed to see the tortuous and dim paths by which it had been imperceptibly guided to that point, without noticing what was happening.

You say that the precautions prescribed by good sense and equity with ordinary men are superfluous with such a monster; that since he has trampled all justice and all humanity underfoot, he is unworthy of having people follow on his behalf the rules inspired by them; that the number and enormity of his crimes is such that making a conviction for each one by itself would entail immense discussions made superfluous by the evidence of them all.

What! Because you conjure up for me a monster like none that ever existed, you want to dispense with the proof that gives sanction to all the others? But who ever claimed that the absurdity of a fact served as its proof, and that to establish the truth of it, it suffices to show that it is unbelievable? What a wide and easy door you open to calumny and imposture if in order to have the right to judge a person definitively without his knowledge and while hiding from him, it suffices to multiply and inflate the accusations, to make them so awful they horrify, so that the less credible they are, the more they must be believed. I don't doubt that a man capable of committing one crime is capable of committing a hundred. But what I know better still is that a man accused of a hundred crimes may not be guilty of any. Piling the accusations is not convicting and cannot dispense with it. The very reason that makes his conviction superfluous for you is for me an additional reason to make it indispensable. To spare the difficulty of so many proofs, I ask only for one, but I want it authentic, invincible, and according to all forms. It is proof of the first offense which gave credibility to all the others. When that one has been proved, I will believe all the others without proofs, but the accusation of a hundred thousand others will never take the place in my mind of the judicial proof of that one.

The Frenchman

You are right. But take a better look at my thought and that of our Gentlemen. They did not pay attention as much to the multitude of J.J.'s crimes as they did to his awful character, discovered at last, albeit late, and now generally recognized. All those who have seen, followed, examined him with the most care agree on this subject and unanimously recognize him, as his virtuous Patron Mr. Hume said so well, to be the shame of the human race and a monster of wickedness. The exact and punctilious discussion of facts becomes superfluous when the result is only what is already known without them. Even if J.J. had not committed any crime, he would be no less capable of them all. He is not being punished for one offense or for another, but he is abhorred for harboring them all in his heart. I see nothing that is not just in that. The horror and aversion of men is due to the wicked person whom they allow to live when their clemency leads them to spare him.

Rousseau

After our earlier discussion, I did not expect this new distinction. In order to judge him by his character independently from the facts, I would have to understand how they so suddenly and so surely recognized this character independently from these same facts. When I consider that this monster lived for forty years generally esteemed and well thought of, without a suspicion of his bad nature, with no one having the least suspicion of his crimes, I cannot understand how these two things can suddenly have become so evident, and I understand even less how one can have become evident without the other. Let us add that since these discoveries were made together and all at once by the same person, that person must necessarily have started by stating facts in order to establish such novel judgments, so contrary to those which had been current to that point; and otherwise what confidence could I place in appearances that are vague, uncertain, often deceptive, without anything precise that one could state? If you see the possibility that for forty years he was thought to be an honest man when he was not, I see even more clearly the possibility that for ten years he has been wrongly thought to be a scoundrel. For there is this essential difference between these two opinions: formerly he was judged fairly and without bias, whereas he is no longer judged except with passion and prejudice.

The Frenchman

And that is precisely the reason people were mistaken formerly and are mistaken no longer now that he is regarded with less indifference. You remind me of what I had to say about those two beings, so different and so contradictory, into which you divided him earlier. His hypocrisy fooled men for a long time because they went no further than appearances and did not look at things very closely. But since they began to spy on him more carefully and to examine him better, they soon discovered his boasting. All his moral ostentation disappeared, his awful character became apparent from all sides. Even the people who knew him before, who loved him, who esteemed him because they were his dupes, blush today for their former folly, and cannot understand how such gross artifices could have deceived them for so long. They see with utmost clarity that while he is different than he appeared then because the illusion has vanished, he is the same as he always was.

Rousseau

I don't doubt that at all. But what does not seem as clear to me as it does to you is that people used to be mistaken about him but are mistaken no longer today. It is harder than you seem to think to see a man exactly as he is when one has a fixed opinion about him in advance, whether it be good or bad. To everything he does, to everything he says one applies the idea that has been formed about him. Each sees and agrees on everything that confirms his judgment, rejects or explains in his own way all that contradicts it. All his movements, his looks, his gestures are interpreted according to this idea. One relates to it what is least related to it. The very same things that a thousand others say or do and that one says or does indifferently oneself take on a mysterious meaning as soon as they come from him. One wants to guess, one wants to be perceptive. It is the natural game of amour-propre:[33] one sees what one believes and not what one sees. A person explains everything according to his prejudice, and consolation for the error he thinks he made comes only from convincing himself that the error was made for want of attention, not for want of penetration. This is so true that if two men have opposite opinions about a third, this same opposition will dominate the observations they make about him. One will see white, the other black; one will find virtues, the other vices in the most indifferent acts that come from him, and each, using subtle interpretations, will prove that it is he who sees correctly. The same object seen at different times with eyes in a different state makes very different impressions on us, and even if we agree that the error comes from our organ we can still deceive ourselves by concluding that we were mistaken before when it is perhaps today that we are mistaken. All this would be true if the only thing to fear were the error of prejudices. What would happen if the influence of the passions were added too. If charitable, ever alert interpreters, constantly anticipated all the favorable ideas that one could draw from one's own observations in order to disfigure, blacken, and poison everything? How much hatred fascinates the eyes is well known. Who knows how to see virtues in the object of his aversion; who does not see evil in everything that comes from an odious man? One always seeks to justify one's own feelings; that too is a very natural disposition. One strives to find hateful what one hates, and if it is true that the biased man sees what he believes, it is even more true that the passionate man sees what he desires. The difference here, then, is that whereas formerly J.J. was seen disinterestedly, and was therefore judged impartially, now bias and hatred no longer allow one to see anything in him except what one wants to find. In your opinion, then, is it to the old or to the new judgments that the prejudice of reason should give greater authority?

If it is impossible, as I believe I have proved to you, that certain knowledge of the truth and even less the evidence of it results from the method that has been adopted to judge J.J.; if the true means of bringing to bear an impartial, infallible, enlightened judgment about him were deliberately avoided, it follows that his condemnation—so stridently and proudly pronounced—is not only arrogant and rash, but strongly to be suspected of the blackest iniquity. I conclude from this that having no right to judge him clandestinely as they have done, they also do not have the right to pardon him, since the pardon of a criminal is only his exemption from a punishment incurred and judicially inflicted. Thus the clemency your gentlemen boast of with regard to him, even if they display genuine good will toward him, is deceptive and false; and when they count as a good deed the exemption they claim to give him from the harm he deserves, they are deceitful and lie, since they have not convicted him of any punishable action. An innocent person who deserves no punishment needs no pardon, and such a word is nothing but an insult to him. They are therefore doubly unjust, in that they take credit for generosity they do not display toward him and in that they make a pretense of sparing his person only to insult his honor with impunity.

Let us now get a sense of that pardon you emphasize so strongly, and see what it consists of. It consists of dragging the one who receives it from disgrace to disgrace and from misery to misery without leaving him any possible means to protect himself. Do you know of any other punishment for a man's heart as cruel as such a pardon? I refer to the picture you drew yourself. What! Is it through goodness, commiseration, or benevolence that they make this unfortunate man the plaything of the public, the laughingstock of the rabble, the horror of the universe; that they deprive him of all human society, suffocate him at whim in mire, amuse themselves by burying him alive? If you or I had to undergo the ultimate torture, would we avoid it at the cost of such a pardon? Would we choose life on the condition of spending it like that? Surely not. There is no torment, no torture that we would not prefer to that, and the most painful end to our ills would seem desirable and sweet rather than to prolong them in such anguish. Oh, what idea do your Gentlemen have of honor if they do not consider infamy a torture? No, no, whatever they may say, it is not bestowing life to make it worse than death.

The Frenchman

You see that our man does not think this way, since in the midst of all his disgrace he continues to live and to be in better health than he ever was. The feelings of a scoundrel must not be judged by those a decent man would have in his position. Infamy is painful only in proportion to the honor a man has in his heart. Base souls, insensitive to shame, find it their element. Scorn has scarcely any effect on one who feels deserving of it: it is a judgment to which his own heart has already completely accustomed him.

Rousseau

The interpretation of this stoic tranquility in the midst of insults depends on the judgment already brought to bear on the person who endures them. Thus, it is not appropriate to judge the man on the basis of this composure, but on the contrary it is through the man that the composure must be assessed. For myself I do not see how the impenetrable dissimulation, the profound hypocrisy you have attributed to him is in harmony with that almost unbelievable baseness which you say here is his natural element. Sir, how is it that such a haughty, proud, arrogant man, full of genius and fire, who according to you could restrain himself and keep silent for forty years in order to astound Europe with the vigor of his pen; a man who so highly values the opinion of others that he sacrificed everything to a false affectation of virtue; a man whose ambitious amour-propre wanted to fill the whole universe with his glory, dazzle all his contemporaries with the brilliance of his talents and his virtues, trample all prejudices underfoot, defy all the powers, and be admired for his fearlessness; this same man now insensitive to so many indignities, avidly quenches his thirst with ignominy and indolently takes his repose in degradation as in his natural element. I beg you, make your ideas more consistent or please explain to me how this brutish insensibility can exist in a soul capable of such effervescence. Insults affect all men, but to a much greater extent those who deserve them and who have no asylum inside themselves to which they can escape. To be moved as little as possible by them, one must feel them to be unjust, and build a rampart of honor and innocence around one's heart, inaccessible to disgrace. Then one can console oneself about the error or injustice of men. For in the former case the insults are not intended by those who make them for the person who receives them, and in the latter they do not make them for him because of the opinion that he is vile and deserves them, but on the contrary because being vile and wicked themselves, they hate those who are not.

But the strength that a healthy soul uses to withstand treatments unworthy of itself does not make these treatments less barbarous on the part of those who make him undergo them. It would be a mistake to give them credit for resources that they could not take away from him and that they did not even foresee, because in his place, they would not find them in themselves. You rattle the words benevolence and pardon in my ears in vain. In the obscure system to which you give these names I see nothing but a refinement of cruelty to crush an unfortunate with miseries worse than death, to give the blackest treachery a look of generosity, and to charge with ingratitude the person they defame because he is not imbued with gratitude for the troubles they take to overwhelm him and deliver him defenseless into the hands of the cowardly murderers who stab him without risk while hiding from his view.

That, then, is the substance of this supposed pardon about which your Gentlemen make so much noise. This pardon would not be one, even for a guilty person, unless he were at the same time the most vile of mortals. That it is one for this daring man who, despite so much resistance and such frightening threats came boldly to Paris to provoke by his presence the iniquitous tribunal that issued a warrant against him when his innocence was perfectly well known; that it is one for this disdainful man who hides so little his scorn for the cajoling traitors who beset him and who hold his destiny in their hands; that, Sir, is what I will never understand. And if he were as they say he is, it would still be necessary to know from him whether he consented to preserve his life and his freedom at this unworthy price. For a pardon, like any other gift, is legitimate only with the consent, at least presumed, of the person who receives it; and I ask you whether the conduct and the discourse of J.J. permit us to presume this consent from him. Now, any gift made by force is not a gift, it is a theft. There is no more wicked tyranny than to force a man to be indebted to us despite himself, and it is an unworthy misuse of the word pardon to attribute it to forced treatment, crueller than the punishment. Here I am assuming that the accused is guilty. What becomes of this pardon if I assume he is innocent, as I can and must do so long as they are afraid to convict him. But, you say, he is guilty; it is a certainty since he is wicked. See how you bandy me about! You have already cited his crimes as proof of his wickedness, and now you cite his wickedness as proof of his crimes. His character was discovered by means of the facts, and you advance his character to avoid the orderly discussion of the facts. Such a monster, you tell me, does not deserve to have the formalities established for the conviction of an ordinary criminal observed with him. There is no need to hear such a detestable scoundrel, his works speak for him! I will grant that the monster you have drawn for me, if he exists, does not deserve any of the precautions established as much for the safety of innocents as for the conviction of the guilty. But they were all needed and more still to verify his existence and be perfectly sure that what you have called his works are really his works. That was where it was necessary to begin, and that is precisely what your Gentlemen forgot. For if the treatment he has been made to suffer would be gentle for a guilty man, it is horrible for an innocent one. Alleging the gentleness of this treatment to avoid the conviction of him who endures it is therefore a sophism as cruel as it is meaningless. Agree moreover that this monster, as they have been pleased to fabricate him for us, is a very strange, very novel, very contradictory personage; an imaginary being such as might be conjured up by the delirium of a fever, confusedly formed of heterogeneous parts which, by their number, their disproportion, and their incompatibility, cannot form a single whole; and the extravagance of this composite, which in itself is a reason to deny its existence, is for you a reason to acknowledge it without deigning to verify it. This man is too guilty to deserve to be heard; he is too far removed from nature for there to be any doubt that he exists. What do you think of this reasoning? It is however yours, or at least that of your Gentlemen.

You assure me that it is through their great goodness, through their excessive benevolence that they spare him the shame of being unmasked. But such generosity bears a strong resemblance to the bravura of braggarts, which they express only far from danger. It seems to me that in their place, and despite all my pity, I would still rather be openly just and severe than charitably deceitful and double dealing; and I will always repeat to you that the benevolence is too bizarre which, making its unfortunate object carry all the disgrace of derision along with all the burden of hate, strives only to deprive him of all means of escape whether he is innocent or guilty. I shall add that all those virtues you boast about to me in the arbiters of his destiny are such that not only do I feel incapable of them, thank Heaven, but that I cannot even conceive of them. How can one love a monster who inspires horror? How can one be imbued with such tender pity for a being so malicious, so cruel, so bloodthirsty? How can one pamper with such solicitude the scourge of the human race, treat him kindly at the expense of the victims of his fury, and for fear of saddening him help him practically to make the world a vast tomb? . . . What, Sir, a traitor, a thief, a poisoner, a murderer! . . . I don't know whether there might be a feeling of benevolence for such a being among the Demons, but among men such a feeling would seem to me a punishable, criminal taste rather than a virtue. No, only one who is like him can love him.

The Frenchman

Whatever you may say about it, it would be a virtue to spare him if in this act of clemency one set out to fulfill a duty rather than follow an inclination.

Rousseau

Here again you are changing the status of the question, and that is not what you were saying before. But let's see.

The Frenchman

Let's assume that the first person who discovered the crimes of this wretch and his awful character believed he was obliged, as he was without any possible contradiction, not only to unmask him to the eyes of the public but to denounce him to the Government; and yet that his respect for old ties did not allow him to want to be the instrument of his downfall. Didn't he, that being the case, have to conduct himself just as he did, placing the pardon of the scoundrel as a condition of his denunciation and dealing with him in such a way, while unmasking him, that while giving him the reputation of a rascal, he was allowed to preserve the freedom of a decent man?

Rousseau

Your assumption contains contradictions about which I could say a great deal. Even in such an assumption, I would have behaved, and you would too I feel sure, along with any other honorable man, in a very different way. First, whatever the cost, I would never have wanted to denounce the scoundrel without coming forward and confronting him, especially in light of the prior relationships you assume, which even more stringently oblige the accuser to give the guilty person prior notice of what duty obligated him to do regarding that person. I would have wished even less to take extraordinary measures to prevent my name, my accusations, my proofs from reaching his ears. Because in any case, an accuser who hides plays a part that is odious, base, cowardly, justly suspected of imposture; and there is no sufficient reason that can oblige an honest man to perform an unjust and dishonoring act. As soon as you assume the obligation to accuse the evil-doer, you also assume that of convicting him, because the first of these two obligations necessarily implies the other, and one must either come forward and confront the accused, or, if one wants to hide from him, be silent about him along with everyone. There is no middle ground. This conviction of the person one accuses is not only indispensable proof of the truth one believes oneself obliged to declare, it is also a duty of the Denouncer to himself from which nothing can dispense him, especially in the case you present. For there is no inconsistency in virtue, and it will never permit imitating an imposter for the purpose of punishing one.

The Frenchman

You don't think the way J.J. does about that. "It is by betraying him that one must punish a traitor."[34] That is one of his maxims. What do you say to that?

Rousseau

Just what your own heart says. It is not surprising that a man who hesitates at nothing has no hesitation about treachery. But it would be extremely surprising for decent people to believe that his example authorizes them to imitate him.

The Frenchman

Imitate him! Not in general, but what harm is done him by following his own maxims with him, to prevent him from taking advantage of them?

Rousseau

Following his own maxims with him! Are you serious? What principles, what morality! If one can, if one should follow their own maxims with people, one would then have to lie to liars, steal from swindlers, poison poisoners, murder murderers, be as much of a scoundrel as one wishes with those who are scoundrels, and if one is no longer obliged to be a decent man except with decent people, this duty will not put anyone to much trouble being virtuous in our era. It is worthy of the scoundrel you have depicted to give lessons in imposture and treachery. But I am sorry for your gentlemen that among so many better lessons that he has given and that would have been more worthwhile to follow, they profited only from that one.

Besides, I don't recall finding anything like that in J.J.'s books. Where did he establish this new precept so contrary to all the others?

The Frenchman

In a line of a comedy.

Rousseau

When was this Comedy presented?

The Frenchman

Never.

Rousseau

Where did he have it published?

The Frenchman

Nowhere.

Rousseau

By my faith, I don't understand you.

The Frenchman

It is a kind of farce he wrote long ago, hastily and almost impromptu in the country in a moment of mirth, which he did not even deign to correct and which our Gentlemen stole from him as they have stolen many other things that they then adjust in their own manner for the edification of the public.

Rousseau

But how is this line used in this play? Is it he himself who delivers it?

The Frenchman

No. It is a young girl, believing herself betrayed by her lover, who says it in a moment of chagrin to give herself the courage to intercept, open, and keep a letter this lover has written to her rival.

Rousseau

What, Sir? Is a word said by a young girl in love and vexed, the lover's intrigue of a farce hastily written long ago which has been neither corrected, published, or performed; this casual word which she uses in her anger to support an act that is not even a betrayal on her part, is this word which you choose to turn into a maxim of J.J. the sole authority on which your Gentlemen have woven the awful web of treachery that envelopes him? Would you have me reply seriously to that? Did you yourself say it seriously to me? No, your look alone as you said it dispensed me from responding. And whether or not it is a duty not to betray him, doesn't every honorable man owe it to himself not to be a traitor toward anyone? Our duties to others may well vary according to the times, the people, the occasions; those to ourselves never vary. And I cannot think that someone who does not believe he is obliged to be decent with everyone is ever decent with anybody at all.

But without belaboring this point any more, let us move on. Let us allow that the Denouncer is a coward and a traitor yet not an imposter and that the Judges are liars and dissemblers yet not iniquitous. If this manner of proceeding were as just and permissible as it is insidious and false, what would its usefulness be in this instance for the purpose you allege? Why is it a necessity, in order to pardon a criminal, not to give him a hearing? Why hide his crimes, with so many machinations and artifices, from him alone when he must know them better than anyone if it is true that he committed them? Why flee, why reject with such fright the surest, most just, most reasonable and most natural way to secure him without inflicting on him any more punishment than that of a hypocrite who finds himself confounded. It is the punishment that best arises from the situation, the one best suited to the pardon they want to accord him, and to the precautions one must take for the future, and the only one that prevents two big scandals, namely that of the publication of the crimes and that of their impunity. However, your Gentlemen allege as the reason for their fraudulent procedures the concern to avoid scandal. But if the scandal consists essentially in publicity, I don't see what scandal is avoided by hiding the crime from the guilty person who cannot be ignorant of it and by divulging it to all other men, who knew nothing of it. The aura of mystery and reserve given to this publicity serves only to accelerate it. No doubt the public is always faithful to the secrets confided to it; they never leave its bosom. But it is laughable that by whispering this secret in everyone's ear and by hiding it very carefully from the only one who necessarily knows it before anyone else does if he is guilty, they thereby intend to avoid a scandal and make this waggish mystery an act of beneficence and generosity. If I felt such tender benevolence for the guilty person, I would have chosen to confound him without defaming him, rather than to defame him without confounding him; and there certainly must have been other reasons for taking the opposite tack which you have not told me and which are not included in this benevolence.

Suppose that instead of digging all these tortuous, subterranean tunnels under his feet, instead of the triple walls of darkness built with such efforts around him, instead of making the public and all Europe the accomplice and witness to the scandal they pretend to want to avoid, instead of allowing him tranquilly to continue and consummate his crimes while being satisfied to see and count them without preventing any of them; suppose, I say, that instead of all this beating around the bush, one were to address him and him alone, openly and directly, that presenting him face to face with his accuser armed with all his proofs, one were to say to him: "Wretch, who pretends to be a decent man and who is only a scoundrel, here you are unmasked, here you are known. Here are the facts about you, here are the proofs; what do you have to respond?" He would deny, you will say, and what does it matter? What can negations do against demonstrations? He would have remained convicted and confronted. Then one could have added, pointing to his denouncer: "Thank this generous man whose conscience forced him to accuse you and whose goodness brings him to protect you. Because of his intercession, we are willing to let you live and to be free. You will not even be unmasked to the eyes of the public unless your conduct makes this step necessary to prevent the continuation of your misdeeds. Remember that piercing eyes are incessantly watching you, that the sword of punishment hangs over your head, and that at your first crime you cannot escape it." In your opinion, was there a simpler, surer, more correct behavior to unite justice, prudence, and charity on his behalf? For myself, I find that had they done this, they would have secured him better through fear than they did with all this immense apparatus of machines which does not prevent him from following his usual pace. There would have been no need to drag him so barbarously or according to you so benignly, through the morass. Justice and virtue would not have had to be decked out in the shameful guises of perfidy and lying. His detractors and his judges would not have been reduced to remaining forever crouched in front of him in their lairs, as though fleeing in guilt the gaze of their victim and fearing the light of day. Finally, along with the double scandal of the crimes and their impunity, this would have prevented the scandal of a maxim as deadly as it is foolish, that your Gentlemen seem to want to establish through his example, namely that provided one has wit and writes fine books, one can commit all sorts of crimes with impunity.

That was the only true path to take if one absolutely wanted to spare such a miserable wretch. But for myself, I tell you that I am as far from approving as I am of understanding the pretended clemency of leaving free, notwithstanding the danger, I don't say an awful monster such as he is portrayed to us, but an evil-doer whoever he may be. I find neither reason, nor humanity, nor safety in this type of pardon, and I find even less that gentleness and that benevolence of which your Gentlemen boast so loudly. To make a man the plaything of the public and the rabble, to chase him successively from all the most remote, the most solitary asylums where he had imprisoned himself and from which he certainly was in no position to do any harm, to have him stoned by the populace, to move him with derision from place to place always subject to new insults, to take from him even the most indispensable resources of society, to rob him of his subsistence in order to give him alms, to make him a stranger everywhere on earth, to make everything that is most important for him to know into impenetrable mysteries for him, to make him so alien, so odious, so contemptible to men that instead of the enlightenment, the help, and the counsel that everyone ought to find among his brothers when he needs it, he finds everywhere only traps, lies, betrayals, insults; in a word, to deliver him without support, without protection, without defense to the clever animosity of his enemies, is to treat him much more cruelly than if his person were to be secured once and for all by a detention in which, along with everyone's safety, he would have found his own, or at least his tranquillity.[35] You told me that he desired, he himself asked for this detention, and that far from granting it to him, this demand was made a new crime, a new source of ridicule. I believe I can see the reason for both the request and the refusal. Unable to find refuge in the most solitary retreats, driven successively from the heart of mountains and the middle of lakes, forced to flee from place to place and to wander endlessly with difficulties and excessive expenses in the midst of dangers and insults, reduced at the beginning of winter to cross Europe in search of asylum without any idea where it might be found, and certain in advance that he would not be left at rest anywhere, it was natural that beaten down, exhausted from so many storms, he wished to end his unhappy days in a peaceful captivity, rather than to see himself in old age pursued, driven away, tossed about from all sides without respite, deprived of a stone where he might rest his head and an asylum where he could draw breath, until by dint of flights and expenses, he would be reduced to die of misery or to live, forever wandering, on the bitter charity of his persecutors eager to reach this stage in order to heap ignominy on him at their leisure. Why didn't they consent to the expedient that was so safe, so quick, so easy which he proposed himself and which he requested as a favor? Isn't it because they did not want to treat him so gently or allow him ever to find this tranquillity he so desired? Isn't it because they did not want to allow him any respite, or put him in a situation where they could not attribute new crimes and new books to him daily, and where perhaps, by dint of gentleness and patience, he would have brought those charged with guarding him to lose the false ideas they wished to spread about him? Finally, isn't it because in the project so desired, so coherent, so well organized to send him to England, there were designs that are well documented by his sojourn in that country and the effects it produced? If anyone can offer other motives for this refusal, let me hear them and I promise to show their falseness.

Sir, everything you have told me, everything you have proved to me is in my view full of inconceivable, contradictory, absurd things which, to be granted, would require still other types of proofs than those which suffice for more complete demonstrations; and it is precisely these same, absurd things that you deprive of the most necessary proof which would sanction all the others. You have fabricated for me at your leisure a being such as never existed, a monster beyond nature, beyond probability, beyond possibility, and made up of dissociated, incompatible parts that are mutually exclusive. As the principle of all his crimes, you have proposed the most raging, most intolerant, most extravagant amour-propre, which he has disguised so well from his birth to his declining years that even today after his misfortunes he stifles or keeps it so well hidden that not the slightest sign of it is seen. Despite all this indomitable pride, you have shown me that this same being is a petty liar, a petty knave, a petty denizen of cabarets and places of ill-repute, a vile and dissolute debauchee rotting with syphilis, who spent his life going to taverns to swindle a few coins here and there from the boors who frequent them. You have asserted that this very person was the same man who for forty years lived esteemed and well regarded by everyone, the Author of the only writings in this era that bring into the soul of their readers the persuasion that dictated them, and about which one feels in reading them that love of virtue and zeal for truth are what cause their inimitable eloquence. You say these books that so move my heart are the games of a scoundrel who felt nothing of what he said with such ardor and vehemence, and who hid the venom with which he wished to infect his readers beneath a veneer of probity. You even force me to believe that these writings—simultaneously so bold, so touching, so modest—were composed amid pitchers and pints and at the houses of prostitution where the Author spent his life; and finally you transform this irascible and diabolical pride into the abjectness of an insensitive, vile heart which is easily glutted with the ignominy wantonly heaped on it by the public's charity.

You have portrayed your Gentlemen, who dispose as they wish of his reputation, his person, and his entire destiny, as models of virtue, marvels of generosity, his angels of gentleness and beneficence; and at the same time you told me that the object of all their tender care was to make him the horror of the universe, the most despised of beings, to drag him from disgrace to disgrace and from misery to misery, and to make him feel at leisure, in the calamities of the most unhappy life, all the anguish that a proud soul can feel seeing itself the plaything and outcast of the human race. You told me that through pity and grace all these virtuous men were willing to remove from him all means of learning the reasons for so many insults, to stoop for his sake to the role of cajolers and traitors, to duck skillfully each time he sought an elucidation, to surround him with tunnels and traps set so that each of his steps was necessarily a fall, and finally to outwit him with such cleverness that although he was the target of everyone's insults, he could never know the reason for anything, learn a single word of truth, ward off any attack, obtain any explanation, find or put his hands on any aggressor; and that attacked at every instant by the cruellest stings, he would feel the flexibility of serpents as well as their venom in those surrounding him.

You have founded the system that is followed with regard to him on duties of which I have no idea, on virtues which inspire horror in me, on principles which in my mind reverse all principles of justice and morality. Picture people who start by each putting on a well-attached mask, who arm themselves to the teeth with swords, who then take their enemy by surprise, grab him from behind, strip him naked, tie up his body, his arms, his hands, his feet, his head so that he cannot move; put a gag in his mouth; poke out his eyes, stretch him out on the ground, and finally spend their noble lives massacring him slowly for fear that if he dies of his wounds, he will stop feeling the pain too soon. Those are the people you would have me admire. Sir, remember your fairness, your rectitude, and feel in your conscience what sort of admiration I could have for them. I acknowledge that you proved to me, to the extent that it could be proved by the method you followed, that the man thus crushed is an abominable monster. But even if that were as true as it is difficult to believe, the Author and directors of the project being executed concerning him would be, I declare it, even more abominable than he in my eyes.

Certainly your proofs have great strength, but it is false that this strength amounts to evidence, as far as I am concerned, since in matters of offenses and crimes this evidence depends essentially on a proof which is put aside here with too much care for there not to be some powerful motive for this omission, which is being hidden from us and which it would be important to know. I admit, however, and I cannot repeat it enough, that these proofs astound me and would perhaps shake me even more if I did not find them to have other faults no less nullifying according to me.

The first is in their very strength, and for the majority in their origin. This would all seem very fine to me in judicial proceedings performed by the public ministry. But for private individuals and worse still for friends to take so much trouble, go to such expense, take so much time making so much information, gathering so many proofs, giving them such strength without being obliged by any duty to do so, they must have been prompted to do it by some very lively passion which, as long as they persist in hiding it, will make me suspicious of everything it produces.

Another defect I find in these invincible proofs is that they prove too much, they prove things that could not naturally exist. You may as well prove miracles to me, and you know I don't believe in them. In all this there are multitudes of absurdities to which, even with all their proofs, my mind cannot acquiesce. The explanations given for them and that everyone, as you assure me, finds so lucid, appear scarcely less absurd to my eyes, and are ridiculous in addition. Your Gentlemen seem to have loaded J.J. with crimes as your Theologians have loaded their doctrine with articles of faith. The advantage of persuading by affirming, the ease of making anything believed has seduced them. Blinded by their passion, they have piled facts on facts, crimes on crimes, without precaution and without measure. And when they finally perceived the incompatibility of it all, they were too late to remedy it, the great care they had taken to prove everything equally forcing them to admit everything on pain of rejecting everything. It was therefore necessary to seek a thousand subtleties to try to fit so many contradictions together. Under the name of J.J. all this labor has produced the most chimerical and the most fanciful being that the delirium of fever can cause anyone to imagine.

A third defect of these invincible proofs lies in the manner in which they are administered with so much mystery and precaution. Why all that? Truth does not seek the darkness like this, and does not walk so timidly. It is a maxim in jurisprudence* that fraud is presumed in one who follows oblique and clandestine roads rather than the straight road. Another one** is that a person who declines a routine judgment and hides his proofs is presumed to support a bad cause. These two maxims are so suitable for the system of your gentlemen one would believe they were made purposely for it if I did not cite the Author. If what is proved about the accused in his absence is never proved according to regulations, what one proves about him while hiding from him so carefully proves far more about the accuser than about the accused; and by that alone the accusation clothed in all its clandestine proofs should be presumed an imposture.

Finally, the great vice of this entire system is that whether it is based on a lie or on the truth, its success is no less assured one way or the other. Assume in place of your J.J. a truly decent man, isolated, deceived, betrayed, alone on earth, surrounded by powerful, clever, masked, implacable enemies who set up their machines at will around him without obstacle from anyone. And you will see that everything that happens to

---

* "Dolus praesumitur in eo qui recta via non incedit, sed per anfractus et diverticula." Menoch: *in Praesump*.

** "Judicium subterfugiens et probationes occultans malam causam fovere praesumitur." *Ibid.*[36]

him if he is wicked and guilty would happen to him to no lesser degree if he were innocent and virtuous. As much because of the substance as of the form of the proofs, it all proves nothing, therefore, precisely because it proves too much.

Sir, when Geometricians moving from proof to proof encounter some absurdity, rather than to accept it although it has been proved, they go back over their steps, and convinced that some paralogism they failed to see slipped into their principles or their reasoning, they don't stop until they find it; and if they cannot discover it, they abandon their supposed proof and take another route to find the truth they seek, certain that it does not admit of absurdity.

The Frenchman

Don't you see that to avoid some supposed absurdities, you fall into another, which, if not greater, is at least more shocking? You justify a single man whose condemnation displeases you at the expense of a whole Nation, or, what am I saying, of a whole generation whom you make into a generation of scoundrels. For really everything is in agreement, the entire public, the entire world without exception has given its consent to the plan which seems so reprehensible to you. All contribute zealously to its execution: no one has disapproved it, no one has committed the least indiscretion that could make it fail, no one has given the accused the least hint, the least glimmer that might have put him in a position to to defend himself. He has not been able to draw from any mouth a single word of elucidation about the atrocious charges that crush him at their whim. Everything eagerly reinforces the darkness with which he is surrounded and it is not clear which is pursued with greater passion: defaming him in his absence or ridiculing him to his face. The conclusion of your reasoning then would have to be that in the present generation not a single decent man, not a single friend of truth, is to be found. Do you accept this consequence?

Rousseau

God forbid! If I were tempted to accept it I would not do so near you, whose unvarying rectitude and sincere equity I know. But I know, too, the power of prejudices and passions over the best hearts and to what extent their illusions are sometimes inevitable. Your objection strikes me as solid and strong. It came to my mind long before you stated it. It strikes me as easier to cast back at you than to resolve, and has to embarrass you at least as much as it does me. For truly, if the public is not completely constituted of wicked people and scoundrels, all in agreement to betray a single man, it is even less constituted without exception of people who are beneficent, generous, free of jealousy, envy, hate, and malice. Are those vices so well extinguished on earth that not the least germ of them remains in the heart of any individual? Yet this is what would have to be acknowledged if this system of secrecy and darkness so faithfully followed toward J.J. were only a work of beneficence and charity. Set aside your Gentlemen, who are divine souls and whose tender benevolence toward him you admire. You told me yourself he has a large number of very ardent enemies in all stations, who assuredly are not trying to make his life pleasant and sweet. Can you imagine that in this multitude of people, all in agreement to spare from worry a rascal they abhor and from shame a hypocrite they detest, there is not a single one who, in order at least to enjoy his confusion, would not be tempted to tell him everything that is known about him? Everything concurs with more than angelic patience to hear him provoke his persecutors in the middle of Paris, call those who obsess him by rather harsh names, say to them insolently: *Speak up, you traitors. Here I am. What do you have to say?* Even with these stimulating reprimands, the most unbelievable patience never for an instant abandons a single man in this entire multitude. Insensible to his reproaches, they all endure them uniquely for his good, and for fear of causing him the slightest pain, they allow him to treat them with a disdain authorized more and more by their silence. For such great gentleness, such sublime virtue generally to animate all his enemies without a single one of them denying this universal forbearance for a moment, you must agree that in a generation which is naturally not too loving, this collaboration of patience and generosity is at least as astonishing as is that of maliciousness, which is the assumption you reject.

The solution to these difficulties must be sought, I think, in some middle ground which does not assume either angelic virtues or demonic wickedness in an entire generation, but rather some disposition natural to the human heart which produces a uniform effect by means skillfully disposed to that end. But while we wait for my own observations to furnish some reasonable explanation of this, allow me to ask you a question that relates to it. Assuming for a moment that after attentive and impartial research, rather than the infernal soul and the monster you now see in J.J., he turned out on the contrary to be a simple, sensitive, and good man, whose innocence—universally recognized by the very people who treated him with such indignity—forced you to give him back your esteem and to reproach yourself for the harsh judgments you made of him. Look deep in your soul, and tell me how you would be affected by this change.

The Frenchman

Cruelly, you can be sure. I feel that while respecting him and doing him justice, I would then hate him more, perhaps, for my errors than I hate him now for his crimes. I would never forgive him for my injustice toward him. I reproach myself for this disposition, I blush for it; but I feel it in my heart despite myself.

Rousseau

Truthful and frank man, I ask no more, and I take note of this admission in order to remind you of it at the proper time and place. For the moment, I am satisfied to let you reflect on it. Moreover, console yourself about this disposition, which is merely one of the most natural developments of amour-propre. You share it with all judges of J.J., with the difference that you are perhaps the only one who has the courage and frankness to admit it.

As for me, in order to resolve so many difficulties and determine my own judgment, I need clarifications and observations that I make myself. Only then will I be able to offer you my thoughts with confidence. It is necessary first of all to start by seeing J.J., and that is what I am determined to do.

The Frenchman

Aha! Have you finally come back then to my proposition, which you so disdainfully rejected? Are you willing then to approach this man, from whom the diameter of the world was still too small a distance away from you for your liking?

Rousseau

Approach him? No, never the rascal you depicted for me, but rather the misrepresented man whom I imagine in his place. That I should go in search of a detestable scoundrel to frequent him, spy on him, and deceive him, is an indignity that will never enter my heart. But if, in doubt about whether this supposed scoundrel may not perhaps be an unfortunate decent man, the victim of the blackest plot, I go to examine for myself what I must think about this, it is one of the finest duties a just heart can impose on itself, and I devote myself to this noble research with as much esteem and contentment about myself as I would have regret and shame in devoting myself to it with the opposite motive.

The Frenchman

Very well. But with the doubt you choose to preserve amid so many proofs, how will you go about taming this nearly unapproachable bear? You will have to begin with those cajoleries you detest so much. And you will be lucky if you have more success with them than do many people who lavish them on him without measure and without scruple, and to whom he reponds with only brusqueness and scorn.

Rousseau

Is that wrong? Let's speak frankly. If this man were easily taken in in this manner, he would be half judged by that alone. After all you have told me about the system that is followed with him, I am not very surprised that he disdainfully rejects most of those who approach him and who very wrongly accuse him on that basis of being distrustful: for distrust presupposes doubt, and he cannot be in any doubt about them. Given how the world perceives him, which cannot escape his notice, what should he think of these wheedling sycophants whose motives he must discern easily in the eagerness they display toward him? He must clearly see that their plan is neither to befriend him in good faith, nor even to study and know him, but merely to outwit him. As I will have neither the need nor the plan to deceive him, I don't at all wish to adopt the crafty airs of those who approach him with that intention. I will not conceal mine from him; if he were alarmed by it, my research would be over and I would have nothing further to do with him.

The Frenchman

It may be harder than you think, perhaps, to distinguish yourself from those who approach him with bad intentions. You don't have the resource of talking with an open heart and stating your true motives to him. If you keep your promise to me, he must remain forever ignorant of what you know about his criminal works and his atrocious character. It is an inviolable secret which must remain forever hidden in your heart when you are near him. He will notice your reserve, he will imitate it, and through that alone, keeping up his guard with you, he will allow himself to be seen only as he wishes to be seen and not as he truly is.

Rousseau

And why do you imply I am the only blind one among all those who approach him daily and who, without inspiring more confidence, have all seen him, and most clearly from what they tell you, exactly as you have depicted him to me. If he is so easy to know and to fathom when one looks at him, despite his distrust and his hypocrisy, despite his efforts to hide, why should I, filled with the desire to appreciate him, be the only one unable to do so, especially when my disposition is so favorable to the truth and I have no other interest than to know it. Is it surprising that having so definitively judged him in advance and approaching this examination with no doubts, they saw him as they wished to see him? My doubts will not make me less attentive and will make me more circumspect. I do not seek to see him as I picture him, I seek to see him as he is.

The Frenchman

Good! Don't you have your ideas too? You desire him to be innocent, I am quite sure. You will do just as they have, but in the opposite direction. You will see in him what you seek.

Rousseau

The case is extremely different. Yes, I desire him innocent, with all my

heart. I would doubtless be happy to find in him what I seek. But it would
be the greatest of misfortunes for me to find what is not there, to believe
he is a decent man and be mistaken. Your Gentlemen are not in a frame
of mind so favorable to truth. I see that their project is a long-standing
and large undertaking which they do not wish to abandon and which
they would not abandon with impunity. The ignominy they have heaped
on him would reflect back on them in its entirety, and they would not
even be sheltered from public outcry. Therefore, whether it is for their
personal safety or for the repose of their consciences, they have too much
at stake in seeing him only as a scoundrel for them and their allies ever
to see anything else in him.

The Frenchman

But truly, can you conceive, can you imagine any solid rejoinder to
the proofs you found so striking? Will everything you see or think you
see ever be able to destroy them? Suppose you do find a decent man
where reason, good sense, and the whole world shows you a scoundrel;
what will follow from that? That your eyes deceive you or that the whole
human race, except for yourself alone, is devoid of sense? Which of these
two assumptions seems more natural to you, and on which of them will
you finally decide?

Rousseau

On neither of the two, and this alternative does not seem as necessary
to me as it does to you. There is another, more natural explanation that
eliminates many difficulties. It is to assume a conspiracy the object of
which is the defamation of J.J. whom the conspiracy has carefully isolated
for that purpose. But why do I say assume? Whatever the motive that
prompted the formation of this conspiracy, it exists. By your own report,
it would seem universal. At the very least it is big, powerful, numerous.
It acts in concert and in the deepest secret from everyone who is not part
of it and especially from the unfortunate person who is its object. To
protect himself from it, he has neither help, nor friends, nor support,
nor counsel, nor enlightenment. Everything around him is snares, lies,
betrayals, darkness. He is absolutely alone and has only himself as a
resource; he must expect neither aid nor assistance from anyone on earth.
Such a singular position is unique in the existence of the human race. The
ordinary forms on which human judgments are established can no longer
be adequate for making sound judgments concerning the person in this
position and everything that relates to him. Even if the accused could
speak and defend himself, I would require extraordinary guarantees to
believe that when he was given back this freedom, he was at the same
time given the necessary knowledge, instruments, and means to be able
to justify himself if he is innocent. For if, although falsely accused, he is

ignorant of all the schemes that bind him, all the snares that surround him, if the only defenders he will find and who will feign great zeal in him are chosen to betray him, if the witnesses who could testify on his behalf are silent, if those who speak out are bribed to accuse him, if false documents are fabricated to blacken him and those which justify him are hidden or destroyed, he will say *no* in vain against a hundred false witnesses who will be made to say *yes*. His negation will be without effect against so many unanimous affirmations, and in the eyes of men he will be no less convicted of offenses he did not commit. In the ordinary order of things, this objection does not have the same strength, because the accused is given all possible means to defend himself, to confound the false witnesses, to reveal the imposture; and because there is not the presumption of this odious conspiracy of many men to ruin one. But here that conspiracy exists, nothing is more certain, you have taught me that yourself; and because of that alone not only are all the advantages of the accused for their defense taken away from him, but in taking them away the accusers can turn them all against him. He is entirely at their discretion. Absolute masters of establishing the facts as they please without fear of any contradiction, they are the sole judges of the validity of their own evidence. Their witnesses, certain to be neither confronted, nor confounded, nor punished, have nothing to fear from their lies. By accusing him, they are assured of the protection of Nobles, the support of Doctors, the approval of Men of letters, and of public favor. By defending him, they are assured of being ruined. That, Sir, is why all the testimony brought against him under the leaders of the conspiracy, that is to say since its formation, has no authority for me; and if there is any that precedes it, which I doubt, I will admit it only after carefully examining whether there is neither fraud, nor predating, and above all after hearing the responses of the accused.

For example, in order to judge his conduct in Venice, I will not foolishly consult what is said about it and, if you will, what is proved about it today and then stop with that; but rather what was proved and acknowledged in Venice, at Court, among the King's ministers and among all those who knew of this affair before the ministry of the Duc de Choiseul, before the ambassadorship of the Abbé de Bernis to Venice, and before Consul Le Blond's trip to Paris.[37] The greater the difference between what has been thought since then and what was thought then, the more I will seek out the causes for such a belated and extraordinary change. In the same way, to decide about his plagiarisms in music, I will not look to M. d'Alembert, nor to his henchmen, nor to all of your Gentlemen, but I will have people who are not suspect, that is who are not known to them, look in the places to see whether there are authentic proofs that these works existed before J.J. gave them out as his.

This is the direction that good sense obliges me to follow in order to verify the offenses, the plagiarisms, and the allegations of all sorts with which he has been continuously charged since the plot was formed, and of which I don't perceive the slightest vestige prior to that. So long as this verification remains impossible for me, nothing will be easier than to present me with as many proofs as one wishes to which I will have no rejoinder, but which will bring about no persuasion in my mind.

To know exactly what faith I can place in your supposed evidence, I would have to know well everything that a whole generation conspiring against one totally isolated man can do to prove to itself anything it pleases about him, and as an extra measure of precaution while hiding very carefully from him. What can power and ruse not accomplish with sufficient time, intrigue, and money, when no one opposes their maneuvers, when nothing stops or undermines their secret operations? To what extent could the public be deceived if all those who lead it either by force, or authority, or opinion, made an agreement to delude it by hidden dealings whose secret it would be incapable of finding out? Who has determined the extent to which powerful, numerous conspirators, unified as they always are for crime, can fascinate the eyes, when people who are not believed to know one another are planning well together; when at opposite ends of Europe, intelligent imposters led by some clever and powerful plotter, will behave according to the same plan, speak the same language, present an identical picture of a man who has been deprived of his voice, his eyes, and his hands and who is delivered bound hand and foot to the mercy of his enemies. So what if your Gentlemen, rather than being such men, are his friends as they proclaim to everyone; so what if in drowning their protégé in insults, they do so only out of goodness, generosity, compassion for him. My point here is not to dispute these new virtues. But your own stories always lead to the conclusion that there is a conspiracy and my reasoning concludes that as soon as a conspiracy exists, it is not enough to follow the ordinary rules in judging the proofs it advances, but it is necessary to establish more rigorous ones to ensure that the conspiracy is not misusing the enormous advantage of planning together, and by that means of deceiving as it certainly can do. Here I see that everything happens among people who prove to one another without resistance and without contradiction what they are very glad to believe. Offering their unanimity then as a new proof to those they wish to bring to their feelings, far from allowing at least the indispensable proof of the rejoinders of the accused, they use the greatest care to conceal from him knowledge of the accusation, of the accuser, of the proofs, and even of the conspiracy. It is a hundred times worse than the Inquisition. For although the prisoner is forced to accuse himself, at least there is not a refusal to hear him, he is not prevented from talking, the fact that he is accused is not hidden from him, and he is not judged until after he has been heard. The Inquisition is willing to have the accused defend himself if he is able, but here they do not want him to be able to do so.

This explanation, which is derived from the facts you yourself exposed to me, ought to make you feel how the public, without being devoid of good sense but seduced by a thousand illusions, can stumble into involuntary and almost excusable error with regard to a man in whom it is basically not very interested, whose singularity shocks its amour-propre, and whom it generally wishes to find guilty rather than innocent; and also how, with a more sincere interest in this same man and more care in studying him oneself, one could see him differently than everyone else does, without being obliged to conclude that the public is in a delirium or that one is deceived by one's own eyes. When poor Lazarillo de Tormes, tied to the bottom of a tub with only his head above water, crowned with Reeds and Algae, was carted from town to town as a sea monster, were the spectators raving mad to take him for that, in their ignorance that he was being prevented from speaking and that if he wanted to cry out that he was not a sea monster, he was instantly forced underwater by a hidden cord?[38] Suppose that a more attentive observer among them perceiving this maneuver and guessing all the rest from that had cried out to them *you are being fooled, this supposed monster is a man*, wouldn't there have been something more than ill-humor to take offense at this exclamation, as at a reproach that they all were senseless. The public, which sees only the appearance of things, can be excused for being deceived by it. But those who claim to be wiser than the public are not excused by adopting its error.

Regardless of the reasons I expose to you, I feel capable, even independent of them, of doubting what has appeared doubtful to no one. I have in my heart evidence stronger than all your proofs that the man you have depicted does not exist, or at least is not where you see him. J.J.'s fatherland alone, which is my own, would suffice to assure me he is not that man. It has never produced beings of that species; they are unknown both among Protestants and in Republics. The crimes of which he is accused are the crimes of slaves, who have never been near free souls. There are none like that in our provinces, and there would have to be many more proofs than those you have provided merely to persuade me that Geneva could have produced a poisoner.

After telling you why your proofs, however evident they seem to you, cannot be convincing for me who does not and cannot have the necessary learning to judge to what degree these proofs may be illusory and deceive me by a false appearance of truth, I admit to you nevertheless once again that while they do not convince me, they worry and disturb me, and I sometimes have trouble resisting them. I would doubtless desire, with all my heart, that they are false, and that the man whom they make into a monster for me is not one. But I desire far more not to lose my way in this research and not to be seduced by my inclination. What can I do in such a situation* to succeed, if it is possible, in unraveling the truth? It is to rejct all human authority in this matter, all proof that is dependent on the testimony of someone else, and to make my determination uniquely on what I can see with my eyes and know by myself. If J.J. is as depicted by your gentlemen, and if he has so easily been seen as such by all those who have approached him, I will be no worse off than they, for I will not bring to the examination less attention, zeal, and good faith, and a being so wicked, so deformed, so depraved should in fact be very easy to see through however little one looks at him. I will stay, then, with my resolution to examine him myself and to judge him through all I will see of him, not by the secret desires of my heart, still less by the interpretations of others, but by the measure of good sense and judgment I may possess, without deferring on this to anyone's authority. I could deceive myself, no doubt, because I am human. But after I have made every effort to avoid this misfortune, if it nonetheless occurs I will offer myself the consoling testimony that neither my passions nor my will are accomplices of my error, and that it was not within my power to preserve myself from it. That is my resolution. Now give me the means to accomplish it and to see our man. For given what you have told me, it is not easy to gain access to him.

The Frenchman

Especially for you, who scorn the only means that could open the way for you. These means, I repeat, are to worm your way in by dint of cleverness, wheedling, stubborn obtrusiveness; to cajole him endlessly; to talk to him rapturously about his talents, his books, and even his virtues, for here lying and falseness are works of piety. The word *admiration* above all, which has an admirable effect on him, expresses rather well in another sense the idea of the feelings inspired by such a monster, and these jesuitical double meanings so sought after by our Gentlemen make their use of this word very frequent with J.J. and very convenient in talking

---

* To excuse the public as much as possible, I assume throughout that its error is nearly invincible. But I—who know in my conscience that no crime ever approached my heart— am sure than every truly attentive, truly just man would discover the imposture through all the art of the plot, because at bottom I do not believe it is possible for lying ever to usurp and appropriate all the characteristics of the truth.

with him.* If all that does not work, no one takes umbrage at his cold reception, his rebuffs are disregarded. Switching immediately to the other extreme, they scold him, they chide him, and adopting the most arrogant tone possible, they try to subjugate him by force. If he says rude things to you, you put up with them as coming from a wretch whose scorn matters very little. If he chases you away, you return. If he shuts the door in your face, you stay until it reopens, you try to slip in. Once inside his lair, you settle in, you stay whatever happens. If he dared to chase you out with force, so much the better: you would make a racket and run everywhere shouting that he murders people who pay him the honor of a visit. There is no other way, I am assured, to insinuate your way in to see him. Are you someone who can do that?

Rousseau

But why haven't you yourself ever wanted to do it?

The Frenchman

Oh, I did not need to see him to know him. I know him by his works. That is enough and even too much.

Rousseau

What do you think of those who, although as decided as you are about him, nonetheless go on seeing him, importuning him, and wishing to get in to his most intimate company at any cost?

The Frenchman

I see you are not satisfied with the answer I already gave to that question.

Rousseau

Nor are you, I see that too. I have my reasons for returning to it. Nearly everything you have said to me in this discussion proves to me that you were not speaking for yourself. After learning from you how others feel, won't I ever learn how you feel? I see that you pretend to establish maxims that you would be in despair to adopt yourself. So speak to me at last more frankly.

The Frenchman

Listen. I don't like J.J., but I hate injustice more, and treachery even more. You have told me things that strike me and that I want to think over. You were refusing to see this unfortunate man. Now you are determined to do so. I refused to read his books. I am changing my mind just as you are, and for good reason. See the man, I will read his books. After that, we will meet again.

* In writing to me, the same frankness obtains. *I have the honor with all feeling due to you, with the most distinguished feeling, with most special consideration, with as much esteem as respect, etc.* With these ambiguous figures of speech, are these Gentlemen lying any less than those who lie openly? No. They are only more false and two-faced; they only lie more treacherously.

SECOND DIALOGUE

The Frenchman
Well, Sir, did you see him?
Rousseau
Well, Sir, did you read him?
The Frenchman
Let us go in turn, I beg you, and allow us to start with you who were the most eager. I have given you plenty of time to study our man well. I know that you have seen him for yourself, and at your leisure. Therefore you are now prepared to judge him or you never will be. So tell me at last what must be thought of this strange character.
Rousseau
No. Saying what must be thought of him is not within my competence. But saying what I think of him, as for myself, I will gladly do if that satisfies you.
The Frenchman
I ask for nothing more. Please go on.
Rousseau
Speaking as I believe, I will tell you then very frankly that according to me he is not a virtuous man.
The Frenchman
Ah! At last you think as everyone else does.
Rousseau
Not entirely, perhaps, because in my view he is still less a detestable scoundrel.
The Frenchman
But then what is all this? You are discouraging with your perpetual riddles.
Rousseau
There is no riddle there unless you put it there yourself. He is a man without malice rather than good, a soul healthy but weak, who adores virtue without practicing it, who ardently loves the good and does hardly any. As for crime, I am as persuaded as I am of my own existence that it never came near his heart, nor did hate. That is the summary of my observations on his moral character. The rest cannot be stated so briefly.

For this man is like none other I know. He requires a separate analysis, made uniquely for him.

The Frenchman

Oh, make this unique analysis for me, then, and show us what you did to find this man without malice, this being so novel for the rest of the world, and whom no one before you managed to see in him.

Rousseau

You are mistaken. On the contrary, it is your J.J. who is this novel man. Mine is the old one, the one I pictured before you talked to me about him, the one whom everyone saw in him before he wrote books, that is until he was forty. Until then, all who knew him, without excepting your Gentlemen themselves, saw him as I see him now. He is, if you will, a man I revive, but assuredly not one I create.

The Frenchman

Watch out that you may yet be mistaken about that and be reviving only an error that was destroyed too late. As I have already told you, this man was able to fool those who judged him by appearances for a very long time; and the proof that he fooled them is that when he became better known to them, they themselves abjured their former error. In reviewing what they had previously seen, they judged it altogether differently.

Rousseau

This change of opinion strikes me as very natural without furnishing the proof you deduce from it. They saw him first with their own eyes; they have seen him since through the eyes of others. You think they were mistaken formerly. I believe it is today they are mistaken. I see no solid reason to support your opinion, and I see a very weighty one supporting mine. It is that there was no conspiracy then and today there is one. Then no one had an interest in disguising the truth and in seeing what was not there, whereas today whoever would dare to say aloud something good he might know about J.J. would be a lost man; to pay one's court and succeed, there is no surer or quicker way than to improve on the accusations that are heaped on him at will, and finally all those who saw him in his youth are sure of advancement for themselves and their family by using the language that suits your Gentlemen when they speak about him. From this I conclude that whoever seeks the truth in sincerity of heart must go back to find it to the time when no one had any interest in disguising it. That is why the judgments that used to be made about this man are authoritative for me and why those made by these same men today no longer are. If you have some good rejoinder to that, you would oblige me by sharing it. For I am not attempting to defend my feeling here nor make you adopt it, and I shall always be ready to abandon it, albeit with regret, when I believe I see the truth in its opposite. However that may be, the point here is not what others have seen, but what I myself saw or believed I saw. That is what you ask, and that is all I have to say. Except that it is for you to accept or reject my opinion, once you know on what I base it.

Let's start with my initial contact. Given the difficulties for which you had prepared me, I thought I should first write to him. Here is my letter and here is his reply.

The Frenchman

What! He answered you?

Rousseau

Immediately.

The Frenchman

That is unusual Let me see this letter, then, which prompted him to make such a great effort.

Rousseau

It is not very elaborate, as you shall see.

(*He reads.*) "I need to see you, to know you, and this need is based on love of justice and truth. It is said you reject new faces. I will not say if you are wrong or right. But if you are the man of your books, open your door to me with confidence. I implore you to do so for my sake, I advise you to do so for yours. If you are not that man, you can still admit me without fear. I will not importune you for long."

Reply. "You are the first led here by this motive. For of all the people who are curious to see me, not one is curious to know me. They all believe they know me well enough. Come then, because of the rarity of that fact. But what do you want from me, and why do you speak of my books? If you have read them and they have left you in any doubt about the feelings of the Author, don't come. In that case, I am not your man, for you could not be mine."

The consistency between this reply and my ideas did not diminish my zeal. I flew to him, I saw him . . . I admit it: even before speaking to him, when I saw him I forecast a good outcome for my project.

Based on the much praised portraits of him that are displayed everywhere and extolled as masterpieces of likeness before he returned to Paris, I expected to see the face of an awful Cyclops like the English portrait or of a grimacing little valet like that of Fiquet; and believing I would find in his face the character traits everyone attributes to him, I warned myself to be on guard against a first impression that is always so powerful for me and to hold in abeyance, despite my repugnance, the prejudice it would inspire in me.

I didn't have that problem. In place of the fierce or mawkish appearance I had expected, I saw only an open, simple physiognomy, which suggested and inspired confidence and sensitivity.

The Frenchman

He must have that physiognomy only for you then. For in general all those who approach him complain of his cold manner and his rejecting welcome, to which they fortunately pay little mind.

Rousseau

It is true that no one in the world hides his antipathy and disdain less than he for those who inspire these feelings in him. But that is not his natural manner of receiving people, although it is very frequent today; and this disdainful greeting for which you reproach him is for me, then, proof that he does not dissimulate as do those who approach him, and that there is no falseness in his face any more than in his heart.

J.J. is certainly not a handsome man. He is short, and looks even shorter when he lowers his head. He is nearsighted, has deep-set little eyes, horrible teeth, and his features altered by age are not very regular. But everything about him belies the idea of him you gave me. Neither his gaze, nor the sound of his voice, nor his accent, nor his bearing belong to the monster you depicted.

The Frenchman

Good! Are you going to divest him of his looks as you did of his books?

Rousseau

But all this fits together well, and would easily appear to me to belong to the same man. I find in him today the features, of Emile's Mentor.[39] Perhaps in his youth I would have found those of Saint Preux. In short, I think that if nature had hidden the soul of a scoundrel behind his physiognomy, she couldn't have done a better job of hiding it.

The Frenchman

I understand. Here you are yielding in his favor to the same prejudice against which you were so well armed if it had worked against him.

Rousseau

No. The only prejudice to which I yield here, because it seems reasonable to me, is much less in his favor than it is against his noisy protectors. They themselves had those portraits made with great expense and care. They announced them with pomp in newspapers, in gazettes; they extolled them everywhere. But if they don't do a better job of depicting the original's moral character than they do his physical appearance, he will surely be badly known through them. Here is a quatrain that J.J. placed below one of these portraits:

Men wise in the art of deceit
In vain would you portray me
When you lend me traits so sweet
It is only yourselves you will see.

The Frenchman

This quatrain must be brand new, for it is rather pretty and I have
never heard it mentioned.

Rousseau

It was written more than six years ago; the Author gave it or recited
it to more than fifty people, all of whom faithfully kept it a secret for him,
although he did not ask them to, and I do not believe you would expect
to find this quatrain in the *Mercure*. I thought I saw peculiarities in this
whole story of the portraits which led me to pursue it, and I found,
especially for the English portrait, some very extraordinary circumstances.
David Hume, closely allied in Paris with your Gentlemen not to mention
the Ladies, becomes, no one knows how, the patron, zealous protector,
and most excessive benefactor of J.J., and in concert with them he finally
manages, despite all of J.J.'s reluctance, to lead him to England. There,
his first and most important concern is to have the portrait of his public
friend J.J. painted by his personal friend Ramsay. He desired that portrait
as ardently as an earnest lover desires that of his mistress. By dint of
importunities, he extracts J.J.'s consent. J.J. is made to wear a very black
hat, a very brown coat, and he is positioned in a very somber place; and
there, in order to paint him seated, he is kept standing, bent over, leaning
with one hand on a very low table, in a posture where his tightly tensed
muscles modify his facial features. The result of all these precautions had
to be a most unflattering portrait even if it were faithful. You saw this
terrible portrait. You will judge the resemblance if you ever see the
original. During J.J.'s sojourn in England, this portrait was engraved,
published, sold everywhere without it being possible for him to see the
engraving. He returns to France and learns there that his portrait from
England is announced, famous, touted as a masterpiece of painting, of
engraving, and above all of likeness. He is finally able, not without
difficulty, to see it. He trembles, and says what he thinks of it. Everyone
ridicules him. All the particulars that concern him appear completely
natural, and far from seeing anything that could cast suspicion on the
rectitude of generous David Hume, they perceive only the most tender
friendship in the care he took to give his friend J.J. the face of a fearsome
Cyclops. Do you agree with the public about this?[40]

The Frenchman

How could I, after such an exposé! On the contrary, I admit that this fact alone if well verified would seem to me to reveal many things. But who will assure me it is true?

Rousseau

The face in the portrait. On the question at hand, this face will not lie.

The Frenchman

But aren't you attributing too much importance to trivia? That a portrait is deformed or bears little resemblance is the least extraordinary thing in the world. Famous men are engraved, distorted, disfigured every day, without anyone concluding from these vulgar engravings anything like what you conclude.

Rousseau

I agree. But these disfigured copies are the work of bad workmen who are greedy, and not the products of distinguished Artists, nor the fruits of zeal and friendship. They are not loudly extolled all over Europe, they are not announced in public papers, they are not displayed in residences, adorned with glass and frames. They are left to rot on the quays, or to decorate the rooms in cabarets and the shops of barbers.

I don't mean to give you as realities all the troubling ideas suggested to J.J. by the profound obscurity in which they persist in surrounding him. The mysteries made for him about everything are so black it is not surprising that they affect his frightened imagination with the same coloration. But among the exaggerated and fantastic ideas he can get from that, there are some that deserve serious examination before being rejected, given the extraordinary way he is treated. He believes, for example, that all the disasters of his destiny since his fatal fame are the fruits of a long-standing plot formed in great secrecy by a few people, who found the way to include gradually all those they needed for its execution: Nobles, Authors, doctors (that wasn't hard), all the powerful men, all the courtesans, all the official bodies, all those who control the administration, all those who govern public opinions. He claims that all the events relating to him that appear accidental and fortuitous are merely successive developments, organized in advance, and so ordered that everything that is to happen to him later is already in place in the picture and must not occur until the indicated moment. All that fits rather well with what you yourself told me and with what I believed I saw under different names. According to you, it is a system of beneficence toward a scoundrel. According to him, it is a plot of imposture against an innocent. According to me, it is a conspiracy the object of which I cannot determine, but of which you cannot deny the existence since you yourself have joined it.

He thinks that from the moment they undertook the complete work of his defamation, in order to facilitate the success of this then difficult enterprise, they resolved to make it gradual, to begin by making him

Jean Jacques Rousseau.
- VITAM IMPENDERE VERO

Top: Portrait of Rousseau by
Maurice Quentin de la Tour
(reproduced with permission, cour-
tesy Musée de St Quentin and Ets.
Bulloz, Paris). Bottom: portrait by
Allan Ramsay in the popularly sold
engraving by Richard Purcell, 1766
(reproduced with permission, cour-
tesy of National Portrait Gallery of
Scotland, Edinburgh).

odious and black, and to end by making him abject, ridiculous, and contemptible. Your Gentlemen, who forget nothing, did not forget his face, and after getting him away from Paris, they worked on giving him one in the eyes of the public that conformed to the character with which they wanted to endow him. The first thing that had to be done was to make the engraving disappear that was done from the portrait painted by La Tour. This was soon accomplished. After his departure for England, using a model made by Le Moine, they had an engraving made such as they desired. But the face was so hideous that in order not to expose themselves too much or too soon, they were obliged to suppress the engraving. Through the good offices of friend Hume, they had painted in London the portrait I have just been talking about, and sparing no artistry to enhance the engraving, they made it less deformed than the preceding one, but a thousand times more terrible and blacker. With the help of your Gentlemen, this portrait was long the admiration of Paris and London, until having fully won the first point and rendered the original as black as the engraving in the eyes of the public, they turned to the second issue, and skillfully darkening that awful coloration, in place of the terrifying and vigorous man painted initially, little by little they made a petty imposter, a petty liar, a petty swindler, a denizen of taverns and low places. It was then that Fiquet's grimacing portrait appeared,[41] which had been held in reserve for a long time until the moment to publish it was ripe, so that the base and laughable expression of the face would correspond to the idea of the original they wished to convey. It was then too that a small, plaster medallion using the costume of the English engraving but on which care was taken to change the terrible and proud look into a treacherous and sardonic smile like that of Panurge buying Dindenaut's sheep[42] or of people who encounter J.J. in the street. And it is certain that since then your Gentlemen are less committed to making him an object of horror than an object of derision. However this does not appear to advance the goal they say they have of putting everyone on guard against him. For one is on guard against people one fears, but not against those one scorns.

That is the idea which the history of these different portraits aroused in J.J. But all these gradations prepared over time certainly look like chimerical conjectures, the rather natural fruits of an imagination beset by so many mysteries and misfortunes. So without either adopting or rejecting these ideas at this point, let's leave all these strange portraits and return to the original.

I had broken through to him, but how many difficulties remained for me to conquer concerning the manner in which I proposed to examine him! After studying man all my life, I believed I knew men. I was mistaken.

I never succeeded in knowing a single one. Not that they are in fact difficult to know; but I went about it badly, and always interpreting according to my own heart what I saw others do, I attributed to them the motives that would have prompted me to act in their place, and I always deluded myself. Paying too much attention to their words and not enough to their actions, I listened to them talk rather than to watch them act. In this era of philosophy and fine words, this led me to take them all for wise men and to judge their virtues by their pronouncements. And if their actions sometimes attracted my attention, it was those actions they selected for the purpose, when they walked on stage to perform some showy work to be admired. In my stupidity, I never thought that they often drew attention to that brilliant work in order to mask a network of sordidness and iniquity in the course of their life. I saw nearly all those who pride themselves on their subtlety and perceptiveness deceive themselves in the opposite direction using that same principle of judging another's heart by one's own. I saw them eagerly pounce on a random trait, a gesture, a thoughtless word, and interpreting it in their own way, congratulate themselves on their wisdom while attributing to every casual movement a man makes some subtle meaning that often existed only in their mind. What witty man never speaks foolishly? What decent man never comes out with a reprehensible remark that his heart did not dictate. If one were to keep a precise record of all the faults committed by the most perfect man, carefully suppressing everything else, what opinion would one give of that man? What am I saying, faults! No, the most innocent actions, the most indifferent gestures, the most sensible speeches; in an impassioned observer, everything increases and nurtures the prejudice in which he takes pleasure, when he removes each word or each fact from its context to place it in the light that suits him.

I wanted to proceed differently in order to study without regard to myself a man who is so cruelly, so superficially, so universally judged. Without stopping at futile speeches that can deceive, or at passing signs that are even more uncertain but so convenient for superficiality and spite, I resolved to study him by his inclinations, his morals, his tastes, his penchants, his habits; to follow the details of his life, the course of his temperament, the bent of his affections; to watch him act while hearing him talk; to look inside him if it were possible; in a word to observe him less by equivocal and transient signs than by his constant way of being; the only infallible rule for correctly judging a man's true character and the passions he may conceal deep in his heart. My dilemma was to push aside the obstacles I foresaw, warned by you, in executing this project.

I knew that being irritated by the treacherous eagerness of those who approach him, he sought only to reject all newcomers. I knew that he judged people's intentions, and I think reasonably enough, by the open or reserved demeanor they assumed with him; and since my promises deprived me of the power to say anything to him, I had to expect that these mysteries would not dispose him to the familiarity I needed for my purpose. I saw no remedy for that except to allow him to see as much of my project as was compatible with the silence imposed on me, and that in itself might even provide me with an initial prejudice for or against him. For if, although well convinced by my behavior and language of the rectitude of my intentions, he nonetheless was alarmed by my purpose, worried by my gaze, sought to mislead my curiosity, and began by being defensive, in my mind he was half judged. Far from seeing any such thing, I was as touched as I was surprised not by the welcome for me that this idea drew from him, for he conveyed no ostensible eagerness, but by the joy it seemed to me to arouse in his heart. His tender looks told me more about him than his caresses would have done. I saw that he was at ease with me; it was the best way to put myself at ease with him. By the way he distinguished me at the outset from all those who importuned him, I understood that he never for a moment mistook my motives. For although everyone tries equally hard to observe him, and the common purpose must give everyone a rather similar appearance, our researches were too different in their objects for the distinction not to be easily made. He saw that all the others sought and wanted to see only the bad; that I was the only one who, seeking the good, wanted to see only the truth; and this motive, which he discerned without difficulty, earned me his confidence.

Of the many examples he gave me of the intention of those who approach him, I shall give you only one. One person had so set himself apart from the others by his more affectionate expressions and by a tenderness extending to tears, that he believed he could open up to him without reserve and read him his *Confessions*. He even allowed him to interrupt the reading to take note of everything he particularly wanted to retain; and he noticed during this lengthy reading that while the person almost never wrote things down from the favorable and honorable parts, he invariably wrote with care in all those where the truth forced him to accuse and blame himself. That is how the remarks of these Gentlemen are obtained. I, too, obtained these, but I did not omit the others as they did, and the whole gave me results that are very different from theirs.

Through the fortunate effect of my frankness, I had the rarest and surest opportunity to know a man well, which is to study him at leisure in his private life and living, so to speak, with himself. For he shared himself without reservation and made me feel as much at home in his house as in mine. I had almost no other abode than his own.

The Frenchman

What! You ate there too?

Rousseau

Every day.

The Frenchman

What precautions did you take, then, in order to do so with impunity?

Rousseau

Just one, which will strike you as more bizarre than useful, but which he made a necessary condition for admission to his table. It was to renounce for the time being the table of your Gentlemen, and especially never to dine with or at the home of any Doctor, however much they might insist, after dining with their knowledge at his house the previous day.

The Frenchman

That, without lying, is a strange precaution! What does it mean, and what can its purpose be? To vindicate one monster, would you claim to create a hundred others?

Rousseau

Ah, I make no such claim, I swear to you. My intention here is not to accuse or to vindicate anyone . God alone knows the truth. For myself, I keep silent and lament. All I know in general is that these Gentlemen are truly of their era and that thank Heaven my J.J. is not of his.*

The Frenchman

But you cannot truly believe this! If perhaps there is a little hidden rancor against J.J. in some doctors, you are not unaware, on the other hand, of how much their body differs from all the others in its great integrity.

Rousseau

Pardon me, Sir. I know it differs, but I was not aware it was in that way.

The Frenchman

You were not aware! Too bad, Sir; you must learn it. But whatever opinion you may have of them and of their principles, be assured that whenever J.J. is concerned, they will not be accused of prevarication.**

Rousseau

How can that be? Their impartiality regarding him is too well established! But let's get back to the point.

---

* I wish, with all my heart, that doing evil oneself in order to accuse those one hates of it were a maneuver foreign to the era in which I have had the misfortune to live.

** There is one whom I believe incapable of it; this declaration is a duty and a pleasure for me. A good man, loving virtue, he may be mistaken just as the public can, but not seduced or corrupted. However, in order not to expose him to scuffles with these Gentlemen, I will refrain from naming him.[43]

Once admitted to his retreat, my first concern was to find out the reasons that kept him confined there. I knew he had always fled high society and loved solitude. But I also knew that in small social groups he had formerly enjoyed the sweetness of intimacy as a man whose heart is made for it. I wanted to learn why being detached from everything now, he had withdrawn himself so completely that only by force could anyone succeed in meeting him any more.

The Frenchman

Wasn't that perfectly clear? He made an effort before, because no one knew him yet. Now that he is well known by all and would gain nothing more by keeping himself in check, he yields completely to his horrible misanthropy. He flees men because he detests them; he lives like a Were-wolf because there is nothing human in his heart.

Rousseau

No, that does not seem as clear to me as it does to you, and this speech I hear everyone make proves to me very well that men hate him, but not that he hates them.

The Frenchman

What! Didn't you see him, don't you see him every day, sought after by many people, harshly refusing their advances? How then do you explain that?

Rousseau

Much more naturally than you do: because flight is a much more natural consequence of fear than of hate. He doesn't flee men because he hates them, but because he is afraid of them. He doesn't flee them in order to harm them, but to try to escape the harm they wish to do to him.[44] They, on the contrary, don't seek him through friendship, but through hate. They seek him and he flees from them just as in the wilderness of Africa, where there are few men and many tigers, the men flee the tigers and the tigers seek the men. Does it follow from that the men are wicked and fierce, and that the tigers are sociable and human? Still, whatever opinion J.J. must have of those who, despite their opinion of him, continue to seek him out, he does not close his door to everyone. He decently receives his old acquaintances, sometimes even newcomers, when they show neither wheedling nor arrogance. I have never seen him harshly refuse any but tyrannical, insolent, and dishonest advances, which clearly revealed the intention of those making them. This open and generous manner of rejecting perfidy and betrayal was never the demeanor of wicked men. If he resembled those who seek him, rather than to escape their advances, he would respond to them in an effort to pay them with the same coin, and returning deceit for deceit, betrayal for betrayal, he would use their own weapons to defend himself and seek revenge on them. But far from ever accusing him of troublemaking in the social groups in which he lived, or setting his friends against each other, or doing a bad turn to anyone with whom he was in contact, the only thing his so-called friends have been able to reproach him with is that he openly broke with them, as he had to do as soon as he stopped respecting them when he found them false and perfidious.

No, Sir, the true misanthrope, if such a contradictory being could exist,* would not flee into solitude. What harm could and would someone who lives alone do to men? Someone who hates them wants to harm them, and in order to harm them, one must not flee them. Wicked men are not in the wilderness, they are in the world. That is where they intrigue and work to satisfy their passion and torment the objects of their hatred. Whatever motive might animate someone who wants to join the crowd and be noticed, he must summon up the vigor to repel those who push him, push aside those who are in front of him, divide the crowd and make his way. Is the mild and gentle man, the timid and weak man who lacks this courage and tries to move to one side for fear of being thrown down and trampled underfoot a wicked man in your estimation then, while the others—stronger, harder, more ardent to push through—are good? I saw this new doctrine for the first time in a discourse published by the philosopher Diderot at precisely the time when his friend J.J. had withdrawn into solitude. *Only the wicked person,* he said, *is alone.*[45] Until that time, the love of seclusion had been regarded as one of the least ambiguous signs of a peaceful and healthy soul, exempt from ambition, envy, and all the ardent passions that are the daughters of amour-propre and are born and ferment in society. Instead, with one unexpected stroke of the pen, this peaceful and gentle taste, formerly so universally admired, was suddenly transformed into an infernal rage. Many respected wise men and Descartes himself were thereby transformed in an instant into so many awful misanthropes and scoundrels. The Philosopher Diderot may have been alone when he wrote that sentence, but I doubt he was alone when he thought of it, and he took great care to circulate it widely in society. Would that it pleased God that the wicked man were always alone! He would scarcely harm himself.

I do believe that those who are forced to be solitary, consumed by spite and regrets in the seclusion where they are captive, can become inhuman, ferocious, and start to hate along with their shackles all those who are not chained as they are. But those who are solitary by taste and by choice are naturally humane, hospitable, tender. It is not because they

---

* Timon was not naturally a misanthrope, and did not even deserve this name. There was more spite and childishness than true wickedness in his deed. He was a discontented madman who was sulking at the human race.

hate men but because they love repose and peace that they flee the tumult and the noise. Their long deprivation of society even makes it pleasant and sweet when it is offered to them without constraint. Then they partake of it with delight, and that is obvious. It is to them like the company of women to those who do not spend their lives with them, but who, in the brief moments when they are together, discover in them charms that are unknown to professional ladies' men.

I don't understand how a man of good sense can accept for a single moment the sentence of the philosopher Diderot. It may well be high-sounding and incisive, it is nonetheless absurd and false. And who does not see, on the contrary, that it is not possible for the wicked man to love living alone and with himself? He would feel himself in company that is too bad, he would be too ill at ease, he would not be able to bear it for very long, or else, with his dominant passion remaining idle, it would have to die out and he would become good again. Amour-propre, the principle of all wickedness, is revived and thrives in society, which caused it to be born and where one is forced to compare oneself at each instant. It languishes and dies for want of nourishment in solitude. *Whoever suffices to himself does not want to harm anyone at all.* This maxim is less resounding and less arrogant, but more sensible and more just than that of the philosopher Diderot, and preferable at least in that it does not tend to offend anyone. Let's not be dazzled by the sententious glitter with which error and lying often cover themselves. Society is not created by the crowd, and bodies come together in vain when hearts reject each other. The truly sociable man is more difficult in his relationships than others; those which consist only in false appearances cannot suit him. He prefers to live far from wicked men without thinking about them, than to see them and hate them. He prefers to flee his enemy rather than seek him out to harm him. A person who knows no other society than that of the heart will not seek his society in your circles. That is how J.J. must have thought and behaved before the conspiracy of which he is the object. Now that it exists and spreads its traps everywhere around him, judge whether he ought to take pleasure in living with his persecutors, in seeing himself the object of their derision, the plaything of their hatred, the dupe of their perfidious caresses through which they malignly allow their insulting, mocking tone to break through, which must make them odious to him. Scorn, indignation, anger cannot leave him while he is in the midst of those people. He flees to spare himself such painful feelings. He flees them because they deserve his hatred and because he was made to love them.

The Frenchman

I cannot evaluate your prejudices in his favor before learning on what you base them. As for what you say in favor of solitaries, that may be true of some unusual men who developed false ideas about wisdom; but at least they gave unambiguous signs of the praiseworthy use of their time. The profound meditations and immortal works with which the philosophers you cite made their solitude famous prove well enough that they used their time in a useful and glorious manner, and that they didn't spend their time uniquely as your man did to hatch crimes and evil deeds.

Rousseau

It seems to me he did not spend his time doing nothing but that either. The *Letter to d'Alembert on the Theatre, Heloise, Emile, The Social Contract,* the *Essays on Perpetual Peace,* and *On Theatrical Imitation,* and other no less estimable writings that have not appeared are the fruits of J.J.'s seclusion. I doubt that any philosopher ever meditated more profoundly, more usefully perhaps, and wrote more in so little time. Do you call all that evil deeds and crimes?

The Frenchman

I know some people in whose eyes that might well be. You know what our Gentlemen think or say about these books. But have you forgotten that he did not write them, and that you yourself persuaded me of it?

Rousseau

I told you what I imagined in order to explain contradictions that I saw then and that I no longer see. But if we continue to shift from one subject to another, we will lose sight of our object and never reach it. Let's pick up the thread of my observations with a little more coherence before moving to the conclusions I drew from them.

My first attention after getting on familiar terms with J.J. was to examine whether our relationship made him change anything about his way of living. And I soon felt every possible certainty that not only did he change nothing for me, but that it had always been the same and perfectly uniform at all times when, as master of the choice, he had been able to follow his inclination in freedom. Five years ago, when he returned to Paris, he took up living there again. At first not wishing to hide in any way, he frequented some houses with the intention of resuming his oldest relationships and even forming new ones. But at the end of one year, he stopped making visits, and resuming in the capital the solitary life he had led for so many years in the country, he divided his time between the daily occupation which he had made his livelihood and the country walks which he made his sole amusement. I asked him the reason for this behavior. He told me that having seen the entire current generation join together in the dark work of which he was the object, he had at first put all his efforts into seeking someone who did not share the public iniquity. That after searching vainly in the provinces, he had come to Paris to continue them, hoping that at least among his old acquaintances he would find someone less dissembling, less false, who would give him the enlightenment he needed to see through the obscurity. That after many useless efforts, he had not found anything even among the most decent people except betrayal, duplicity, lying, and that while they all hastened to welcome him, to warn him, to attract him, they appeared so happy about his defamation, contributed to it so willingly, gave him such false caresses, praised him in a tone so insensitive to his heart, showered him with extreme admiration with so little respect and consideration, that tired of these mocking and deceitful displays, and indignant at being thus the plaything of his supposed friends, he stopped seeing them, withdrew without hiding his disdain from them, and after seeking a man without success for a long time, he extinguished his lantern and shut himself up completely within himself.

It was in this state of absolute seclusion that I found him when I undertook to know him. I was attentive to all that could reveal his interior to my eyes, on guard against any precipitous judgment, resolved to judge him not on a few scattered words nor on a few special circumstances, but on the coherence of his speech, his actions, his habits, and on that consistent way of being which alone infallibly reveals a character but which requires, in order to be perceived, more persistence, more perseverance, and less confidence in the first glance than the lukewarm love of justice—divested of all other interest and opposed by the trenchant decisions of amour-propre—inspires in ordinary men. Consequently, I had to begin by seeing everything, hearing everything, taking note of everything before reaching a verdict about anything, until I had assembled enough material on which to base a solid judgment that was not the work of either passion or prejudice.

I was not surprised to see him tranquil. You had warned me that he was. But you attributed his tranquillity to baseness of soul. It could come from a very opposite cause. I had to determine which was true. That was not difficult; for unless that tranquillity was always unchangeable, all that had to be done to discover its cause was to see what could disturb it. If it were fear, you would be right. If it were indignation, you would be wrong. This verification did not take long, and I soon knew which was the case.

I found him busy copying music at so much per page. This occupation had struck me, as it had you, as ridiculous and affected. I bent my efforts first to finding out whether he devoted himself to it seriously or as a game, and then to knowing exactly what motive had prompted him to return to it, and this required more research and care. I had to know exactly what his resources and the status of his fortune were, verify what you had told me about his affluence, examine his way of life, learn the details of his little household, compare his expense and his income; in short, know his current situation in other ways than through his word and the contradictory word of your Gentlemen. To his I gave the greatest attention. I believed I saw that this occupation pleased him, although he was not terribly good at it. I sought the cause of this strange pleasure, and I found that it came basically from his nature and his disposition, about which I did not yet have any idea and which I began to penetrate on this occasion. He joined this work to a recreation in which I followed him with equal attention. His long sojourns in the country had given him a taste for the study of plants. He continued to devote himself to this study with more ardor than success; whether because his failing memory started to refuse to work altogether, or because, as I thought I observed, he made this occupation into more of a child's game than a true study. He was more devoted to creating pretty herbals than to classifying and characterizing the genuses and species. He spent an incredible amount of time and trouble drying and flattening the branches, stretching and spreading out the little leaves, preserving the natural colors of the flowers. So that carefully pasting these fragments on papers which he decorated with little frames, he joined the brilliance of the miniature and the charm of imitation to the whole truth of nature.

I saw him finally cool toward this recreation, which had become too tiring for his age, too costly for his purse, and which took away necessary time for which he was not compensated. Perhaps our relations contributed to detaching him from it. It is apparent that the contemplation of nature always had a great attraction to his heart. He found in it a supplement to the attachments he needed. But he would have given up the supplement for the thing itself if he had had the choice, and he did not confine himself to talking with plants until his efforts to talk to humans proved vain. I will gladly leave the society of plants, he told me, for that of men at the first hope of finding it again.

Since my initial research had thrown me into the details of his domestic life, I applied myself particularly to it, persuaded that for my object I would derive more certain enlightenment from that than from all he might have said or done in public, which in addition I would not have seen for myself. It is in the familiarity of intimate commerce in the continuity of private life that a man eventually lets himself be seen as he really is, when the incentive for self-awareness relaxes, and forgetting the rest of the world, one yields to the impulse of the moment. This method is certain, but lengthy and hard. It requires a patience and persistence that only true zeal for justice and truth can sustain, and that is easily dispensed with by substituting some chance and fleeting remark for the slow but solid observations provided by an even and consistent examination.

I therefore looked to see whether disorder or regulation, constraint or freedom prevailed in his home; whether he was sober or dissolute, sensual or vulgar; whether his tastes were depraved or healthy; whether he was somber or gay at meals, dominated by habit or subject to whims; stingy or prodigal in his household; unyielding, imperious or tyrannical in his small sphere of authority, or on the contrary perhaps too gentle and too soft, fearing dissensions still more than he loves order, and for the sake of peace tolerating the things most contrary to his taste and his will. How he bears adversity, scorn, public hatred. What types of affection are habitual for him. What types of pain or pleasure most affect his disposition. I followed him in his most constant manner of being and in those little uneven times, no less inevitable, no less useful perhaps in the calm of private life than slight variations of air and wind in the calm of the loveliest days. I wanted to see how he gets angry and how he calms down, if he vents or holds back his anger, if he is spiteful or hot-headed, easy or difficult to appease; if he worsens or redeems his mistakes, if he knows how to bear and pardon those of others; if he is gentle and easy to live with, or harsh and cross in familiar commerce; if he likes to be outgoing or concentrated inward on himself, if his heart opens easily or closes to endearments, if he is always prudent, circumspect, master of himself, or if letting himself be dominated by his impulses, he indiscreetly shows every feeling that moves him. I captured him in the most diverse, the most contrary states of mind that it was possible for me to grasp: sometimes calm and sometimes agitated, in a fit of rage and in an outpouring of tenderness, in sadness and downheartedness; in those brief but sweet moments of joy with which nature still provides him and of which men have not been able to deprive him; in the gaiety of a slightly prolonged meal; in those unpredictable circumstances when an ardent man does not have time to disguise himself and when the first impulse of nature prevents all reflection. In following all the details of his life, I did not neglect his speech, his maxims, his opinions. I left out nothing that would acquaint me well with his true feelings about the matters he treats in his writings. I sounded him out on the nature of the soul, on the existence of God, on the morality of human life, on true happiness, on his thoughts about the doctrine in fashion and its authors, in short on everything that can make known, along with a man's true feelings about the use of this life and its destination, his true principles of conduct. I carefully compared everything he said to me with what I saw him do in practice, accepting as true only what this test confirmed.

I studied especially those aspects of him which relate to amour-propre, sure that pride irascible enough to have created a monster must have strong and frequent explosions, difficult to contain and impossible to disguise from the gaze of a man attentive to examining that aspect of him, especially in the cruel position in which I found him.

By the ideas that most frequently preoccupy a man consumed with amour-propre, by his favorite topics of conversation, by the unforeseen impact of unexpected news, by his manner of reacting to things he is told, by the impressions he receives from the faces and tone of the people who approach him, by his looks when he hears his enemies or his rivals praised or discredited, by the way he himself speaks of them, by the degree of joy or sadness he feels about their good fortunes or setbacks, it is eventually possible to look within him and read in his soul, especially when an ardent temperament deprives him of the power to repress his first impulses (if it is possible, however, for a passionate temperament and extreme amour-propre to coexist in the same heart). But it is above all in talking about talents and books that authors withhold least and reveal themselves most. So I did not fail to examine him about this. I often led him to this topic, and saw others do so at various times and on various occasions. I sounded him out what he thought of literary glory, what value he attached to its enjoyment, and which type of reputation he most valued: that which shines because of talent or the less brilliant one conferred by an estimable character. I wanted to see whether he was curious about the story of rising or declining reputations, whether he maliciously scrutinized those that were talked of most; how he reacted to the successes or failures of books and of Authors, and how he himself tolerated the harsh reproofs of the critics, the malicious praise of rivals, and the conceited scorn of the brilliant writers of this century. Finally, I examined every part of him where my gaze could penetrate, and without seeking to interpret anything according to my desire, but letting my observations shed light on one another in order to discover the truth, I did not forget for a moment in my research that my life's fate depended on not being mistaken in my conclusion.

The Frenchman

I see that you looked at many things. Will I learn, finally, what you saw?

Rousseau

What I saw is better seen than said. What I saw suffices for me, who saw it, to determine my judgment, but not for you to arrive at yours on the basis of my report. For this has to be seen to be believed, and after the way you warned me, I myself would not have believed it based on another's report. What I saw were only things very common in appearance, but very rare in fact. Besides, they are stories ill-suited to my telling, and to do so with propriety requires being someone other than myself.

The Frenchman

What, Sir! Do you hope to mislead me so easily? Is this how you fulfill your engagements, and will I receive nothing in return for the advice I gave you? Isn't the enlightenment it procured for you to be shared by us both, and after shaking my persuasion, do you think you can leave me with doubts you aroused if you have what is needed to remove them?

Rousseau

It is easy for you to leave your doubts behind, by following my example of taking the advice you say you gave me. It is unfortunate for J.J that Rousseau cannot say everything he knows about him. These declarations are impossible from now on because they would be useless and because the courage to make them would only bring me the humiliation of not being believed.

For example, do you wish to have a concise idea of my observations? Take the exact opposite of everything, the good as well as the bad, of your gentlemen's J.J. and you will have very precisely the person I found. Theirs is cruel, fierce, and harsh to the point of depravity. Mine is gentle and compassionate to the point of weakness. Theirs is intractable, inflexible, and always rejecting. Mine is easygoing and soft, unable to resist endearments he believes to be sincere, and letting himself be subjugated, when the right approach is used, by the very people he does not respect. Theirs, a ferocious misanthrope, detests men. Mine, humane to excess and overly sensitive to their troubles, is as moved by the ills they do to one another as by those they do to him. Theirs seeks only to attract attention in the world at the expense of the tranquillity of others and of his own. Mine prefers repose to all else, and would rather be ignored by everyone on earth provided he were left in peace in his little corner. Theirs, consumed with pride and the most intolerant amour-propre, is tormented by the existence of his fellows, and would like to see the whole human race disappear before his eyes. Mine, loving himself without making comparisons, is no more susceptible to vanity than to modesty; content to feel what he is, he does not seek what his place is among men, and I am sure that in his life it never entered his mind to measure himself against another in order to know who is greater or smaller. Theirs, full of ruse and art, covers his vices with the greatest skill and hides his wickedness under apparent candor. Mine, quick-tempered and even violent in his initial responses that pass like lightning, spends his life making large and small mistakes and atoning for them with ardent and lengthy repentance. In addition, lacking prudence, presence of mind, and being an incredible blunderer, he offends when he wants to please, and in his naivete which is more heedless than frank, he says equally what is to his advantage and what harms him without even sensing the difference. Finally, theirs is a diabolical, sharp, penetrating mind. Mine, thinking only very slowly and with much effort, fears the fatigue it causes, and often able to understand the most ordinary things only by thinking them over at his leisure and alone, he can scarcely pass for a man of wit.

Isn't it true that if I were to multiply these oppositions, as I could do, you would take them for imaginary games that would have no reality? And yet I would be telling you nothing that had not been witnessed with my own consciousness rather than, as in your case, asserted by others. This simple, but scarcely credible manner of disproving the noisy assertions of passionate people by the peaceful but certain observations of an impartial man, would therefore be useless then, and produce no effect. Besides, in certain respects J.J.'s situation is even too incredible for it to be capable of being well unveiled. However, to know him well, it is necessary to know his situation to the bottom: it is necessary to know both what he endures and what makes him bear it. Now all of that cannot be well stated; it has to be seen to be believed.

But let's see if there isn't some other route, as direct and less traveled, to reach the same goal; if there would not be some way to make you feel all at once, through a simple and immediate impression, what I cannot persuade you of, given the opinions you hold, by proceeding gradually, without constantly attacking the incisive assertions of your Gentlemen with hard negations. To do so, I would like to try to sketch for you here the portrait of my J.J. as its idea has become imprinted in my mind after a long examination of the original. First, you can compare this portrait to the one they have drawn, judge which of the two is better unified in its parts, and seems to better form a single whole, which more naturally and more clearly explains the conduct of the person represented, his tastes, his habits, and everything that is known about him not only since he has written books, but from his childhood and at all times. After this, it will remain entirely for you to verify for yourself whether I have seen well or badly.

The Frenchman
Nothing could be better. Speak then; I am listening.
Rousseau
Of all the men I have known, the one whose character is derived most completely from his temperament alone is J.J. He is what nature made him. Education has changed him very little. If his faculties and strengths had developed all at once right after his birth he would have been been found then to be just about the same as when he reached maturity, and

now after sixty years of cares and miseries, time, adversity and men have still changed him very little. While his body ages and breaks down, his heart remains ever youthful. He still maintains the same tastes, the same passions as in his younger years, and until the end of his life, he will not cease to be an elderly child.

But this temperament which has given him his moral form has some singularities requiring more sustained attention in order to be unraveled than the superficial glance cast on a man believed to be known and who has already been judged. I can even say that it is his vulgar exterior and in what is most common about him which, in looking more closely, I found him most singular. This paradox will clarify itself as you listen to me.

If, as I have told you, I was surprised at the first contact to find him so different from how I had pictured him based on your stories, I was even more surprised at the lack of brilliance, not to say at the stupidity, of his conversation. Having had the opportunity to live with men of letters, I have always found them brilliant, sharp, pithy, sententious as oracles, subjugating everything with their scholarly fluency of speech and the loftiness of their decisions. But this person, saying scarcely anything but commonplaces, and saying those without precision, without finesse, and without force, seems always tired of talking even when he talks very little, or of the effort of listening, often not even listening as soon as one says something a bit subtle, and never answering with relevance. So that if by chance he finds some felicitous word, he is so pleased that in order to say something he repeats it eternally. In conversation, he would be taken not for a thinker full of lively and new ideas, thinking forcefully and expressing himself with precision, but for a schoolboy at a loss about his choice of words and subjugated by the self-importance of people who know more than he does. I had never seen such timid and awkward demeanor in our lowliest scribbler of pamphlets, how could I conceive of it in an author who, trampling underfoot the opinions of his age, seemed in all ways less disposed to receive the law than to make it. If he had done nothing except say trivial and flat things, I could have believed he was playing the fool to disarm the spies he feels are surrounding him. But whoever may be listening to him, far from adopting the least precaution with them, he stupidly blurts out a hundred thoughtless propositions, which provide great holds on him, not because these propositions are basically reprehensible, but because it is possible to attribute to them a bad meaning, which, without ever entering his mind, does not fail to be preferred in the minds of those listening to him, and who are looking for just that. In short, I almost always found him ponderous in his thinking, clumsy in his speech, always exhausting himself in search of the right word which never came to him, and tangling up ideas that were already unclear by his poor manner of expressing them. I add in passing that if in our first conversations I had been able to suspect this extreme difficulty in speaking, using your arguments I would have drawn from that a new proof that he did not write his books. For if according to you he could not have composed music since he sight-read it so badly, all the more reason he could not have written so well because he knew so badly how to speak.

Such ineptness was already very astonishing in a man clever enough to have succeeded for forty years in using false appearances to deceive all who approached him. But that isn't all. This same man, whose dull eye and effaced physiognomy seem in the course of indifferent conversation to announce only stupidity, suddenly changes aspect and demeanor as soon as a subject matter that interests him draws him out of his lethargy. His dim physiognomy is animated, vivified, becoming eloquent, expressive, and promising wit. Judging by the brilliance his eyes still have at his age, they must have shot lightning bolts in his youth. In his impetuous gesture, in his agitated countenance, one can see that his blood is boiling, one could believe that flames will emerge from his mouth; but not so. All this effervescence produces only commonplaces, confused, badly ordered, which without being any more expressive than is ordinarily the case, are only more ill-considered. He raises his voice a lot, but what he says becomes noisier without becoming more vigorous. A few times, however, I found energy in his expression, but it was never at the moment of a sudden outburst. It was only when this outburst, having preceded, had already produced its initial effect. Then that prolonged emotion, acting with greater order, seemed to act with more strength and suggest to him vigorous expressions, full of the feeling that still moved him.[46] From that I understood how this man could, when the subject warmed his heart, write with strength, although he spoke feebly, and how his pen could speak the language of the passions better than his tongue.

The Frenchman

All that is not as contrary as you think to the ideas I was given of his character. The confusion first of all and this timidity you ascribe to him are now recognized generally as the surest signs of amour-propre and pride.

Rousseau

From which it follows that our little shepherds and our poor village maidens overflow with amour-propre, and that our brilliant academicians, our young abbés, and our worldly ladies are marvels of modesty and humility? Oh unhappy nation, where all ideas of the lovable and the good are reversed and where the arrogant amour-propre of worldly people transforms the virtues they trample underfoot into pride and vices!

The Frenchman

Don't get angry. Let's leave this new paradox, which is debatable, and return to the sensitivity of our man, about which you agree and which can be deduced from your observations. Profoundly indifferent about everything that does not touch his small person, he never becomes animated except in his own interest. But every time he is the subject, the violent intensity of his amour-propre must indeed stir him to the point of delirium, and it is only when this agitation moderates that he begins to vent his anger and his bile, which in the first moments are concentrated with strength around his heart.

Rousseau

My observations, from which you draw this conclusion, provide me with one that is the complete opposite. It is certain that unlike all our Authors he is not generally moved by every slightly subtle question that arises, and that for a discussion to interest him, it is not enough that his wit could sparkle in it, I have always seen, I acknowledge, that in order to conquer his reluctance to talk and to move him in conversation, there must be some other interest than the vanity of babble, but I hardly saw that the interest capable of animating him was his own interest, that of his own person. On the contrary, when the subject is himself, whether he is being cajoled with flattery or covertly insulted, I have always found him to have a nonchalant and disdainful air, which did not show that he placed much stock in all these speeches, nor in those who were making them, nor in their opinions concerning him. But the greater, nobler interest that animates and impassions him is that of justice and truth, and I never saw him listen calmly to any doctrine he thought harmful to the public good. His difficulty in speaking can often prevent him from exposing both himself and the good cause vis-à-vis those brilliant speechmakers who know how to garb their cruel philosophy in seductive and magnificent terms. But it is easy to see the effort he makes to keep silent then, and how his heart suffers in allowing the propagation of errors he thinks fatal to the human race. Indiscreet defender of the weak and oppressed whom he does not even know, I have often seen him quarrel impetuously with the powerful oppressor who, without appearing offended by his audacity, readied himself beneath his look of moderation to make him pay dearly someday for this indiscretion. So that while one person is judged to be a madman by his quick tempered-zeal, another, secretly meditating evil deeds, appears to be a wise man in command of himself. And thus judging always on appearances, men most often misconstrue the truth.

I have seen him grow impassioned in the same way, and often moved to tears, over good and beautiful things which struck him in nature's marvels, in the works of men, in virtues, in talents, in the fine arts, and generally in everything that has a character of strength, grace, or truth worthy of moving a sensitive soul. But above all something I have seen in him alone in the world is an equal attachment to the works of his cruelest enemies, and even to those works that make a brief against his own ideas, when he found in them beauties that touched his heart, savoring them with the same pleasure, praising them with the same zeal as if his amour-propre had not been wounded by them, as if the Author had been his best friend; and becoming just as indignant about the cabals aimed at depriving them of their just reward along with the approval of the public. His great misfortune is that all this is never ruled by prudence, and that he throws himself impetuously into whatever impulse excites him without foreseeing the effect and the consequences, or without caring about them. He is incapable of moderate animation. He must be either fire or ice; when he is lukewarm, he is nothing.

Finally, I noticed that the activity of his soul lasted only a short time, that it was brief in proportion to its vivacity; that the ardor of his passions consumed them, devoured them; and that after strong and rapid explosions, they promptly faded and let him fall back into that initial torpor that delivers him to the sway of habit alone and seems to me to be his permanent and natural state.

That is the summary of the observations from which I drew my knowledge of his physical constitution and, through necessary consequences confirmed by his conduct in all instances, of his true character. These observations and the others that relate to it offer as their outcome a mixed temperament composed of elements that appear contradictory: a sensitive heart, ardent or easily excited; a compact, heavy brain whose solid and massive parts can be shaken only by a lively and prolonged agitation of the blood. I don't raise these apparent contradictions as a physician, and what do they matter to me? What did matter was to assure myself of their reality, and that was all I did. But in order for you to see it in its full light, this result needs some explanations I am going to try to provide.

I have often heard J.J. reproached, as you have just done, for an excess of sensitivity, and from that the obvious conclusion reached that he was a monster. This is above all the aim of a new English book entitled *Research on the Soul*, in which it is proved, by means of I know not how many fine anatomical and completely conclusive details, that there is no soul, since the Author saw none at the origin of the nerves;[47] and it is established in principle that sensitivity in man and especially in J.J. (which must always be inferred) is the sole cause of his vices and his crimes, that he is wicked in proportion to this sensitivity, although through an exception to the rule, the Author agrees that this same sensitivity can sometimes engender virtues. Without disputing the impartial doctrine of the philosopher-surgeon, let's try to start by understanding well this word *sensitivity,* to which, for want of precise notions, such vague and often contradictory ideas are constantly applied.[48]

Sensitivity is the principle of all action. A being, albeit animated, who would feel nothing, would never act, for what would its motive for acting be? God himself is sensitive since he acts. All men are therefore sensitive, and perhaps to the same degree, but not in the same manner. There is a purely passive physical and organic sensitivity which seems to have as its end only the preservation of our bodies and of our species through the direction of pleasure and pain. There is another sensitivity that I call active and moral which is nothing other than the faculty of attaching our affections to beings who are foreign to us. This type, about which study of nerve pairs teaches nothing, seems to offer a fairly clear analogy for souls to the magnetic faculty of bodies. Its strength is in proportion to the relationships we feel between ourselves and other beings, and depending on the nature of these relationships it sometimes acts positively by attraction, sometimes negatively by repulsion, like the poles of a magnet. The positive or attracting action is the simple work of nature, which seeks to extend and reinforce the feeling of our being; the negative or repelling action, which compresses and diminishes the being of another, is a combination produced by reflection. From the former arise all the loving and gentle passions, and from the latter all the hateful and cruel passions. Please recall at this point, Sir, along with the distinctions made in our first conversations between love of oneself and amour-propre, the manner in which each of them acts on the human heart. Positive sensitivity is directly derived from love of oneself. It is very natural that a person who loves himself should seek to extend his being and his enjoyments and to appropriate for himself through attachment what he feels should be a good thing for him. This is a pure matter of feeling in which reflection plays no part. But as soon as this absolute love degenerates into amour-propre and comparative love, it produces negative sensitivity, because as soon as one adopts the habit of measuring oneself against others and moving outside oneself in order to assign oneself the first and best place, it is impossible not to develop an aversion for everything that surpasses us, everything that lowers our standing, everything that diminishes us, everything that by being something prevents us from being everything.

Amour-propre is always irritated or discontent, because its wish is that each person should prefer us to all else and to himself, which is impossible. It is irritated by the preferences it feels others deserve even when they don't obtain them. It is irritated by the advantages someone else has over us, without being appeased by those for which it feels compensated. The feeling of inferiority in a single respect therefore poisons the feeling of superiority in a thousand others, and what one has more of is forgotten in devoting attention only to what one has less of. You can feel that in all this there is little that would dispose the soul to benevolence.

If you ask me the origin of this disposition to compare oneself, which changes a natural and good passion into another passion that is artificial and bad, I will answer that it comes from social relations, from the progress of ideas, and from the cultivation of the mind. So long as we are occupied solely by absolute needs, we confine ourselves to seeking what is truly useful to us, we scarcely cast an idle glance at others. But as society becomes more closely knit by the bond of mutual needs, as the mind is extended, exercised, and enlightened, it becomes more active, embraces more objects, grasps more relationships, examines, compares. In these frequent comparisons, it doesn't forget either itself, its fellows, or the place it aspires to among them. Once we have started to measure ouselves this way, we never stop, and from then on the heart occupies itself only with placing everyone else beneath us. It is also noted generally, in confirmation of this theory, that witty people and especially literary people are of all men those with the most intense amour-propre, the least inclined to love, and the most inclined to hate.

You will tell me, perhaps, that nothing is more common than fools consumed by amour-propre. That is true only when some distinctions are made. Very often fools are vain, but they are rarely jealous, because since they think themselves securely in first place, they are always very content with their lot. A witty man scarcely enjoys the same happiness. He feels perfectly both what he lacks and the advantage in terms of merit or talent someone else may have over him. He admits it only to himself, but he feels it despite himself, which is what amour-propre cannot forgive.

These clarifications seemed necessary to me to shed light on those imputations of sensitivity, which some turn into praise and others into reproach, with neither knowing very well what they mean by that, for want of conceiving that there are types of sensitivity of different and even contrary natures, which cannot merge together in the same individual. Let us move on now to the application.

J.J. appeared to me endowed with physical sensitivity to a rather high degree. He depends a great deal on his senses, and he would depend on them even more if his moral sensitivity did not often divert him. And frequently it is even through the latter that the former exerts such a lively effect on him. Beautiful sounds, a beautiful sky, a beautiful landscape, a beautiful lake, flowers, odors, beautiful eyes, a gentle look: all these react so strongly on his senses only when they have in some way gotten through to his heart. I saw him walk two leagues a day during almost an entire Spring to go and listen to the nightingale in Bercy as it suited him. There had to be water, greenery, solitude, and woods to make this bird's song touching to his ear, and the countryside itself would have less charm in his eyes if he didn't see in it the attentions of the common mother who takes pleasure in adorning the dwelling place of her children. It is the mixture in most of his sensations that tempers them, and depriving the purely material ones of the seductive appeal of the others makes them all act more moderately on him. Thus his sensuality, though lively, is never impetuous, and feeling the privations less than he does the enjoyments, in a sense he could call himself temperate rather than sober. However, total abstinence can be costly to him when he is tormented by his imagination, whereas moderation costs him nothing once he has something, because then his imagination is no longer active. If he loves to enjoy, it is only after having desired, and he doesn't wait to stop until his desire stops; it is enough that it has abated. His tastes are healthy, even delicate, but not refined. Good wine and good food please him greatly, but his preference is for things that are simple, common, without special preparation, but well chosen from their species, and he attaches no importance concerning anything to the value conferred uniquely by rarity. He hates fancy dishes and food that is too elaborate. Game rarely enters his house, and would never do so if he had better control there. His meals, his feasts consist of a single dish, which is unchanged until it is finished. In a word, he is perhaps more sensual than one should be, but not enough to be that alone. People like that are maligned. Yet they follow, in all its simplicity, the instinct of nature that leads us to seek what pleases us and flee what is loathsome to us. I don't see what harm can come from such an inclination. The sensual man is the man of nature. The reflective man is the man of opinion; it is he who is dangerous. The former can never be so even if he falls into excess. It is true that this term sensuality must be confined to the meaning I am giving it and not extended to those showy voluptuaries who make a vanity of being so, or who in their wish to exceed the limits of pleasure fall into depravity; or who, seeking in the refinements of luxury not so much the charms of enjoyment as those of exclusiveness, disdain those pleasures available to all men and confine themselves to those that make people envious.

J.J. enslaved to his senses is nonetheless not affected by all sensations, for something to make an impression on him, a distinct feeling of pleasure or pain that attracts or repels him must accompany the simple sensation. The same is true of ideas that may strike his brain: if the impression doesn't reach his heart, it is nothing. Nothing that is indifferent for him can remain in his memory, and it is almost impossible to say that he perceives those things that he only perceives. All this means there never was a man on earth less curious than he about the affairs of others and of what doesn't touch him in any way, nor is there a worse observer, although he long believed he was a very good one, because he always thought he saw well when he merely felt strongly. But a person who can see only those things that touch him does a bad job of determining relationships; and however delicate a blind man's touch may be, it will never take the place of a two good eyes. In short, everything that is only a matter of pure curiosity—whether it is in the arts, in society, or in nature—does not tempt or appeal to J.J. in any way, and he will never be seen voluntarily attending to it for a single moment. All this relates too to that laziness about thinking which, already overtaxed for his own wishes, prevents him from being affected by indifferent objects. This is also the explanation of those continual distractions that prevent him from hearing almost anything of what is said in ordinary conversations, and extend sometimes to stupidity. These distractions are not due to his thinking about something else, but to his thinking about nothing, and to his inability to bear the fatigue of listening to what is of little importance for him to know. He appears distracted without really being so, and is in fact merely sluggish.

From this come the indiscretions and blunders he incessantly commits and which have harmed him more than the most odious vices would have done, because such vices would have forced him to pay attention to himself in order to disguise them from the sight of others. People who are clever, false, evil-doers are always on guard and provide no hold over themselves through their speech. One is much less careful to hide the bad when one feels the good that redeems it and when there is no risk in showing oneself as one is. What decent man is there without vice or fault and—always displaying himself completely—never says or does anything reprehensible? The sly man who shows himself only as he wishes to be seen, appears never to do or say anything reprehensible, at least in public. But let's be wary of perfect people. Even independently of imposters who disfigure him, it would always have been difficult for J.J. to appear at his full worth, because he doesn't know how to show off his worth, and his clumsiness constantly displays his faults. Such are the good and bad effects of his physical sensitivity.

As for his moral sensitivity, I never knew any man so subjugated by it, but here it is necessary to understand what I mean, for I have found in him only that which acts positively, which comes from nature, and which I have previously described. His need to attach his heart, satisfied with more speed than selectivity, has caused all the misfortunes of his life. But although he is frequently animated, and often in a very lively way, I have never seen him perform those affected and convulsive demonstrations, those stylish apings, which are so nervewracking. His emotions can be perceived although he does not become agitated; they are natural and simple like his character. Among all those who rant about sensitivity, he is like a beautiful woman without rouge, who looks pale among all the painted faces because she has only the colors of nature. As for the repelling sensitivity, which becomes exalted in society (and from which I distinguish the lively and rapid first impression that produces anger and not hate), I found vestiges of this in him only in that aspect that relates to moral instinct. Which is to say that hatred of injustice and wickedness may well make the unjust and wicked man odious to him, without his mixing into this aversion anything personal that comes from amour-propre. None of the amour-propre of the Author or man of letters can be felt in him. No feeling of hatred or jealousy of any man ever took root deep in his heart. He has never been heard to devalue or disparage famous men in order to damage their reputations. He has never in his life tried, even during his brief successes, to create a faction, or proselytes, or to excel anywhere. In all the social groups in which he has lived, he always let others set the tone, being among the first to follow their lead because he found them deserving and because their minds spared his the effort. So that in none of these societies was there any suspicion of the prodigious talents the public acknowledges in him today in order to make them the instruments of his crimes. And even now, if he were to live among uninformed people who did not know he had written books, I am sure that far from believing that he was capable of doing so, they would all agree in finding him without the taste or vocation for that trade.

This same ardent and gentle nature is constantly felt in all his writings as it is in his speech. He neither seeks nor avoids talking about his enemies. When he does speak of them, it is with pride without disdain, humor without rancor, reproach without bitterness, frankness without spite. And in the same way, he speaks of his rivals for glory only with deserved praises that conceal no hidden venom, which can certainly not be said of the praise they sometimes give him. But what I find in him that is most rare in an Author and and even in a sensitive man is the most perfect tolerance in matters of feelings and opinions, and the putting aside of all partisan spirit, even in his own favor; wanting freely to state his opinion and his reasons when the issue demands it, and even doing so with passion when his heart is agitated; but not blaming people for not adopting what he feels any more than he puts up with anyone's wish to deprive him of his feeling; and giving everyone the same freedom of thought as he insists on having for himself. I hear everyone talk about tolerance, but he is the only truly tolerant person I have known.

Finally, the type of sensitivity I found in him might make those governed by it rather unwise and very unhappy, but it doesn't turn them into either hotheads or monsters. It merely makes them thoughtless and often in contradiction with themselves if, uniting a lively heart and a slow mind as he does, they start by following only their inclinations and end by wanting to turn back, but too late, when their belated reason finally warns them they are going astray.

This opposition between the primary elements of his constitution makes itself felt in most of the qualities that grow out of them, and in all of his conduct. There is little order in his actions, because since his natural movements and his well-thought-out projects never take him along the same path, the former constantly distract him from the route he has traced for himself, and although very active, he doesn't advance at all. There is nothing great, beautiful or generous of which he is not capable in spurts, but he tires very quickly, and falls back promptly into his inertia. It is in vain that for a few moments he has the courage for noble and beautiful actions; the laziness and timidity which soon follow hold him back, overwhelm him, and that is how—despite feelings that are sometimes lofty and great—he was always small and of no account in his conduct.

Do you want to know his behavior and morals to the bottom then? Study carefully his inclinations and his tastes; knowledge of these will give you perfect knowledge of the other, for no man ever behaved less on the basis of principles and rules, or followed his penchants more blindly. Prudence, reason, precaution, foresight: for him all these are only meaningless words. When he is tempted, he succumbs; when he is not, he remains in languor. From that you see that his behavior must be uneven and jerky, impetuous for brief moments, and almost always soft or worthless. He doesn't walk; he leaps and falls back in the same place; even his activity tends only to return him to the place from which he is pulled away by the strength of things; and if he were driven only by his most constant desire, he would remain forever immobile. In short, there never existed a being more sensitive to emotion and less formed for action.

J.J. did not always flee from men, but he has always loved solitude. He enjoyed himself with the friends he believed he had, but he enjoyed himself still more alone. He valued their society, but he sometimes needed to withdraw, and he would perhaps have preferred to live always alone than always with them. His fondness for the Novel *Robinson Crusoe* made me judge that he would not have thought himself as unhappy as Crusoe did confined to his desert island.[49] For a sensitive man, without ambition and without vanity, it is less cruel and less difficult to live alone in a desert than alone among one's fellows. Moreover, although this inclination for a withdrawn and solitary life is certainly in no way bad or misanthropic, it is nonetheless so unusual that I have seen it to this degree in him alone, and that I absolutely had to unravel its precise cause or abandon the idea of knowing well the man in whom I noticed it.

I clearly saw first that the bounds of ordinary societies governed by apparent familiarity and real reserve could not suit him. The impossibility of softening his language and hiding the movements of his heart placed him at an enormous disadvantage vis-à-vis all other men who—knowing how to hide what they feel and who they are—show themselves only as it suits them to be seen. Only a perfect intimacy could reestablish equality between them and him. But when he adopted it, they adopted only the appearance of it. It was an imprudence on his part, and a snare on theirs; and once he felt it this deceit of which he was the victim had to distance him from them forever.

But finally losing the comforts of human society, what did he substitute that could compensate him for it and cause him to prefer this new state to the other despite its drawbacks? I know that the din of the world frightens loving and tender hearts; that they withdraw and constrict themselves in the crowd, expand and flourish among themselves, that there is no true effusiveness except in private conversations, and finally that the delectable intimacy which is the true enjoyment of friendship can scarcely form and be nurtured elsewhere than in seclusion. But I also know that absolute solitude is a state that is sad and contrary to nature: affectionate feelings nourish the soul, communication of ideas enlivens the mind. Our sweetest existence is relative and collective, and our true *self* is not entirely within us.[50] Finally, such is man's constitution in this life that one never is able to enjoy oneself well without the cooperation of another. Solitary J.J. therefore ought to be somber, taciturn, and always discontent with life. In fact, this is how he appears in all his portraits, and this is how he has always been depicted to me since his misfortunes. He is even made to say in one published letter that he has laughed only twice in his whole life, and both times it was a wicked laugh. But people used to speak to me very differently about him, and I saw him become totally different himself as soon as he felt at ease with me. I was especially struck to find him in the gayest and most serene spirits when he had been left alone and tranquil, or on return from his solitary walk, so long as no sycophant had approached him. His conversation was then even more open and gentle than usual, like that of a man who has just experienced pleasure. What, then, occupied him all alone, he who having become the laughingstock and horror of his contemporaries sees only subjects for tears and despair in his sad destiny?

Oh providence! Oh nature! Treasure of the poor, resource of the unfortunate. The person who feels, knows your holy laws and trusts them, the person whose heart is at peace and whose body does not suffer, thanks to you is not entirely prey to adversity. Despite all men's plots, all the successes of the wicked, he cannot be absolutely miserable. Divested by cruel hands of all the goods of this life, hope compensates him for them in the future, imagination gives them back to him in the present. Happy fictions take the place of real happiness for him. And what am I saying? Only he is securely happy, because earthly goods can escape at any moment, in a thousand ways, from a person who believes he holds them firmly, but nothing can take those of the imagination away from whoever knows how to enjoy them. He possesses them without risk and without fear. Chance and men are unable to deprive him of them.

Visions are a feeble resource, you will say, against great adversity! Oh Sir, these visions may possibly have more reality than all those apparent goods about which men make so much ado, for they never bring a true feeling of happiness to the soul, and those who possess them are equally forced to project themselves into the future for want of finding enjoyments that satisfy them, in the present.

If you were told that a mortal, in other repects most unfortunate, regularly spent five or six hours a day in delightful company, composed of men who are just, true, gay, likeable, simple but very enlightened, gentle with great virtues; of charming and wise women, full of feeling and graces, modest without shame, droll without giddiness, using the ascendancy of their sex and the empire of their charms only to nurture among men the emulation of great things and zeal for virtue; that this mortal being known, esteemed, and cherished in these elite societies lived with everything composing them in an intercourse of confidence, attachment, and familiarity; that he found there his choice of true friends, faithful mistresses, tender and solid female friends who are perhaps more valuable still: don't you think that the half of each day spent in this manner would easily outweigh the hardships of the other half? Wouldn't the ever-present memory of such a sweet life and the certain hope of its prompt return sweeten well enough the bitterness of the remaining time; and do you believe, all things considered, that the happiest man on earth enjoys more moments as sweet in the same period of time? For myself, I think and you will too, I feel sure, that this man could pride himself despite his hardships on thus spending a life as full of happiness and enjoyment as any other mortal. Well, Sir, that is J.J.'s state in the midst of his afflictions and his fictions, this J.J. so cruelly, so obstinately, so unfairly blackened, dishonored, defamed, and who, with concern, effort, enormous expense, his clever, powerful persecutors have tried for so long without respite to render the most unhappy of beings. In the midst of all their successes, he escapes them, and taking refuge in the ethereal regions, he lives there happily despite them. Even with all their machines, they will never pursue him that far.

Yielding to amour-propre and its pathetic retinue, men no longer know the charm and effect of the imagination. They pervert the use of this consoling faculty, and instead of using it to alleviate the feeling of their ills, they use it only to aggravate it. More preoccupied with the objects that wound them than with those that soothe them, they see some subject of pain everywhere, they always maintain some saddening memory; and then when they meditate in solitude about what has affected them most, their ulcerated hearts fill their imagination with a thousand fatal objects. Competitions, preferences, jealousies, rivalries, offenses, revenges, discontents of all sorts, ambition, desires, projects, means, obstacles fill their brief leisure hours with disquieting thoughts. And if some pleasant image dares to appear with hope, it is erased or obscured by a hundred painful images which the doubtfulness of success quickly puts in its place.

But the person who, breaking out of the narrow prison of personal interest and petty earthly passions, rises on the wings of imagination above the vapors of our atmosphere, one who, without exhausting his strength and his faculties fighting against chance and destiny, knows how to soar to the ethereal regions, hover and sustain himself there by sublime contemplations, can brave from there the blows of fate and the senseless judgments of men. He is beyond their reach; he doesn't need their suffrage to be wise or their favor to be happy. In short, such is the empire and influence of the imagination over us that it gives birth not only to the virtues and vices, but to the goods and ills of human life; and it is mainly the manner in which men yield to it that makes them good or bad, happy or unhappy on this earth.

An active heart and a lazy nature must inspire the taste for reverie. This taste emerges and becomes a very lively passion if it is helped in the slightest by the imagination. This is what very often happens to Orientals. It is what happened to J.J., who resembles them in many respects. Being too subjected to his senses to throw off their yoke as his imagination plays its games, he would not easily rise to purely abstract meditations, and he would not maintain himself there for very long. But this weakness of understanding may be more advantageous to him than a more philosophical head would be. The collaboration of sensible objects makes his meditations less dry, sweeter, more illusory, more suited to him entirely. For him, nature dresses itself in the most charming forms, paints itself in his eyes with the liveliest colors, populates itself for his use with creatures after his very heart. And which is more consoling in times of misfortune: profound conceptions that fatigue or cheerful fictions that ravish and transport the person who surrenders to them to the bosom of happiness? He reasons less, it's true, but he enjoys more. He doesn't lose a moment of enjoyment, and as soon as he is alone, he is happy.

Reverie, however sweet it may be, exhausts and tires eventually, it needs a respite. This is found by letting the mind repose and letting only the senses receive the impression of external objects. The most indifferent spectacle becomes sweet through the relaxation it provides for us, and as long as the impression is not totally null, the slight movement it causes in us is enough to keep us from lethargic torpor and to nurture our pleasure in existing without giving exercise to our faculties. Contemplative J.J., who pays so little attention at all other times to the objects surrounding him, often has great need for this rest, and then tastes it with a childlike sensuality, which our wise men hardly suspect. He perceives nothing except perhaps some movement at his ear or in front of his eyes, but that is enough for him. Not only do a parade at a fair, a review, an exercise, a procession amuse him, but the crane, the windlass, the sheep, the working of some machine, a boat that passes by, a windmill that turns, a cowherd at work, people bowling or playing with a racquet, the flowing river, the flying bird attract his gaze. He even stops at sights without movement, as long as variety takes its place. Trinkets on display, books of which he reads only the titles lying open on the quay, images on walls at which he gazes with a stupid eye, all these things stop him and amuse him when his tired imagination needs rest. But our modern wise men who follow and spy on him in all this lounging draw their own conclusions about the motives for his attention, always in the delightful character with which they obligingly gratify him. One day I saw him stop for a rather long time in front of an engraving. Some young people, anxious to know what occupied him so strongly, but polite enough— which was unusual—not to interject themselves between the object and him, waited with laughable impatience. As soon as he left, they rushed over to the engraving and found that it was the plan for the attacks on the Fort of Kehl.[51] I then saw them engaged in lengthy and lively fashion in a most animated discussion, from which I understood that they were wracking their brains to figure out what crime could be meditated while examining the plan of attacks on the Fort of Kehl.

That, Sir, is a great discovery about which I was extremely happy, because I consider it the key to the other singularities of this man. From this inclination to sweet reveries I saw derived all J.J.'s tastes, inclinations, and habits, even of his vices and whatever virtues he may have. He has scarcely enough consistency in his ideas to develop true projects, but enflamed by the lengthy contemplation of an object, he sometimes makes strong and hasty resolutions in his room that he forgets or abandons before he has reached the street. All the vigor of his will is exhausted in resolving; he has none left for executing. Everything about him follows from an initial inconsistency. The same opposition presented by the elements of his constitution is found again in his inclinations, his morals, and his conduct. He is active, ardent, laborious, indefatigable; he is indolent, lazy, without vigor. He is proud, audacious, foolhardy; he is fearful, timid, awkward. He is cold, disdainful, rejecting to the point of harshness; he is gentle, affectionate, easygoing to the point of weakness, and doesn't know how to guard against doing or enduring what he likes least. In short, he shifts from one extreme to the other with incredible speed without even being aware of it or recalling what he was the moment before. And to link these diverse effects to their primitive causes, he is lax and soft as long as reason alone excites him; he becomes completely enflamed the moment he is animated by some passion. You will say all men are like that. I think the very opposite, and you yourself would think this way if I had put the word *interest* in place of the word *reason*, which basically means the same thing here. For what is practical reason if not sacrificing a present and temporary good to the means for procuring greater or more solid ones someday, and what is interest if not the augmentation and continuous extension of these same means? The interested man thinks less of enjoying than of multiplying for himself the instrument of enjoyments. He has no passions as such, just as the miser doesn't, or he overcomes them and through an excess of foresight works only to attain a status that will allow him to satisfy at his leisure those which might come to him someday. True passions, which are rarer than one might think among men, become even more so day by day. Interest erodes them, diminishes them, swallows them all up, and vanity, which is only a folly of amour-propre, helps to stifle them more. The motto of Baron de Feneste can be read in big letters in all the actions of the men of today: *It is for appearances.*[52] These habitual dispositions are hardly suited to allowing the true movement of the heart to act.

J.J., incapable of the slightest sustained foresight and completely engulfed by each feeling that rocks him, does not even know while the feeling lasts that he can ever cease being affected by it. He thinks of his interest, that is to say of the future, only when he is absolutely calm; but he then falls into such a torpor that he might as well not think about it at all. He can truly say, in contrast to those people in the Gospel and those in our day, that where his heart is, there too is his treasure.[53] In short, his soul is strong or weak to excess according to the relations under which one sees it. His strength is not in action but in resistance; all the powers of the universe would not sway for an instant the directions of his will. Only friendship would have had the power to lead him astray; he is safe from everything else. His weakness does not consist in allowing himself to be diverted from his goal, but in lacking the vigor to reach it and in being stopped short by the first obstacle encountered, although it would be easy to surmount. Judge whether these dispositions enabled him to make his way in the world, where one moves only by zigzag?

From his earliest years, everything converged to detach his soul from the places where his body lived and to lift and establish it in those ethereal regions of which I spoke before. Plutarch's famous men were his first reading at an age when children rarely know how to read. The outline of these men of antiquity made impressions on him that have never been effaced. These readings were followed by that of *Cassandra* and old novels which, tempering his Roman pride, opened this nascent heart to all the expansive and tender feelings to which it was already only too well disposed.[54] From then on, he made for himself romantic and false ideas about men and society, of which he has never been completely cured even by so many deadly experiences. Finding nothing around him that fulfilled his ideas, he left his homeland when he was still a young adolescent, and confidently embarked into the world in search of the Aristides, the Lycurguses, and the Astreas he believed filled it. He spent his life throwing his heart into those he believed would open in welcome, believing he had found what he sought, and being disappointed. During his youth, he found souls that were good and simple but lacking warmth and energy. In his maturity, he found minds that were lively, enlightened, and subtle, but false, duplicitous, and evil, who appeared to like him as long as they were at the top, but who used his trust only to heap him with opprobrium and misfortune as soon as they believed he overshadowed them. Finally, seeing that he had become the laughingstock and the plaything of his era without knowing how or why, he understood that he had nothing further to hope for from men while growing old in the hatred of the public, and shedding too late the illusions under which he had labored for so long, he surrendered completely to those he could realize daily, and ended by nurturing his heart—which was always consumed by the need to love— with his chimeras alone. All his tastes, all his passions thus have their objects in another sphere. This man is less attached to this sphere than any other mortal I know. It is no way to become beloved by those who inhabit it and who, feeling dependent on everyone, also want everyone to depend on them.

These causes based on the events of his life could by themselves have made him flee the crowd and seek solitude. Natural causes based on his constitution could by themselves have produced the same effect. Judge whether he could have escaped from the convergence of these different causes that make him what he is today. To get a better sense of this necessity, let's set aside all the facts for a moment,[55] let's suppose that the only thing known is the temperament I described to you; and let's see what would naturally result from that in a fictional being about whom we would have no other idea.

Endowed with a very sensitive heart and a very lively imagination, but slow to think, arranging his thoughts with difficulty and his words with more difficulty still, he will flee situations that are painful to him and seek out those that are comfortable; he will delight in the feeling of his advantages, he will enjoy delightful reveries at his convenience, but he will have the strongest repugnance for displaying his awkwardness in assemblies; and the useless effort to be ever attentive to what is said and to always have his mind alert and prepared to answer make unimportant social groups as tiring as they are displeasing to him. Memory and reflection will further reinforce this loathing, by making him hear after the fact a multitude of things he was unable to hear at first, and to which he responded inappropriately for lack of time to think because he was forced to reply instantly. But born for true attachments, the society of hearts and intimacy will be very precious to him, and he will feel all the more at ease with his friends because, well known by them or believing that he is, he will not fear that they will judge him by the foolish things that may escape him in the rapid chatter of conversation. Also, the pleasure of living with them exclusively will be clearly sensible in his eyes and his manners; but an unexpected arrival will make his confidence and gaiety disappear instantly.

Feeling his inner worth, the feeling of his invincible outer ineptness can often make him disgusted with himself and sometimes with those who force him to show it. He must take an aversion for the entire stream of compliments that are nothing but the art of drawing compliments to oneself and provoking a fencing match with words. This art is used and cherished above all by women, certain of what they have to gain from it. Consequently, whatever tendency our man has toward tenderness, whatever his natural taste for women, he can't bear ordinary contact with them in which he must furnish a perpetual tribute of sweet nothings which he feels incapable of rendering. He might speak the language of love as well as another in tête-à-tête, but he speaks that of gallantry worse than anyone in a gathering.

Men, who can judge others only on the basis of what they perceive, finding in him nothing but what is mediocre and common will at best value him beneath his worth. His eyes, lively at times, would vainly promise what he cannot do. They would sometimes shine in vain with a fire that is very different from that of wit. Those who know only wit and don't find it in him would go no further and judging him by this appearance they would say: he is a man of wit in painting, a fool in the original. Even his friends could be mistaken as the others are about his measure, and if some unforeseen event were finally to force them to acknowledge that he has more talent and wit than they had granted him at first, their amour-propre would never forgive him for their first error concerning him, and they could hate him for their entire lives uniquely because they did not know how to appraise him correctly from the beginning.

Intoxicated by his contemplation of nature's charms, his imagination filled with the types of virtue, beauty, and perfection of all sorts, this man would have to seek far and wide in the world for subjects in which he would find them all. By dint of desiring, he would often believe he had found what he sought. The slightest appearances would seem to him to be real qualities, the slightest protestations would take the place of proofs for him; in all his attachments, he would always believe he had found the feeling he himself brought to it; always deceived in his expectation and always cherishing his mistake, he would spend his youth believing he had realized his fictions. Maturity and experience at last would barely be able to show them to him for what they are, and despite the errors, mistakes, and expiations of a long life, possibly only the convergence of the cruelest misfortunes could destroy his cherished illusion and make him feel that what he seeks is not to be found on earth, or is found here only in an order of things far different from where he sought it.

The contemplative life discourages action. There is no more seductive attraction than the fictions of a loving and tender heart which, in the universe it creates to its liking, dilates and expands at its ease, freed from the hard obstacles that confine it in this one. Reflection and foresight, mother of cares and worries, scarcely approach a soul intoxicated by the charms of contemplation. All the tiring tasks of the active life become unbearable to it, and appear superfluous. And why give oneself so much trouble in the remote hope of such impoverished, such uncertain success, while one can at that very moment in a delicious reverie enjoy at one's ease all the felicity of which one feels capable and in need? He would therefore become indolent, lazy by taste and even by reason if he were not so by temperament. And if from time to time some project involving glory or ambition could stimulate him, he would follow it at first with ardor, with impetuousness, but the slightest difficulty, the slightest obstacle would stop him, discourage him, return him to inaction. The uncertainty of success alone would detach him from any dubious undertaking.

His nonchalance would show him the folly of counting on anything in this world, of being tormented for such a precarious future, and the wisdom of renouncing foresight in order to be attached only to the present, which alone is in our power.

Thus systematically surrendering to his gentle idleness, he would fill his leisure with enjoyments that suited him, and neglecting those masses of supposed duties which human wisdom prescribes as indispensable, he would be thought to trample the proprieties underfoot because he would disdain pretenses. Finally, far from cultivating his reason in order to learn to behave prudently among men, he would in fact use it only to find new motives to live apart from them and surrender totally to his fictions.

This indolent and voluptuous disposition, always attending to cheerful objects, would consequently turn him away from painful and unpleasant ideas. Sad memories would be erased promptly from his mind. The authors of his ills would retain no more space than the ills themselves, and completely and quickly forgotten, all of it would soon be as nothing for him unless the ill or the enemy he still had to fear were to remind him of what he had already suffered. Then he could be extremely frightened of the ills to come, not so much specifically because of these ills as by the troubled rest, the deprivation of leisure, the necessity of acting one way or another that would inevitably follow and that would alarm his laziness more than the fear of the ill would appall his courage. But all this sudden and momentary fright would be without sequel and sterile in its effects. He would fear suffering less than action. He would prefer to see his ills increase and remain tranquil than to torment himself to temper them: a disposition that would give quite an advantage to the enemies he might have.

I have said that J.J. was not virtuous; our man would not be virtuous either. And how could he be, feeble and subjugated by his inclinations, always having only his own heart as a guide, never his duty or his reason. How could virtue, which is nothing but work and struggle, preside in the bosom of indolence and sweet leisures. He would be good, because nature would have made him so. He would do good, because it would be sweet for him to do so. But if it were a matter of fighting his fondest desires and breaking his heart to fulfill his duty, would he do that also? I doubt it. The law of nature, or its voice at least, does not extend that far. There must then be another voice that commands, and nature must be silent.

But would he place himself in those violent situations from which such cruel duties arise? I doubt that even more. From the tumult of social groups arise a multitude of new and often opposing relationships that pull in opposite directions those who march with zeal along the social route. Then they hardly have any other good rule of justice than to resist all their inclinations, and always do the opposite of what they desire for the sole reason that they desire it. But the person who stands aside and flees these dangerous conflicts has no need to adopt this cruel morality, since he is not carried off by the flood nor forced to surrender to its impetuous ardor or stiffen in order to resist it. He finds himself naturally subject to that great precept of morality, yet destructive to the entire social order, never to put himself in a situation in which his advantage lies in someone else's misfortune.[56] A person who wishes to follow this precept rigorously has no other means of doing it than to withdraw completely from society; and the person who does live apart, by that alone follows this precept without needing to think about it.

Our man will not be virtuous, then, because he will not need to be, and for the same reason he will be neither vicious nor wicked. For indolence and idleness, which are such a great vice in society, are so no longer in anyone who has renounced the advantages of society in order not to endure its work. The wicked man is wicked only because of his need for others, because some don't favor him enough, because others form an obstacle for him, and because he can neither use them nor push them aside at will. The solitary needs only his subsistence, which he prefers to obtain through his work in seclusion than through his intrigues in the world, which would be much more work for him. Moreover, he needs others only because his heart needs attachments; he provides himself with imaginary friends because he could not find real ones. He flees men only after searching among them in vain for what he should love.

Our man will not be virtuous because he will be weak and virtue belongs only to strong souls. But who will admire, cherish, adore that virtue which he cannot attain more than he does? Who has a livelier imagination to paint its divine simulacrum better? Who, having a more tender heart, will be more intoxicated with love for it? Order, harmony, beauty, perfection are the objects of his sweetest meditations. An idolater of the beautiful in all its genres, would he remain cold to the supreme beauty alone? No, with its immortal charms it will adorn all those cherished images that fill his soul, that feed his heart. All his initial movements will be lively and pure; the second ones will have little sway over him. He will always want what is good, he will sometimes do it, and if he often allows his will to be extinguished by his weakness, it will be to fall back into his languor. He will cease doing good; he will not even start when the enormity of the effort alarms his laziness. But he will never voluntarily do something wicked. In short, if he rarely acts as he should, he will even more rarely act as he should not, and all his faults, even the worst ones, will be only sins of omission. But that is precisely why he will scandalize men, who—having reduced morality to little formulas—count abstention from evil for nothing and the etiquette of little procedures for everything, and are far more attentive to noticing one's failed duties than to considering those one fulfills.

Such will be the man endowed with the temperament I spoke of; such did I find the one I have just studied. His soul, strong in that it cannot be distracted from its object but weak in overcoming obstacles, almost never moves in bad directions, but follows the good one slackly. When he is something, he is good, but more often he is nothing, and it is for that very reason that without being persevering he is firm, that the traits of adversity have less of a hold on him than they would have on any other man, and that despite all his misfortunes, his feelings are still more affectionate than painful. Avid for happiness and joy, his heart can retain no painful impression. Pain can tear him apart for a moment without being able to take root. A distressing thought has never preoccupied him for long. During the greatest calamities of his unhappy life I have seen him shift rapidly from the deepest distress to the purest joy, and when that happens not the slightest trace remained for the moment in his soul of the pains that were just tearing him apart, were going to tear at him again, and constituted his habitual state at the time.

The affections toward which he is most inclined are even visible in physical signs. If he is moved in the slightest, his eyes promptly fill with tears. Yet pain alone never made him shed a tear. But any tender and sweet or great and noble feeling the truth of which reaches his heart inevitably draws tears from him. He can weep only out of compassion or admiration; tenderness and generosity are the only two sensitive chords by which he can be truly affected. He can view his misfortunes with a dry eye, but he weeps when he thinks of his innocence and of the reward his heart deserved.

There are misfortunes for which a decent man is not even allowed to be prepared. Such are the ones people destined for him. Taking him unawares, they began by knocking him down; that had to be, but they were not able to change him. He may have allowed himself to be degraded momentarily to baseness and cowardice, never to injustice, falseness, betrayal. Once recovered from this initial surprise, he picked himself up and seemingly will not be knocked down again, because his nature reemerged; finally knowing which people he is dealing with, he is prepared for anything; and after they exhausted all the arrows of their rage on him, they were no longer in condition to do anything worse to him.

I saw him in a unique, almost unbelievable situation, more alone in the middle of Paris than Robinson on his island, and sequestered from intercourse with men by the crowd itself, eager to surround him in order to prevent him from allying with anyone. I saw him willingly collaborate with his persecutors to make himself ever more isolated, and while they worked without stopping to keep him separated from other men, he distanced himself increasingly from others and from them. They want to stay to be a barrier for him, to watch over all those who might approach him in order to trick them, win them over, or push them aside; to observe his speech and his countenance; to drink in slowly the sweet sight of his misery; to seek out with a curious eye whether there remains a spot in his torn heart where they can still wound him. For his part, he would like to move them away or rather move himself away from them because their spite, their duplicity, their cruel gazes wound his eyes everywhere, and the spectacle of hatred afflicts and distresses him even more than its effects. Then his senses subjugate him, and as soon as they are struck by a painful object, he is no longer in control of himself. The presence of someone malevolent upsets him to the point where he cannot disguise his anguish. If he sees a traitor cajoling him in order to surprise him, indignation seizes him, emerges everywhere in his accent, his gaze, his gestures. If the traitor disappears, he is forgotten instantly, and the idea of the black deeds someone is going to brew cannot involve him for even a minute in seeking ways to protect himself. He wants to be alone in order to remove that painful object whose sight torments him. He wants to be alone to live at his ease with the friends he has created for himself. But all that is only an additional reason for those who don the mask of friendship to obsess him more closely. If they can help it they don't even want to leave him the resource of fictions in this life.

I saw him, caught in their snares, struggling very little to get out; surrounded by lies and darkness, waiting without a murmur for light and truth; buried alive in a coffin, remain rather still without even invoking death. I saw him poor passing for rich, old passing for young, gentle passing for ferocious, obliging and weak passing for inflexible and hard, gay passing for somber, and finally simple to the point of stupidity passing for crafty to the point of blackness. I saw him handed over by your Gentlemen to public derision, basely flattered, bantered, mocked by decent people, serving as a plaything for the rabble, see it, feel it, bemoan it, deplore human wretchedness and patiently endure his state.

In that state, should he have had such a lack of respect for himself to the extent of seeking out in society the ill-disguised indignities which they took pleasure in heaping on him? Should he have made a spectacle of himself for those barbarians who, making his troubles a subject of amusement, sought only to break his heart by all the hardships of distress and pain to which he was most sensitive? That is what made the way of life he resorted to, or rather to which they reduced him, indispensable.

Because that was what they aimed for, and they persisted in making the frequentation of men so cruel and so devastating for him that he was finally forced to renounce it completely. *You ask me,* he said, *why I flee from men. Rather ask them, they know still better than I.* But does an expansive soul change its nature in this way, and does it thus become detached from everything? All his misfortunes came only from that need to love that consumed his heart from childhood, and that worries and upsets him still, to the point that remaining alone on earth, he awaits the time when he will leave it in order to realize at last his favorite visions and find, in a better order of things, a homeland and friends.

He attained and passed maturity without thinking of writing books, and without feeling for a moment the need for that fatal celebrity which was not made for him, of which he has tasted only the bitterness and for which he has paid so dearly. His cherished visions took the place of everything for him, and in the ardor of youth his lively imagination—overloaded, weighed down with charming objects that constantly filled it—kept his heart in a state of continual intoxication that left him without the power to organize his ideas or to establish them, without the time to write them or the desire to communicate them. It was only when these great movements began to calm down, when his ideas assumed a more orderly, slower pace, that he was able to follow the outline well enough to take note of it. It was only then, I say that the use of the pen became possible for him, and that following the example and at the urging of the men of letters with whom he then lived, he got the whim of communicating to the public these very ideas that had nurtured him for so long and that he believed useful to the human race. It was even, in a way, by surprise and without forming the project that he found himself thrust into that fatal career where possibly even then people were digging out under his feet those caverns of misfortunes into which he was thrown.

During his youth he often asked himself why he did not find all men good, wise, happy as they seemed to him made to be. He sought in his heart the obstacle that prevented them from being so, and he did not find it. If all men, he said to himself, were like me, there would doubtless be much languor in their industriousness. They would not have much activity and would have it only in sudden and infrequent jolts. But they would live together in a very sweet society. Why don't they live like that? Why, always blaming Heaven for their miseries, do they work ceaselessly to increase them? While admiring the progress of the human mind, he was amazed to see that public calamities increased proportionately. He glimpsed a secret opposition between the constitution of man and that of our societies. But it was more of a dumb feeling, a confused notion than a clear and developed judgment. Public opinion had sujugated him too greatly for him to dare contest such unanimous decisions.

An unfortunate question from an Academy that he read in the *Mercure* suddenly made the scales fall from his eyes, unscrambled this chaos in his head, showed him another universe, a true golden age, societies of simple, wise, happy men, and fulfilled in hopes all his visions through the destruction of the prejudices that had subjugated even him but from which at that moment he believed he saw all the vices and miseries of the human race flow.[57] From the lively effervescence that developed then in his soul came those sparks of genius that have glittered in his writings during ten years of delirium and fever, but of which no vestige had appeared before then and which presumably would not have sparkled subsequently if, once this paroxysm had passed, he had wanted to continue to write. Enflamed by the contemplation of these great objects, they were always present in his thought, and comparing them to the real state of things, he saw them each day in relationships that were totally new to him. Deluded by the ridiculous hope of making reason and truth triumph at last over prejudices and lies, and of making men wise by showing them their true interest, his heart—excited by the idea of the future happiness of the human race and by the honor of contributing to it—dictated to him a language worthy of such a great undertaking. Constrained by that to deep and lengthy preoccupation with the same subject, he submitted his head to the fatigue of reflection, he learned to meditate profoundly, and for a time he astounded Europe by productions in which vulgar souls saw only eloquence and wit, but in which those who occupy our ethereal regions joyfully recognized one of their own.

The Frenchman

I have let you speak without interruption, but allow me to stop you for a moment now. . .

Rousseau

I can guess why . . . . There's a contradiction, isn't there?

The Frenchman

No, I saw what appeared to be one. It is said that this appearance is a trap which J.J. enjoys setting for careless readers.

Rousseau

If that is so, he is well punished for it by readers of bad faith, who pretend to be caught in order to accuse him of not knowing what he is saying.

The Frenchman

I'm not one of that class, and I try not to be one of the others either. So it is not a contradiction for which I reproach you here, but rather a clarification for which I ask you. You were persuaded earlier that the books that bear the name J.J. are no more written by him than that translation of Tasso, so faithful and so flowing, which is so pretentiously circulated under his name. Now you appear to believe the opposite. If in fact you have changed your opinion, kindly tell me the basis for this change.

Rousseau

This research was the first object of my attentions. Certain that the Author of these books and the monster you had portrayed could not be the same man, I confined myself to resolving this question in order to remove my doubts. However, without even thinking about it, I managed to resolve it by the opposite method. I wanted first to know the author in order to decide about the man, and it is by knowing the man that I decided about the Author.

To make you feel how doing one part of these two pieces of research eliminated the need for me to do the other, I must go into the details of what I did to that end. You will deduce for yourself, very easily, the consequences I drew from them.

I told you that I had found him copying music at ten sols a page, an occupation ill-suited to the dignity of an Author and scarcely resembling those which gave him such a reputation as much for good as for ill. This first item already provided me with two topics of research to be done: first, whether he devoted himself to this work sincerely, or just to mislead the public about his true occupations; the other whether he really needed this trade to live, or whether it was an affectation of simplicity or poverty to copy an Epictetus or Diogenes as your Gentlemen claim.[58]

I began by examining his work, feeling quite sure that if he were doing it as a matter of form, I would find traces of the boredom it must give him over such a long period of time. His ill-formed notation appeared to me to be done with a heavy hand, slowly, without fluency, without grace, but with precision. It is apparent that he tries to make up for the aptitudes he lacks by means of labor and care. But since the cares he puts into it are perceived only on examination and produce their effect only when executed, about which the Musicians, who don't like him, are not always sincere, they don't offset the defects that are visible right away in the eyes of the public.

Since he doesn't keep his mind on anything, he doesn't keep it on his work either, especially when he is forced by the crowds of chance visitors to combine it with chit-chat. He makes many mistakes and then corrects them by erasing his paper, wasting time and having incredible difficulties. I saw nearly whole pages that he had preferred to erase in this way rather than to start a fresh sheet, which would have been finished much sooner.

But in his laboriously lazy turn of mind, he cannot reconcile himself to start afresh something he has already done once, albeit badly. He makes the correction with an obstinacy that can be satisfied only with effort and time. Moreover, the most lengthy, the most boring work cannot exhaust his patience, and often, making mistake after mistake, I saw him erase and erase over again until he made a hole in the paper, on which he then pasted repairs. Nothing led me to judge that this work bored him, and after six years he appears to turn to it with the same taste and the same zeal as if he were just beginning.

I knew he kept a record of his work. I desired to see this record. He shared it with me. I saw there that in these six years he had made simple copies of more than six thousand pages of music, some of which—Music for Harp and Clavecin or Violin solos and concerti, very complex and on larger size paper—requires great attention and takes considerable time. He invented, in addition to his notation by numbers, a new way of copying ordinary music, which makes it easier to read; and to prevent and resolve all difficulties, he wrote a large number of pieces of all types in this manner, partitions as well as separate parts.

Beyond this work and his Opera *Daphnis and Chloe*,[59] of which one act is completed and a good part of the remainder well underway, and the *Village Soothsayer* for which he rewrote the music almost entirely, in the same period he has composed more than one hundred pieces of Music in various genres, most of them vocal works with accompaniments, which he did as much to oblige people who provided him with the words as for his own entertainment. He made and distributed copies of this music both in partition and in separate parts transcribed from the originals which he kept. The issue here is not whether he composed all this music or stole it from others. Even if he didn't compose it, it is certain that he did write and notate it several times in his own hand. If he didn't compose it, what a lot of time it must have taken him to look for and choose in music already written what was well suited to the words that were given to him, or to fit the music to them so well that it was perfectly matched, which is a particular merit of the music he claims to be his. In such a theft there is doubtless less invention, but there is more art, more work, especially more time consumed; and for the moment that was the unique object of my research.

All that work he placed before my eyes, either directly or in precisely detailed lists, adds up to more than eight thousand pages of Music,* all written by hand since his return to Paris.

These occupations did not prevent him from devoting himself to the amusement of botanizing, to which he gave the majority of his time for

* See the note on page 167 [Pléiade, I, 875]

several years. By extensive and frequent herborizing, he made an immense collection of plants. He dried them with infinite care, glued them with great neatness onto paper which he decorated with red frames. He was careful to preserve the aspect and color of the flowers and the leaves, to the extent of making these herb books prepared in this way into collections of miniatures. He gave and sent some to various people, and what he has left* would be enough to persuade those who know how much time and patience this work requires that it is his sole occupation.

The Frenchman

Add to that the time it took to study in depth the properties of all these plants, to reduce them to powder, extract them, distill them, prepare them in such a way as to obtain the applications he intends. For however biased toward him you may be, you surely know, I think, that no one studies botany for nothing.

Rousseau

No doubt. I understand that the charm of studying nature is something for all sensitive souls, and a great deal for a solitary person. As for the preparations of which you speak and which have no relationship whatever to botany, I didn't see the least vestige of them at his home. I didn't notice that he had made any study of the properties of plants, nor even that he believed very much in these. "I know the vegetable organization and the structure of plants," he said to me, "by what my eyes see, by the testimony of nature which shows it to me and doesn't lie. But I know about their virtues only by the testimony of men, who are ignorant and liars. Their authority generally has too little sway over me for me to confer much in that area. Besides, that study, true or false, isn't undertaken out in the fields as the study of botany is, but in laboratories and with sick people. It requires a focused and sedentary life, which neither pleases nor suits me." In fact, I saw nothing at his home that demonstrated a taste for pharmacology. I saw there only cartons filled with the stalks of plants about which I have just told you, and seeds sorted into little, classified boxes, corresponding to the plants that furnish them according to the Linnaean system.[61]

The Frenchman

Ah, little boxes! And these little boxes, Sir, what are they for? What can you say about them?

Rousseau

What a question! For poisoning people, whom he forces to swallow all these seeds by the bowlful. For instance, you unwittingly swallow one or two ounces of poppy seeds that will put you to sleep forever, and so on for

---

* This remainder has been given almost entirely to Mr. Malthus[60] who bought my botanical books.

all the rest. And approximately the same is true for the plants. He makes you chew them like fodder, or else he makes you drink their juice in sauces.

The Frenchman

Oh no, Sir! It's well known that it is not in this way that it can be done, and our Doctors, who wanted to have it like this, have been proved wrong by educated people. One bowlful of hemlock juice wasn't enough for Socrates; a second one was needed. Therefore J.J. would have to make his guests drink tubs of herb juices or eat buckets of seeds. But this is not how he goes about it! By dint of operations and manipulations, he knows how to concentrate the poisons of plants so much that they act even more potently than those of minerals. He conceals them and makes you swallow them without noticing; he even makes them act from a distance like sympathetic powder; and like the basilisk, he knows how to poison people just by looking at them. He took a chemistry course a long time ago, nothing is more certain.[62] Now you understand fully what happens, what might be involved when a man who is neither a Doctor nor an Apothecary nonetheless takes courses in chemistry and engages in botanizing! However, you say you never saw any vestige of chemical preparations in his home. What, no still, no ovens, no heads, no converters? Nothing related to a laboratory?

Rousseau

Forgive me, truly! In his tiny kitchen I saw a small stove, tin coffeepots, dishes, pots, earthenware bowls.

The Frenchman

Dishes, pots, bowls! But truly that is just fine! Nothing more is needed to poison the whole human race.

Rousseau

Witness Mignot and his successors.[63]

The Frenchman

You will tell me that poisons prepared in bowls have to be eaten with a spoon, and that soups cannot be concealed. . . .

Rousseau

Oh no, I won't tell you that at all, I swear, or anything of the kind. I'll be content to admire. Oh the learned, the methodical process of learning botany to become a poisoner. It's as if one were to learn Geometry in order to become a murderer.

The Frenchman

I see you smile very disdainfully. Will you always be so taken with that man?

Rousseau

So taken with him! Me! Do more justice to me, and even rest assured that Rousseau will never defend J.J. accused of poisoning.

The Frenchman

Then let's stop all this banter and resume your stories. I am listening attentively. They interest me more and more.

Rousseau

They would interest you even more, I'm quite sure, if it were possible or allowed for me to say everything here. It would take unfair advantage of your attention to share all the precautions I took to ascertain the actual use of his time, the nature of his occupations, and the spirit in which he performs them. It would be better to limit myself to the results, and leave to you the task of verifying it all yourself, if this research interests you enough to do that.

I must however add to the details I have just been explaining that in the midst of all this manual work, J.J. also spent six months within that time both examining the constitution of an unfortunate Nation and proposing his ideas about the corrections to make in this constitution; and he did so at the insistence, reiterated to the point of obstinacy, of one of the leading patriots of that nation, who imposed the task on him as a humanitarian duty, and who, as his total thanks for the zeal and time he devoted to this work, informed him subsequently that he did not want to have any obligation to him at all and then wanted to send him some wine.* But this is only a sample of that destiny which, though he consecrated his life to deserve good things from men, caused him to spend it in their bad graces.[64]

Finally, despite the resolution he made when he arrived in Paris not to pay any further attention to his misfortunes or to write any more about this subject, the continual indignities he suffered, the unceasing harassment he underwent because of the fear that he would write, the impudence with which new books were constantly attributed to him, and the stupid or spiteful credulity of the public about this having exhausted his patience and making him feel that he gained no rest by keeping silent, he made one more effort, and attending once again to his destiny and to his persecutors despite himself, he wrote a kind of judgment of them and of himself in the form of a Dialogue, rather like the one that may result from our conversations. He often complained to me that this piece of writing was, of all he had done in his life, the one he undertook with the most repugnance and executed with the most boredom. He would have abandoned it a hundred times over if the ever-increasing insults, finally pushed to the greatest extremes, hadn't forced him despite himself to continue. But far from ever devoting himself to it for long periods, he

---

* I must be considered a great wine fancier, because the Duc de Grammont also wanted to send me some for various bits of music I had composed for him at his request. But this offer was much more appropriate and could even have been accepted.

could not even have withstood the anguish of writing it if his daily work had not come to interrupt and make him forget it. So that he rarely spent more than a quarter of an hour on it each day, and that choppy and interrupted manner of writing is one of the causes of the lack of continuity and continual repetitions that prevail in this writing.

After making sure that this music copying wasn't a game, I still needed to know if in fact it was necessary for his subsistence, and why, having other talents he could put to work more usefully for himself and for the public, he had preferred that one. To shorten this research without breaking my promises to you, I indicated my curiosity to him in a natural way and without telling him everything you had told me about his wealth, I was satisfied to repeat to him what I had heard a thousand times: that from the sales of his books alone and without fleecing his publishers, he must be rich enough to live comfortably on his income.

"You are right," he said, *"if by that you mean only what might be true; but if you propose to conclude that it really is and that I am in fact rich, you are mistaken, at the very least. For a cruel sophism could be hidden beneath that error."*

Then he detailed what he had received from his publishers for each of his books, all his resources from other sources, the expenses he has had to assume during the eight years that others have taken pleasure in forcing him and his companion, now his wife, to travel at great cost. And from all these things, carefully calculated and confirmed, the result was that, including some cash coming from his agreement with the Opera as well as from the sale of his botanical books and the remainder of a savings fund of a thousand ecus that he had in Lyon and that he withdrew to get himself established in Paris, his entire current fortune consists of eight hundred francs of uncertain life annuity to which he has no title, and three hundred francs of annuity, also for life, but guaranteed at least as long as the person who must pay it is solvent. "That is a very faithful accounting," he told me "of my entire wealth. If someone says he knows I have some other savings or income whatsoever, I say he is lying and I can show it. And if someone says he owes me something, let him give me one quarter of it and I will discharge him of the remainder.

"You could say as many have," he continued "that for an austere philosopher eleven hundred francs of annuity, at least when I have it, ought to be enough for me to subsist on, without my needing to add to it by work to which I am ill suited and which I do with greater ostentation than necessity. To that I respond first that I am neither a philosopher nor austere, and this hard life that it pleases your Gentlemen to make my duty has never been either to my taste nor in accord with my principles, as long as by just and honest means I have been able to avoid being reduced to it. In becoming a music copyist, I made no pretense of adopting an austere state of self-mortification, but rather chose an occupation to my taste, that didn't tire my lazy mind, and that could provide me with the commodities of life which my scanty income could not procure without this supplement. In renouncing very gladly everything that constitutes luxury and vanity, I didn't renounce the real pleasures, and it was rather in order to taste them in all their purity that I separated out everything that derives only from opinion. Neither dissolute acts nor excesses have ever been to my taste, but without ever being rich, I have always lived comfortably, and it is completely impossible for me to live comfortably with my small household on eleven hundred francs of annuity even if it were assured, let alone with the three hundred to which I can be reduced any day. But let's set aside this foresight. Why would you want me unnecessarily, in my old age, to make the harsh apprenticeship of a more frugal life to which my body is not accustomed, when a labor, which is only a pleasure for me, procures for me the continuation of those same commodities that habit has transformed into needs, and which in any other way would be less available to me or cost me much more? Your Gentlemen, who have not adopted for themselves the austerity they prescribe for me, are happy to plot or borrow rather than to subject themselves to manual work which strikes them as ignoble, usurious, unbearable, and doesn't suddenly procure sums of fifty thousand francs. But I, who don't think as they do about true dignity, I, who find a very sweet enjoyment in the alternation of work and recreation, through an occupation to my taste that I can pursue at will, I add what is missing from my small fortune to procure a comfortable subsistence, and I enjoy the sweetness of a calm and simple life to the extent that it depends on me. Absolute inaction would subject me to boredom, would perhaps force me seek amusements that are always costly, often painful, rarely innocent; whereas after work, simple rest has its charm, and along with walking provides me with all the amusement I need. Finally, it is perhaps a care I owe myself in such a sad situation at least to contribute to it all the amenities that remain available to me to try to sweeten its bitterness, for fear that the feeling of my hardships sharpened by an austere life would ferment in my soul and produce hateful and vindictive dispositions such as would make me wicked and more unhappy. I have always found it good to arm my heart against hatred with all the enjoyments I could procure. The success of this method will always make it dear to me, and the more deplorable my destiny, the more I try to sprinkle it with sweet things, so that I will always remain good.

"But, they say, among so many occupations from which he can choose, why does he prefer to pick the one to which he seems least suited and that will earn the least? Why copy music rather than write books? He would earn more and not debase himself. I will gladly answer that question by turning it around. Why write books instead of copying music, when that work pleases me, suits me more than any other, and when its result is a just, honest profit that suffices for me? Thinking is very painful work for me, which tires, torments, and displeases me. Working with my hands and letting my head rest refreshes and amuses me. If I sometimes like to think, it is freely and without constraint, letting my ideas flow at will without subjecting them to anything. But thinking of this or of that as an obligation, as a trade, making my productions correct, methodical is for me the work of a galley slave, and thinking as a livelihood seems to me the most painful as well as the most ridiculous of occupations. Let others use their talents as they please; I will not blame them. But for myself, I have never wanted to prostitute my talents such as they are by attaching a price to them, certain that this venality itself would have destroyed them. I sell the work of my hands, but the products of my soul are not for sale. Their disinterestedness alone can give them strength and eminence. What I would do for money would hardly be worth any and would bring me even less.

"Why wish that I write more books when I have said all I had to say and my only recourse, too petty in my view, would be to go back and repeat the same ideas? What good is it to say badly a second time what I said once as well as I could? Those who always have the itch to talk always find something to say. That is easy for whoever wants only to string words together. But I have never been tempted to take up my pen except to say things that are great, new, and necessary, and not to be repetitive. I've written books, it's true, but I was never a book factory. Why pretend to want me to write more books, when in fact there is so much fear that I will do so, and such vigilance to deprive me of all the means for doing it? Access to all houses except for those fomenting the conspiracy is closed to me. Everyone's residence and address are hidden from me with the greatest care. The Swiss guards and Doormen all have secret orders regarding me, different than those of their masters. No further communication with humans is allowed to me, even to talk; would I be allowed to write? Perhaps I would be allowed to express my thinking in order for it to be known, but I would certainly be prevented from saying it to the public.

"In my position, if I were to write books, I should and would want to do so only to defend my honor, to confound and unmask the imposters who defame it. I can no longer treat any other subject without failing in what I owe myself. Even if I had the necessary enlightenment to see through the abyss of darkness into which I have been thrust and to shed light on all these underground schemes, does it make sense to assume I would be allowed to act, and that the people who dispose of me would tolerate my teaching the public about their maneuvers and my fate? To whom would I turn for a publisher who was not one of their emissaries or who did not become one immediately? Have they left me anyone in whom I can confide? Isn't it known every day, every hour, to whom I've talked, what I've said; and do you doubt that since we began our talks, you are not as much under surveillance as I? Is there anyone who can't see that surrounded on all sides, kept in sight as I am, it is impossible for me to make the voice of justice and truth heard anywhere? If they appeared to allow me the means for doing so, it would be a trap. If I had said *white,* they would make me say *black* without my even knowing it*, and since they openly falsify my old writings which everyone has in hand, would they refrain from falsifying those that haven't yet appeared and about which nothing could prove the falsification since my protests count for nothing? Ah, Sir, can't you see that the great, the only crime they fear from me, a horrible crime the fear of which keeps them in continuous dread, is my justification?

"Writing books to make a living would have made me dependent on the public. From then on, the issue would have been not to teach and correct, but to please and succeed. That could no longer be done by following the route I had taken. The times were too changed, and the public had changed too much for me. When I published my first writings, the public was still left on its own, it hadn't yet completely adopted a sect and could hear the voice of truth and reason. But completely subjugated today, it no longer thinks, no longer reasons, it is no longer anything by itself, and no longer follows anything but the impressions given to it by its guides. The sole doctrine it can henceforth taste is that which puts its passions at ease and covers the irregularity of its morals with a veneer of wisdom. Only one path remains for anyone who aspires to please the public. It is to follow in the track of the brilliant Authors of this century and to preach as they do, with hypocritical morality, the love of virtues and the hatred of vice, but after starting by pronouncing as do they that all this is words empty of meaning, made to amuse the people; that there is neither vice nor virtue in the heart of man, since there is neither freedom in his will nor morality in his actions, that everything including this will itself is the work of blind necessity, and finally that conscience and remorse are only prejudices and chimeras, since one can neither applaud oneself for a good action one has been forced to do, nor reproach oneself for a

* As they will certainly do with the contents of this writing if its existence is known to the public and it falls into the hands of these Gentlemen, which naturally appears inevitable.

crime from which one didn't have the power to abstain.* And what warmth, what vehemence, what tone of persuasion and truth could I convey even if I wanted to in these cruel doctrines which, flattering the happy and the rich, crush the unfortunate and the poor by removing all restraint, all fear, all reserve from the former and from the latter all hope, all consolation. And finally how could I make them fit with my own writings, which are full of refutations of all these sophisms? No, I said what I knew, what I at least believed to be true, good, consoling, useful. I said enough for whoever would listen to me with a sincere heart, and much too much for the century in which I had the misfortune to live. Anything further I might say would have no effect, and I would say it badly, being animated neither by the hope of success like popular authors, nor as long ago by that height of courage which uplifts and is inspired only by the love of truth unmixed with any personal interest."

Seeing the indignation which these ideas generated in him, I refrained from talking to him about that hodgepodge of books and pamphlets he is said to scribble and publish every day with as much secrecy as good sense. Under such surveillance, by what inconceivable foolishness could he hope to be able to maintain anonymity even for a moment; and how could he, who is reproached so much for being mistakenly wary of everyone, be so stupidly confident about those whom he would charge with the publication of his manuscripts. And if he had this inept confidence in someone, is it believable that in his awful position, he would utilize him only to publish dry translations and frivolous pamphlets?** Finally, is it thinkable that seeing himself thus exposed daily, he simply continued on his way with the same mystery, with the same well-kept secret, either by continuing to confide in the same traitors or by choosing new confidants who were just as faithful?

I stress this on purpose. Without resuming the trade of an Author which he so dislikes, why didn't he at least turn to some more honorable or more lucrative talent as a resource? If it's true he knew music, why didn't he write or teach it instead of copying it? If he didn't know music, he had or was thought to have other knowledge about which he could give lessons. Italian, Geography, Arithmetic; how do I know! Everything, since it is so easy in Paris to teach what one doesn't know oneself. The most mediocre talents were more profitable to cultivate to help him earn a living than the least of all, which he possessed badly and from which he

---

* That is what they have openly taught and published to this point, and no one has dreamt of issuing a warrant against them for this doctrine. This punishment was reserved for the *Blasphemous System of Natural Religion*. Now they make J.J. state all that; they keep silent, or cry blasphemy, and the public goes along with them. *Risum teneatis, amici.*[65]

** Today they are bound books. But in the operation concerning me, there is a progression which was not easy to foresee.

derived so little profit, even charging so much for his work. He would not have become dependent, as he did, on whoever turns up with a shred of music spouting their gibberish, nor on insolent valets who come with their arrogant demeanor to reveal the hidden feelings of their masters. He would not as often have gone unpaid for his work, been scorned by the people and called a Jew by the philosopher Diderot because of this very work. All these paltry profits are scorned by great souls. Illustrious Diderot, who doesn't dirty his hands with mercenary work and disdains little, usurious profits, is a Wise man as virtuous as he is disinterested in the eyes of all Europe. And the copyist J.J. who takes ten sols per page for his work to help make his living is a Jew whose greed makes him universally scorned. But despite its harshness, in this instance fortune seems to have put everything in its proper place, and I don't see that the usurious practices of the Jew J.J. have made him very rich nor that the disinterestedness of the philosopher Diderot has impoverished him. And is it possible not to feel that if J.J. had taken up the trade of music copyist uniquely to mislead the public or through affectation, he would not have failed, in order to deprive his enemies of this weapon and take credit for his trade, to perform it at the same price as others or even less?

The Frenchman

Greed doesn't always reason well.

Rousseau

Animosity often reasons worse still. That becomes wonderfully clear in examining the demeanor of your Gentlemen and their singular reasonings that would betray them very rapidly to anyone who would look at them and didn't share their passion.

I had all these objections in mind when I began to observe our man, but seeing him familiarly, I soon felt and I feel more strongly each day that the true motives which determine his actions in everything he does are rarely in his best interest and never in the opinions of the multitude. They must be sought closer to him, if one is not to be constantly mistaken.

First, how can one not feel that in order to profit from all those little talents that are spoken of, there would have to be another one that he lacks, namely the talent of asserting them. He would have to plot, rush from house to house at his age, pay court to Nobles, to the rich, to women, to artists, to all those he would be allowed to approach. For the same choice would be given to the people he would be permitted to approach as is given to those allowed to approach him, among whom I would not figure were it not for you.

In Lyons, he had a public and memorable experience of the manner in which musicians would treat him if he put himself at their mercy for the execution of his works, as he would have to in order to benefit from them.[66] I add that even if he could succeed through trickery, he would always find success purchased at this price too costly. For myself at least, thinking differently than the public about true honor, I find there is much more honor in copying music at so much per page at home than in rushing from door to door to suffer the rebuffs of valets, the caprices of masters, and to ply the trade of cajoler and flatterer everywhere. Every judicious mind should feel this on its own. But specific study of the man adds new weight to all that.

J.J. is indolent, lazy like all contemplative people, but this laziness is only in his head. He thinks only with effort, he tires when he thinks, he becomes fearful about everything that forces him to do so to whatever small degree it may be, and if he must reply to a greeting stated with a special turn, he will be tormented by it. Yet he is lively and laborious in his own way. He cannot tolerate absolute idleness. His hands, his feet, his fingers must move, his body must be exercised, and his head must remain at rest. That is the source of his passion for walking, which allows him to move without being obliged to think. In reverie, one is not active. Images are traced in the brain, where they combine as in sleep without the collaboration of the will. All that is allowed to follow its course, and one enjoys without acting. But when one wishes to stop and stare at objects, to organize and arrange them, that is another matter; one puts something of one's own into it. As soon as reasoning and reflection are involved, meditation is no longer a repose. It is a very painful action, and it is that pain which terrifies J.J., and just the idea of it weighs him down and makes him lazy. I never found him like that except in any work where the mind must be active, however little that may be. He is stingy with neither his time nor his effort; he can't remain idle without suffering. He would willingly spend his life digging in a garden in order to dream at his ease. But it would be the cruelest torture for him to spend it in an armchair tiring his brain looking for trivia to amuse the ladies.

Moreover, he detests bother as much as he loves occupation. Work costs him nothing as long as he does it when he chooses and not when someone else does. He bears the yoke of the necessity of things without difficulty, but not so the yoke of the will of men. He will prefer to do twice the work taking his time than an easier one at a prescribed moment.[67]

If he has some business, a visit, a trip to make, he will go immediately if nothing presses him; if he must go promptly, he will balk. The moment when he got rid of his watch, renouncing all thought of becoming rich in order to live from day to day, was one of the sweetest days of his life. Heaven be praised, he cried in a fit of joy, I won't need to know what time it is any longer.

If he has difficulty submitting to the whims of others, it is not because he has many whims of his own. Never was a man less an imitator and yet less capricious. It is not his reason that prevents him from being so, it is his laziness. For caprices are jolts of the will, and he would fear that they are tiring. Rebellious to any other will, he doesn't even know how to obey his own, or rather he finds it so tiring even to will that he prefers in the course of living to follow a purely mechanical impression that carries him along without his having to direct it. Never did a man more fully bear, right from his youth, the yoke that belongs to weak souls and the aged, namely that of habit. It is through habit that he likes to do again today what he did yesterday, without any other motive than that he did it yesterday. Since the path has been cleared, he has less trouble following it than making the effort to go in a new direction. It is incredible to what extent this laziness of the will subjugates him. It can even be seen in his walks. He will always repeat the same one until some motive absolutely forces him to change. His feet carry him back by themselves to where they have already carried him. He likes to walk straight ahead always, because that can be done without his needing to think about it. He would go along like this, constantly daydreaming, as far as China without realizing it and without being bored. That is why he likes long walks. But he doesn't like gardens where a little change of direction is needed at the end of every path, in order to turn and retrace one's steps; and in a group he places himself without thinking behind others so he won't need to think about his route. Thus he has never remembered any route unless he walked it alone.

All men are naturally lazy, even their interest doesn't animate them, and the most pressing needs make them act only in spurts. But as amour-propre is progressively aroused, it excites them, pushes them, keeps them going constantly breathless because it is the only passion that always speaks to them. That is why they are all seen out in the world. The man who is not dominated by amour-propre and who does not go seeking his happiness far from himself is the only one who knows heedlessness and sweet leisure, and J.J. is that man as far as I can determine. Nothing is more uniform than his way of life. He gets up, goes to bed, eats, works, goes out and returns at the same hours, without willing it and without knowing it. All days are cast in the same mold. The same day is always repeated. His routine takes the place of all other rules: he follows it very precisely without fail and without thought. This weak inertia does not influence only his indifferent actions, but his entire conduct, even the affections of his heart; and when he so passionately sought relationships that suited him, he never really formed any others than those that came to him by chance. Indolence and the need to love have given a blind ascendancy to all who approach him. A fortuitous encounter, the occa-

sion, the need of the moment, the habit too rapidly adopted have determined all his attachments and through them his entire fate. His heart
asked him in vain to make a choice; his easygoing disposition did not
allow him to make one. He is perhaps the only man in the world from
whose relationships it is impossible to draw any conclusions, because his
own taste never brought about any of them, and because he always found
himself subjugated before he had the time to choose. Moreover, habit
does not lead to boredom for him. He would live forever on the same
food, repeat the same tune endlessly, reread the same book always, see
only the same person always. Finally, I never saw him develop a distaste
for anything that had once given him pleasure.

It is through these observations and others related to them, through
attentive study of the nature and tastes of the individual, that one learns
to explain the singularities of his behavior, and not by the frenzies of
amour-propre that devour the hearts of those who judge him without
ever getting close to his heart. It is through laziness, through nonchalance,
through aversion for dependency and penury that J.J. copies music. He
does his work when and as it suits him. He is not accountable to anyone
for his day, his time, his work, his leisure. He doesn't need to arrange
anything, foresee anything, worry about anything; he has nothing to
expend his mind on; he is himself and on his own all day every day. And
in the evening when he relaxes and walks, his soul leaves its calm only to
surrender to delectable emotions without any cost to himself and without
upholding the burden of celebrity by brilliant or learned conversations
which would be the torment of his life without soothing his vanity.

He works slowly and ponderously, makes many mistakes, erases or
starts over ceaselessly; all of which forces him to charge a high price for
his work even though he feels its imperfection more than anyone. However, he spares neither expense nor effort to make it worth the price, and
he brings to it attention that is not without effect and would be sought
in vain from other copyists. However high it is, this price would perhaps
be below theirs if what they take pleasure in making him lose, either by
not picking up or not paying for the work that was ordered from him or
by distracting him from his work in a thousand ways from which other
copyists are exempt, were deducted from it. If he abuses his celebrity in
that respect, he feels it and laments it. But it is a very tiny advantage
compared to all the ills it brings him, and he cannot do otherwise without
exposing himself to inconveniences he doesn't have the courage to bear.
Whereas with this slender supplement earned by his work, his current
situation is on the comfortable side precisely as his disposition requires.
Free from the chains of fortune, he enjoys with moderation all the real
goods it offers. He has eliminated those of opinion, which are only

apparent and are the most costly. If he were poorer, he would feel deprivation and suffering; richer, he would have the burden of wealth, worries, business; he would have to renounce heedlessness, the sweetest of the sensual delights for him. By possessing more, he would enjoy far less.

It's true that since he is already old, he cannot hope to occupy himself much longer with his work; his already trembling hand refuses to function with ease, his notes become misshapen, his activity diminishes, it takes him more time to do less work less well. A time will come,* if he ages a great deal, when with the withdrawal of the resources he has preserved, he will be forced to make a belated and difficult apprenticeship in very austere frugality. He has no doubt that your Gentlemen already have a new plan of beneficence for this time which is approaching and which they may be able to hasten. That is, new ways to make him eat the bread of bitterness and drink the cup of humiliation. He feels and foresees all that very well, but being so close to the end of life, he doesn't see that it is a great inconvenience. Besides, since this inconvenience is inevitable, it would be folly to torment himself about it and it would be rushing into it prematurely to seek to prevent it. He provides for the present as best he can, and leaves the care of the future to providence.

I have therefore seen J.J. entirely immersed in the occupations I have just described to you, always walking alone, thinking little, dreaming a lot; working almost mechanically, incessantly occupied with the same things without ever balking; and gayer, more content, healthier leading this almost automatic life than he was the entire time he devoted himself, so cruelly for him and with so little utility for others, to the sad trade of Author.

But let's not overestimate the value of this conduct. The moment this simple and hardworking life is not a pretense, it would be sublime in a famous writer who could reduce himself to it. In J.J. it is only natural, because it is not the work of either effort or reason, but a simple impulsion of temperament determined by necessity. The sole merit of the person who yields to it is that he gave in without resistance to nature's bent, and was not deterred by unwarranted shame or foolish vanity. The more I examine in detail how this man spends his days, the uniformity of this mechanical life, the taste he appears to have for it, the contentment he finds in it, the advantages he derives from it for his disposition and his health, the more I see that this is the way of living for which he was born.

---

* Another very serious inconvenience will force me finally to abandon this work, which the bad will of the public also makes more burdensome than useful for me. It is the frequent intrusion of foreign or unknown fellows who enter my home with this pretext, and who are then able to cling there despite me, without my being able to penetrate their plan.

Men, always believing him to be like themselves, saw him sometimes as a profound genius, sometimes as a petty charlatan, at first a prodigy of virtue, then a monster of villainy, and always as the world's strangest, most bizarre being. Nature made him only a good artisan, albeit sensitive to the point of transport, an idolater of the beautiful, impassioned for justice, capable of vigor and loftiness during brief moments of effervescence, but whose habitual state was and will always be inertia of mind and mechanical activity; and to state it all in a word, someone who is rare only because he is simple. One of the things on which he congratulates himself is that in his old age he finds himself in just about the same rank as the one into which he was born, without ever having gone either up or down very much in the course of his life. Fate returned him where nature placed him; he applauds this collaboration daily.

These resolutions—so simple and for me so clear—of my initial doubts made me feel more and more that I had taken the only correct route to reach the source of the singularities of this man who is judged so much and known so little. The great mistake of those who judge him isn't that they did not guess the true motives for his conduct. Such subtle people never suspected what they were.* But it is never having wanted to learn what they are, to have lent all their heart to the means taken to prevent him from stating them and themselves from knowing them. Even the most equitable people are likely to seek bizarre causes for extraordinary behavior, and on the contrary it is by virtue of being natural that J.J.'s is quite uncommon. But that is what one cannot feel without having made an attentive study of his temperament, his disposition, his tastes, his entire constitution. Men don't go to such lengths to judge one another. They respectively attribute the motives which could make the one judging act as the one judged does if he were in his place, and often they hit it right, because they are all guided by opinion, by prejudices, by amour-propre, by all the artificial passions that follow in its wake, and especially by this lively interest—foresighted and provident —that always throws them far away from the present and is nothing for the man of nature.

But they are so far from reaching back to the pure impulses of this nature and of knowing them that if they were finally able to understand that it isn't through ostentation that J.J. behaves so differently from them,

* I don't know two Frenchmen who could succeed in knowing me, even if they desired to do so with all their heart. The primitive nature of man is too far removed from all their ideas. I don't say, however, that there are none. I say merely that I don't know two.[68]

* Clever people, totally transformed by amour-propre, haven't the slightest idea of nature's true movements, and will never have any understanding of decent souls, because they see nothing but evil everywhere except in those whom they have an interest in flattering. Since the observations of clever people are in harmony with the truth only by chance, they have no authority at all for the wise.

the majority would conclude immediately that it is therefore through baseness of soul, a few perhaps that it is through a heroic virtue, and all would be equally mistaken. There is baseness in voluntarily choosing an occupation worthy of scorn, or in receiving from charity what could be earned from one's work; but there is none at all in living by honest work rather than by charity or rather intriguing to succeed. There is virtue in conquering one's inclinations to do one's duty; but there is none in following them to devote oneself to occupations that are to one's taste although unworthy in the eyes of men.

The cause of false judgments made about J.J. is that it is usually assumed that he had to make great efforts to be different from other men, whereas, given his constitution, he would have had to make great efforts to be like them. One of my most certain observations, which is least suspected by the public, is that although he is impatient, touchy, subject to the liveliest angers, he is nonetheless unacquainted with hatred, and no idea of revenge ever entered his heart. If someone could ever admit a fact so contrary to the ideas held about the man, its cause would promptly be seen as a sublime effort, the painful victory over amour-propre, the great but difficult virtue of pardoning one's enemies; yet it is simply a natural result of the temperament I described. Always preoccupied with or for himself, and too avid for his own good to have time to think about the ill of another, he isn't aware of those jealous comparisons of amour-propre from which the hateful passions of which I spoke arise. I even dare to say that there is no constitution more removed than his from wickedness. For his dominant vice is to pay more attention to himself than to others, and that of wicked men, in contrast, is to pay more attention to others than to themselves. And it is precisely for this that taking the word *egoism* in its true sense, they are all egoists and he is not, because he does not place himself either beside or above or below anyone, and no one's displacement is necessary to his happiness. All his meditations are sweet because he loves enjoyment. In painful situations, he thinks about them only when he is forced to do so. Every moment he can take away from them is given to his reveries. He knows how to get away from unpleasant ideas and to transport himself to somewhere other than where he is uncomfortable. Since he spends so little time on his troubles, how would he spend much on those who make him suffer? He takes revenge by not thinking about it, not in a spirit of revenge but to spare himself the torment. Lazy and voluptuous, how could he be hateful and vindictive? Would he want to transform into tortures his consolations, his enjoyments, and the sole pleasures that remain to him on this earth? Bilious and wicked men seek retreat only when they are sad, and retreat saddens them still more. The leavening of revenge ferments in solitude through the pleasure taken in indulging in it. But this sad and cruel pleasure devours and consumes one who indulges in it. It makes him nervous, active, scheming. The solitude he sought soon becomes the torture of his hateful and tormented heart, he doesn't taste that pleasant heedlessness, that sweet nonchalance that constitutes the charm of true solitaries; his passion animated by his gloomy reflections seeks satisfaction, and soon abandoning his somber retreat, he rushes back into the world to feed the fire with which he wants to consume his enemy. If writings emerge from the hand of such a solitary, they will surely resemble neither *Emile* nor *Heloise*; whatever art the Author uses to disguise himself, they will bear the taint of the bitter bile that prompts them. The fruits of J.J.'s solitude attest to the feelings on which he feeds himself there. He was ill-tempered so long as he lived in the world; he was so no longer as soon as he lived alone.

This dislike of feeding himself with black and unpleasant ideas can be felt in his writings as well as in his conversation, and especially in those lengthy ones where the Author had more time to be himself and where his heart is, so to speak, more at ease. Carried away by his subject, indignant at the spectacle of public morals, excited by the people living with him and who already, perhaps, held their views at that point, in his first works he sometimes allowed himself to depict wicked people and vices with lively and poignant traits, but those were always quick and rapid, and it can be seen that he didn't take pleasure except in the happy images with which he has always liked to occupy himself. He congratulates himself at the end of *Heloise* for having sustained interest through six volumes without the help of a single wicked person or a single bad action. That, it seems to me, is the least equivocal testimonial to the true tastes of an Author.[69]

The Frenchman

How you do deceive yourself! Good people depict wicked ones without fear. They aren't afraid to be recognized in their portraits. But a wicked person doesn't dare paint his ilk. He fears its application.

Rousseau

Sir, is this very natural interpretation one you made up?

The Frenchman

No, it comes from our Gentlemen. I would never have had the wit to find it!

Rousseau

At least do you seriously accept it as correct?

The Frenchman

But, I admit I don't like to live with wicked people, and I don't believe it follows from that that I am wicked myself.

Rousseau

It is the very opposite that follows, and not only do the wicked like to live among themselves, but their writings as well as their speeches are filled with horrible depictions of all sorts of wickedness. Sometimes good men attempt in the same way to depict them, but only in order to make them odious; whereas wicked men use the same pictures only to render odious not so much the vices as the persons they have in mind. These differences make themselves felt very much in reading, and the lively but general censures of the former are easily distinguished from the personal satires of the latter. Nothing is more natural for an Author than to prefer to treat subjects that are the most to his taste. J.J.'s taste, in attaching him to solitude, attests through the products he worked on there, to the sort of charm that could attract and keep him there. In his youth and during brief periods of prosperity when he did not yet have anyone to complain about, he didn't like retreat any less than he likes it in his wretchedness. He then divided his delectations between the friends he believed he had and the sweetness of meditation. Now that he is so cruelly disabused, he completely surrenders to his dominant taste. This taste neither torments nor troubles him. It makes him neither sad nor somber. He was never more satisfied with himself, less worried about anyone else's affairs, less preoccupied with his persecutors, more content or happier, to the degree that one can make oneself happy living in adversity. If he were as they represent him to us, the prosperity of his enemies, the opprobrium they heap on him, the impossibility of revenging himself would already have made him die of rage. He would have found nothing but despair and death in the solitude he seeks. He finds there peace of mind, sweetness of soul, health, life. All the mysterious arguments of your Gentlemen will never undermine the certainty provided by that argument in my mind.

But is there some virtue in that sweetness? None. There is only the inclination of a loving and tender nature which, filled with delicious visions, cannot pull itself away from them to focus on deadly ideas and destructive feelings. Why suffer when one can enjoy? Why drown one's heart in rancor and bile when one can flood it with good will and love? However, this very reasonable choice isn't made by either reason or will. It is the work of pure instinct. It lacks the merit of virtue, doubtless, but neither does it have its instability. One who has surrendered only to the impulses of nature for sixty years is certainly never going to resist them.

If these impulses do not always take him along the best route, they rarely take him along the worst. The few virtues he has never did much good to others, but his much more numerous vices harm only himself. His morality is less a morality of action than of abstinence. His laziness gave it to him and his reason has often confirmed him in it. Never to do evil seems to him a more useful, more sublime, and much more difficult maxim even than to do good, for often the good one does from one viewpoint becomes an evil from a thousand others. But in the order of nature, there is no true evil except positive evil. Often there is no other way to abstain from harming than to abstain altogether from acting; and according to this, the best regime both morally and physically is a purely negative regime. But it is not one that is suited to an ostentatious philosophy, which wants only showy works and teaches the members of its sect nothing so much as to show off a great deal. This maxim of doing no harm is very similar to another that he also owes to his laziness, but that becomes a virtue in anyone who makes a duty of it. It consists in never getting into a situation that makes him find his own advantage in someone else's detriment. No man fears such a situation. They are all too strong, too virtuous ever to fear that their interest would tempt them against their duty, and in their proud confidence they fearlessly provoke the temptations to which they feel so superior. Let's congratulate them on their strength, but let's not blame weak J.J. for not daring to trust his strength and for preferring to flee temptations rather than to have to conquer them, feeling too uncertain of the success of such a fight.[70]

This indolence alone would have been his downfall in society even if he hadn't added to it other vices. Little duties to perform made society unbearable for him, and neglect of these little duties did him a hundred times more harm than unjust actions could possibly have done. The morality of worldly people, like that of the pious, has been put into minute practices, little formulas, rules of etiquette that take the place of everything else. Whoever devotes himself scrupulously to all these little details can, in addition, be black, false, treacherous, a scoundrel, wicked; it matters very little. As long as he is precise about the rules of etiquette, he is always a decent enough man. The amour-propre of those who are left out in such a case portrays this omission as a cruel outrage or a monstrous ingratitude, and a person who would give his purse and his blood for another will never be forgiven for omitting a detail of civility in some encounter. By his disdain for everything that is pure formality and done both by good and bad people, by friends and those who are indifferent, in order to devote himself to solid duties that have nothing to do with ordinary custom and cause little sensation, J.J. provided the pretexts your Gentlemen have so skillfully used. He may have quietly fulfilled great duties about which no one would have said a word; but the neglect of useless little details caused his downfall. These little details are sometimes also duties that it is not permissible to disregard, and I don't mean by that to excuse him. I am only saying that even this evil, which is not one in its source and which befalls only him, again comes from that indolence of character which dominates him and makes him neglect his interests no less than his duties.

J.J. seems never to have coveted very ardently the goods of fortune, not because of any moderation for which he might be honored but because those goods, far from procuring those for which he is avid, take away their enjoyment and taste. He has never been very affected by real losses and frustrated hopes. He desired happiness too greatly to have much desire to be rich, and if he had a few moments of ambition, his desires like his efforts were lively and brief. At the first obstacle he could not overcome with the first blow, he gave up and, falling back immediately into his languour, he forgot what he could not attain. He was always so inactive, so unsuited to the stratagems necessary to succeed in any undertaking, that when the things that were easiest for others became difficult for him, his laziness made it impossible for him to spare the necessary efforts to get them. Another prop for his laziness in any affair that was a little lengthy was the uncertainty time places on successes which seem the most assured in the future, a thousand unforeseen events being capable of aborting the best conceived plans at any moment. Life's instability alone reduces all future events for us to simple probabilities. The effort that must be made is certain, the reward for it is often dubious, and remote projects can appear to be only lures for dupes to whoever has more indolence than ambition. J.J. is and always was like that. Ardent and lively by temperament, he could not have been exempt from all sorts of covetousness in his youth, and he is likely still to be much the same. But whatever desire he may have formed, and whatever its object may have been, if he was unable to obtain it on the first try, he was always incapable of prolonged perseverance in aspiring to it.

Now he seems to desire nothing more. Indifferent about the rest of his career, he sees its end approach with pleasure, but without accelerating it even through his wishes. I doubt whether another mortal has ever said better and more sincerely to God, *Thy will be done*, and it is doubtless not a very praiseworthy resignation for someone who sees nothing more on this earth capable of soothing his heart. But in his youth, when the fire of temperament and his age must often have enflamed his desires, he was able to form some that were lively enough but rarely durable enough to conquer the occasionally very surmountable obstacles that stopped him. Desiring much, he must have obtained very little, because it is not impulses of the heart alone that suffice to attain the object, and other means that he never knew how to apply are necessary. The most unbelievable timidness, the most excessive indolence would perhaps have yielded on occasion to the strength of desire, had he not found in this very strength the art of eluding the efforts it seemed to require; and here again, of all the keys to his character, this is the one that best reveals its mechanical parts. By dint of attending to the object he covets, by dint of reaching out for it with his desires, his beneficent imagination reaches its goal by leaping over the obstacles that stop or frighten him. It does more. Removing from the object everything that is foreign to his covetousness, it presents it to him only as suited to his desire in all respects. In this way, his fictions become even sweeter to him than the realities themselves, removing the defects along with the difficulties, offering them especially prepared for him, and making the desiring and the enjoying one and the same thing for him. Is it surprising that a man so constituted should have no taste for the active life? In order to pursue a few imperfect and uncertain enjoyments that are remote, it would deprive him of those which are worth a hundred times more and are always in his power. He is happier and richer possessing the imaginary goods he creates than he would be possessing those that really exist, which are more real, if you wish, but less desirable.

But this very imagination, so rich in pleasant pictures full of charms, obstinately rejects objects of sadness and pain, or at least it does not depict them so vividly for him that his will cannot erase them. Uncertainty about the future and the experience of so many misfortunes can make him overly frightened about the ills that threaten him by occupying his mind with finding ways to avoid them. But have these ills actually happened? He feels them keenly for a moment and then forgets them. By looking at everything in the future at its worst, he is comforted and reassured. Once the misfortune has happened, it must no doubt be endured but there is no further need to think about it in order to prevent it from happening. It is one less source of great torment in his soul. By counting in advance on the ill he fears, he removes its greatest bitterness. When it happens, he is ready to bear it, and if it doesn't happen, that is something good which he relishes with all the more joy because he wasn't counting on it at all. Since he prefers enjoyment to suffering, he turns away from sad and unpleasant memories that are useless, in order to surrender his whole heart to those which are soothing. When his destiny was such that he found in it nothing that was agreeable for him to remember, he lost all memory of it, and going back to the happy times of his childhood and youth, he went over them again and again in his recollections. Leaping forward sometimes into the future for which he hopes and which he feels is his due, he tries to draw for himself its delights by comparing them to the ills he has been made to suffer unjustly in this world. More often, letting his senses collaborate with his fictions, he forms beings in accord with his heart and living with them in a society of which he feels worthy, he soars to the highest heaven, surrounded by charming and almost angelic objects. Do you conceive that in a tender soul of such disposition the leavening of hatred ferments easily? No, no, Sir; you can be sure that a person who could feel for a moment the habitual delectations of J.J. will never contemplate evil deeds.

The most sublime of virtues, that which requires the most greatness, courage, and strength of soul is the pardon of wrongs and the love of one's enemies. Can weak J.J., who doesn't attain even mediocre virtues, achieve that? I am as far from believing it as from affirming it. But what does it matter, if his loving and peaceful nature leads him to the same place to which he would have been led by virtue? What would hatred have done to him if he had known it? I don't know; he himself doesn't know. How could he know where a feeling that never entered his heart would have led him? He had no battle to wage on that issue because he never had the temptation. The temptation of depriving his faculties of their pleasures in order to surrender them to irascible and wrenching passions does not exist for him. That is the torment of hearts consumed by amour-propre and which know no other love. They don't have that passion by choice; it tyrannizes them and leaves no others in their power.

When he undertook his *Confessions*, that work unique to mankind, the reading of which he profaned by offering it to the listeners least suited to hear it, he had already passed middle age and was still ignorant of adversity. He carried out this project in a dignified way until the time of his misfortunes; at that point he found himself forced to renounce it.[71] Accustomed to his sweet reveries, he found neither the courage nor the strength to sustain the meditation of so many horrors. He would not even have been able to recall its horrible web by persisting. His memory refused to be sullied with these atrocious memories. He can remember only the image of times he would see return with pleasure. Those when he was the prey of wicked men would be erased forever along with the cruel people who made them so deadly, if the harm they continue to do to him did not occasionally revive, despite himself, the idea of all they had already made him suffer. In short, a loving and tender nature, a languid soul that carries him to the sweetest enjoyments of the senses, making him reject any sorrowful feeling, removes from his memory any disagreeable object. He does not have the merit of forgiving offenses, because he forgets them. He doesn't love his enemies, but he doesn't think about them. That puts all the advantage on their side, because since they never lose sight of him and are ceaselessly involved in enmeshing him more fully in their traps, and since they find him neither attentive enough to see them nor active enough to defend himself, they are always sure to take him off his guard when and how they wish, without fear of reprisals. While he is occupied with himself, they are occupied with him too. He loves himself and they hate him. That is the occupation of both. He is everything to himself; he is also everything to them. For as for them, they are nothing either to him or to themselves; and as long as J.J. is miserable, they need no other happiness. Thus he and they, each from his own vantage point, have two great experiments to make: they, to heap all the hardships conceivable to man onto the soul of an innocent man, and he, to use all the resources that innocence can draw from itself alone to endure them. What is priceless in it all is to hear your benign Gentlemen lament in the midst of their horrible plotting about the harm done by hatred to one who indulges in it and to pity their friend J.J. tenderly for being the prey of such a tormenting feeling.

He would have to be insensitive or stupid not to see and feel his position. But he pays too little attention to his troubles to be much affected by them. He turns to himself for consolation about the injustices of men. Withdrawing into his own heart, he finds very sweet compensations there. So long as he is alone, he is happy; and when the spectacle of hatred distresses him, or when scorn and derision fill him with indignation, it is a passing mood that ends as soon as the object that elicits it has disappeared. His emotions are prompt and lively, but rapid and of short duration, and that is visible. His heart, transparent as crystal, can hide nothing of what happens within it. Every mood it feels is transmitted to his eyes and face. One sees when and how he gets upset or calms down, when and how he gets angry or is softened, and as soon as what he sees or hears affects him, it is impossible for him to withhold or dissimulate its impression even for a moment. I have no idea how he managed to deceive the whole world for forty years about his character. But however little he is drawn out of his cherished inertia, which unfortunately is only too easy to do, I defy him to hide what is happening at the bottom of his heart from anyone; and yet it is from this same nature, as ardent as it is indiscreet, that the cleverest hypocrite and the most devious scoundrel who could exist have been drawn by an admirable illusion of magic.

This remark was important, and I gave it the greatest attention. The foremost art of all wicked people is prudence, that is to say dissimulation. Having so many projects and feelings to hide, they know how to compose their exterior; govern their looks, expression, bearing; become masters of appearances. They know how to work to their own advantage and cover with a veneer of wisdom the dark passions that consume them. Lively hearts are impetuous, carried away, but everything evaporates externally. The wicked are cold, composed; venom collects and hides deep within their hearts, to do its work only at a certain time and place. Until then, nothing escapes, and to make the effect greater or more certain, they slow it down at will. These differences come not only from temperaments, but also from the nature of the passions. Because those of ardent and sensitive hearts are the work of nature, they show themselves despite the person who has them. Their initial, purely mechanical explosion is independent of his will. All he can do by resisting is to stop its progress before it has produced its effect, but not before it has been manifested either in his eyes, or by his blush, or by his voice, or in his bearing, or through some other palpable sign.

But since amour-propre and the impulses derived from it are only secondary passions produced by reflection, they do not act so sensibly on the machine. This is why those governed by that sort of passion have more mastery over appearances than those who surrender to the direct impulses of nature. In general, if ardent and lively natures are more loving, they are also more easily carried away, less patient, more wrathful. But these noisy transports are without consequence, and as soon as the sign of anger disappears from the face, it is also extinguished in the heart. On the contrary, phlegmatic and cold people—so gentle, so patient, so moderate on the outside—are hateful, vindictive, implacable within. They know how to preserve, disguise, nurture their rancor until the moment to satisfy it is at hand. In general, the former love more than they hate; the latter hate much more than they love, if they even know how to love. Souls of high calibre are nonetheless often among the latter, as if above the passions. True wise men are cold, I have no doubt. But in the class of common men, without the counterweight of sensitivity, amour-propre will always tip the scales, and if they do not remain nothing, it will make them wicked.

You will tell me there are lively and sensitive men who are also wicked, hateful, and spiteful. I don't believe it, but it is necessary to understand what I mean. There are two types of liveliness: that of the feelings and that of ideas. Sensitive souls are strongly and quickly affected. The blood, inflamed by sudden agitation, carries those impetuous movements which indicate passion to the eye, the voice, the face. On the contrary, there are lively minds joined to frigid hearts, which draw from the brain alone the agitation that also appears in their eyes, in their gestures, and that accompanies their words, but through very different signs; mimes and actors rather than animated and impassioned people. These people, rich in ideas, produce them with extreme ease. They have words at their command, their ever alert and pentrating mind continuously gives them new thoughts, flashes of wit, felicitous replies. Whatever strength and whatever finesse is put into what might be said to them, they are astounding by the promptness and piquancy of their replies, and are never caught short. Even in matters of feeling, they have a little patter so well organized that one would believe they are moved to the bottom of the heart if this very precision of expression didn't bear witness that only their mind is at work. The others, completely involved in their feelings, attend too little to their words to arrange them with so much art. The cumbersome sequence of speech is unbearable to them. They chaff against its slow progression. From the speed of the impulses they feel, it seems to them that what they feel should become apparent and penetrate from one heart to another without the cold intermediary of words. Ideas usually present themselves to men of wit in prearranged phrases. That is not true of feelings. It is necessary to search, to combine, to choose language suited to convey what is felt; and what sensitive man would have the patience to suspend the flow of the affections that agitate him to attend every moment to this selecting. A violent emotion can sometimes suggest energetic and vigorous expressions. But these are lucky chances which the same situations don't always provide. Besides, is a man who is strongly moved in a condition to give minute attention to everything that may be said to him, to everything that is happening around him, in order to tailor his reply or his remarks to it? I am not saying that everyone will be as distracted, as heedless, as stupid as J.J., but I doubt that anyone who has received from Heaven a truly ardent, lively, sensitive, and tender nature was ever a man of very lively repartee.

So let's not repeat society's error of mistaking for sensitive hearts hotheads whose desire to shine is the only thing animating their speech, their actions, their writings, and who pretend as best they can to have the sensitivity they lack in order to be applauded by young people and women. Entirely devoted to their sole object, that is to say celebrity, they aren't provoked by anything in the world, they don't take a true interest in anything. Their heads, agitated by rapid ideas, leave their hearts empty of all feeling except that of amour-propre, which, being habitual to them, gives them no impulse that is palpable and noticeable on the outside. Thus tranquil and cold-blooded about everything, they think only of the advantages relative to their own little selves, and letting no opportunity escape, they are constantly busy, with a success that is hardly surprising, disparaging their rivals, scattering their competitors, shining in society, excelling in letters, and depreciating everything that is not connected to their wagon. It is no miracle that such men are wicked and evil-doing; but that they experience any passion other than the egoism that dominates them, that they have true sensitivity, that they are capable of attachment, of friendship, even of love is what I deny. They don't even know how to love themselves; they only know how to hate what is not themselves.

A person who knows how to govern his own heart, keep all his passions under control, over whom personal interest and sensual desires have no power, and who both in public and in private with no witness does only what is just and honest on every occasion, without regard for the secret wishes of his heart, he alone is a virtuous man. If he exists, I rejoice for the honor of the human race. I know that masses of virtuous men existed formerly on earth. I know that Fénelon, Catinat, others less known, did honor to modern times, and among us I have seen George Keith still follow in their sublime paths.[72] With that exception, I have seen in the apparent virtues of men only boasting, hypocrisy, and vanity. But what is a little closer to ourselves, what is at least much more in the order of nature, is a well born mortal who has received from Heaven only expansive and gentle passions, loving and lovable inclinations, a heart that desires ardently but that is sensitive and affectionate in its desires, that has no wish for glory or treasures, but only for real enjoyments, true attachments, and who, counting the appearance of things for nothing and the opinion of men for little, seeks his happiness within, without regard for customs and received prejudices. This man will not be virtuous, because he will not conquer his inclinations, but in following them, he will do nothing contrary to what would be done by a person who heeds only virtue by overcoming his. Goodness, commiseration, generosity, these first inclinations of nature which are only emanations of love of oneself, will not set themselves up in his mind as austere duties. But they will be his heart's needs, which he will satisfy more for his own happiness than by a principle of humanity that he will scarcely dream of reducing to rules. The instinct of nature is less pure, perhaps, but certainly more secure than the law of virtue. For one is often in contradiction with one's duty, never with one's inclination, in order to do evil.

The man of nature enlightened by reason has appetites that are more delicate but not less simple than in his initial coarseness. Fantasies of authority, celebrity, preeminence are nothing to him. He wants to be known only in order to be loved, he wants to be praised only for what is truly praiseworthy and what he indeed possesses. Wit and talents are merely the ornaments of merit for him, and do not constitute it. They are necessary developments in the progress of things, and they have their advantages for the amenities of life, but these are subordinate to the more precious faculties that make man truly sociable and good, and that make him prize order, justice, rectitude, and innocence above all other goods. The man of nature learns to bear the yoke of necessity in all things and to submit to it, never to grumble against providence, which began by loading him with precious gifts, which promises his heart goods more precious still, but which, to mend the injustices of fortune and men, chooses its hour and not ours, and whose vision is too far beyond ours for her to be accountable to us about her means. The man of nature is subjected by it and for his own preservation to irascible and momentary fits, to anger, to outbursts, to indignation. Never to hateful and lasting feelings, harmful both to the person who is prey to them and to the one who is their object, and which lead only to harm and destruction without serving for anyone's good or preservation. Finally, the man of nature, without exhausting his weak forces building tabernacles on earth, enormous machines for happiness or pleasure, enjoys himself and his existence without much worry about what men think of it and without much concern about the future.

Such was the indolent J.J. I saw, without affectation, unstudied, given by taste to his sweet reveries, thinking profoundly sometimes, but always with more fatigue than pleasure, and preferring to be governed by a cheerful imagination rather than to govern his head by reason. I saw him lead an even, simple, and routine life by taste, without ever becoming disheartened by it. The uniformity of this life and the sweetness he finds in it show that his soul is at peace. If he were ill at ease with himself, he would finally tire of living this way. He would need diversions which I don't see him seek, and if by a turn of mind difficult to conceive he persisted in imposing such torture on himself, the effect of this constraint would eventually be visible in his disposition, in his complexion, in his health. He would become jaundiced, he would languish, he would become sad and somber, he would waste away. On the contrary, he is in better health than ever.* He no longer has those chronic pains, that thinness, that pallor, that moribund look which he had constantly for ten years of his life; that is during the entire time when he was mixed up in writing, a trade as fatal for his constitution as it was contrary to his taste, and that would finally have landed him in the grave if he had pursued it longer. Ever since he has resumed the sweet leisures of his youth, he has resumed its serenity. He keeps his body busy, and rests his head. It agrees with him in every way. In short, just as I found the man of nature in his books, I found in him the man of his books, without having needed to look expressly at whether it were true that he was their Author.

I had only one bit of curiosity I wanted to satisfy; it was on the subject of the *Village Soothsayer*. What you had told me about it had struck me so greatly that I would not have been satisfied without being enlightened about it in particular. It is hardly conceivable how a man endowed with some genius and talents through which he can aspire to deserved glory, would intrude unnecessarily on every occasion to show his ineptness in order to boast shamelessly of a talent he didn't have. But in the middle of Paris and of the artists least disposed to be indulgent toward

---

* Everything comes to an end in this world. If my health is declining and succumbing at last to so many uninterrupted afflictions, it still remains astounding that it resisted for so long.

him, for such a man to present himself unceremoniously as the Author of a work he is incapable of writing, for a man so timid, so inadequate to set himself up among masters as the preceptor of an art about which he understands nothing and for him to accuse them of not listening, is surely one of the most unbelievable things anyone could propose. Besides, there is such baseness in boasting in this way of another's remains, this maneuver presumes such an impoverished mind, such childish vanity, such limited judgment, that whoever could resort to it will never do anything great, lofty, beautiful in any genre, and despite all my observations, it would forever have remained impossible in my view that J.J., falsely stating himself to be the Author of the *Village Soothsayer*, wrote any of the other writings he claims, and which certainly have too much strength and loftiness to have come out of the little head of an impudent little plagiarizer. All that seemed to me so incompatible that I kept going back to my first conclusion of *everything or nothing*.

One more thing prompted my zeal in this research. The Author of the *Village Soothsayer*, whoever he is, is not an ordinary Author, nor is the author of the other works that bear the same name. There is a sweetness, a charm, above all a simplicity in that piece which sensibly distinguish it from all other productions of the same genre. The words contain neither lively situations, nor beautiful sentences, nor a pompous moral. The Music has neither learned features nor labored passages, nor colored songs, nor pathethic harmony. The subject is more comical than moving, and yet the piece touches, stirs, moves one to tears. One feels moved without knowing why. What is the source of this secret charm that flows thus into the heart? This unique source into which no one else has dipped is not the Hippocrene;[73] it comes from somewhere else. Its Author must be as singular as the piece is original. If, already acquainted with J.J., I had seen the *Village Soothsayer* for the first time without the Author being named to me, I would have said without wavering that it is the author of the *Nouvelle Héloïse*, it is J.J. and it can be no one else. Colette is interesting and touching like Julie without the magic of situations, without the preparation of romantic events, the same nature, the same sweetness, the same accent. They are sisters, or I am much mistaken. That is what I would have said or thought. Now I am assured, to the contrary, that J.J. claims falsely to be the Author of this piece, and that it is by someone else. Show me that someone else, then, so I can see how he is made. If it is not J.J., he must at least be very much like him, since their productions—so original and so characteristic—are so much alike. It is true that I cannot have seen J.J.'s musical productions since he cannot write music. But I am sure that if he could, they would have a character very like that. If I rely on my own judgment, that music is by him. The proofs I am given say it isn't. What should I believe? I resolved to seek the truth by myself on this point so well that I could have no further doubt about it, and I went about it in the quickest and surest way to succeed.

The Frenchman

Nothing could be simpler. You did what everyone else does: you gave him some music to read and seeing that he just muddled around, you drew your conclusions and did nothing more.

Rousseau

That isn't what I did, and that wasn't the point, either. For as far as I know, he has never claimed to be either a crooner or a Cathedral chorister. But in presenting Music as his own, he did claim to know how to write it. That is what I had to verify. I therefore proposed that he write, rather than read, some music. It seemed to me that this was the most direct way possible to address the real point of the question. I asked him to write this music in my presence to accompany words that were unknown to him and that I gave him on the spot.

The Frenchman

You are most generous, for when he assured you that he didn't know how to read music, wasn't he also assuring you that he didn't know how to compose it?

Rousseau

I don't really know. I see no impossibility at all for a man who is too full of his own ideas to know neither how to grasp nor how to render those of others; and since it isn't due to lack of wit that he speaks so badly, it may also not be due to his ignorance that he reads music so badly. What I do know is that if it is valid to conclude the possibility from the act, seeing him compose music right before my eyes assured me that he knew how to compose.

The Frenchman

On my honor, how curious! Well, Sir, with what evasion did he reward you? He took umbrage, no doubt, and rejected the proposition with disdain?

Rousseau

No, he saw my motive too clearly to be able to take offense, and he even seemed to me more grateful than humiliated by my proposition. But he begged me to compare the situations and ages. "Take into consideration," he said to me, "the difference that an interval of twenty-five years, lengthy heartaches, annoyances, discouragement, old age must make in the productions of the same man. Add to that the constraint you impose, which pleases me because I see the reason for it, but which nonetheless hinders the ideas of a man who has never been able to compel them, nor produce anything except when he chose, at his leisure, and at will."

The Frenchman

So when all is said and done, with well-turned phrases he refused the test you proposed?

Rousseau

On the contrary. After that little preamble, he undertook it wholeheartedly, and did better than he himself hoped to do. A little slowly but in my presence the whole time, he wrote music as fresh, as lilting, as well developed as that of the *Soothsayer,* and in a style, rather similar to the style of that piece but less novel than it was then, that is just as natural, just as expressive, and just as pleasant. He himself was surprised by his success. "The desire I saw you had to see me succeed," he said, "made me succeed better. Distrust stupefies me, burdens me, and shrivels my brain just as it does my heart. Confidence animates me, gladdens me, and makes me soar on wings. Heaven made me for friendship: it would have given new momentum to my faculties, and my worth would have doubled through it."

That, Sir, is what I wanted to verify for myself. If this experiment isn't enough to prove that he wrote the *Village Soothsayer*, it is at least enough to destroy the proof he did not write it which you yourself have held. You know why all the other proofs are not authoritative in my view. But here is another observation that completes the destruction of my doubts, and confirms or brings me back to my long-standing persuasion.

After this test, I examined all the music he had composed since his return to Paris, which adds up to a considerable collection, and I found it had a uniformity of style and technique that might sometimes become monotonous if it were not authorized or excused by the close relationship to the words he most frequently chose. J.J., with his heart too inclined to tenderness, always had a lively taste for the rustic life. All his music, although varied according to the subjects, shows the imprint of this taste. One believes one hears the pastoral accent of the shepherd's pipe, and this accent makes itself felt everywhere just as it is in the *Village Soothsayer*. A connoisseur cannot mistake it any more than one can be mistaken about the technique of a painter. In addition, all this music has a simplicity, I daresay a truth, that no other modern music has among us. Not only does it have no need for trills, or grace notes, or embellishments, or ornaments of any sort, but it cannot even tolerate anything like that. Its expressiveness consists solely in the nuances of loud and soft, which is the true characteristic of good melody. This melody is always unified and well-marked; the accompaniments enliven it without obscuring it. There is no need to shout repeatedly to the accompanists: *soft, softer*. All this also applies to the *Village Soothsayer*, alone. If he didn't write that piece, he must have had its Author at his beck and call always, to compose new music for him every time he wished to produce some under his name, because only he writes like that. I am not saying that on picking over all that music one won't find resemblances or reminiscences or touches taken or imitated from other Authors. That isn't true of any music I know. But whether these imitations are chance similarities or true plagiarisms, I say that the manner in which they are used by the Author makes them his own. I say that the abundance of ideas of which he is full and which he associates with the others leaves no room to presume that he adopts them because his own resources are sterile. It may be laziness or haste, but it isn't poverty: it is too easy for him to produce for him ever to need to plagiarize.*

I advised him to assemble all this music and try to sell it off to help him live when he could no longer continue his work, but above all to try to see that this collection fell only into faithful and safe hands that would not allow it to be destroyed or divided. For when passion no longer dictates the judgments about him, this collection, it seems to me, will provide powerful proof that all the music that it contains is by one and the same author.**

---

* There are only three passages in the *Village Soothsayer* that are not uniquely by me. As I have repeatedly stated from the outset to everyone, all three are in the divertimento. First, the words of the song which are in part, and at least the idea and refrain, by M. Collé. Second, the words of the Arietta, which are by M. Cahusac who induced me to write this Arietta afterward to please Mademoiselle Fel who was complaining that there was nothing brilliant for her voice in her role. Third, the entrance of the Shepherdesses, which at the lively insistence of M. d'Holbach I arranged from a piece for Clavecin in a collection he gave me. I won't say what M. d'Holbach's intention was, but he urged me so strongly to use something from this collection that I could not obstinately resist his desire concerning such a trifle. As for the love song, which I am said to have derived from Switzerland or Languedoc or our Psalms or some other place, I took it from my own head like the entire piece. Recently returned from Italy, I composed it, feeling passionately fond of the music I had heard there, which was then unknown in Paris. When knowledge of it began to spread, my plagiarisms would soon have been discovered if I had done what French composers do, because they lack ideas, don't even know true song, and their accompaniments are nothing but scribbling. They had the impudence to put M. Vernes' love song ceremoniously in the collection of my writings, to make the public believe I attributed it to myself. My entire reply was to write two other tunes for the love song that were better than that one. My argument is simple: the person who wrote the better tunes had no need to claim the worse one falsely.

** I faithfully included in this collection all the music of all types that I have composed since my return to Paris, and from which I would have eliminated a great deal had I left in only what I considered good. But I wanted to omit nothing of what I really wrote, so that it would be possible to distinguish everything that is attributed to me as falsely as it is impudently even of this genre to the public, in newspapers, and even in collections of my own writings. As long as the words are gross and dishonest, as long as the tunes are dull and flat, I am willingly acknowledged the talent to compose that Music. There is even the pretense of attributing to me the tune of a good song written by others, to make it appear

Everything that came from J.J.'s pen during the period of his effervescence bears a stamp that is impossible to mistake and more impossible to imitate. His music, his prose, his verse, everything during those ten years has a coloration, a hue that no other will ever match. Yes, I repeat, if I did not know the Author of the *Village Soothsayer*, I would feel it from this conformity. The removal of my doubt about that piece completes the removal of any remaining doubts I had about its Author. The strength of the available proofs that it is not by him now serves only to destroy in my mind those of the crimes of which he is accused, and all that leaves me with only one surprise: which is how so many lies can be so well proven.

J.J. was born for music. Not to be consumed in its execution, but to speed its progress and make discoveries about it. His ideas on the art and about the art are fertile, inexhaustible. He has found clearer, more convenient, simpler methods some of which facilitate composition, others execution; and the only thing lacking for their acceptance is that they be proposed by someone other than himself. He has made a discovery about harmony that he does not even deign to announce, certain in advance that it would be rejected or that it would only bring down on him, as with the *Village Soothsayer*, the charge of taking possession of someone else's property. He willl compose ten tunes for the same words without having this abundance be costly or exhausting for him. I have also seen him read music very well, better than many of those who teach it. In this art, he even displays an *impromptu* quality of execution which he lacks in everything else, when nothing intimidates him, nothing troubles the presence of mind he rarely enjoys, easily loses, and can no longer recover once he has lost it. Thirty years ago he was seen in Paris singing everything with an open book. Why can he now no longer do this? It is because no one suspected the talent that everyone now denies him, and a single ill-disposed spectator is enough to trouble his head and his eyes. Let a man in whom he has confidence give him some music that is not known to him. I will bet that unless it is queer or says nothing, he can still sight-read it immediately and sing it passably well. But if in reading that man's heart he sees that he is ill-intentioned, he won't sing a note, and then the spectators draw a conclusion without further examination. About music and about the things he knows best, J.J. is like he used to be with chess. If he played against someone stronger than he whom he believed weaker, he most often beat him; if he played a against a weaker person whom he thought stronger, he got beaten. The adequacy of others intimidates and

---

that I attribute them to myself and adopt as mine the works of others. Depriving me of my own productions and attributing theirs to me has been the most constant maneuver of these gentlemen for twenty years, and the most certain to discredit me.

unnerves without fail. In this respect opinion has always subjugated him, or rather as he himself says, in all things it is the degree of his confidence that determines how high his capabilities rise. The greatest harm that comes from this is that feeling his own capability, he surrenders without fear to occasions to show it in order to convince those who are in doubt about it, always planning that this time he will remain in control of himself; and always intimidated no matter what he does, he always shows only his ineptness. Experience teaches him in vain about this; it has never cured him.

Aptitudes usually announce propensities and vice versa. That is also true of J.J. I have never seen another person as passionate about music as he is, but only for music that speaks to his heart. That is why he prefers to write it than to hear it, especially in Paris, because there is none there so well suited to him as his own. He sings it with a voice that is weak and cracked, but still lively and sweet. He accompanies it, not without difficulty, with fingers trembling less from age than from invincible timidity. He has indulged in this entertainment for several years with more ardor than ever, and it is easy to see that he makes it a pleasant diversion from his hardships. When sorrowful feelings distress his heart, he seeks on his clavier the consolations men refuse him. In this way, his sorrow loses its dryness and supplies him with both songs and tears. In the street, he distracts himself from the insulting looks of passersby by thinking up tunes in his head. Several of the love songs he has written, with a sad and languishing but tender and sweet song, have had no other origin. Everything that has the same character pleases and charms him. He is passionate for the nightingale's song, he likes the cooing of the Turtledove and has imitated it to perfection in the accompaniment of one of his tunes. The regrets that accompany attachment interest him. His liveliest and vainest passion was to be loved. He believed he was made to be loved. He at least satisfied this fantasy with animals. He always lavished his time and his attentions to attract them, caress them. He was the friend, almost the slave of his dog, his cat, his canaries. He had pigeons that followed him everywhere, that flew to his arms, to his head to the point of inconvenience. He tamed birds and fish with incredible patience, and at Monquin he succeeded in having swallows nest in his room so confidently that they allowed themselves to be shut in without startling. In short, his amusements, his pleasures are innocent and gentle like his work, like his inclinations. There is not a taste in his soul that is unnatural or costly or criminal to satisfy; and to be as happy as it is possible to be on this earth, wealth would have been useless to him, and celebrity even more so; all he needed was health, the necessities, repose, and friendship.

I have described for you the principal traits of the man I saw, and limited my descriptions not only to what can be seen in the same way by anyone else if he brings an attentive and unbiased eye to this examination, but to what cannot for long be simulated by hypocrisy, being intrinsically neither good nor bad. As to what is not credible although true, all that is known only to Heaven and to myself but would have deserved to be known by men, or what cannot be said of oneself with decency even when it is known to others, don't hope that I will talk about that with you any more than do those who know him. If his entire worth comes from the approval of men, that much will be lost forever. I will not speak to you about his vices either. Not that he doesn't have very great ones, but because they have never harmed anyone but himself, and he doesn't have to account to others for them. Evil that does no harm to another can remain unspoken when the good that redeems it is unspoken. He was not so discreet in his *Confessions*, and perhaps that was not all to the good. Except for that, all the details I might add to what I have said are nothing more than consequences that everyone can easily fill in by reasoning well. They are sufficient for knowing the nature of the man to the bottom. I cannot go further without breaking the promises to which you bound me. As long as they remain, all I can require and expect of J.J. is that he give me, as he has done, a natural and reasonable explanation of his conduct on all occasions. For it would be unjust and absurd to require that he answer to charges of which he is ignorant and which may not be stated to him. And all I can add of my own to that is to assure myself that the explanation he gives me agrees with everything I have seen of him for myself, giving it my total attention. That is what I have done, so I can stop. Either make me feel how I am deceiving myself or show me how my J.J. can fit the J.J. of your Gentlemen, or agree finally that these two beings, so different, were never the same man.

The Frenchman

I have listened to you with an attentiveness that must please you. Rather than countering your ideas with mine, I have followed you in yours, and if I have interrupted you mechanically at times, it was when I shared your opinion and wanted to have your reply to objections that are often raised which I was afraid I would forget. Now, I ask in return a bit of the attention I have given you. I will avoid being diffuse; if you can, avoid being impatient.

I begin by fully granting your conclusion, and I readily agree that your J.J. and that of our Gentlemen cannot be the same man. The one, I also agree, seems to have been made deliberately in opposition to the other. I even see incompatibilities between them that may strike no one other than myself. The empire of habit and taste for manual work are, for example, in my view things that are unreconcilable with the dark and stormy passions of the wicked, and I reply that a determined scoundrel will never make pretty miniature flower books nor write eight thousand pages of music in six years.* Thus, right from the first sketch, our Gentlemen and you cannot agree. There is certainly error or lying on one of the two sides. There is no lying on yours, I am very sure of that. But there may be error. Who will assure me there is not, in fact? You accuse our Gentlemen of being biased when they discredit him; isn't it you who is biased when you honor him? Your fondness for him makes this doubt very reasonable. To unravel the truth with certainty, it would be necessary to have impartial observations, and whatever precautions you took, yours are no more impartial than theirs. Whatever you may say, everyone has not joined in the plot. I know decent men who don't hate J.J., that is who don't profess toward him that treacherous kindliness which according to you is only a more murderous hatred. They esteem his talents without either loving or hating his person, and they don't have much confidence in all that noisy generosity that is admired in our Gentlemen. However on many points these equitable people agree in thinking like the public with regard to him. What they have seen for themselves, what they have learned from one another gives a rather unfavorable idea of his morals, his rectitude, his gentleness, his humanity, his disinterestedness, all the virtues he displayed with such ostentation. He must be excused for some faults, even some vices, because he is a man. But some of them are too base to germinate in a decent heart. I am not looking for a perfect man, but I despise an abject man, and will never believe that the felicitous inclinations you find in J.J. can be compatible with vices such as those of which he is accused. You can see that I do not stress facts as well proved as anything in the world, but concerning which the omission of a single formality weakens all the proofs, according to you. I say nothing about the creatures he takes pleasure in raping, although nothing is so unnecessary; of the ecus he swindles from passersby in taverns and that he later denies borrowing, of the copies for which he charges twice, of those for which he makes false accounts; of the money he pilfers in payments made to him, and of a thousand other allegations of that sort. I concede that all these things, although proved, are subject to quibbling like the others. But what is widely seen by everyone cannot be. This man in whom you see the modesty and timidity of a virgin is so well known to be a satyr full of impudence that in the very houses that tried to attract him on his arrival in Paris, the daughter of the house was removed as soon as he

---

* Having done part of this calculation in advance and simply by extrapolation, I underestimated everything, and that is what I am clearly discovering as I proceed in my listing, since at the end of only five and a half years I already have more than nine thousand pages well enumerated and about which there can be no disagreement.

appeared, so she would not be exposed to the brutality of his talk and his manners. This man who seems to you so gentle, so sociable flees everyone without exception, disdains every caress, rejects all overtures, and lives alone like a werewolf. He feeds on visions, you say, and goes into ecstasies over chimeras. But if he scorns humans and pushes them away, if his heart is closed to their society, what does the society with imaginary beings you ascribe to him matter to them? Ever since they had the idea of picking him apart more carefully, he has been found to be not only different from what he was believed to be, but contrary to everything he pretended to be. He said he was decent and modest; he was found to be cynical and dissolute. He boasted of good morals; and he is rotting with syphilis. He said he was disinterested; and he is of the basest greed. He said he was humane, compassionate; he harshly pushes away anyone who asks him for help. He said he was pitying and gentle; he is cruel and bloodthirsty. He said he was charitable and he gives nothing to anybody. He said he was affable, easy to subjugate; and he arrogantly rejects all the courtesies that are heaped on him. The more one seeks him out, the more one is disdained by him. In accosting him, it is useless to adopt a sanctimonious look, a wheedling, mournful, lamentable tone; to write him letters that will make him weep; to show him outright that one will kill oneself on the spot if not allowed in. Nothing moves him, he is a man who would allow that if anyone were foolish enough to do it; and the plaintiffs who flock to his door all leave without consolation. In a situation like his, seeing himself so closely watched, shouldn't he apply himself to making everyone who approaches him satisfied with him, to making them give up their black impressions of him by means of gentleness and good manners, to substituting in their souls benevolence for the esteem he has lost and to obliging them at least to pity him since they can no longer honor him. Instead of that, he contributes through his wild disposition and his rude manners to substantiate as much as possible their bad opinion of him. Finding him so hard, so rejecting, so intractable, they easily recognize the fierce man who was depicted to them, and they come back convinced for themselves that no one exaggerated his character and that he is as black as his portrait.

You will doubtless repeat that this is not the man you saw. But it is the man seen by everybody except you. You speak, you will say, only from your own observations. Most of those whom you contradict also speak only from theirs. They saw black where you see white. But they are all in agreement about that color black; the white is apparent to no other eyes than yours. You are alone against all. Are appearances on your side? Does reason allow giving more weight to your unique vote than to the unanimous votes of the entire public? Everything is in agreement concerning this man whom you alone obstinately believe to be innocent, despite so many proofs to which you yourself can find no rejoinder. If these proofs are only so many impostures and sophisms, what then must be thought of the whole human race? What? An entire generation agrees to calumny an innocent man, heap mud on him, to suffocate him, so to speak, in the quagmire of defamation? Whereas all that is necessary, according to you, is to open one's eyes and look at him to be convinced of his innocence and of the blackness of his enemies? Watch out, M. Rousseau. It is yourself who proves too much. If J.J. were as you saw him, would it be possible for you to be the first and only person to have seen him in that light? Are you really the only just and sensible man left on earth? If there is another one left who doesn't think as you do about this, all your observations are annihilated, and you stand alone charged with the accusation you bring against everyone: that you saw what you desired to see and not what was really there. Respond to this one objection, but respond correctly and I will yield on everything else.

Rousseau

To return frankness for frankness here, I begin by declaring that this one objection to which you summon me to respond is, in my view, an abyss of darkness in which my understanding loses itself. J.J. himself understands no more about it than I do. He admits that he is incapable of explaining, of understanding the conduct of the public with regard to him. This harmony with which an entire generation eagerly adopts such an execrable plan makes it incomprehensible to him. He sees in it neither good people, nor bad people, nor humans. He sees beings about whom he has no idea. He doesn't honor them, nor does he despise them or have a conception of them. He doesn't know what it is. His soul, incapable of hate, prefers to rest in this total ignorance rather than to yield, through cruel interpretations, to feelings that are always painful to the person who feels them when their object is beings whom he cannot respect. I approve of that disposition, and I adopt it insofar as I can to spare myself a feeling of disdain for my contemporaries. But in the end I often discover that I am judging them despite myself: my reason performs its task despite my will, and I take Heaven as a witness that it is not my fault if this judgment is so disadvantageous to them.

Therefore, if you make your assent to the result of my research depend on the solution to your objection, it appears likely that leaving me to my opinion, you will maintain your own. For I admit that this solution is impossible for me, though this impossibility does not destroy my persuasion, which began with the clandestine and tortuous progress of your Gentlemen and was confirmed after that by direct acquaintance with the man. All your proofs to the contrary, drawn from further afield, break down against the axiom which carries me on irresistibly, that the same thing cannot be and not be; and everything your Gentlemen say they saw is, by your own admission, entirely incompatible with what I am certain I saw myself.

My practice in my judgment about this man is like that in my belief concerning matters of faith. I yield to direct conviction without stopping at the objections I cannot resolve; as much because these objections are founded on principles that are less clear, less solid in my mind than those that determine my persuasion, as because in yielding to these objections, I would come up against others still more invincible. In making this change, I would therefore lose the strength of evidence without avoiding the obstacle of difficulties. You say that my reason chooses the feeling that my heart prefers, and I don't deny it. That is what happens in all deliberations where judgment is not enlightened enough to reach a decision without the help of the will. Do you believe that in taking the opposite view with so much ardor, your Gentlemen are influenced by a more impartial motive?

Since I don't seek to surprise you, I owed you this declaration at the outset. Now, let's take a look at your difficulties, if not to resolve them at least to look for some sort of explanation for them if possible.

The principal one, which is the foundation for all the others, is what you suggested earlier about the unanimous collaboration of the entire current generation in a plot of imposture and iniquity against which it would be either too harmful for the human race to assume that not one human being would protest against it if he saw its injustice, or—given how obvious this injustice seems to me—too proud of me and too humiliating for common sense to believe that this is not perceived by anyone else.

Let's make this trivial assumption for a moment that all men have jaundice and that you alone do not. I can anticipate the interruption you are preparing for me. . . . *What a dull comparison! What is this jaundice thing all about? . . . How did everyone catch it except you? You are only posing the same question in different terms, but you're not resolving it, you're not even shedding light on it.* Did you want to say something else in interrupting me?

The Frenchman
No, go on.
Rousseau
I will reply then. I think I am shedding light on it, whatever you may say, when I state that there are, so to speak, epidemics of the mind, which conquer men one after another like a kind of contagion, because the human mind, being naturally lazy, likes to spare itself some effort by thinking the way others do, especially in whatever matters agree with its

own leanings. This tendency to be led around in this way, extends further to the inclinations, tastes, passions of men. General infatuation, a very common sickness in your country, has no other cause, and you won't contradict me when I cite you as an example for yourself. Remember the admission you made to me before in assuming the innocence of J.J., that you would never forgive him for your injustice toward him. Thus because of the discomfort his memory would give you, you would prefer to make it worse rather than redress it. Can this feeling, which is natural in hearts consumed by amour-propre, be so in yours which is governed by love of justice and reason? If you had reflected about that to seek within yourself the cause of a feeling that is so unjust and so foreign to you, you would soon have discovered that in J.J. you hate not only the scoundrel who was depicted to you, but J.J. himself; that this hate which was elicited at first by his vices had become independent of them, had become attached to his person, and that whether he was innocent or guilty, without your perceiving it he had become the object of your aversion. Now that you listen to me in a more impartial way, if I remind you of your reasonings in our first conversations, you will feel that they weren't the product of judgment on your part, but that of impetuous passion that dominated you without your knowledge. That, Sir, is the strange cause that seduced your heart and bewitched your judgment, which are so just and so healthy in their natural state. You found a bad side to everything that came from this unfortunate man, and a good one to everything that tended to defame him. Acts of perfidy, betrayals, lies lost all their blackness in your eyes when they were aimed at him, and so long as you yourself were not involved, you became accustomed to seeing them in others without horror. But what was only a temporary aberration for you became a habitual delirium for the public, a constant principle of conduct, a universal jaundice, the fruit of acrid and widespread bile that alters not only the sense of sight but corrupts all dispositions and in the end kills the moral man who would have remained in good health without that. If J.J. had not existed perhaps the majority of them would have had nothing to be ashamed of. Take away this one object of a passion that carries them away, in all other respects they are decent people like everyone else.

This animosity, livelier and more active than simple aversion, seems to me the general disposition of the entire current generation toward J.J. Simply the look that is given him when he walks through the streets clearly shows this disposition, which is held back and constrained sometimes in those who meet him, but which comes through and is visible despite them. From their coarse and idle eagerness to stop, turn around, stare at him, follow him; from the sneering whispers that direct their impudent looks to converge on him, they would be taken not so much for decent people who have the misfortune to meet a frightful monster as for a bunch of thieves, all delighted to have their prey in hand, and who make a game worthy of them by insulting his misfortune. Picture him entering the theatre suddenly surrounded by a close circle of outstretched arms and canes within which you can envisage how at ease he feels! What is the purpose of this barrier? If he wants to break through it, will it resist? Doubtless not. Then what is it for? Uniquely to give them the amusement of seeing him enclosed in this cage, and to make him feel very much that all those surrounding him take pleasure in being so many cops and constables with respect to him. Is it goodness, too, that makes them spit on him without fail every time he passes by within close range and they can do so without being seen by him? Sending a wine of honor to the same person one spits on is making the honor even more cruel than the outrage. All the signs of hatred, of scorn, even of rage that can tacitly be shown to a man without accompanying them with an open and direct insult are showered on him from all quarters; and while heaping him with the most insipid compliments by feigning the sweet little solicitudes tendered to pretty women, if he were truly in need of assistance, he would joyfully be left to perish without the slightest help. I saw him take a dangerous fall almost under a carriage on the rue St.-Honoré. People ran to him, but as soon as they recognized J.J., they dispersed, passersby resumed their way, merchants returned to their shops, and he would have remained alone in that condition if a poor haberdasher, rustic and uneducated, hadn't made him sit down on his little bench, and if a servant girl, equally removed from being a philosopher, hadn't brought him a glass of water. Such, in reality, is the very lively and tender interest of which fortunate J.J. is the object.

Animosity of this kind, when it is strong and durable, does not follow the shortest route but rather the route most certain to sate itself. Now since this route was already mapped out in the plan of your Gentlemen, the public they artfully placed in their confidence had only to follow it, and sharing the same secret among themselves, they all worked together to execute the plan. That is what has happened; but how could it have happened? That is your objection which continually reemerges. Nothing is easier to conceive than that once this animosity was aroused, it changed the faculties of those who surrendered to it to the point where they saw goodness, generosity, clemency in all of the blackest perfidy. Everyone knows too well that violent passions, which always begin by leading reason astray, can make a man unjust and wicked in what he does and, so to speak, unbeknownst to himself, without his having stopped being just and good in his soul or at least loving justice and virtue.

But how did they manage to ignite this venomous hatred? How could they make so odious the human being least destined for hatred, who never had either the interest or desire to harm another, who never either did, wished, or rendered harm to anyone; who, without jealousy, without competitiveness, without aspiration, and always keeping to himself, was not an obstacle to anyone else, and who, instead of the advantages connected with celebrity, found in his own only outrages, insults, wretchedness, and defamation. I discern in all this the secret cause that unleashed the fury of the authors of the plot. The route J.J. had taken was too contrary to their own for them to forgive him for providing an example they didn't wish to follow and for generating comparisons that were uncomfortable for them to endure. In addition to these general causes and those you yourself designated, this primitive and radical hatred of your Ladies and Gentlemen has other causes that are specific and relative to each individual, which are neither acceptable to state nor easy to believe, and about which I will abstain from speaking; but the strength of their effects make them too palpable for anyone to doubt their reality, and the violence of this same hatred can be judged by the art devoted to keeping it hidden while it is being sated. But the more this individual hatred is disclosed, the less understandable is the participation of everyone in it, and even those who could not be affected by any of the motives that gave rise to it. Despite the cleverness of the leaders of the plot, the passion that guided them was too visible for the public not to become wary about everything that came from them. Removing such legitimate suspicions, how did they succeed in making the public so easily and completely share their views to the extent of making the public as ardent as they themselves to fulfill them? That is not easy to understand and explain.

Their underground ways of proceeding are too obscure for it to be possible to follow them. I believe I only perceive an occasional air vent in one spot or another above these tunnels which may indicate their windings. You yourself described to me in our first discussion several of these maneuvers you assumed were legitimate as having for their object the unmasking of a wicked man. Destined, on the contrary, to make a man who is furthest from being wicked appear so, they will be equally effective. He will necessarily be hated, whether he deserves to be or not, because the measures certain to make him odious will have been taken. Up to this point, it is still understandable. But here the effect goes further. It is not only a matter of hatred, but of animosity. It is a matter of the very active cooperation of all in the execution of the project devised by a small number who alone ought to take a great enough interest in it to act so vigorously.

The idea of wickedness is terrifying in itself. The natural impression one receives from a wicked person from whom one has nothing personal to complain is to fear him and to flee from him. Content not to be his victim, no one takes it upon himself to become his executioner. A well-established wicked person, who can and wants to do much evil, can elicit animosity through fear; and the evil that is dreaded may inspire efforts to prevent it. But impotence combined with wickedness can produce only scorn and aversion. A wicked person without power can inspire horror but not animosity. One trembles at the sight of him; far from pursuing him, one flees him, and nothing is further from the effect produced by meeting him than an insulting and mocking smile. Leaving the punishment he deserves to the public authorities, a decent man doesn't stoop to desiring participation in it. Even when this punishment consists in inflicting only dishonor and exposure to public ridicule, what honorable man would lend a hand in this work of justice and place the guilty party in the pillory. So true is it that animosity is not generally felt toward offenders, that if one of them is seen being pursued by justice and nearly caught, far from helping to hand him over, the majority will try to save him if possible, his peril making them forget that he is criminal so that they can remember that he is human.

That is all that is brought about by the hatred of good men for the wicked. It is a hatred composed of repugnance and aversion, even of horror and fear, but not of animosity. It flees its object, averts its eyes, disdains to pay attention to it. But the hatred for J.J. is active, ardent, tireless. Far from fleeing its object, it pursues him eagerly, to use him at its pleasure. The web of his misfortunes, the contrived work of his defamation indicates a very tight, very active conspiracy into which everyone is eager to enter. Each one rushes in with the greatest emulation to encircle him, surround him with betrayals and traps, prevent any useful opinion from reaching him, deprive him of all means of justification, all possibility of repelling the attacks against him, of defending his honor and his reputation; to hide from him all his enemies, all his accusers, all their accomplices. They tremble for fear he will write in his own defense; they worry about everything he says, everything he does, everything he might do. Everyone appears upset by the fear of seeing some apology by him appear. They watch him, they spy on him with the greatest care to try to avoid this misfortune. Precise surveillance is maintained over everything around him, over everyone who approaches him, over everyone who says a single word to him. His health, his life are fresh subjects of worry for the public. They fear that such youthfulness in old age will refute the idea of the shameful ills from which they happily predicted he would die. They fear that with time, the precautions they have accumulated will not longer suffice to prevent him from talking. If the voice of innocence were finally to make itself heard above the din, what an awful misfortune it would be for the corps of men of letters, for that of Doctors, for the Nobility, for magistrates, for everyone? Yes, if by forcing his contemporaries to acknowledge him to be an honest man, he were finally to confound his accusers, his complete vindication would be public desolation.

All this proves irrefutably that the hatred of which J.J. is the object is not hatred of vice and wickedness, but hatred of the individual himself. It doesn't matter whether he is wicked or good. Consecrated to the public hatred, he can no longer escape it, and however little one knows of the workings of the human heart, one sees that recognition of his innocence would serve only to make him still more odious, and to transform the animosity of which he is the object into rage. He is not forgiven now for shaking off the heavy yoke everyone wants to place on him; he would be forgiven even less for wrongs about which they would reproach themselves, and since you yourself have briefly experienced such an unjust feeling, would these people, so imbued with amour-propre endure without bitterness the idea of their own baseness compared to his patience and gentleness? And you can be sure that if he were in fact a monster, they would flee him more, but they would hate him much less.

For myself, in order to explain such dispositions, I can't think of anything except that in order to arouse this violent animosity in the public, they used motives similar to those that had been born in the souls of the Authors of the plot. They had seen this man, adopting principles totally opposite to their own, not wishing, not following either a party or a sect, saying only what seemed to him true, good, useful to men, without consulting his own advantage or that of anyone in particular in doing so. This process and the superiority it conferred on him over them was the great source of their hatred. They could not forgive him for not twisting his morality to his own benefit as they do, for caring so little about his self-interest and theirs, and for so openly showing the abuse of writing and the bragging in the Author's trade, without worrying about the application to himself that would surely be made with these maxims he was establishing, or about the fury he would inspire in those who boast of being the arbiters of fame, the dispensers of glory and reputation for actions and men, but who do not boast, as far as I know, of doing this dispensing with justice and disinterestedness. Detesting satire as much as he loved truth, he always set individuals apart in honorable ways and gratified them with sincere praise when he proposed general truths about which they might have taken offense. He made it felt that evil is grounded in the nature of things, and good in the virtues of individuals. Both for his friends and for Authors he judged worthwhile, he made the same exceptions he believed he deserved, and the pleasure his heart took in these honorable exceptions is felt when one reads his works. But those who felt themselves to be less worthy than he believed them to be, and whose conscience secretly rejected his praise, growing irate in proportion to how little they deserved it, never forgave him for having so well unraveled the abuses of a trade they were trying to make the vulgar admire, or for having through his conduct tacitly, albeit involuntarily, devalued their own. The venomous hatred to which these reflections gave rise in their hearts suggested to them the means to elicit similar hatred in the hearts of other men.

They began by denaturing all his principles, by parodying an austere republican as a seditious bungler, his love for legal freedom as unbridled license, and his respect for the laws as aversion for Princes. They accused him of wanting to overturn the entire order of society because he was indignant that daring to consecrate the most fatal disorders by that name, they insulted the miseries of the human race by presenting the most criminal abuses as the laws of which they are the ruin. His anger against public plunder, his hatred for the powerful rascals who uphold the plunder, his intrepid audacity in speaking truths unpleasant to all stations were means used to make them all become irritated with him. In order to make him odious to those in all stations, he was accused of scorning them personally. His harsh but general reproaches were all transformed into so many specific satires, which were artfully given the most malicious applications.

Nothing inspires as much courage as the testimony of an upright heart, which draws from the purity of its intentions the audacity to state aloud and without fear the judgments dictated solely by love of justice and truth. But at the same time, nothing exposes someone to so many dangers and risks coming from clever enemies as this same audacity, which thrusts a passionate man into all the traps they set for him, and surrendering him to an impetuosity without rules, cause him to make a thousand mistakes contrary to prudence, into which only a frank and generous soul falls but which they know how to transform into so many atrocious crimes. Ordinary men, incapable of lofty and noble feelings, never assume feelings other than self-interested ones in those who become impassioned; and unable to believe that love of justice and the public good could arouse such zeal, they always invent personal motives for them, similar to those they themselves conceal under pompous names and without which they would never be seen getting excited about anything.

What is least forgiven is well-deserved scorn. The scorn which J.J. had displayed for that entire pretended social order, which in fact hides the most cruel disorders, fell much more on the constitution of the different estates than the subjects filling them and who, by this very constitution, must of necessity be what they are. He had always made a very judicious distinction between persons and conditions, often respecting the former although they had surrendered to the spirit of their estate, when nature periodically regained ascendancy over their interest, as frequently occurs in those who are well born. The art of your Gentlemen was to present things from a completely different point of view and to label as hatred of men the hatred which, for love of them, he bears toward the harm they do to each another. It appears that they did not stop with these general allegations, but attributing to him speeches, writings, works in conformity with their views, they spared neither fictions nor lies to provoke their amour-propre against him, both in all estates and among all individuals.

J.J. even has an opinion which, if it is just, can help explain this general animosity. He is persuaded that in the writings circulated under his name, particular care has been taken to make him brutally insult all the estates of society, and to transform into odious personalities the frank and strong reproaches he sometimes makes to them. This suspicion came to him * when, in several letters, anonymous and otherwise, things are brought to his attention as being in his writings which he never dreamed of including. In one, he was said to have *questioned very humorously whether sailors were men.* In another, an officer modestly admits that according to J.J.'s expression he, a military man, *talks drivel in good faith like most of his fellow soldiers.* He thus receives daily quotations of passages falsely attributed to him with the greatest confidence and which are always insulting to someone. He learned a little while ago that a man of letters who was among his oldest acquaintances and for whom he had maintained his respect, having perhaps displayed too openly some remaining affection for him, was cured of it by being persuaded that J.J. was working on a bitter criticism of his writings.

These are just about all the mechanisms they have been able to put into play to ignite and foment that very lively and very general animosity of which he is the object, and which—focusing especially on his defamation—hides beneath a false interest in him the care to debase him further by this appearance of favor and commiseration. For myself, I can imagine only this means to explain the different degrees of hatred people feel toward him, in proportion to how much those who indulge in it see themselves as deserving the reproaches he states about his century and his contemporaries. Public rascals, conspirators, ambitious men whose maneuvers he reveals, passionate destroyers of all religion, all conscience, all freedom, all morality, touched more to the quick by his reproofs, must hate him and do in fact hate him even more than do decent men in error.

---

* It is impossible for me to verify this, because these Gentlemen don't allow a single copy of the writings they fabricate or have fabricated under my name to reach me.

Even when they only hear his name, the former can hardly contain themselves, and the moderation they try to feign quickly flags if they don't need a mask to satisfy their passion. If hatred of the man were merely hatred of vice, the ratio would be reversed, the hatred of good men would be more marked; that of the wicked would be more indifferent. The opposite observation is general, striking, incontestable, and could explain many inconsistencies. Let's be satisfied here with the confirmation I derive from it about the justness of my explanation.

Once this aversion has been inspired, it spreads, is communicated from one person to another within families, within social groups, and it becomes in a way an innate feeling that is established for children through education and for young people through public opinion. It should also be noted that with the exception of the secret confederation of your Ladies and Gentlemen, the remainder of the generation in which he lived does not feel as venomous a hatred toward him as that which is propagated in the following generation.[74] All youth have been fed with this feeling through a special effort of your Gentlemen, the cleverest of whom have taken charge of this department. It is from them that all apprentice philosophers make their connections, it is through their hands that placements are made of children's Tutors, fathers' secretaries, mothers' confidants. Nothing that happens within families occurs without their direction, without any appearance of their involvement. They have discovered the art of circulating their doctrine and their animosity in seminaries, colleges, and the entire nascent generation is devoted to them right from birth. Great imitators of the ways of the Jesuits, they were their most impassioned enemies, no doubt because they were jealous of their trade; and now, governing minds with the same control, with the same dexterity as the others governed consciences, cleverer than they in that they know how to hide themselves better as they act, and little by little substituting philosophic intolerance for the other kind, they become as dangerous as their predecessors without anyone being aware of it. It is through them that this new generation—which certainly owes to J.J. being less tormented in infancy, healthier and better developed at all ages—far from being grateful to him for this is fed with the most odious prejudices and cruelest feelings with respect to him. The venom of animosity which it suckled practically with its first milk makes this generation seek to debase him and push him down with even greater zeal than those who raised it in these hateful dispositions. Picture the unfortunate J.J. on the street or on walks surrounded by people who, less out of curiosity than in derision, since most of them have already seen him a hundred times, turn around and stop to stare at him with a gaze that surely has nothing to do with French urbanity. You will always find that the most insulting, the most mocking, the most assiduous are young people who, with an ironically polite expression, amuse themselves by giving him all the insulting, hateful signs they can inflict on him without compromising themselves.

All that would have been less easy to do in any other century. But this one is particularly hateful and malevolent in character.* This cruel and wicked spirit makes itself felt. in every group, in all public affairs; it is sufficient by itself to make those who stand out in that way fashionable and brilliant in society. The proud despotism of modern philosophy has carried the egoism of amour-propre to its furthest extreme. The taste that all the youth have developed for such a convenient doctrine has led them to adopt it with a frenzy and preach it with the liveliest intolerance. They have grown accustomed to carrying into society that same proprietary tone with which they pronounce the oracles of their sect, and to treating with obvious scorn, which is only more insolent hatred, everyone who dares to hesitate about submitting to their decisions. This taste for domination has not failed to arouse all the irascible passions related to amour-propre. The same bile that flows along with their ink in the writings of the masters fills the hearts of the disciples. Having become slaves in order to be tyrants, they ended up by prescribing in their own name the laws the others had dictated to them, and seeing the guiltiest rebellion in any resistance. A generation of Despots can be neither very gentle nor very peaceful, and such a haughty doctrine—which in addition admits of neither vice nor virtue in the heart of man—is not suited to restrain the pride of its sectaries by a morality indulgent toward others and repressive toward oneself. From this come the hateful tendencies that distinguish this generation. There is no longer moderation in souls or truth in attachments. Everyone hates everything that is not himself more readily than he loves himself. People pay too much attention to others to know how to pay attention to themselves. The only thing still known is hating, and no one stays with his own side because of attachment or still less because of esteem, but uniquely because of hatred for the other side. Those are the general dispositions in which your Gentlemen found or placed your contemporaries, and which they then had only to turn against J.J.**, who, as ill-equipped to receive the law as to make it, for that reason alone could not fail in this new system to be the object of the hatred of the

---

* Fréron had just died. It was asked who would write his epitaph. *The first to spit on his tomb*, M. Marmontel replied promptly. If the author of this had not been named to me, I would have guessed it came from a philosopher's mouth and was from this century.

** In this generation nurtured on philosophy and bile, nothing is easier for conspirators than to make this general appetite for hatred fall on anyone they choose. Their prodigious successes in this regard are proof not so much of their talents as of the dispositions of the public, whose apparent testimonials of esteem and attachment for some are in fact only acts of hatred for others.

leaders and the resentment of the disciples. The crowd, eager to follow the route that leads it astray, doesn't view with pleasure those taking the opposite path, who by doing that seem to reproach it for its error.

Someone who would know well all the contributing causes,* all the different mechanisms put to work to stimulate this hateful infatuation in all estates would be less surprised to see it become by degrees a general contagion. Once it has been set in motion, each person following in the stream increases its momentum. How can one mistrust one's feeling when he sees it is the same as everyone else's? How can it be doubted that the object of such universal hatred is truly an odious man? Then the more absurd and unbelievable the things attributed to him are, the readier people are to accept them. Each fact that makes him odious or ridiculous is well proved by that alone. If it were a matter of a good action he had done, no one would believe his own eyes or soon a subtle interpretation would change it from white to black. The wicked believe neither in virtue nor even in goodness. It is necessary to be good oneself already to believe that other men are better than oneself, and it is nearly impossible for a truly good man to remain so or to be recognized as such in a generation of wicked men.

With hearts thus disposed, everything else became easy. From that point on your Gentlemen could have persecuted J.J. openly, in a straight-forward way, with public approval, but they would only half satisfy their vengeance, and to commit any blunder with respect to him was to risk discovery. The system they adopted fits better with all their views and forestalls all drawbacks. The masterpiece of their art was to transform the precautions they took for their own safety into consideration for their victim. A veneer of humanity concealing the blackness of the plot completed the seduction of the public, and everybody hastened to collaborate in this good work. It is so sweet to satisfy a passion in a saintly way and blend the merit of virtue with the venom of animosity! Everybody, glorying himself for betraying an unfortunate person, told himself complacently: "Ah, how generous I am! I am defaming him for his own good; I am debasing him to protect him. And far from feeling my kindness, the ingrate takes offense at it! But that won't prevent me from going right on and helping him in this way despite himself." That is how, under the pretext of providing for his safety, they all become satellites of your Gentlemen against him, while admiring themselves, and, as J.J. wrote to

* Perhaps I should have emphasized here the favorite trick of my persecutors, which is to satisfy all their hateful passions at my expense, do evil through their satellites and see to it that it is ascribed to me. In this way they successively attributed to me the *System of Nature*, the *Philosophy of Nature*, the note in the novel by Madame d'Ormoy, etc. In this way they tried to make the people believe it was I who stirred up the thieves who were in their pay when the price of bread went up.[75]

M. Dusaulx, *are so proud to be traitors*.* With such a frame of mind, can you conceive that one could be equitable and see things as they are? One could see Socrates, Aristides, one could see an Angel, one could see God himself with eyes thus fascinated and still believe one were seeing an infernal monster.

But however easy this inclination, it's still quite amazing, you say, that it is universal, that everyone without exception goes along with it, that not a single person resists or protests, that the same passion leads an entire generation blindly along, and that there is universal consent in such a reversal of the right of nature and of nations.[77]

I agree that the fact is very extraordinary, but in assuming its certainty, I would find it more extraordinary still if its principle were virtue. For the entire current generation would have to be elevated by that unique virtue to a sublimity it surely displays in nothing else, and among all the enemies J.J. has, there could not be a single one who had the malicious frankness to spoil the marvelous work of all the others. In my explanation, a small number of clever, powerful, conspiratorial people, united for a long time, deceiving some people by false appearances and stirring up others by passions to which they are already only too inclined, brings everything together against an innocent person whom they have carefully accused of crimes while depriving him of every means to absolve himself. The other explanation requires that the most hateful of all generations suddenly transform itself completely and without exception into as many celestial angels for the sake of the lowest of scoundrels whom they insist on protecting and allowing to remain free despite the outrages and crimes he continues to commit at his leisure, without anyone daring to think of preventing him from doing them, or even of reproaching him so fearful are they of displeasing him. Which of these two assumptions appears the more reasonable and the more admissible to you?

Besides, this objection based on everyone's unanimous collaboration in the execution of an abominable plot may be more apparent than real. First, the art of the initiators of the whole scheme has been not to reveal it equally to all eyes. They kept the principal secret of it among a small number of conspirators. They let the remaining men see only what was necessary to get them to collaborate. Each person saw only the aspect of the object that could move him, and was initiated into the plot only as much as required by the part of its execution entrusted to him. There

---

* M. Dusaulx and I had a lively and brief correspondence, worthy perhaps of some curiosity. Based on a statement made to me by one of these Gentlemen, I have reason to think that in my absence and without my knowledge they are arranging this correspondence as they wish, just like everything else. It would possibly have been a bit harder to do in my presence, but that's a drawback they know how to prevent.[76]

may be no more than ten people who know what the real basis of the scheme is, and of these ten there may not even be three who know their victim well enough to be sure that they are sullying an innocent man. The secret of the initial plot is tightly kept between two men who are not about to reveal it.[78] All the other accomplices, more or less guilty, delude themselves about maneuvers which, according to them, are intended not so much to persecute innocence as to secure a wicked man. Each was lured through his particular character, through his favorite passion. If it were possible for this multitude of collaborators to come together and enlighten each other by sharing confidences, they would themselves be struck by the absurd contradictions they would find in the facts that have been proved to each of them, and by the motives—not only different but often contradictory—by which they have all been made to collaborate in the common work without any of them seeing its true goal. J.J. himself can distinguish between the rabble into whose hands he was thrown in Môtiers, Trye, and Monquin, and persons of true worth who—deceived rather than seduced and, without being exempt from blame, pitiable in their error—despite the opinion they had of him continued to seek him out as eagerly as the others did, although with less cruel intentions. Three quarters, perhaps, of those who joined in the plot remain only because they haven't seen all its blackness. There is even more baseness than maliciousness in the indignities which the majority heaps on him, and it can be seen by their look, by their tone, in their manners that they consider him much less with horror as an object of hatred than with derision as an unfortunate person.

Moreover, although no one openly challenges the general opinion, which would be compromising oneself to no purpose, do you think that everyone really agrees with it? How many individuals seeing so many maneuvers and underground mines perhaps become angry about them, refuse to collaborate, and secretly moan about oppressed innocence! How many others, not knowing what to think about a man caught up in so many traps, refuse to judge him without a hearing, and judging only his clever persecutors think that people for whom ruse, falseness, and betrayal cost so little might well be no more scrupulous about imposture. Caught between the strength of the proofs alleged to them and the proofs of the maliciousness of the accusers, they cannot fit such zeal for the truth with such aversion for justice, nor such generosity for the person they accuse with such art in dodging him and evading his defenses. One can abstain from iniquity without having the courage to combat it. One can refuse to be the accomplice in a betrayal without daring to unmask the traitors. A man who is just but weak withdraws then from the crowd, stays in his corner, and not daring to show himself, quietly pities the oppressed, fears the oppressor, and remains silent. Who can know how many decent men there are like this? They are neither seen nor felt. They leave the way open for your Gentlemen until the moment comes when they can speak without danger. Based on the opinion I've always had of the natural rectitude of the human heart, I believe that must be so. On what reasonable basis can one maintain that it is not? Sir, that is all I can say in response to the unique objection to which you reduce yourself and which, besides, I don't undertake to resolve to your satisfaction or even to mine, although it cannot shatter the direct persuasion my research has produced in me.

I saw you ready to interrupt me and I understood it was to reproach me for the superfluous care I took to establish for you one fact about which you yourself so thoroughly agree that you turn it into an objection against me, namely that it isn't true that everyone has joined in the plot. But notice that while appearing to agree on that point, we nonetheless have feelings that are very opposite, in that according to you those who are not in the plot think the same of J.J. as those who are, and according to me they must think very differently. Thus your exception, which I do not admit, and mine, which you don't admit either, concerning different people are mutually exclusive or at least not in agreement. I have just told you the basis for mine. Now let's examine yours.

Decent men whom you say have not joined in the plot and do not hate J.J. nevertheless see in him everything his most mortal enemies say they see in him. As if there were any who agreed to be his enemies and didn't boast of loving him! In raising that objection, you didn't remember this, which anticipates and destroys it. If there is a plot, its effect is to make everything easy to prove to the very people who are not part of the plot, and when they believe they are seeing with their eyes, they see, without realizing it, through the eyes of another.

If these people you speak of are not of bad faith, at least they are certainly prejudiced like the entire public, and must because of that alone see and judge as it does. And how would your Gentlemen, once having the possibility of making everything believed, have neglected to take this advantage as far as it would go? Those of this general persuasion who set aside the surest proof for distinguishing true from false, may well not be part of the plot in your eyes; that alone makes them part of it in mine. And I who feel in my conscience that where they believe they see certainty and truth, there is only error, lies, and imposture, can I be in doubt that they are to blame for their persuasion, and that if they had sincerely loved the truth, they would soon have unraveled it from the artifices of the scoundrels who misled them. But those who have irrevocably judged the object of their hatred ahead of time and will not give it up, seeing in him only what they want to see, twist and turn everything at the whim of their passion, and by means of subtleties give the things most contrary to their ideas an interpretation that can make them compatible. Have the people you believe are impartial taken the necessary precautions to overcome these illusions?

The Frenchman

But M. Rousseau, are you serious, and what are you expecting of the public? Have you been able to believe it would examine the matter as scrupulously as you have?

Rousseau

It would have been excused from doing so had it abstained from such a cruel decision. But in passing sentence like a sovereign on the honor and destiny of a man, it could not, without committing a crime, neglect any of the essential and possible ways to ensure that it passed its sentence justly.

You say you scorn an abject man and will never believe that the good inclinations I believed I saw in J.J. can be compatible with vices as base as those of which he is accused. I think exactly as you do on this article. But I am as sure as of any other truth I know that this abjectness for which you reproach him is, of all vices, the most remote from his nature. Far closer to the opposite extreme, he has too much loftiness in his soul to be able to tend toward abjectness. J.J. is weak, without doubt, and not very able to overcome his passions! But he can have only passions that are relative to his character, and base temptations cannot come near his heart. The source of all his consolations is in his self-esteem. He would be the most virtuous of men if his strength responded to his will. But even with all his weakness, he cannot be a vile man, because there is not an ignoble inclination in his soul to which he would be ashamed to yield. The only one that could have led him to evil is false shame[79,] against which he has battled all his life with efforts as great as they have been futile, because it comes from his timid disposition which presents an invincible obstacle to the ardent desires of his heart, and forces him to mislead them in a thousand often blameworthy ways. That is the unique source of all the evil he may have done, but from which nothing can emerge that bears any resemblance to the indignities of which you accuse him. How can you not see how removed your Gentlemen themselves are from this scorn for him they want to inspire in you? How can you not see that the scorn they feign is not real, that it is only the very transparent veil covering an esteem which tears them apart and a rage which they hide very badly? The proof of this is manifest. One doesn't worry in this way about people one scorns. One looks away, one lets them be for what they are. One does with respect to them not what your Gentlemen do with respect to J.J. but what he himself does with respect to them. It is not surprising that having stoned him, they also cover him with mud. All these proceedings are very consistent on their part. But those they impute to him are hardly consistent for him, and are these indignities to which you come back better proved than the crimes you no longer emphasize? No, Sir, after our earlier discussions, I see no middle ground between accepting everything and rejecting everything.

Of the testimonials you assume to be impartial, some involve facts that are absurd and false but made credible by means of bias. Among these are rape, brutality, debauchery, cynical impudence, base knavery. The others involve facts that are true but falsely interpreted. Among these are his harshness, his disdain, his angry and rejecting disposition, his obstinacy in closing his door to new faces, especially to unknown cajolers and weepers and to arrogant boors.

Since I will never defend J.J. accused of murder and poisoning, I don't intend to justify him either as a rapist of girls, a monster of debauchery, a petty crook. If you can seriously adopt opinions of this sort about him, I can only pity him and pity you as well, you who cherish ideas that would make you blush as a friend of justice if you take a closer look and do what I did. Him debauched, brutal, impudent, cynical toward women! Oh, I'm afraid it is the opposite excess that caused his downfall, and if he were what you say, he would be far less unhappy today. It's easy to make the daughters of the household withdraw on his arrival. But what does that prove except the malicious attitude of parents toward him?*

Is there an example of some fact that made such a bizarre and affected precaution necessary? And what must he have thought about it when he arrived in Paris, he who had just been living very casually in a very worthy home in Lyons, where the mother and three charming daughters, all in the flower of age and beauty, overwhelmed him by vying with each other for friendship and caresses? Was it because he abused that familiarity with those young people, was it because of his manners or free speech with them that he deserved the unworthy and novel welcome that awaited him in Paris when he left them; and even today are very wise mothers afraid to bring their daughters to the home of this terrible satyr with whom

---

* At the moment I transcribe this, I am receiving several consecutive visits from the daughter of an English Lord, a young woman of eighteen, very likeable, very modest, who is not afraid to spend entire mornings with me at her father's request and her own. I am in ignorance, I must admit, of the true motive of these visits. But whatever it may be, it is still certain that this young Lady's father does not seem to be afraid of the dangers from which the parents who invited me to their homes removed their daughters so ostentatiously. What is noteworthy is that this contrast in behavior with respect to me is occurring with two Ministers, from different countries, it's true, but both at the same Court. The one who makes his daughter disappear when I arrive is a plenipotentiary of France; the one who sends his daughter all alone to my house is the Ambassador from England.[80]

those other people don't dare leave their daughters for a moment, even at their own homes and in their presence? Truly, that such crude farces can fool sensible people for a moment must be seen to be believed.

Assume for a moment that they had dared make all that known ten years earlier, when the esteem of decent men which he always enjoyed since his youth was at its highest point. Would these opinions, even though supported by the same proofs, have obtained the same acceptance among those who now rush to adopt them? Doubtless not. They would have rejected them with indignation. They would all have said, "When a man has reached this age with the esteem of the public, when without homeland, without fortune, and without refuge, in a situation of want, and forced for subsistance to have recourse constantly to expedients, he has never used any except honorable ones and has always generated consideration and good will in his distress, he doesn't start after reaching maturity and when all eyes are on him to turn away from the straight route in order to plunge into the muddy ways of vice; he doesn't mix the baseness of the most vile knaves with the courage and loftiness of proud souls, nor love of glory with the maneuvers of cheats; and if forty years of honor allowed someone to deviate belatedly to this degree, he would soon lose that vigor of feeling, that energy, that intrepid frankness that is not combined with base passions and never outlives honor. A rascal can be cowardly, a wicked man can be arrogant. But the sweetness of innocence and the pride of virtue can unite only in a beautiful soul."

That is what they all would have said or thought, and they certainly would have refused to believe he was tainted with such base vices, unless he were convicted of them before their very eyes. They would at least have wanted to study him themselves before judging him so emphatically and so cruelly. They would have done what I did, and if they had the impartiality you assume, they would have drawn from their research the same conclusion I draw from mine. They did none of that. The most obscure proofs, the most suspect testimony sufficed for them to decide the worst without further verification, and they carefully avoided all clarification that might show them their error. Therefore, whatever you may say, they are part of the plot. For what I call being part of it is not just knowing the secret of your Gentlemen; I presume that few people are allowed to do so. But it is adopting their iniquitous principle. It is making it a law for oneself, as they do, to state to everyone and hide from the accused person alone the evil one thinks or pretends to think about him and the reasons on which this judgment is based, in order to make it impossible for him to reply and to make his own reasons heard. For as soon as one allows oneself to be persuaded that he must be judged not only without hearing him but without being heard by him, all the rest must follow; and it isn't possible to resist so much testimony so well arranged and sheltered from the worrisome test of the accused person's responses. Since the entire success of the scheme depended on this important precaution, its Author will have put all the sagacity of his mind into giving this injustice the most specious presentation, and even to cover it with a veneer of beneficence and generosity which would not have fooled any impartial mind, but which people hastened to admire with regard to a man who was respected only by force, and whose singularities weren't well viewed by anyone at all.

Everything relates to the initial accusation which made him suddenly lose the title of decent man, which he had borne until then in order to substitute that of most awful scoundrel. Anyone who has a healthy soul and truly believes in probity doesn't easily give up the well-founded esteem he has conceived for a good man. I could see Mylord Maréchal commit a crime, if that were possible,* or perform a base act, and I would not believe my eyes. When I believed everything you proved to me about J.J., it was on the assumption he had been convicted. Changing opinions to this extent about a man who has been esteemed during his entire life isn't an easy thing. But also once the first step is taken, all the rest follows from that. From one crime to another, a man guilty of one becomes, as you said, capable of all. Nothing is less surprising than the passage from wickedness to abjectness, and it isn't worth it to measure with such care the distance that sometimes separates a scoundrel from a rascal. One may therefore debase at leisure the man one has begun by sullying. When it is believed there is only evil in him, nothing but that is seen any longer; his good or his indifferent actions soon change appearance with many prejudices and a little interpretation, and then judgments are retracted with as much assurance as if those which are substituted for them were better established. Amour-propre makes people always want to have seen for themselves what they know or believe they know from elsewhere. Nothing is so manifest as soon as it is scrutinized. People are ashamed not to have observed it sooner; but this is because they were so distracted or so prejudiced they didn't pay attention to it. It's because they are so good themselves, they can't assume the wickedness of others.

When the spreading infatuation finally reaches an excess, believing everything is no longer adequate. People try to embellish in order to join in the party, and everyone who latches on to this system takes pride in

---

* It is true that Mylord Maréchal is of illustrious birth and J.J. is a man of the people. But it must be understood that Rousseau, who is speaking here, doesn't have a very sublime opinion in general of the high virtue of the well born, and that the story of J.J. naturally does little to improve that opinion.

bringing something personal to adorn or strengthen it. The eagerness of some people to invent is matched by the eagerness of others to believe. Every imputation passes for an invincible proof, and if it were learned today that a crime had been committed on the moon, tomorrow it would be proved clearer than day to all that J.J. was its author.

Once the reputation he had been given was well established, it is very natural that it resulted in the effects you spelled out to me, even among men of good faith. If he makes an accounting mistake, it will always be on purpose. Is it in his favor? It's cheating. Is it against him? It's a ruse. A man seen this way, regardless of how subject he is to slips, distractions, and blunders, is no longer allowed any of those. Everything he does by inadvertence is always seen as done on purpose. On the contrary, the slips, the omissions, the oversights of others regarding him are no longer believed in anyone's mind. If he points them out, he lies. If he puts up with them, it is in vain. Heedless women, vapid youths will make blunders for which he gets blamed. And it would be surprising if lackeys, bribed or unfaithful, only too well instructed of the feelings their masters have toward him, aren't sometimes tempted to get something out of it at his expense, certain that the matter will not be clarified in his presence and that if that should happen a little insolence abetted by the prejudices of the masters, would easily get them out of trouble.

I assumed, as you did, that those who deal with him are all sincere and of good faith. But if they were trying to deceive him in order to find him at fault, what assistance wouldn't his vivacity, his heedlessness, his distractions, his bad memory offer to that end?

Other causes, too, may have contributed to these false judgments. Through his *Confessions*, which they call his memoirs, this man gave your Gentlemen a hold on him which they have taken care not to neglect. This reading which he lavished on so many people, but of which so few were capable and still fewer worthy, initiated the public into all his weaknesses, all his most secret faults. The hope that these *Confessions* would not be seen until after his death gave him the courage to say everything, and to treat himself with a justice that is often even too rigorous. When he saw himself distorted among men to the point of being considered a monster, conscience—which made him feel more good than bad in himself—gave him the courage that perhaps he alone had and will ever have to show himself as he was. He believed that by fully manifesting his soul and revealing his *Confessions*, the very frank, simple, and natural explanation of all that might have been found to be bizarre in his conduct, bearing with it his own testimony, would make felt the truth of his declarations and the falseness of the horrible and fantastic ideas he saw being spread about him without being able to discover their source. Far from being suspicious of your Gentlemen, then, the confidence in them of this very untrusting man extended not only to reading to them this history of his soul but to leaving it with them in trust for a rather long time. The use they made of this imprudence was to exploit it to defame the person who committed it, and the most sacred trust of friendship became the instrument of betrayal in their hands. They travestied his flaws as vices, his faults as crimes, the weaknesses of his youth as evildoings of his maturity. They denatured the effects, ridiculous at times, of all the lovable and good things nature placed in his soul; and what are only peculiarities of an ardent temperament restrained by a timid nature became, through their attentions, a horrible depravity of heart and of taste. Finally, all their ways of proceeding with regard to him and from the looks of things I have caught wind of, I am led to believe that to discredit his *Confessions*, after taking from them every possible thing to use against him, they conspired and maneuvered in all the places where he had lived and about which he provided them with information, in order to distort his whole life, to fabricate with artistry lies that would make his *Confessions* appear to lie, and to deprive him of the merit of frankness even in the admissions he makes against himself. Ah! Since they know how to poison his writings which are right under everyone's eyes, why wouldn't they poison his life, which the public knows only through their report?

The *Heloise* had turned the glances of women to him. They had rather natural rights to a man who described love in that way. But knowing hardly anything about it except the physical side, they believed that only very lively senses could inspire such tender feelings, which might have given them a higher opinion of the person expressing them than he perhaps deserved. Suppose that a few of them carried this opinion to the point of curiosity, and that this curiosity was not guessed or satisfied promptly enough by the person who was its object. You can easily conceive the consequences of this blunder for his destiny.

As for the cold and harsh welcome he gives certain arrogant or weeping persons who come to him, I have often witnessed this myself, and I agree that in such a situation this conduct would be very imprudent on the part of an unmasked hypocrite, who is only too fortunate that anyone would pretend to be misled, and who ought to join in with a dissimulation equal to this pretense and the apparent considerations people would feign for him. But do you dare reproach an insulted man of honor for not behaving as though he were guilty, and for not having the cowardice of a vile scoundrel in his misfortunes? How would you want him to view the perfidious eagerness of the traitors who obsess him, and who—while affecting the purest zeal—have in fact only the goal of enmeshing him more and more in the traps of those who employ them? In order to welcome them, he would have to be in fact just as they assume he is. He would have to be as much an imposter as they are, and pretending not to see through them, return betrayal for betrayal. His entire crime consists in being as frank as they are false. But after all, what does it matter to them whether he receives them well or badly? The most manifest signs of his impatience or his disdain contain nothing that shocks them. He could insult them openly and they would not go away because of that. Acting together to abandon at his door any feelings of honor they might have, they all show him only insensitivity, duplicity, cowardice, perfidy, and act with him as he would with them if he were as they represent him. And how would you expect him to show them esteem which they have gone to such lengths not to allow him. I agree that the scorn of a man whom one scorns oneself is easy to bear. But still, isn't it necessary to go to him to seek signs of it? Despite all this insidious wheedling, if he believes he glimpses the least bit of naturally decent feelings and a few good dispositions deep down in their souls, he still lets himself be subjugated. I laugh at his simplicity, and I make him laugh about it himself. He always hopes that by seeing him as he is, at least a few will no longer have the courage to hate him, and believes that by virtue of frankness he can finally touch those hearts of bronze. You can imagine how well he succeeds. He sees it himself, and after so many sad experiences, he should finally know what to expect.

If you have once made the reflections suggested by reason and the searches required by justice before judging an unfortunate person so severely, you would have felt that in a situation like his and as the victim of such detestable plots, he should at least no longer surrender to his natural inclinations with regard to what is around him, inclinations which your Gentlemen have used for so long and so successfully to catch him in their nets. He can no longer act in any matter according to the simplicity of his heart without throwing himself into these nets. Thus he must no longer be judged by his present works, even if it were possible to have a faithful account of them. It is necessary to go back to the time when nothing prevented him from being himself, or else to fathom him more intimately, *intus et in cute,*[81] in order to read directly the true dispositions of his soul, which so many misfortunes have been unable to embitter. By following him during the happy times in his life and even during those when he was already the prey of your Gentlemen but didn't yet suspect it, you would have found the kindly and gentle man that he was and was accepted as being before they disfigured him. Everywhere he used to live, in the habitations where he was allowed to stay long enough to leave traces of his character, the regrets of the inhabitants always followed him on his departure; and alone perhaps of all the foreigners who ever lived in England, he saw the people of Wootton[82] weep when he left. But your Ladies and Gentlemen have taken such care to erase all these traces, it is only when they were fresh that they could be detected. Montmorency, which is closer to us, offers a striking example of these differences. Thanks to some people whom I don't wish to name and to the Oratorians[83] who have somehow become the most ardent satellites of the conspiracy,* you will no longer find any vestige of the attachment and I dare say the veneration which people there used to feel for J.J., both while he lived there and after he left. But at least the traditions about it still remain in the memory of the decent people who then frequented that place.

In those outpourings to which he still likes to surrender, often with more pleasure than prudence, he sometimes confided his troubles to me, and I've seen that the patience with which he bears them didn't lighten in any way the impression they made on his heart. Those which are least softened by time come down to two main ones, which account for the only true ills that his enemies have done him. The first is to have deprived him of the sweetness of being useful to men and helpful to the unfortunate, either by depriving him of the means to do so or by no longer allowing anyone under this passport to approach him except imposters who seek to interest him in themselves only to insinuate themselves into his confidence, spy on him, and betray him. The way they present themselves, the tone they adopt in talking to him, the dull praises they give him, the wheedling they add to this, the bile they can't refrain from mixing in with it, everything reveals them to be grimacing little actors who don't know how or don't care to do a better job in their role. The letters he receives, along with bookish commonplaces and pompous lessons about his duties toward those who write them, are nothing but stupid declamations against Nobles and the rich, by means of which they think they will bait him; bitter sarcasms about all estates; shrill reproaches to fortune for depriving a great man like the Author of the letter and by implication the other great man to whom it is addressed of the honors

---

* The most dangerous enemies there ever were, not only because of the body they form and the colleges they govern, but because they know even better than the philosophers how to hide their cruel animosity under a saintly and mawkish look. During my sojourn at Montmorency they had the best time in the world with me, because of the respect I had for them and the blind confidence that resulted from it. I was also ensnared there by two Priests in disguise who were writing the ecclesiastical gazettes and who were following with respect to me the orders of M. D'Alembert, with whom they lodged in Paris. In the security of innocence and without the least suspicion of any plot, I jumped into their traps with both feet, until this finally resulted in that fine decree and the explosion to which it led. All that was still not enough to open my eyes. But when the Oratorians later dispatched to Monquin a Jacobin who was the brother of one of them, he finally made me feel through his monkish works what I had been so stupid as not even to suspect until then.

and goods which were their due in order to heap them on the unworthy; proofs based on this that providence doesn't exist; pathetic declarations about the prompt assistance that is needed followed by proud protestations of wanting none nevertheless. Usually it all ends with confiding the firm resolve to kill oneself, and with the warning that this resolve will be executed at the appointed time if one doesn't speedily receive a satisfactory response to this letter.

After having been very foolishly duped by these suicide threats several times, he ended up by laughing both at them and at his own stupidity. But when they no longer found an easy entry with this pathos, they soon resumed their natural demeanor and substituted the ferociousness of tigers for the flexibility of serpents to force their way in. It is necessary to have seen the assaults his wife is forced to sustain ceaselessly, the insults and outrages she suffers daily from all these humble admirers, all these virtuous unfortunate people, when they encounter the slightest resistance, in order to judge the motive that brings them and the people who send them. Do you believe he is wrong to get rid of all this rabble and not wish to be subjugated by them? It would take him twenty years of concentration just to read all the manuscripts people bring him to review, correct, rewrite. For his time and effort cost your Gentlemen nothing.* He would have to have ten hands and ten secretaries to write all the requests, petitions, letters, memoirs, compliments, verses, bouquets for which they flock to him owing to the great eloquence of his pen and the great goodness of his heart. For that is always the habitual refrain of these sincere people. Using the word humanity which these swarms of wasps have learned to buzz around him, they riddle him with their stings just as they wish, and he doesn't dare pull away from them. And the best that can come of it for him is to get out with some money for which they thank him later with insults.

After nursing so many serpents in his bosom, a very simple reflection finally convinced him to behave as he does with all these newcomers. By means of kindnesses and generous attentions, your Gentlemen— successful in making him detested by everyone—left him with the esteem of no one. Any man of rectitude and honor can no longer do anything except to abhor and flee from a being so disfigured. No sensible man can expect anything good from him. In this position, what then should he think of those who choose to come to him, seek him out, heap him with praises, ask him either for services or for his friendship; who despite the

---

* I should be fair, however, to those who offer to pay me for my efforts, of whom there are many. At the very moment I'm writing this, a provincial Lady has just offered me twelve francs, and possibly more, to write a fine letter to a Prince. It's a shame I didn't think to set up shop under the charnel house of the innocents. I could have done a good business there.

opinion they have of him still desire to be linked or indebted to the lowest of scoundrels? Can they possibly be unaware that far from having credit, power, or favor with anyone, the interest he might take in them would only harm them as well as himself, that the effect of his recommendation would be to ruin them if they had recourse to him in good faith, or to turn them into new betrayers, destined to snare him through his own good deeds. Whatever is assumed, given the judgments of him circulating in society, isn't whoever still has recourse to him a condemned man, and what decent man can take an interest in such wretches! If they weren't imposters, wouldn't they still be infamous; and isn't someone who would implore a man he scorns for favors even more worthy of scorn than he?

If all these eager people came only to see and find out how things are, doubtless he would be wrong to get rid of them. But not a single one has that purpose, and you would have to know very little about men and about J.J.'s situation to look for either truth or faithfulness from all those people. Those who are being paid want to earn their pay, and they know very well that they have only one way to do that, which is to state not what is but what pleases, and that they will not be well received if they say good things about him. Those who spy on him of their own accord, moved by their passion, will never see anything except what flatters it. No one comes to see what he sees, but rather to interpret it in his own way. Black and white, pro and con are equally useful to them. He gives alms? Ah, the sanctimonious man! He refuses them? See how the man is so charitable! If he is impassioned in talking about virtue, he's a Tartuffe; if he is animated in talking about love, he's a Satyr. If he reads the gazette,* he is meditating a conspiracy. If he picks a rose, they try to find out what poison there is in roses. With a man who is viewed like this, I defy you to find a statement that is innocent, an action that is not a crime.

If the public administration itself had been less biased or of good faith, the constant uniformity of his balanced, simple life would soon have disabused it. It would have understood that it would never see any but the same things, and that it was a real waste of money, time, and trouble to spy on a man who lived like this. But since it isn't the truth that is sought, since they seek only to sully the victim, and rather than to study his character they want only to defame it, it matters little whether he behaves well or badly, and whether he is innocent or guilty. All that matters is to be knowledgeable enough about his behavior to have fixed

---

* To the great satisfaction of my very nervous patrons, I give up this sad reading which has become indifferent to a man who has been made into a total stranger on earth. I no longer have either a homeland or brothers. Inhabited by beings who mean nothing to me, the earth is like any other sphere, and from now on I have as little curiosity about what is happening in the world as I do about what is happening at Bicêtre or the Petites Maisons.[84]

points on which to hang the system of impostures of which he is the object, without taking the risk of being convicted of lying; and it is solely to that end that the spying is aimed. If you reproach me here for turning back onto his accusers the accusations they make about him, I will readily agree, but with the difference that when he talks about them, Rousseau doesn't hide. I think and say all this only with the greatest repugnance. I wish with all my heart I could believe the government commits an error in good faith with regard to him, but it is impossible for me to do so. If I had no other proof of the opposite, the method that is followed with him would provide me with an invincible one. All those things aren't done to wicked men; it is wicked men who do them to others.

Weigh the consequence that follows from that. If the administration, if the police itself participates in the plot to deceive the public about J.J., what person in the world, however wise he may be, could be protected from error regarding him?

How many reasons make us feel that in the strange position of this unfortunate man, no one is able to judge about him with certainty any longer, based either on another person's report or on any kind of proof. Even seeing is not sufficient; it's necessary to verify, compare, delve more deeply into everything for oneself, or else abstain from judging. Here, for example, it's as clear as day that based on the testimony of others, the reproach of harshness and lack of commiseration, deserved or not, will always be just as inevitable. Because assume for a moment that he fulfills with all his strength the duties of humanity, charity, beneficence which constantly surround all men. Who would give him credit in public for having fulfilled them? It wouldn't be himself, unless he did it with that philosophic ostentation that spoils the deed by the motive. It wouldn't be those toward whom he had fulfilled them, who become, the moment they approach him, the ministers and creatures of your Gentlemen. Still less would it be your Gentlemen themselves, who are no less zealous to hide the good he might seek to do than they are to publicize loudly the good they say they do for him in secret. By forming duties for him of their choosing in order to blame him for not fulfilling them, they would remain silent about the true ones he had fulfilled wholeheartedly, and criticize him in the same way with equal success. This reproach therefore proves nothing. I note only that he was beneficent and good when, left unhampered to his own nature, he followed his inclinations in total freedom. And now that he feels caught in a thousand traps, surrounded by spies, informers, inspectors, now that he can't say a word that isn't collected, make a movement that isn't noted, this is the time he chooses to remove the mask of hypocrisy and surrender to that belated harshness, to all those petty thefts of which the public accuses him today! You'll have to agree he would be a very stupid hypocrite and a very clumsy deceiver! Even if I had seen nothing for myself, this reflection alone would have made me suspicious of the reputation he is now given. All this is very like the income attributed to him with such magnificence. In his position, if it were real wouldn't he have to be an imbecile to try to conceal it from public knowledge for even a moment?

These reflections on the knavish tricks he has undertaken and the good deeds he no longer does can extend to the books he still writes and publishes, concerning which he hides so successfully that as soon as they appear everyone knows immediately that he is their author. What, Sir, this very temperamental and sullen mortal, who can scarcely see a single man approach him without knowing or believing him to be a traitor, who knows or believes that the vigilant Magistrate specifically in charge of the two departments of the police and publishing[85] holds him caught in inextricable nets, never stops eternally scribbling books by the dozens and entrusting them without fear into the hands of third and fourth parties to have them printed in great secrecy. These books are printed, published, sold openly under his name, even with ridiculous affectation as though he were afraid of not being known; and my lout, without seeing, without even suspecting this very public maneuver, without ever believing he has been discovered, always goes right along prudently on his way, always scribbling, always publishing, always confiding in such discreet confidants, and always in ignorance that they are making fun of him! What stupidity for such a shrewd person! What confidence for such a suspicious man! Does all this really seem to you so well organized, so natural, so believable? For myself, I didn't see in J.J. either of these two extremes. He isn't as shrewd as your Gentlemen, but neither is he as stupid as the public, and wouldn't be taken in as the public is with such blunders. When one bookseller comes conspicuously to his door, when others write him friendly letters, propose beautiful editions, pretend to have close relationships with him, he is not unaware that this neighborliness, these visits, these letters come from somewhere else; and while so many people labor over making him the author of books of which the lowest pedant would blush to be the Author, he weeps bitterly over the ten years of his life spent writing books that were a little less insipid.

These, Sir, are the reasons that forced him to change his behavior toward those who approach him, and to resist his heart's inclinations in order not to ensnare himself in the traps set all around him. To this I add that his timid nature and his taste which is removed from all ostentation are not suited to display his inclination to do good, and can even, in such a sad situation, stop him when he would appear to be allowing himself to be seen. In a very animated neighborhood of Paris, I saw him refrain despite himself from an opportunity to do a good deed, unable to bring himself to have the hostile gaze of two hundred people focused on him; and in a neighborhood close by but less crowded, I saw him behave differently in a similar situation. This false shame or this blameworthy pride seems very natural to me in an unfortunate man who is certain in advance that everything good he might do will be badly interpreted. It would doubtless be better to brave the public's injustice. But with a lofty soul and a timid nature, who could resign himself to performing a good act that will be reproached as hypocrisy, to read in the eyes of the onlookers the unfair judgment they make about it. In such a situation, a person who still wishes to do good would hide it from them as though it were an evil deed, and that secret could not be spied on for publicizing.

As for the second and most palpable of the punishments inflicted on him by the barbarians who torment him, he swallows it in secret, it remains in reserve deep in his heart, he has shared it with no one, and I myself wouldn't know about it if he had been able to hide it from me. Because it deprives him of all the consolations remaining within his reach, they used it to make his life as burdensome to him as the life of an innocent person can be. Judging the true goal of your Gentlemen by all their behavior toward him, this goal seems to be to lead him gradually and always without appearing to do so to the most violent despair, and under the appearance of interest and commiseration, to force him, by means of secret agonies, to end by setting them free of him. As long as he lives, they will never be without uneasiness about being discovered, despite all their vigilance. Despite the triple walls of darkness around him which they reinforce ceaselessly, they always tremble for fear a shaft of light will enter through some chink and shed light on their underground works. They hope to enjoy their work more tranquilly when he is no longer alive. But until now they have refrained from doing away with him altogether, either because they fear that they couldn't keep that attack as hidden as the others, or because they still have a scruple about themselves executing the act which they have none about forcing him to do; or finally because being attached to the pleasure of tormenting him some more, they prefer to wait for his hand to offer them the complete proof of his misery. Whatever their true motive, they used every possible means to make him, through ravages, the minister of the hatred of which he is the object. They worked especially hard to devastate him with deep and repeated wounds to every sensitive spot in his heart. They knew how ardent and sincere he was in all his attachments, so they worked without respite to leave him without a single friend. They knew that with his sensitivity to the honor and esteem of decent men, he thought little of reputations acquired by talent alone, so they pretended to extol his talents while heaping opprobrium on his character. They praised his mind in order to dishonor his heart. They knew him to be open and frank to the point of imprudence, detesting the mysterious and false; so they surrounded him with betrayal, lies, darkness, duplicity. They knew how much he cherished his homeland; they spared nothing to make it contemptible and to make him hated there. They knew his disdain for the trade of Author, how he deplored the brief period of his life that he wasted in this sad trade and among the brigands who exercise it; they make him scribble books endlessly and take great care to have these books—very worthy of the pens that write them—dishonor the name they make them carry. They have made him detested by the people whose wretchedness he deplored, by the good whose virtues he honored, by women whom he idolized, by all those whose hatred could grieve him most. By means of bloody but silent insults, by means of mobs, whispering, sneering, cruel and fierce or insulting and mocking gazes, they were able to drive him out of every meeting, every entertainment, cafés, public promenades; their project is to drive him in the end from the streets, shut him in his home, hold him there surrounded by their henchmen, and finally make his life so sorrowful for him that he can no longer endure it. In short, by simultaneously showering him with all the blows they knew he would feel the most without his being able to parry any of them, and leaving him only one means of escape, it's clear they wanted to force him to take it. But they calculated everything, no doubt, except for the resources of innocence and resignation. Despite age and adversity, his health has improved and remains good. The calm of his soul seems to rejuvenate him. And although he has nothing more to hope for among men, he has never been further from despair.

I have shed whatever clarification I could on your objections and doubts. This clarification, I repeat, cannot remove the obscurity, even in my eyes, because the assembling of all these causes falls too far short of the effect for there not to be some other more powerful cause which I am unable to imagine. But even if I were to find no reply whatever to you, I would still maintain my feeling, not through ridiculous stubbornness, but because I see fewer intermediaries between me and the person being judged, and because of all the eyes I must rely on, those I have least reason to distrust are my own. I agree that proofs have been given for things I have not been able to verify, and which perhaps would still leave me in doubt if there were not equally good proofs of things I know with certainty to be false. And what authority to be believed in any matter can remain with those who know how to give lies all the signs of truth. Besides, remember that I do not pretend here that my judgment should become authority for you. But after the details into which I have just gone, you can't blame me for accepting it, and whatever apparatus of proofs may be displayed for me while hiding from the accused, as long as he isn't convicted in person, and in my presence, of being what your Gentlemen have depicted, I will believe myself well-founded in judging him as I saw him myself.

Now that I've done what you desired, it's your turn to explain yourself, and to tell me according to your reading how you saw him in his writings.

The Frenchman

It's late now. I'm leaving for the country tomorrow. We shall see one another on my return.

THIRD DIALOGUE

Rousseau

You had a long stay in the country.

The Frenchman

The time flew by for me. I spent it with your friend.

Rousseau

Oh! If only he could be yours someday!

The Frenchman

You'll judge that possibility by the effect of your advice. I finally read those books that are so justifiably detested.

Rousseau

Sir!

The Frenchman

I've read them, not enough yet to understand them well, but enough to have found, enumerated, collected the irremediable crimes that couldn't have failed to make their Author the most odious of monsters and the horror of the human race.

Rousseau

What are you saying? Is it really you talking, and is it your turn to make riddles? For pity's sake explain yourself at once.

The Frenchman

The list I'm giving you will provide both the reply and the explanation. Reading it, no reasonable man would be surprised about the destiny of the Author.

Rousseau

Let me see this strange list then.

The Frenchman

There it is. I could easily have made it ten times more ample, especially if I had included the numerous articles about the trade of Author and the corps of men of letters. But they are so well known that it is enough to give one or two as examples. In those of all types to which I limited myself and which I noted down in the order in which they came, I did nothing except extract and transcribe the passages faithfully. You'll judge for yourself the effects they had to produce and the names their Author must have hoped to be called once he could be accused of them with impunity.

EXTRACTS

MEN OF LETTERS

1. "Who denies that the learned know countless true things which the ignorant will never know? Are the learned thereby closer to the truth? On the contrary, they get farther from it in advancing; because the vanity of judging makes even more progress than enlightenment does, each truth that they learn comes only with a hundred false judgments. It is entirely evident that the learned companies of Europe are only public schools of lies. And there are very certainly more errors in the Academy of Sciences than in a whole nation of Hurons." *Emile*, Book 3.[86]

2. "A man who plays the free thinker and philosopher today would, for the same reason, have been only a fanatic at the time of the League." *Preface of the Discourse of Dijon.*[87]

3. "Men should never be half taught. If they must remain in error, why not leave them in ignorance? What good are so many schools and universities if they teach them nothing of what is important for them to know? What, then, is the object of your colleges, your academies, all your learned establishments? Is it to mislead the people, modify its reason at the outset, and prevent it from going to the truth? Professors of the lie, it is to lead it astray that you pretend to instruct it, and like those brigands who place beacons on reefs, you enlighten it in order to destroy it." *Letter to M. de Beaumont.*[88]

4. "One read these words carved in marble at Thermopylae: *Passer-by, tell them at Sparta that we died here to obey her holy laws*. It is quite obvious that it was not the Academy of Inscriptions which wrote that." *Emile*, Book IV.[89]

THE DOCTORS[90]

5. " A frail body weakens the soul. This is the origin of the empire of medicine, an art more pernicious to men than all the ills it claims to cure. As for me, I do not know of what illness the doctors cure us; but I do know that they give us quite fatal ones: cowardice, pusillanimity,[91] terror of death. If they cure the body, they kill courage. What difference does it make to us that they make cadavers walk? It is men we need, and none is seen leaving their hands.

"Medicine is the fashion among us. It ought to be. It is the entertainment of idle people[92] who, not knowing what to do with their time, pass it in preserving themselves. If they had had the bad luck to be born immortal, they would be the most miserable of beings. A life they would never fear losing would be worthless for them. These people need doctors who frighten [93] them in order to cater to them and who give them every day the only pleasure of which they are susceptible—that of not being dead.

"I have no intention of enlarging on the vanity of medicine here. My object is to consider it only from the moral point of view. I can, nevertheless, not prevent myself from remarking that men make, concerning its use, the same sophisms as they make concerning the quest for truth, they always assume that, in treating a sickness, one cures it[94] and that, in seeking a truth, one finds it. They do not see that it is necessary to balance the advantage of a cure effected by the doctor against the death of a hundred sick persons killed by him, and the usefulness of a truth discovered against the harm done by the errors which are established[95] at the same time. Science which instructs and medicine which cures are doubtless very good. But science which deceives and medicine which kills are bad. Learn, therefore, to distinguish them. That is the crux of the question. If we knew how to be ignorant of the truth, we would never be the dupes of lies; if we knew how not to want to be cured in spite of nature, we would never die at the doctor's hand. These two abstinences would be wise; one would clearly gain by submitting to them. I do not, therefore, deny[96] that medicine is useful to some men, but I say that it is harmful[97] to mankind.

"I will be told, as I am incessantly, that the mistakes are the doctor's, while medicine in itself is infallible. That is all very well. But then let it come without the doctor, for so long as they come together, there will be a hundred times more to fear from the errors of the artist than to hope from the helps [98] of the art." *Emile*, Book I.

6. "Live according to nature, be patient, and drive away the doctors. You will not avoid death, but you will feel it only once, whereas they bring it every day into your troubled imagination; and their lying art, instead of prolonging your days, deprives you of the enjoyment of them. I shall always ask what true good this art has done for men. Some of those it cures would die, it is true, but thousands[99] whom it kills would remain alive. Men of sense, do not wager in this lottery where too many chances are against you. Suffer, die, or get well, but above all live until your last hour." *Emile*, Book I.[100]

7. "Will we inoculate our pupil? Yes and no, depending on the occasion, the times, the places, the circumstances. If he is given smallpox, one will have the advantage of foreseeing and knowing his illness ahead of time; that is something. But if he gets it naturally, we will have preserved him from the doctor. That is even more." *Emile*, Book III.[101]

8. "Is it a question of looking for a nurse? They let the obstetrician choose her. What is the result of that? That the best nurse is always the one who paid him best. I shall not hence, look for[102] an obstetrician about

Emile's nurse; I shall take care to choose her myself. I will not reason[103] so fluently about the issue as a surgeon, but I will certainly be in better faith, and my zeal will deceive me less than his avarice." *Emile,* Book I.[104]

THE KINGS, THE NOBLES, THE RICH

9. "We were made to be men; laws and society have plunged us once more into childhood. The kings, the nobles, the rich[105] are all children who, seeing that men are eager to relieve their misery, derive a puerile vanity from that very fact and are very proud of care that one would not give to them if they were grown men." *Emile,* Book II.[106]

10. "Thus there must have come a time when the eyes of the people were so bewitched that their leaders had only to say to the smallest of men: Be great, you and all your line; immediately he appeared great in everyone's eyes as well as in his own, and his descendants were exalted even more in proportion to their distance from him. The more remote and uncertain the cause, the more the effect augmented; the more idlers one could count in a family, the more illustrious it became." *Discourse on Inequality.*[107]

11. "Once peoples are accustomed to masters, they are no longer able to do without them. If they try to shake off the yoke, they move all the farther away from freedom because, mistaking for freedom an unbridled license which is its opposite, their revolutions almost always deliver them to seducers who under the lure of freedom only make their chains heavier." *Dedicatory Letter of the Discourse on Inequality.*[108]

12. " *'This little boy that you see there,'* said Themistocles to his friends, *'is the master of Greece, for he governs his mother, his mother governs me, I govern the Athenians, and the Athenians govern Greece.'* O what little leaders would often be found in the greatest States, if from the prince one descended by degrees to the first hand which secretly sets things in motion!" *Emile,* Book II.[109]

13. "I assume that I am rich; therefore I must have exclusive pleasures, destructive pleasures. This is an entirely different affair. I need lands, woods, guards, rents, seignorial honors, and, above all, incense and holy water.

"Very well. But this land will have neighbors jealous of their rights and desirous of usurping those of others. Our guards will squabble, and so perhaps will their masters. Now there are altercations, quarrels, hatreds, lawsuits, at the very least. Already things are no longer very agreeable. My vassals will not take pleasure in seeing their wheat ripped up by my hares and their beans ripped up by my boars. Not daring to kill the enemy who destroys his work, each will at least want to drive him from his field. After having spent the day cultivating their lands, they will have to spend the night guarding them. They will have watchdogs, drums, cornets, bells. With all this racket they will disturb my sleep. In spite of myself, I shall think of the misery of these poor people and will not be able to refrain from reproaching myself for it. If I had the honor of being a Prince, all this would hardly touch me. But as I would be a parvenu who had recently become rich, I would still have a trace of a plebeian heart.

"That is not all. The abundance of the game will tempt hunters. There will soon be poachers whom I shall have to punish. I shall need prisons, jailers, armed guards, galleys. All this appears rather cruel. The wives of these unfortunate men will come to besiege my doors and to importune me with their cries; they will have to be driven away and maltreated. Those among the poor who have not poached and whose harvest has been foraged by my game will also come to complain. The former group will be punished for having killed the game, and the latter ruined for having spared it. What a sad choice! I shall see only examples of misery on all sides; I shall hear only groans. It seems to me that this ought greatly to disturb the pleasure of massacring at one's ease—practically under one's feet—throngs of partridges and hares.

"Do you wish to disengage the pleasures from their pains? Then remove exclusiveness from the pleasures. . . . The pleasure is not any less, then, and the inconvenience is removed when one has neither land to guard nor poachers to punish nor unfortunate people to torment. Here, then, is a solid reason for preference. No matter what the situation, one does not torment men endlessly without also receiving some discomfort from it; and the continued maledictions of the people sooner or later make the game bitter." *Emile*, Book IV.[110]

14. "Aren't all the advantages of society for the powerful and the rich? Aren't all the lucrative jobs filled by them alone? Aren't all the pardons and all the exemptions reserved for them? And isn't public authority entirely in their favor? When an esteemed man steals from his creditors or cheats in other ways, isn't he always sure of impunity? The beatings he gives, the violent actions he commits, even the murders and assassinations he is guilty of, aren't these fleeting rumors[111] passed over in silence and forgotten after six months? If this same man is robbed himself, the forces of law and order go into action immediately, and woe to the innocents whom he suspects. Does he have to travel through dangerous places? He is escorted through the countryside. Does the axle of his carriage break? Everyone rushes to his aid. Is it noisy near his door? He says a word and all is silent. Does the crowd annoy him? He gives a sign and everything becomes orderly. Is a cart driver in his way? His men are ready to beat him. And fifty honest pedestrians going about their business will be trampled a hundred times[112] before an idle good-for-nothing's

coach is slowed down. All these attentions don't cost him a penny; they are the rich man's right, and not the price of riches. How different is the picture of the poor man! The more humanity owes him, the more society refuses him. All doors are closed to him when he has the right to make them open. And if he sometimes obtains justice, it is with greater difficulty than another would obtain pardon. If there are corvees to do, troops to be raised, he is given preference. In addition to his own burden, he always bears the one from which his richer neighbor has the influence to be exempted. At the slightest accident that happens to him, everyone abandons him. If his poor cart tips over, far from being helped by anyone, he will be[113] lucky if he avoids the passing insults of the flippant servants of some young duke. In short, all free assistance flees him when needed, precisely because he has nothing with which to pay for it. And I consider him a lost man if he has the misfortune to have an honest soul, an attractive daughter, and a powerful neighbor." *Discourse on Political Economy*.[114]

WOMEN

15. "Women of Paris and London, forgive me, but if a single one of you has a truly decent soul, I understand nothing about our institutions." *Emile*, Book IV.[115]

16. "He is held in the public's esteem; he deserves to be. That being the case, there should be no hesitation even if he were the least important of men; for it is better to forfeit nobility than virtue, and the wife of a charcoal-burner is more respectable than the mistress of a Prince." *Nouvelle Héloïse*, Part V, Letter 13.[116]

THE ENGLISH

17. "Things have changed since I wrote this (in 1756), but my principle will still be true. It is, for example, very easy to foresee that twenty-five years from now* England, with all its glory, will be ruined, and moreover will have lost its remaining freedom. Everyone asserts that agriculture is flourishing on that island, but I bet that it is dying. London grows larger each day, therefore the kingdom is becoming depopulated. The English want to be conquerors; therefore it won't be long before they are slaves." *Extract from the Project for Perpetual Peace*.[117]

18. "I know that the English greatly vaunt their humanity and the good nature of their people[118] whom they call *good natured people*. But however much they may shout that, no one repeats it after them." *Emile*, Book II.[119]

You would have too much to do if it were necessary to finish, and you

---

* It is worthy of note that this was written and published in 1760, the period of England's greatest prosperity during the ministry of Mr. Pitt, now Lord Chatham.

can see that isn't necessary. I knew all estates were ill-used in the writings of J.J. But seeing them all so tenderly interested in him anyhow, I was far from understanding to what extent his crime toward each of them was unpardonable. I understood it as I read, and reading only these articles, you must feel as I do that a man who is isolated and without support, who in the current century dares to talk like this about medicine and Doctors, cannot fail to be a poisoner; that one who treats modern philosophy like this can only be an abominable blasphemer; that one who appears to have so little respect for gallant ladies and the mistresses of Princes can only be a monster of debauchery; that one who doesn't believe in the infallibility of fashionable books must see his own burned by the executioner's hand; that one who, refusing the new oracles, dares to continue to believe in God should be burned himself by the philosophical inquisition as a hypocrite and a scoundrel; that one who dares to claim the common rights of nature for these peasant riffraff against such respectable hunting rights should be treated by Princes like the wild animals they protect only to kill them at their convenience and in their own way. With respect to England, the last two passages explain too well the ardor of J.J.'s friends to send him there, and David Hume's zeal to take him, for one to have any doubt about the kindness of the protectors and the ingratitude of the protégé in that whole affair. All these unpardonable crimes, made even worse by circumstances of time and place, prove that there is nothing surprising about the fate of the guilty person, and nothing that he did not well earn. Molière, I know, teased Doctors. But other than that he was only teasing, he was not at all afraid of them. He was well connected. He was loved by Louis XIV; and the Doctors—who hadn't as yet succeeded the spiritual Directors in the government of women—weren't versed then as they are today in the art of secret intrigues. Everything has greatly changed for them, and for the past twenty years they have had too much influence in private and public affairs for it to be prudent—even for people in good standing—to dare to speak freely about them. So you can judge how well a J.J. was received! But without launching into useless and dangerous details at this point, just read the last article of this list; it alone surpasses all the others.

19. "But if it is difficult for a large State to be well governed it is even more so for it to be governed by one man alone, and everyone knows what happens when the king appoints agents.

"An essential and inevitable defect, which will always place monarchical government below republican, is that in the latter the public voice almost never raises to high positions any but enlightened, capable men, who fulfill them with honor; whereas those who attain them in monarchies are most often petty troublemakers, petty rascals, petty intriguers, whose petty talents—which lead to high positions in royal courts—serve only to reveal their ineptitude to the people as soon as these men are in place. The people makes a mistake in its choice much less often,[120] and a man of real merit is nearly as rare in a ministry as a fool at the head of a republic.[121] So it is that when, by some lucky chance, one of those men who are born to govern takes control of public affairs in a monarchy that has been wrecked by this bunch of fine managers, people are all amazed at the resources he finds, and it is epoch-making for the whole country." *Social Contract*, Book III, chapter 6.[122]

I will add nothing about this last article; simply reading it has told you all. Actually, Sir, there is only one thing in all this that surprises me. It's that an isolated foreigner, without family, without support, caring about nothing in this world and wanting to say all those things thought he could do so with impunity.

Rousseau

But he didn't believe that, I assure you. He must have expected the cruel vengeance of all those who are offended by the truth, and he did expect it. He knew that the Nobles, the Viziers, the Lawyers, the Financiers, the Doctors, the Priests, the philosophers, and all the sectarian people who truly plunder society would never forgive him for having seen and shown them as they are. He must have expected hatred, persecutions of all kinds; not dishonor, opprobrium, defamation. He must have expected to live overwhelmed with miseries and adversities, but not with infamy and scorn. There are, I repeat, types of misfortune for which it is not even permissible that a decent man be prepared, and it is precisely those that were chosen to overwhelm him. Since they caught him unprepared, he was knocked down by the first shock, and did not pick himself up again without difficulty. He needed time to regain his courage and tranquillity. To preserve them always, he would have needed foresight that is not in the order of things any more than the fate that was being prepared for him. No, Sir, don't believe that the destiny in which he is buried is the natural fruit of his zeal for saying without fear all he believed to be true, good, salutary, useful. It has other causes—more secret, more fortuitous, more ridiculous—which have nothing whatever to do with his writings. It is a plan meditated for a long time and even before he was famous. It is the work of an infernal but profound genius, who could have taught Job's persecutor a great deal about the art of making a mortal unhappy. If this man had never been born, J.J., despite the audacity of his censures, would have lived in poverty and glory, and the ills that would still have been used to overwhelm him, far from debasing him would make him more illustrious. No, such an execrable project would never have been invented by the very people who have devoted themselves to its execution with the most ardor. That is one justice J.J. still likes to render to the nation that hastens to cover him with opprobrium. The plot was formed in the bosom of that nation, but it didn't come from there. The French are its ardent executors. That's too much, no doubt, but at least they are not its Authors. A well-meditated and thoughtful blackness of which they are incapable was necessary for being that. Whereas to be its ministers, the only requirement is an animosity which is nothing but the chance effect of certain circumstances and their inclination for infatuation as much with evil as with good.

The Frenchman

Whatever may be true about the cause and Authors of the plot, the effect is no longer surprising for anyone who has read the writings of J.J. The harsh truths he stated, although general, are arrows whose wounds never heal in the hearts of those who feel struck by them. Of all those who so ostentatiously become his patrons and protectors, there is not a single one who has not been wounded to the quick by one of these arrows. Of what stamp, then, are these divine souls, from whom the most stinging attack only elicited benevolence and love, and—in the most striking of all prodigies—who have made a scoundrel they ought to abhor the object of their most tender solicitude?

If that is virtue, it is bizarre, but it is magnanimous, and can only belong to strong souls that are above vulgar little passions. But how can such sublime motives be reconciled with the unworthy means used by those who claim to be animated by them? You know that however biased, however irritated I was with J.J., whatever bad opinion I held of his character and morals, I have never been able to relish our Gentlemen's system, nor resolve to practice their maxims. I always found as much baseness as falseness in that malevolent ostentation of beneficence, the only purpose of which was to debase its object. It's true that in conceiving of no flaws in so many clear proofs, I didn't doubt for a moment that J.J. was a detestable hypocrite and a monster who should never have been born, and with that simply granted, I admit that given the easy job they said they had to confound him, I admired their patience and gentleness in letting themselves be provoked by his clamors without ever getting upset, and with no other effect than to bind him more tightly in their nets as their entire response. Since they were able to convict him so easily, I saw it as heroic moderation not to do so, and even in blaming the method they wanted to follow, I couldn't help but admire their stoic phlegmatism in keeping to it.

In our first conversation, you shook the confidence I had in proofs that were so strong yet administered with so much mystery. In thinking it over since then, I was more struck by the extreme care taken to hide

them from the accused than I had been by their strength, and I began to
find the motives that were alleged for this conduct sophistic and weak.
These doubts were increased by my reflections on this affectation of
interest and benevolence for such a scoundrel. Virtue may be able to
generate hatred only for vice, but it is impossible for it to make the vicious
loved; and to persist in allowing him to remain free despite the crimes he
is seen continuing to commit, there must certainly be some stronger
motive than natural commiseration and humanity, which would even
require the opposite behavior. You had said that to me; I felt it, and the
very peculiar zeal of our Gentlemen for the impunity of the guilty person
as well as for his defamation presented me with throngs of contradictions
and inconsistencies, which began to disturb my initial security.

I was in this frame of mind when, prompted by your exhortations, in
starting to look through J.J.'s books I happened successively on the
passages I have transcribed, about which I previously had no notion. For
in talking to me about his harsh sarcasms, our Gentlemen had kept secret
those that involved them; and from the way in which they concerned
themselves with the Author, I would never have thought that they had
any personal grievances against him. This discovery and the mystery they
made of it finished enlightening me about their true motives. All my
confidence in them vanished, and I no longer had any doubt that what I
had accepted on their word as beneficence and generosity was the work
of a cruel animosity artfully masked by an exterior of goodness.

Another reflection reinforced the preceding ones. Such sublime virtues
aren't found by themselves. They are only branches of virtue. I looked
for the trunk and didn't find it. How could our Gentlemen—otherwise
so vain, so full of hate, so spiteful—decide for a single time in their lives
to be humane, generous, debonnaire other than in words; and to do so
precisely toward the mortal who was according to them least worthy of
this commiseration which they showered on him despite himself? I ought
to have been suspicious of this virtue, so new and so misplaced, if it had
been displayed openly, without disguise, without shadows. What was I
to think seeing it buried so carefully in obscure and tortuous paths, and
surprising by treachery the person who was its object to cover him despite
himself with their ignominious benefits.

Adding my own observations in this way to the reflections you had
caused me to make, the more I meditated on this same subject, the
more amazed I became at my blindness up to that point concerning our
Gentlemen, and my confidence in them faded away to the point where I
could no longer doubt their falseness. But the duplicity of their maneuver
and the cleverness with which they hid their true motives did not shake
the certainty of their proofs in my eyes. I judged that they were executing

an act of justice based on unjust views, and all I concluded about the art with which they ensnared their victim was that one wicked man was prey to other wicked men.

What had confirmed me in this opinion was the opinion you yourself held that J.J. was not the Author of the writings that bear his name. The only thing that could have made me think well of him were these very writings, which you had so beautifully praised and about which I had sometimes heard others speak favorably. But as soon as he was not their Author, I had no favorable idea of him left that could outweigh the horrible impressions I had been given concerning him, and it wasn't surprising that a man who was so abominable in everything was impudent and vile enough to claim the works of another as his own.

Such were more or less the reflections I made about our first conversation and the scattered and rapid reading that disabused me concerning our Gentlemen. I had begun that reading only as a sort of accommodation to the interest you appeared to take in it. The opinion I continued to have that these books were by another Author left me with scarcely more than curiosity as an interest in reading them.

I didn't get very far before adding to that another motive that better corresponded with your views. In reading these books, it wasn't long before I felt I had been deceived about their contents, and that what I had been told were fatuous declamations, adorned with fine language but disconnected and full of contradictions, were things that were profoundly thought out, forming a coherent system which might not be true but which offered nothing contradictory. In order to judge the true goal of these books, I didn't apply myself to picking apart a few scattered and separate sentences here and there; but rather consulting myself both during these readings and as I finished them, I examined as you desired the dispositions of soul into which they placed and left me, judging as you do that it was the best means to penetrate through to that of the Author when he wrote them and the effect he proposed to produce. I don't need to tell you that in place of the bad intentions that had been attributed to him, I found only a doctrine that was as healthy as it was simple, which without epicureanism and cant was directed only to the happiness of the human race. I felt that a man truly imbued with these feelings must attach little importance to fortune and the affairs of this life, and I myself would have been more fearful in surrendering too much to them of falling into negligence and quietism than of becoming factious, turbulent, and mischief-making as the Author was supposed to be and as he was supposed to want to render his disciples.

If it were only a question of that Author, I would from that point on have been disabused concerning J.J. But in filling me with the most sincere esteem for the one, this reading left me in the same position as before with regard to the other, because in appearing to see in them two different men, you had inspired me with as much veneration for one of them as I felt aversion for the other. The only thing this reading gave me, compared to what our Gentlemen had said about it, was that since they were persuaded these books were by J.J. and interpreting them in a totally different spirit than the one in which they were written, they had deceived me about what they contained. My reading, therefore, only completed what our conversation had begun, namely to take away all the esteem and confidence that had made me surrender to the impressions of the conspiracy, but without changing my feeling about the man it defamed. The books I was told were so dangerous were anything but that. They inspired feelings just the opposite of those attributed to their author. But if J.J. were not the author, in what way did they serve to justify him? The care you made me take was useless for making me change my opinion of him, and remaining in the opinion you gave me that these books were the work of a man of an entirely different character, I could not be amazed enough that up to this point you had been the first and only person to feel that a brain nourished on such ideas was incompatible with a heart full of blackness.

I eagerly awaited the story of your observations to know what I ought to believe concerning our man. Because already vacillating about the judgment based on so many proofs that I had reached before, and anxious since our conversation, I had become even more so since my readings had convinced me of the bad faith of our Gentlemen. Being able to esteem them no longer, was it necessary to esteem no one and to find only wicked people everywhere? Little by little, I felt the wish grow within me for J.J. not to be one. To feel alone and full of good sentiments and find no one who shares them is too cruel a condition. It is tempting, then, to believe one is the dupe of one's own heart, and to take virtue for a chimera.

The story of what you had seen struck me. I found in it so little relation to the accounts of others that, being forced to opt for excluding one, I was inclined to exclude entirely those for whom I had already lost all esteem. The very strength of their proofs held me back less. Having found them deceitful about so many things, I began to believe that they might well be so about everything, and to familiarize myself with the idea that had to that point seemed so ridiculous: that J.J. was innocent and persecuted. That required, it's true, assuming that in such a web of impostures there was artistry and magical illusions that seemed inconceivable to me. But I found still more absurdities heaped up in the obstinacy of my first feeling.

Before reaching my final conclusion, however, I resolved to reread his writings with more consistency and attention than I had to that point. I had found ideas and maxims that are very paradoxical, and others that I had not been able to understand well. I believed I had felt inequalities, even contradictions. I hadn't grasped the whole sufficiently to make a sound judgment about a system that was so new to me. Those books are not, like those of today, collections of detached thoughts on each of which the reader's mind can rest. They are the meditations of a solitary person. They require a consistent attention that is not too much to our nation's taste. When one persists in following its thread well, one must reread with effort, and more than once. I had found him impassioned for virtue, freedom, order, but with a vehemence that often carried him beyond the goal. In all respects I felt him to be a very ardent, very extraordinary man, but whose character and principles weren't yet well enough developed for me.

I believed that by meditating on his works very attentively and carefully comparing the Author with the man whom you had portrayed, I would succeed in having each of these two objects shed light on the other and in ascertaining whether everything fit together and belonged without question to the same individual. If this question were settled it seemed to me it would completely remove my irresolution about him; and taking a livelier interest in this research than I had to that point, I made it my duty, following your example, to reach a point where by putting together my reflections with the enlightenment I had from you, I would finally rid myself of the doubt into which you plunged me and judge the accused man for myself after having judged his accusers.

To undertake this research with more consistency and composure I went to the country for several months, and I took with me J.J.'s writings to the extent I could distinguish them among the fraudulent collections published under his name. From my first reading, I had felt that these writings proceeded in a certain order which it was necessary to find in order to follow the chain of their contents. I believed I saw that this order was the reverse of their order of publication, and that going backward from one principle to the next, the Author reached the first ones only in his final writings.[123] To proceed by synthesis, then, it was necessary to begin with these, which is what I did, by focusing first on the *Emile*, with which he finished, the other two writings that he has published since then no longer being part of his system and destined only to the personal defense of his homeland and his honor.

Rousseau

You no longer attribute to him, then, these other books that are published daily under his name, and carefully used to stuff collections of his writings so it will no longer be possible to discern which are really his?

The Frenchman

I was capable of being mistaken as long as I made my judgments about them on the basis of somebody else's word. But after reading him myself, I soon knew what I was doing. After following the maneuvers of our Gentlemen, I am surprised, given the ease of attributing books to him, that they don't attribute more to him. Because in the disposition they have established in the public concerning him, nothing is too dull or too punishable for them not to rush to the belief that he wrote it as soon as they wish to affirm it.

As for me, even if I didn't know that he stopped writing twelve years ago, a glance at the writings they attribute to him would suffice for me to feel that they couldn't be by the Author of the others. Not that I believe I am an infallible judge in matters of style. I know that very few people are, and I don't know to what extent a clever Author can imitate another's style the way Boileau imitated Voiture and Balzac. But it is about the things themselves that I believe I can't be mistaken. I found the writings of J.J. full of affections of the soul which penetrated mine. I found in them ways of feeling and seeing that distinguish him easily from all the writers of his time and most of those who preceded him. He is, as you said, an inhabitant of another sphere where nothing is like it is here. His system may be false, but in developing it, he portrayed himself truthfully in a manner so characteristic and so sure that it's impossible for me to mistake it. Before I reach page two of his stupid or malicious imitators I feel the aping,* and while they think they sound like him, how far they are from feeling and thinking like him. Even when they copy him, they denature him by the way they frame his work. It is easy to counterfeit his turns of phrases; what is hard for anyone else is to grasp his ideas and express his feelings. Nothing is so contrary to the philosophic spirit of this era, into which his false imitators always fall back.

In this second reading, better organized and more reflective than the first, following the thread of his meditations as best I could, I saw

---

* See for example the *Philosophy of Nature* that was burned at the Châtelet.[124] It is an execrable book and double edged sword written for the purpose of attribution to me, at least in the provinces and abroad, in order to take appropriate action and propagate at my expense the doctrine of these Gentlemen under the mask of mine. I've never seen this book and hope I never will, but I read all that too clearly in the indictment to be able to be mistaken about it, and I am certain that there can be no true resemblance between this book and mine because there is none between the souls that dictated them. Note that since it became known that I read this indictment, new measures have been taken so nothing like that can happen in the future.

throughout the development of his great principle that nature made man happy and good, but that society depraves him and makes him miserable. The *Emile*, in particular—that book which is much read, little understood, and ill-appreciated—is nothing but a treatise on the original goodness of man, destined to show how vice and error, foreign to his constitution, enter it from outside and insensibly change him. In his first writings, he tries even more to destroy that magical illusion which gives us a stupid admiration for the instruments of our misfortunes and to correct that deceptive assessment that makes us honor pernicious talents and scorn useful virtues. Throughout he makes us see the human race as better, wiser, and happier in its primitive constitution; blind, miserable, and wicked to the degree that it moves away from it. His goal is to rectify the error of our judgments in order to delay the progress of our vices, and to show us that where we seek glory and renown, we in fact find only errors and miseries.

But human nature does not go backward, and it is never possible to return to the times of innocence and equality once they have been left behind. This too is one of the principles on which he has most insisted. So that his object could not be to bring populous peoples or great States back to their first simplicity, but only to stop, if it were possible, the progress of those whose small size and situation have preserved from such a swift advance toward the perfection of society and the deterioration of the species. These distinctions deserved to be made and were not. He was stubbornly accused of wanting to destroy the sciences, the Arts, the theaters, the Academies and to plunge the universe back into its first barbarism; and on the contrary he always insisted on the preservation of existing institutions, holding that their destruction would only remove the palliatives while leaving the vices and substituting brigandage for corruption. He had worked for his homeland and for little States consti-tuted like it. If his doctrine could be of some utility to others, it was in changing the objects of their esteem and perhaps thus slowing down their decadence, which they accelerate with their false appreciations. But despite these distinctions, so often and forcefully repeated, the bad faith of men of letters and the foolishness of amour-propre which persuades everyone that they are always the focus of attention even when they aren't even being thought of, made the large nations apply to themselves what had been intended only for small republics; and people stubbornly insisted on seeing a promoter of upheavals and disturbances in the one man in the world who maintains the truest respect for the laws and national constitutions, and who has the greatest aversion to revolutions and con-spirators of every kind, who make him pay dearly for it.

Gradually grasping this system in all its ramifications through a more reflective reading, I still paid less attention at first to the direct examination of the doctrine than to its relationship to the character of the person whose name it bore; and on the basis of the portrait you had drawn of him for me, this relationship seemed so striking to me that I could not refuse my assent to its obviousness. Where could the painter and apologist of nature, so disfigured and calumnied now, have found his model if not in his own heart? He described it as he himself felt. The prejudices that did not subjugate him, the factitious passions to which he was not prey did not hide from his eyes as they did from others those original traits so generally forgotten or misjudged. These traits so novel for us and so true once they are traced could still find, deep in people's hearts, the attestation of their correctness, but they would never have sought them out themselves if the historian of nature hadn't started by removing the rust that hid them. A retired and solitary life, an active taste for reverie and contemplation, the habit of looking within oneself and seeking, in the calm of the passions, those original traits that have disappeared in the multitude, could alone enable him to rediscover them. In short, a man had to portray himself to show us primitive man like this, and if the Author hadn't been as unique as his books, he would never have written them. But where is this man of nature who lives a truly human life, who— discounting the opinion of others—behaves uniquely according to his inclinations and his reason, without regard to what the public approves or blames? He would be sought in vain among us. With a fine veneer of words, everyone tries in vain to mislead everyone else about his true goal. No one is deceived about it, and not a one is the dupe of the others although they all talk like him. They all seek their happiness in appearances, none is concerned about reality. They all place their being in appearance. Slaves and dupes of amour-propre, they live not to live but to make others believe they lived. If you hadn't portrayed your J.J. to me, I would have believed that the natural man no longer existed, but the striking relationship between the person you depicted and the Author whose books I read would not leave me in any doubt that they are one and the same person even if I had no other reason to believe it. This clear relationship is decisive for me, and without worrying about the J.J. of our Gentlemen, even more monstrous by his distance from nature than yours is unique for remaining so close to it, I fully adopt the ideas you've given me about him; and if your J.J. has not become entirely mine, he has the additional honor of wresting my esteem without benefit of any help from my inclination. Perhaps I will never love him, because that does not depend on me. But I honor him because I want to be just, because I believe he is innocent, and because I see him oppressed. The wrong I did him by thinking so ill of him was the effect of an almost invincible error for which I cannot in any way reproach my will. Even if the aversion I had for him remained at full strength, I would be no less disposed to esteem and pity him. His destiny is perhaps a unique example of all possible humiliations and an almost invincible patience to endure them. Finally the memory of the illusion from which I am emerging leaves me with a great preventive against arrogant confidence in my own understanding and against the adequacy of false knowledge.

Rousseau

It's truly to profit from experience, and even to make the error useful, to learn in this way from the error into which one may have fallen to rely less on the oracles of our judgments, and never to neglect—when one wishes to dispose arbitrarily of the honor and fate of a man—any of the means prescribed by justice and reason to determine the truth. If despite all these precautions we are still mistaken, it is the result of human misery, and we will at least not have to reproach ourselves for failing through our own fault. But nothing can excuse those who—stubbornly and unreasonably rejecting the most inviolable forms, and full of pride for sharing a work of iniquity with Nobles and Princes—fearlessly condemn an accused person and imperiously dispose of his destiny and his reputation uniquely because they like finding him guilty and because it gives them pleasure to see justice and evidence where fraud and imposture would jump out at unbiased eyes.

I will not have to reproach myself for doing this with respect to J.J., and if I deceive myself in judging him innocent, at least it is only after taking all the measures within my power to preserve me from error. You can't say quite as much yet, since you have neither seen nor studied him by yourself, and in the midst of so many magic tricks, illusions, prejudices, lies, and false witnesses, that, I believe, is the only sure method to know him. This method leads to another which is no less indispensable and ought to be the first if the natural order could be followed here. That is debate about the facts by the parties themselves, such that the accusers and the accused are placed in confrontation and his responses are heard. The terror which this sacred formality appears to inspire in the former, and their stubbornness in refusing it cause, I admit, a very strong, very reasonable prejudice against them, which by itself would suffice to condemn them, if the number and strength of their very striking, dazzling proofs didn't in a way block the effect of this refusal. It can't be known what the accused might respond, but until he has either given or refused to give his responses, no one has the right to announce for him that he has nothing to respond; nor, assuming one is entirely instructed about what he can or cannot say, to maintain that he is convicted as long as he has not been, or completely absolved so long as he has not confounded his accusers.

That, Sir, is what is still missing from the certainty of our judgments in this matter. Being men and subject to error, we can be mistaken in judging a guilty person innocent just as we can in judging an innocent one guilty. The first error, it's true, seems more excusable. But can one be excused for an error that can do harm and that could have been prevented? No, so long as there remains a possible means of clarifying the truth and it is neglected, the error is not involuntary and must be imputed to the person who wishes to remain in error. If, therefore, you take sufficient interest in the books you have read to want to reach some decision about their Author, and if you hate injustice enough to want to make amends for the injustice which in such a cruel way you may have committed with respect to him, I propose first of all that you see the man. Come, I will get you into his home without difficulty. He is already informed. I told him everything I could about you without breaking my commitments. He knows in advance that if ever you appear at his door, it will be in order to know him and not to deceive him. After refusing to see him so long as you judged him the way everyone else did, your first visit will be consoling proof for him that you no longer despair of owing him your esteem and of having wrongs to repair toward him.

As soon as you stop seeing him through the eyes of your Gentlemen and see him through your own, I have no doubt that your judgments will confirm mine, and that rediscovering in him the Author of his books, you will remain persuaded as I am that he is the man of nature and not at all the monster who has been portrayed to you under his name. But then, since each of us could be wrong in judgments that lack positive and regular proofs, we will always be left with a just fear based on the possibility of being in error and the difficulty of explaining in a satisfactory manner the facts alleged against him. Only one step then remains for us to take to establish the truth, to pay him homage and to demonstrate it to all eyes: it is to come together to force your Gentlemen at last to explain themselves openly in his presence and to confound such an impudent guilty man, or at least release us from the secrecy they demanded of us, by allowing us to confound him ourselves. Such a legitimate instance as this will be the first step. . . .

The Frenchman

Stop. . . . I tremble just listening to you. I made you a straightforward admission of what I believed I owed to justice and truth. I want to be just, but without temerity. I don't want to sacrifice myself uselessly without saving the innocent person for whom I make the sacrifice, and that is what I would do by following your advice. It is what you yourself would do by wanting to put it into practice. Learn what I can and want to do, and expect nothing beyond that from me.

You claim I should go and see J.J. to verify with my own eyes what you've told me about him and what I infer myself from reading his writings. This confirmation is superfluous for me, and without resorting to it I know in advance what to think about the matter. It is odd that I am now more decided than you about the feelings you had such trouble making me adopt. But there is, however, a reasonable basis for that. You still stress the strength of the proofs advanced against him by our Gentlemen. That strength is henceforth null for me since I looked more closely and unraveled its artifice. I know so many facts about it of which you are unaware. I so clearly read in their hearts, along with the keenest anxiety about what the accused would say, the most ardent desire to take away from him every means of defending himself. I saw so much cooperation, care, activity, warmth in the measures taken to achieve this, that proofs administered in this manner by such impassioned people lose all authority in my mind compared to your observations. The public is deceived; I see it, I know it. But it likes being deceived, and would not want to be disabused. I've been in the same position myself and didn't get out of it without difficulty. Our Gentlemen had my confidence because they gratified the inclination they gave me; but I never fully esteemed them, and when I praised their virtues to you, I could not resolve to imitate them. I never wished to approach their prey to cajole, deceive, outwit him following their example, and the same repugnance I saw in your heart was in mine when I sought to fight it. I approved of their maneuvers without wishing to adopt them. Their falseness, which they called benevolence, could not seduce me, because in place of the benevolence of which they boasted, I sensed only antipathy, repugnance, aversion for the one who was its object. I was very relieved to see them nurture a kind of scornful and mocking affection for him, which had all the effects of the most mortal hatred. But I could not mislead myself in the same way, and they had made him so odious to me that I hated him with all my heart, without sham and completely openly. I would have been afraid to approach him just as I would a horrible monster, and I preferred not to have the pleasure of harming him in order to avoid the horror of seeing him.

By gradually bringing me back to reason, you inspired me with as much esteem for his patience and gentleness as with compassion for his misfortunes. His books finished the work you had started. In reading them, I felt the passion that gave so much energy to his soul and vehemence to his diction. It isn't a fleeting explosion; it is a dominant and permanent feeling which can sustain itself like that for ten years and produce twelve volumes[125] always filled with the same zeal, always extracted by the same persuasion. Yes, I feel and assert just as you do: the moment he is the Author of the writings that bear his name, he can only have the heart of a good man.

This attentive and reflective reading fully completed in my mind the revolution you had started. It was while doing this reading with the care it requires that I felt all the maliciousness, all the detestable cleverness of his bitter commentators. In everything I read by the original writer, I felt the sincerity, the rectitude of a soul that was lofty and proud but frank and without bile, which shows itself without precaution, without fear; which censures openly, praises without reticence, and has no feeling to hide. On the contrary, everything I read in the responses displayed fierce brutality or insidious, treacherous politeness, and covered with the honey of praises the bile of satire and the poison of calumny. One should read carefully the honest but frank letter to M. d'Alembert on the theater, and compare it with his [d'Alembert's] response to it, a response so carefully measured, so full of affected circumspection, of bittersweet compliments, so suited to induce thinking the worst while feigning not to say it. One should then seek to discover on the basis of these readings which of the two authors is the wicked one. Do you believe there is a mortal in the universe impudent enough to say it is J.J.?

This difference is apparent from the start in their epigraphs. That of your friend, taken from the *Aeneid*,[126] is a prayer to Heaven to protect good men from such a fatal error and to leave error to the enemies. Here is M. d'Alembert's, taken from La Fontaine:

> Give me your scythe, instrument of harm.[127]

One thinks only of preventing an evil. The other, from the outset, forgets the question to think only of harming his adversary, and in examining the utility of theaters, addresses very appropriately to J.J. the same verse which the serpent addresses to the man in La Fontaine.[128]

Ah, subtle and crafty d'Alembert, if you don't have a scythe—a very useful instrument whatever the serpent may say—you have instead a well sharpened pen, which is scarcely, and especially in your hands, a tool of beneficence.

You see that I am more advanced than you in your own research, since you still have scruples about this that I no longer have. No, Sir, I don't even need to see J.J. to know what I think about him. I saw the maneuvers of which he is the victim at too close a range to allow the slightest authority for anything that may come from it to remain in my mind. What he was in the eyes of the public at the time his first work was published, he has become in mine, because the magic of all that has been done since then to disfigure him is destroyed, and because in all the proofs that still impress you, I no longer see anything except fraud, lies, illusion.

You asked whether a plot existed? Yes, without any doubt one exists, and such as there never has been and never will be another like it. Wasn't that clear as early as the year of the decree in the brusque and incredible outburst in all the printed works, all the newspapers, all the gazettes, all the brochures against this unfortunate man. This decree was the tocsin for all this fury. Can you believe that the Authors of all that—however jealous, however wicked, however vile they might be—could attack all together in this way, like mad Wolves, a man who was then and from that point forward the prey of the cruelest adversities? Can you believe that the collections of his own writings would have been insolently stuffed with such black libels if those who wrote them and those who used them hadn't been inspired by this conspiracy which, for a long time, had been silently progressing and which then emerged in public for the first time. Reading J.J.'s writings made me read at the same time those venomous productions so attentively mixed with them. If I had done this reading earlier, I would have understood everything from then on. It isn't hard for someone who can go through them calmly. The conspirators themselves felt this, and they soon adopted another method that worked far better. This was to attack J.J. in public only by innuendos, and most often without naming either him or his books. But to do it in such a way that the application of what was said was so clear that everyone would make it immediately. The ten years of following this method have proved more effective than gross insults, which because of their grossness alone can displease the public or elicit its suspicions. It is in private conversations, in circles, in secret little committees, in all those little literary tribunals over which women preside, where the daggers are sharpened in order to riddle him underhandedly. Impetuous Voltaire at first went about vigorously spewing forth a flood of his usual insults. But sly d'Alembert, on the pretext of a trip to Italy that he had no wish to make and did not make,* went to Ferney, and there, getting together with him completely at leisure, gave him to understand that this open manner of saying and doing was not within the system of the conspiracy and didn't have its approval. That he ought to conform to the agreed upon method of always acting without ever being seen, of speaking well of J.J. and of his talents in public, and even with showiness, of always appearing to be tenderly interested in him, but to try, through secret and continual indignities, to

---

* I guessed that this trip to Italy was only a sham by the affectation with which it was spoken of long before departure. Could this affectation escape me, from whom everything was kept a mystery, even the most indifferent things?

force him to kill himself finally out of despair, which would easily be interpreted by the public as if he had killed himself out of madness. For that, you may be sure, is the true hidden goal of the conspiracy which, whatever you may say about it, it has not yet despaired of achieving. "Be silent," d'Alembert said to Voltaire. "Don't talk about him at all and let us take care of things. Soon we will all be rid of that B——." Since then he has followed that advice, always awaiting the results of the promise, which he is eager to see happen.

It is inconceivable how the defamation of a private person without a job, a project, a party or credit could become such an important and such a universal affair. It is even much more inconceivable how such an enterprise could have seemed attractive enough so that all classes, without exception, were eager to collaborate in it, *by fair means or foul*, as though it were the most glorious work. If the Authors of this amazing plot, if the leaders who took over its direction had put half the care, trouble, work, time, expense they lavished on the execution of this fine project into some honorable enterprise, they could have been crowned with immortal glory at far less expense* than what it cost them to carry out this shadowy work, which can result in neither good nor honor for them, but only in the pleasure of secretly satisfying the most cowardly of all the passions, yet which the patience and gentleness of their victim will never allow them to enjoy fully.

It is impossible for you to have a just idea of the position of your J.J. or of the manner in which he is enmeshed. Everything is so well organized concerning him that an Angel could descend from Heaven to defend him without being able to do so. The plot of which he is the subject isn't one of those impostures hastily put together, which have a prompt but fleeting effect and which are discovered and destroyed in an instant. As he himself felt, it is a long-meditated project, whose slow and gradual execution functions with as much precaution as method, erasing as it advances both all trace of the paths it has taken and the all vestiges of the truth it has caused to disappear. In so carefully avoiding all types of explanations, can you believe that the Authors and leaders of this plot neglect to destroy and denature everything that might one day serve to confound them; and in more than fifteen years of full execution, haven't they had all the time they needed to do so successfully? The further they move into the future, the easier it is for them to obliterate the past or give it the aspect that

---

* I will be reproached, I'm quite sure, for attributing prodigious importance to myself. Ah, if I didn't have more importance in the eyes of others than in my own, how much less pitiable my fate would be! I beg those who will reproach me for this to explain only two things in a manner that could satisfy a sensible man. One is the invasion of Corsica; the other, the construction of the city of Versoix.[129]

suits them. The moment should come when having all witnesses at their disposition, they can without risk lift the impenetrable veil they placed over the eyes of their victim. Who knows if this moment hasn't already come; if with the measures they have had the time to take, they couldn't expose themselves right now to confrontations that would confound innocence and make imposture triumph? Perhaps they still avoid them only in order not to appear to change maxims and, if you will, through a remnant of fear linked to lying that not everything has been well enough foreseen. I tell you again that they have worked ceaselessly to arrange everything so as to have nothing to fear from a regular discussion if they were ever forced to agree to one, and it seems to me they have had all the time and means to protect the success of their enterprise from any unforeseen event. Why, what would the resources of J.J. and his defenders be henceforth if he dared present some? Where would he find judges who were not in the plot, witnesses who were not suborned, faithful counsels who would not lead him astray? Alone against a whole conspiring generation, from whom would he demand the truth without getting a lie for an answer instead? What protection, what support would he find to resist this general conspiracy? Is there, can there be among the people in power, a single man with enough integrity to condemn himself, enough courage to dare defend an oppresed man consecrated for so long to the hatred of the public; enough generosity to be moved to such zeal with no other interest than that of equity? You may be sure that regardless of the credibility or authority of the person who would dare speak out in his favor and demand the first laws of justice for him, he would be lost without saving his client, and the entire conspiracy united against this daring protector, beginning by removing him in one way or another, would end by holding its victim at its mercy as before. Nothing can protect him from his destiny any longer, and all a wise man interested in his fate can do is to seek out silently the vestiges of the truth in order to guide his own judgment, but never to have it adopted by the multitude, which is incapable of using reason to renounce the position that passion has made it take.

As for myself, I want to make my straightforward confession to you at this point. I believe that J.J. is innocent and virtuous, and this belief is such, deep in my soul, that it has no need for some other confirmation. Well persuaded of his innocence, I will never be so unworthy as to talk about him contrary to my thinking, nor will I join my voice to that of the public against him, as I have done up until now holding a different opinion. But don't expect either that I will thoughtlessly go about displaying myself openly as his defender and forcing his detractors to drop their mask in order to accuse him aloud to his face. That would be undertaking a step as imprudent as it would be useless, to which I don't want to expose myself. I have a status, friends to preserve, a family to support, patrons to satisfy. I don't want to play Don Quixote in this and fight the powers in order to be the center of attention for a moment and be lost for the rest of my life. If I can make amends for my wrongs toward the unfortunate J.J. and be of use to him without exposing myself, well and good. I will do so with all my heart. But if you expect me to take some flamboyant step that compromises me and exposes me to the blame of my peers, you are quite mistaken. I will never go to that point. You yourself can't go any further than you have without breaking your word and placing us both in an embarrassing situation from which neither of us can get out as easily as you have presumed.

Rousseau

Please set your mind at rest. I would far rather go along with your resolutions than require of you anything that displeases you. In the steps I would have wished to take, my object was more our complete and shared satisfaction than it was bringing either the public or your Gentlemen around to feelings of justice and the path of truth. Although inside I am as persuaded of J.J.'s innocence as you are, I have not been properly convinced, since, unable to inform him about the things imputed to him, I couldn't either confound him by his silence or absolve him through his responses. In this regard, I confine myself to the immediate judgment I made about the man, without pronouncing on the facts that contradict that judgment, since they are lacking in the characteristic that alone can confirm or destroy them in my eyes. I don't have enough confidence in my own understanding to believe it can never deceive me, and I would perhaps still be in doubt here if the most legitimate and strongest of prejudices didn't come in support of my own remarks and show me the lie of the side that refuses the test of truth. Far from fearing a cross-examination, J.J. has not ceased to seek one, to provoke his accusers with his outcries, and to say aloud whatever he had to say. They, on the contrary, have always dodged, ducked their heads, talked softly among themselves, hiding from him with the greatest care their accusations, their witnesses, their proofs, above all their persons, and fleeing with the most obvious fear any kind of confrontation. Therefore, they have strong reasons to fear it, those they allege being inept to the point of being insulting to those to whom they offer them, and who, I don't know how, are still satisfied with them. But for myself, I will never be satisfied, and that being the case, all their clandestine proofs are without authority for me. There you are in the same situation as I am, but with a lesser degree of certainty about the innocence of the accused, since not having examined him with your own eyes, you judge him only by his writings and on the basis of my testimony. Therefore your scruples ought to be greater than mine if the maneuvers of his persecutors, which you followed more closely, were not a counterbalance for you. In this position, I thought the best thing we could do to be assured of the truth was to put it to its final and most certain test, precisely the one which your Gentlemen avoid so carefully. It seemed to me that without overly compromising ourselves, we could have said to them: "We are unable to approve that at the expense of justice and public safety you give tacit pardon to a scoundrel which he doesn't accept and says is nothing other than horrible barbarousness which you cover up with a fine name. Even if this truly were a pardon, its nature changes because it is conferred by force. Instead of being a benefit, it becomes a cruel insult, and nothing is more unjust and tyrannical than to force a man to be obligated to us despite himself. No doubt it is one of J.J.'s crimes that in place of the acknowledgment he owes you, he has only the most scornful disdain for you and your maneuvers. This impudence on his part in particular deserves a fitting punishment, and this punishment that you owe to him and to yourselves is to confound him, so that being forced at last to acknowledge your indulgence, he no longer casts doubts on the motives that prompt you. Let the confusion of such an arrogant hypocrite be his only punishment, if you will, but let him feel it for edification, public safety, and the honor of the current generation, which he appears to disdain so greatly. Only then will there be no risk in allowing him to wander among us with shame, when he has been very authentically convicted and unmasked. How long will you tolerate the odious scandal that with the security of innocence, crime insolently dares to provoke virtue, which flinches before it and hides away in darkness. It is he who must be reduced to the unworthy silence you maintain in his presence. Without this the future will never want to believe that the person who shows himself alone and without fear is guilty and the person who, though well accompanied, doesn't dare wait for him is innocent."

By talking to them like this, we would have forced them to explain themselves openly or to concur tacitly about their imposture, and through the cross-examination of the facts, we could have made a decisive judgment about the accusers and the accused, and pronounced definitively between them and him. You say that because the judges and the witnesses are all in the conspiracy, it would have been very easy for prevarication to occur, very difficult to discover it, and that must be so. Yet it isn't impossible that the accused would have found some unforeseen and decisive reply that would have undone all their devices and revealed the plot. Everything is against him, I know: power, ruse, money, intrigue, time, prejudices, his ineptness, his distractedness, his lack of memory, his difficulty in expressing himself, everything really except for innocence and truth which alone have given him the confidence ardently to seek, demand, and provoke these explanations which he would have so many reasons to fear if his conscience were working against him. But his lukewarm desires are no longer animated either by the hope of a success which he can no longer expect except through a miracle, or by the idea of a reparation that could soothe his heart. Put yourself in his place for a moment, and feel what he must think of the current generation and of its behavior toward him. After the pleasure it has taken defaming him while cajoling him, what importance should he attach to the return of its esteem, and what value in his eyes could there be in the sincere caresses of the same people who lavished such false ones on him with hearts full of aversion for him. Can their duplicity, their betrayal, their perfidy have left him with the slightest favorable feeling for them, and wouldn't he be more indignant than flattered to see himself sincerely celebrated by them with the same demonstrations they derisively used for such a long time to make him the plaything of the rabble.

No, Sir, even if his contemporaries—as repentant and true as they have been false and cruel up to now toward him—were finally to retract their error or rather their hatred, and making amends for their long-lasting injustice were to try by means of honors to make him forget their insults, could he forget the baseness and unworthiness of their behavior; could he stop saying to himself that even if he had been the scoundrel they wished to see in him, their way of dealing with this supposed scoundrel, though less iniquitous, would be still more abject, and that debasing oneself in relation to a monster with so many insidious tricks was to place oneself beneath him? No, it is no longer in the power of his contemporaries to take away the disdain they went to such trouble to inspire in him. Having even grown insensitive to their insults, how could he be touched by their praise? How could he accept the belated and forced return of their esteem when he can no longer feel any esteem for them? No, this change on the part of a public so deserving of scorn can no longer bring him any pleasure nor give him any honor. He would be more importuned, without being more satisfied by it. Thus the juridical and decisive explanation which he was never able to obtain and which he ceased desiring was more for ourselves than for him. It could no longer, even with the most dazzling justification, bring any true comfort to his old age. He is henceforth too much of a stranger here below to take any personal interest in what happens here. No longer having a sufficient reason to act, he remains tranquil while waiting for death to bring an end to his troubles, and looks only with indifference on the fate of the few days that remain for him to spend on earth.

Some consolation, nonetheless, is still within his reach. I consecrate my life to giving it to him, and I entreat you to join me in this. Neither you nor I has become party to the secrets of the conspiracy of which he is the object. We have not shared the falseness of those who compose it. We have not sought to overtake him with perfidious caresses. As long as you hated him, you fled from him, and I sought him out only in the hope of finding him worthy of my friendship; and the test necessary for making an enlightened judgment about his case having been as sought after by him as it was avoided by your Gentlemen constitutes a prejudice that takes the place of that test insofar as possible, and confirms what I thought of him after an examination that was as long as it was impartial. He told me a hundred times that he would have been consoled about the public injustice if he had found a single human heart that opened up to his, felt his sorrows, and pitied them. The frank and full esteem of one single person would have compensated him for the scorn of all the others. I can give him this compensation, and I pledge it to him. If you join me in this good work, we can give him back in his old age the sweetness of true society which he lost so long ago and no longer hoped to find again here below. Let the public remain in the error that delights it and that it deserves, and let's show only the person who is its victim that we don't share it. He is already no longer mistaken about me, he will not be about you, and if you come to him with the feelings that are his due, you will find him ready to return them to you. Ours will be all the more sensible to him because he no longer expects them from anyone; and with the heart I know he has, he didn't need such a long deprivation to make him feel their value. Let his persecutors continue to triumph; he will not be troubled by their prosperity. The desire for revenge never tortured him. In the midst of all their successes, he still pities them, and believes they are far more unhappy than he. Indeed, even if the sad enjoyment of the harm they have done to him could fill their hearts with true contentment, can it ever protect them from the fear of someday being discovered and unmasked? Don't all the attention they give and all the measures they have taken, without respite, for so many years indicate the terror of never having taken enough? In vain they enclose the truth in triple walls of lies and impostures which they continually reinforce; they always tremble for fear it will escape through some crack. The immense edifice of shadows they have built around him does not suffice to reassure them. As long as he lives, an unforeseen accident can unveil their mystery to him and expose them to finding themselves confounded. Even his death, far from calming them, must increase their alarms. Who knows whether he hasn't found some discreet confidant who, once public animosity has ceased to be aroused by the presence of the condemned man, will seize the moment when eyes begin to open to make himself heard? Who knows whether some faithful trustee won't at some time and place produce such proofs of his innocence that the public—forced to acknowledge them—will feel and deplore its long-standing mistake? Who knows whether among the infinite number of their accomplices there isn't someone who will be forced by his own repentance and remorse to speak out? Even if one foresees or arranges all the imaginable combinations, there is always the fear that something remains which has not been foreseen and which will cause the truth to be discovered just when it is least expected. Foresight labors in vain, fear is more active still, and the authors of such a project, without realizing it, have sacrificed the repose of their remaining days to their hatred.

If their accusations were true and J.J. were as they have portrayed him, having unmasked him once as a matter of conscience and deposited their secret with those who must watch over public order, they would rely on them for the rest, cease to be preoccupied with the guilty person, and think no more about him. But the anxious and vigilant eye they maintain constantly focused on him, the emissaries with whom they surround him, the measures they constantly take to close off all means of explanation from him, so that he should have no way whatever to escape from them, reveal along with their alarms the cause that maintains and perpetuates them. They can no longer stop no matter what they do. Living or dead, he will always worry them, and if he loved revenge, he would have one well guaranteed in the fright by which, despite all the precautions built up, they will never again stop being agitated.

That is the counterpart of their success and all their prosperity. They have used all the resources of their art to make him the most unhappy of beings. By dint of adding one means to another, they have exhausted them all and far from achieving their ends, they have produced the opposite effect. They have caused J.J. to find resources within himself that he would not even know without them. Having done the worst they could to him, they put him in the position of having nothing more to fear either from them or from anyone, and of viewing all human events with the most profound indifference. There is no wound his soul might feel that they didn't inflict on it. But by doing him all the harm they could, they forced him to seek refuge in asylums which it isn't within their power to enter. He can now defy them and laugh at their impotence. Unable to make him more unhappy, it is they who grow more so each day, seeing that so many efforts resulted only in worsening their situation and soothing his. Having become powerless, their rage has become irritated in the attempt to satisfy itself.

Besides, he has no doubt that despite so many efforts, time will eventually lift the veil of imposture and reveal his innocence. The certainty that the value of his patience will be felt someday contributes to maintaining it, and in taking everything away from him, his persecutors have been unable to take away his confidence and hope. "If all memory of me were to disappear along with me," he said, "I would be reconciled to being so badly known by men, who would soon forget me. But since my existence must be known after me through my books and even more through my misfortunes, I admit that I can't muster enough resignation to think without a sense of impatience—I who feel that I am better and more just than any man I know—that I will only be remembered as a monster; and that my writings, in which the heart that dictated them is imprinted on every page, will pass for the declarations of a Tartuffe who sought only to deceive the public. What purpose will my courage and zeal have served if their monuments, far from being useful to good people* only embitter and foment the animosity of the wicked, if everything that love of virtue has made me say without fear and without self-interest only generates suspicion and hatred for me in the future as it does now, and never produces any good. If instead of the benedictions I deserved, my name— which everything ought to have made honorable—is uttered in the future only with a curse! No, I will never tolerate such a cruel idea. It would absorb all the courage and constancy I have left. I would easily consent to have no existence at all in the memory of men, but I cannot consent, I admit it, to remain defamed. No, Heaven will not allow it, and regardless of the status to which destiny has brought me, I will never lose hope in providence, knowing very well that it chooses its own hour and not ours, and that it likes to strike at the moment when it is no longer expected. It isn't that I still attach any importance, and above all in relation to myself, to the few days remaining in my life, even if I could see all the sweet things reborn for me that have so carefully been cut off. I have known the wretchedness of human prosperity too well to be sensitive at my age to its belated and vain return, and however hard it is to believe, it would be easier for it to come back than for me to resume my taste for it. I no longer hope and I have very little desire to see in my lifetime the revolution that must disabuse the public concerning me. Let my persecutors enjoy in peace, if they can, all their lives the happiness they derived from the wretchedness of mine. I don't desire to see them either confounded or punished, and as long as the truth is known at last, I don't ask that it be at their expense. But I cannot consider as something indifferent to men

---

* The speech of a man who is believed to say the opposite of what he thinks will never move those who are of that opinion. All those who, thinking ill of me, say their virtue has benefited from the reading of my books are lying, and even very foolishly. It is they who are truly Tartuffes.

the reinstatement of my memory and the return of the public esteem due
to me. It would be too great a misfortune for the human race if the way
in which I was treated were to serve as a model and an example; if the
honor of individuals were dependent on every clever imposter; and if
society, trampling underfoot the most sacred laws of justice, were no
longer anything more than a shadowy brigandage of secret betrayals
and impostures adopted without confrontation, without contradiction,
without verification, and without any defense allowed to the accused.
Soon, men at one another's mercy would have strength and activity only
to tear each other apart, without having any at all for resisting. Good
people, thrown entirely to the wicked, would at first become their prey,
and finally their disciples. Innocence would no longer have a refuge, and
the earth, having become a hell, would be covered only with Demons
busy tormenting each other. No, Heaven will not allow such a fatal
example to open a new path, unknown until now, to crime. It will uncover
the wickedness of such a cruel plot. A day will come, I am justly confident,
when decent men will bless my memory and weep over my fate. I am sure
of it, although I don't know when it will happen. That is the basis of my
patience and my consolations. Order will be reestablished, sooner or later,
even on earth, I have no doubt . My oppressors can delay the moment of
my justification, but they cannot prevent it from coming. That is enough
to make me tranquil in the midst of their deeds. Let them continue to do
what they will to me while I live; but let them hurry. I shall soon escape
from them."[130]

Such are J.J.'s feelings about this, and mine are the same. Due to a
decree whose depth I cannot sound, he must live his remaining days in
scorn and humiliation. But I have the most lively presentiment that after
his death and the death of his persecutors, their plots will be uncovered
and his memory vindicated. This feeling seems so well founded to me
that however little one thinks about it, I can't see that there can be any
doubt about it. It's a generally accepted axiom that the truth is uncovered
sooner or later, and this is confirmed by so many examples that experience
no longer allows it to be a matter for doubt. In this case, at least, it is
inconceivable that such a complicated plot should remain hidden in future
ages. It shouldn't even be presumed that it will remain so for long in
ours. Too many signs divulge it for it to escape the first person who
wishes to look carefully, and that wish will surely occur in several people
as soon as J.J. is no longer alive. Of the many people engaged in fascinating
the eyes of the public, it isn't possible that a large number won't perceive
the bad faith of those who lead them, and feel that if this man were really
such as they make him it would be unnecessary to deceive the public
concerning him, and use so many impostures to accuse him of things he

doesn't do and disguise those he does. If interest, animosity, and fear make them collaborate easily today in these maneuvers, a time may come when their calmed passion and changed interest will make them view in a very different light the secret works to which they are now witnesses and accomplices. Is it believable then that none of these subordinate cooperators will speak in confidence to someone about what he saw, what he was made to do, and the effect of all that in deceiving the public; that, finding decent men eager to seek out the disfigured truth, they won't be tempted to become necessary again by uncovering it just as they are now to keep it hidden; to confer importance on themselves by showing they were admitted to the confidence of Nobles and that they know anecdotes of which the public is ignorant? And why shouldn't I believe that regret for having contributed to defaming an innocent man will make a few of them indiscreet or truthful, especially at the hour when ready to leave this life, they are urged by their consciences not to carry off their guilt with them? Finally, why shouldn't the reflections that you and I make today occur to the minds of several people then, when they calmly examine the behavior that occurred and the ease it offered for portraying this man as they wished? It will be felt that it is far more unbelievable that such a man really existed, than it is that the imposters, emboldened by the credulity of the public, were led to portray him like that gradually and with increasing escalation without perceiving that they were exceeding the limits of the possible. That progression, very natural to passion, is a trap that divulges it and from which it rarely protects itself. A person who would keep an exact record of what, according to your Gentlemen, he did, said, wrote, printed since they took hold of his person, added to what he really did, would find that a hundred years wouldn't be time enough for so many things. All the books attributed to him, all the statements put in his mouth are as harmonious and natural as the deeds they ascribe to him, and it is always so well proved that by admitting a single one of these deeds, one no longer has the right to reject any other.

However, with a little calculation and common sense, it will be seen that so many things are incompatible, that he could never have done all that or be in so many different places in so little time. That consequently there are more fictions than truths in all these accumulated anecdotes, and finally that the same proofs that don't prevent some from being lies, can't establish that the others are truths. The very strength and number of all these proofs will suffice to make the plot suspicious, and from that point on all proofs that haven't undergone a legal test will lose their strength, all the witnesses who haven't confronted the accused will lose their authority, and the only solid charges remaining against him will be those that are known to him and about which he has been unable to justify himself. That is to say that except for the faults which he was the first to declare and which your Gentlemen have exploited so thoroughly, there will be nothing at all for which to reproach him.

It is this persuasion, which seems reasonable to me, that consoles him about the insults of his contemporaries and their injustice. Whatever they may do, his books transmitted to posterity will show that their Author was not as they strove to portray him, and his ordered, simple, uniform life—unchanged for so many years—will never be consistent with the dreadful character they want to confer on him. The fate of this shadowy plot, formed in such profound secrecy, developed with such great precautions, and pursued with such zeal, will be like that of all the works of men's passions, which are transitory and perishable as they are. A time will come when the century in which J.J. lived will be viewed with the same horror this century shows toward him, and when this plot, immortalizing its Author like Erostratus,[131] will be thought of as a masterpiece of genius and even more so of wickedness.

The Frenchman

I heartily join my wishes to yours for this prediction to be realized, but I admit that I am not as confident about it, and seeing the direction this affair has taken, I would judge that multitudes of characters and events described in history may have no other basis than the invention of those who took it upon themselves to affirm them. That time allows truth to triumph must happen very often, but how can one know that it always happens, and on what proof can one vouch for it? Long-hidden truths are finally revealed by some chance circumstances. A hundred thousand others may remain forever obscured by lies without our having any means to recognize them and point them out. For as long as they remain hidden, it is as if they are nonexistent for us. Take away the chance that reveals one, it would continue to be hidden, and who knows how many remain for which this circumstance will never come? So let's not say that time always allows truth to triumph, because that is what is impossible for us to know, and it is far more credible that erasing all its traces step by step, time more often allows lying to triumph, especially when men have an interest in supporting it. The conjectures on which you believe that the mystery of this plot will be unveiled appear to me—having seen it at closer range—much less plausible than they do to you. The conspiracy is too strong, too numerous, too tightly woven to be able to be easily undone, and as long as it remains the way it is, it is too perilous to detach oneself from it for anyone to dare do so without some other interest than that of justice. Of all the threads that make up its web, each one of those people who lead it sees only the thread he must govern and at most those right beside it. The general assembling of the whole is perceived only by the directors, who work ceaselessly to unravel whatever gets tangled up, remove frictions and contradictions, and make the whole function in a uniform manner. The multitude of mutually incompatible things that J.J. is made to say and do is, so to speak, only the supply of materials from which the builders, making a selection, will choose at their leisure those matching things that can go well together; and rejecting those which are contrasting, repugnant, and self-contradictory, are soon able to have them forgotten after they have produced their effect. *Keep on inventing*, they say to subordinate conspirators; *we will be responsible for choosing and arranging later on.* Their project, as I have told you, is to do a general recasting of all the anecdotes collected or made up by their satellites, and to arrange them in a historical body disposed so artfully and worked out so carefully that everything absurd and contradictory, far from appearing to be a tissue of crude fables, will appear to be the result of the inconsistency of the man who, with his diverse and monstrous passions, wanted both black and white, and spent his life doing and undoing, for want of being able to carry out his evil schemes.

This work, which has been in preparation for a long time so that it can be published first after his death, should so firmly establish the public's judgment of his memory through the documents and proofs with which it is replete, that no one will even consider formulating the slightest doubt about it. They will feign the same interest and affection for him whose well-orchestrated appearance was so effective during his lifetime, and to emphasize their impartiality, and appear sad to confer a dreadful character on him, they will add to this the most exaggerated praises of his pen and talents, but expressed in such a way as to make him more odious because of it, as though saying and proving the pro and the con equally, persuading about everything and believing nothing had been the favorite game of his mind. In a word, the writer of his life, admirably chosen for it, will know like Tasso's *Alethes*

> Clever liar, learned in the art of harming
> *In the form of praise clothing the satire.*[132]

His books, you say, transmitted to posterity will testify in favor of their Author. I admit that this will be a very strong argument for those who will think as you and I do about these books. But do you know how much they can be disfigured, and doesn't everything that has already been done about that with the greatest success prove that anything can be done without the public believing or finding it bad. This argument based on his books has always worried our Gentlemen. Unable to annihilate them, and their most malicious interpretations not yet sufficing to discredit them at their whim, they began the process of falsifying them, and this enterprise, which seemed almost impossible at first, has become extremely easy to carry out through the connivance of the public. The Author made only one edition of each work. These scattered printings have long since disappeared, and the few copies that may remain hidden in some bookshelves have not excited anyone's curiosity about comparing them with the collections that are destined to inundate the public. All these collections,—expanded by insulting criticisms, venomous libels, and done for the unique purpose of disfiguring the Author's productions, altering his maxims, and changing their spirit little by little—have been arranged and falsified with great artistry to that end, at first only by the omissions which, suppressing the necessary clarifications, changed the meaning of what was left; then by apparent carelessness that could be passed off as printing errors, but which produced terrible false meanings and which, faithfully transcribed in each new printing finally substituted these false lessons for the true ones by tradition. To make this project more successful, they imagined making fine editions which, because of their typographical perfection, would be preferred to preceding ones and remain in libraries. And to give them even more credibility, they tried to interest the Author himself in this by the lure of profit, and to do so they had the publisher in charge of these maneuvers make him such magnificent offers as would naturally have to tempt him. The project was to establish the public's confidence in this way, to show the Author only correct proofs and to print without his knowledge the pages destined for the public, on which the text was modified according to the views of our Gentlemen. Nothing would have been easier, because of the manner in which he is entangled, than to hide this little stratagem from him and make him thus authorize the fraud of which he was to be the victim and of which he would have been ignorant, believing he was transmitting to posterity a faithful edition of his writings. But whether because of distaste, laziness, or having gotten wind of the project, not only did he refuse the proposition, but he signed a protest disavowing everything that would henceforth be printed under his name. They therefore decided to do without him and continue as if he were participating in the enterprise. The Edition is by subscription and is printed, they say, in Brussels, on fine paper, with beautiful typeface, and beautiful engravings. Nothing will be spared to extol it throughout Europe and especially to praise its exactness and its fidelity, which will not be any more subject to doubt than was the likeness of the portrait published by his friend Hume. Since it will contain many new pieces reworked or fabricated by our Gentlemen, great care will be taken to furnish them with titles that are more than adequate for a public which asks nothing other than to believe everything and which will think so belatedly of raising objections about their authenticity.

Rousseau

But how can this be! Won't the declaration by J.J. that you have just mentioned be of any use in protecting him from all these frauds; and regardless of what he may say will your Gentlemen have everything they please to print under his name pass without obstacle?

The Frenchman

More than that; they have found a way to turn even his disavowal against him. By printing it themselves, they derived an additional advantage for themselves, by publishing that when he saw his bad principles uncovered and recorded in his writings, he tried to exculpate himself by casting suspicion on their fidelity. Cleverly passing over the real falsifications in silence, they let it be understood that he accused of falsification passages everyone knows very well are not, and focusing all the attention of the public on these passages, they thus distracted it from verifying their infidelities. Suppose that a man says to you: J.J. says some pears have been stolen from him and he is lying, because he has all his apples, so nobody stole any pears from him. They reasoned exactly like that man, and using this reasoning they ridiculed his declaration. They were so sure about its lack of effect that at the same time they printed it, they printed also that supposed translation of Tasso just for the purpose of attributing it to him, and which they did attribute to him in fact without the least objection on the part of the public. As if this dry and choppy style of writing, without continuity, without harmony, and without grace were in fact his. So that according to them, at the same time as he protested against everything that would henceforth appear under his name or be attributed to him, he nevertheless published this twaddle not only without hiding, but very fearful of not being believed to be the Author, as shown by the mimicking preface they placed at the beginning of the book.

Do you believe that such a gross blunder, such an extravagant contradiction ought to open everyone's eyes and cause disgust for the impudence of our Gentlemen, carried here to the point of stupidity? Not at all. By regulating their maneuvers by the disposition into which they put the public and the credulity they gave it, they are far more assured of success than if they acted with more finesse. As soon as it is a question of J.J., there is no need to put either good sense or plausibility in the things that are uttered about him, the more absurd and ridiculous they are, the more eager people are not to doubt them. If d'Alembert or Diderot took it upon themselves today to affirm that he has two heads, everyone who saw him pass in the street tomorrow would see his two heads very distinctly, and everyone would be very surprised that they hadn't perceived this monstrosity sooner.

Our Gentlemen feel this advantage and know how to exploit it so well that in their most effective ruses they use maneuvers full of daring and impudence to the point of being unbelievable, so that if he learns about them and complains, no one wants to believe him. For example, when the honest printer Simon says publicly to everyone that J.J. comes to his place often to see and correct the proofs of these fraudulent editions they make of his works, who would believe that J.J. doesn't know the printer Simon and hadn't even heard of these editions when he hears this statement. And in another case, when his name is seen pompously displayed on the list of subscribers to deluxe editions of books, who now and in the future will imagine that all these supposed subscriptions are placed there without his knowledge or despite him, merely to give him an aura of opulence and pretentiousness which belie the tone he has adopted. And yet . . .

Rousseau

I know that is so, because he assured me he had subscribed only to one thing in his life, namely to the statue of M. de Voltaire.[133]

The Frenchman

Well, Sir, that sole subscription he made is the only one about which nothing is known. For the discreet d'Alembert who received it did not publicize it much. I understand very well that this subscription is less a matter of generosity than of revenge. But it is a revenge in the style of J.J. and one that Voltaire will not reciprocate.

You must feel from these examples that whatever he does and at whatever time, he cannot reasonably hope that the truth about him will emerge through the nets held tightly around him and in which he becomes more entangled as he struggles. Everything that happens to him is too far removed from the usual order of things ever to be believed, and his very protests will only attract to him reproaches of impudence and lying that his enemies deserve.

Give J.J. one piece of advice, perhaps the best one left for him to follow, surrounded as he is by traps and snares into which every step he takes can't fail to draw him. It is to remain immobile if he can, not to act at all*; to agree to nothing that is proposed to him under any pretext whatsoever, and to resist even his own impulses to the extent he can abstain from following them.[134] Under whatever advantageous aspect something to say or do presents itself to his mind, he should expect that as soon as he has the power to carry it out, it is because they are sure of

---

* I cannot allow myself to follow this advice as regards the just defense of my honor. Until the end I must do everything within my power if not to open the eyes of this blind generation at least to enlighten one that is more equitable. All the means for doing have been taken away from me I know. But without any hope of success, all efforts possible even though useless are nonetheless my duty, and I will not stop making them until my final breath is drawn. *Do what you ought, come what may.*

being able to turn the effects against him and make it deadly for him. For example, to keep the public on guard against the falsifications of his books and against the pseudonymous writings that are circulated each day under his name, what appeared better and less subject to being used to his detriment than the declaration about which we just spoke? And yet you would be amazed at all that was obtained from this declaration for the very opposite effect, and he must have felt that himself in the care taken to print it without his knowledge. For he surely couldn't have believed that this care was taken to give him pleasure. The Manuscript on the Government of Poland* which he undertook only because of the most earnest entreaties, with the most perfect disinterestedness, and for motives of the purest virtue, seemed only to honor its Author and make him respectable, even if this writing had been nothing but a tissue of errors. If you knew by whom, for whom, why this writing was solicited, the use to which it was eagerly put and the distortion they were able to give it, you would feel perfectly how desirable it would have been for the Author that, resisting all cajoling, he had refused the lure of this good work which, on the part of those who solicited it so insistently, had as a goal only making it pernicious for him. In short, if he knows his situation he must understand, however little he thinks about it, that any proposition being made to him, whatever color it is painted, always has a purpose that is being hidden from him and would prevent him from consenting to it if this purpose were known to him. He must feel above all that the motive of doing good can only be a trap for him on the part of those who propose it, and a real means for them to do harm to him or through him in order to impute it to him later on. That having placed him in a position where he can do nothing useful for others or for himself, he can no longer be offered such a motive except to deceive him. And finally, that no longer able in his position to do any good, the best thing he can

---

* That Manuscript fell into the hands of M. d'Alembert perhaps as soon as it left mine, and God knows what use he made of it. Count Wielhorski[135] informed me when he came to say good-bye on the occasion of his departure from Paris that horrible things about him had been put in the Holland gazette. From the way he said it, I judged when I thought about it again that he believed I was the Author of the article and I have no doubt that d'Alembert had something to do with this affair, as well as with that of a certain Count Zanowisch, a Dalmatian, and of an adventurous Polish priest who tried a thousand times to gain entry to my house. The maneuvers of this M. d'Alembert no longer surprise me; I'm completely used to them. I assuredly can't approve of Count Wielhorski's behavior with respect to me. But aside from this article which I won't endeavor to explain, I always regarded and still do regard this Polish Lord as a decent man and good patriot; and if I had the whim and the means to place articles in Gazettes, I would surely have more pressing things to say, things more important for myself, than Satires about Count Wielhorski. The success of all this scheming is a necessary effect of the system of behavior that is followed with respect to me. What could prevent the success of all that is undertaken against me, about which I know nothing, about which I can do nothing, and that everyone promotes?

do from now on is to abstain entirely from acting, for fear of doing harm without being aware of it or wanting to, as will inevitably happen every time he gives in to the entreaties of the people around him and who always have their lesson prepared about the things they should ask him. Above all, he should not allow himself to be moved by the reproach that he is refusing to do some good deed. Certain, to the contrary that if it were really a good deed, far from exhorting him to collaborate on it, everyone would unite to prevent him from doing so for fear of his getting credit for it and of something in his favor resulting from it.

By the extraordinary measures taken to alter and disfigure his writings and attribute to him others of which he never dreamed, you must judge that the object of the conspiracy is not limited to the current generation, for whom these efforts are no longer necessary, and since, with his books in front of their eyes approximately as he composed them, they did not take from them the objection that appears so obvious to you and me against the dreadful character being attributed to the Author. Since, on the contrary, his books have been ranked among his crimes, since the profession of faith of the Vicar has become a blasphemous writing, the *Heloise* an obscene Novel, the *Social Contract* a seditious book; since *Pygmalion* has been performed in Paris, despite him, for the express purpose of generating that laughable scandal that made no one laugh and about which no one felt the comic absurdity; finally, since these writings such as they exist have not protected their Author from defamation during his lifetime, will they protect him any better after his death when they will have been turned into the condition planned to make his memory odious and when the Authors of the plot will have had plenty of time to erase all traces of his innocence and of their imposture? Having taken all their measures, as foresighted and provident people who think of everything, would they have forgotten the assumption you make about the repentance of some accomplice, at least at the hour of death, and the inconvenient declarations that could result from that if they don't attend to it? No, Sir, you can be sure that all their measures are so well taken that there remains little for them to fear on that side.

Among the peculiarities that distinguish our century from all others is the methodical and consistent spirit that has guided public opinions for twenty years. Until now, these opinions meandered without order and regulation at the whim of men's passions, and these passions, continuously colliding, made the public go back and forth from one to the other with no steady direction. It is no longer the same today. Prejudices themselves have their progression and rules, and these rules to which the public is subject without suspecting of it are based solely on the views of those who direct it. Ever since the philosophic sect organized itself into a body with leaders, these leaders—who have become the arbiters of public opinion through the art of intrigue to which they have applied themselves—are through that the arbiters of the reputation and even the destiny of individuals and through them of that of the State. Their first attempt was made on J.J. and the enormity of its success, which must have astonished even themselves, make them feel how far their credit could extend. Then they had the idea of associating with powerful men in order to become arbiters of society with them, especially with those who, being inclined as they were to secret intrigues and underground plots, wouldn't fail often to encounter and divulge their own. They made them feel that by working together they could spread their roots so far under men's feet that no one would find safe footing any longer and would be able to walk only on countermined turf. They gave themselves principal leaders who—secretly directing all the public forces from their side based on plans agreed upon among themselves—make the execution of all their projects infallible. These leaders of the the philosophic conspiracy scorn it and are not esteemed by it, but common interest keeps them tightly united, because ardent and hidden hatred is the great passion of them all, and through a very natural coincidence, this common hatred has fallen on the same objects.* That is how our century has become the century of hatred and secret plots, the century in which everything acts in concert without affection for anyone, in which no one adheres to his party through attachment but rather through aversion for the opposite party; in which provided one harms something else, no one worries about his own good.

Rousseau

Yet it was among all these people full of hatred that you found such tender affection for J.J.

The Frenchman

Don't remind me of my wrongs. They were less real than apparent. Although all those conspirators fascinated my mind with a certain dazzling jargon, all those ridiculous virtues so pompously displayed were nearly as shocking to my eyes as they were to yours. I sensed in them a bragging that I didn't know how to unravel, and my judgment, subjugated but not satisfied, sought the clarifications you have given me, without knowing how to find them by itself.

---

* At this moment, France has just divided itself into two parties: one consists of the Court and the Duc de Choiseul who leads everything under the veil; the other of the city and the philosophers who direct public opinion. At the head of each of these two parties are my most implacable enemies. In general, any party man, by that alone an enemy of the truth, will always hate J.J. The French have no personal existence. They think and act only in groups; each one of them by himself is nothing. Now there is never any disinterested love of justice in these collective bodies. Nature engraved it only in the hearts of individuals

With the plots organized in this way, nothing was easier than to put them into execution by the means suited to that end. The oracles of Nobles always enjoy great credibility with the people. The only other thing done was to add an air of mystery to them in order to make them travel faster. In order to preserve a certain gravity, in becoming leaders of factions the philosophers gave themselves multitudes of little students whom they initiated into the secrets of the sect and whom they established as so many emissaries and perpetrators of secret iniquities. And using them to spread the blackness they invented and themselves pretended to want to hide, they thereby expanded their cruel influence into all ranks without exception even for the highest. To obtain the inviolable loyalty of their creatures, the leaders began by using them to do evil, just as Cataline made his conspirators drink the blood of a man, certain that through this evil in which they had been immersed, they would hold them bound for the rest of their lives. You have said that virtue unites men only with very fragile bonds, whereas the chains of crime are impossible to break. The experience of this can be felt in the story of J.J. Everything that was attached to him by the esteem and benevolence that his rectitude and the sweetness of his company must inspire naturally, dissipated forever at the first test or remained only in order to betray him. But the accomplices of our Gentlemen will never dare either to unmask them, whatever happens, for fear of being unmasked themselves, or to detach themselves from them, for fear of their revenge, being too well informed of what they know how to do to see it happen. Remaining thus united by fear to a greater degree than good men are united by love, they form an indissoluble body from which each member can no longer be separated.

For the purpose of using their disciples to prevail over public opinion and the reputation of men, they matched their doctrine to their views, they made their followers adopt the principles best suited to keeping them inviolably attached to them, whatever use they wish to make of them; and to prevent the directive of some importuning morality from coming into opposition with theirs, they undermined it at its roots by destroying all Religion, all free will, consequently all remorse, at first with some cautiousness through the secret preaching of their doctrine and then very openly, when they no longer had any powerful reprimand to fear. While appearing to disagree with the Jesuits, they aimed for the same goal nonetheless using roundabout routes by making themselves leaders of factions as they do. The Jesuits became all-powerful by exercising divine authority over consciences and in the name of God making themselves the arbiters of good and evil. The philosophers, unable to usurp the same

---

where it is soon extinguished by the spirit of conspiracy. One can imagine the equity that I, a poor isolated man, can expect from the public in the midst of all these cabals.

authority, worked hard to destroy it, and then while appearing to explain nature* to their docile sectaries and making themselves its supreme interpreters, they established themselves in its name as an authority no less absolute than that of their enemies, although it appears to be free and to govern wills through reason alone. This mutual hatred was at bottom a power struggle like that between Carthage and Rome. Those two bodies, both imperious, both intolerant, were consequently incompatible, since the fundamental system of each was to rule despotically. Each one wishing to rule alone, they could not share the empire and rule together; they were mutually exclusive. The newer, following more skilfully the bad habits of the other, supplanted it by corrupting its supporters, and through them was successful in destroying it. But it can already be seen advancing along its tracks with just as much audacity and more success, since the other always encountered resistance and this no longer encounters any. Its intolerance, more hidden and no less cruel, doesn't appear to exert the same rigor because it no longer encounters rebels. But if a few true defenders of Theism, of tolerance, or of morality were to reappear, one would soon see the most terrible persecutions directed toward them. Soon a philosophical inquisition more wily and no less bloody than the other would burn without mercy whoever would dare to believe in God.[136] I will not hide from you that deep in my heart I have remained a believer myself just as you have. On that subject, I think as J.J. does, that each person is naturally moved to believe what he wishes, and that a person who feels himself worthy of the reward of just souls, cannot prevent himself from hoping for it. But about this as about J.J. himself, I don't wish to profess loudly and uselessly feelings that would bring my downfall. I want to try to combine prudence with rectitude and make my true profession of faith only when I am forced to do so on pain of lying.

Now this doctrine of materialism and Atheism preached and propagated with all the ardor of the most zealous missionaries, does not have as its object only to make the leaders dominate their proselytes, but in the secret mysteries in which they use them, to fear from them no indiscretion during their life nor any repentance when they die. Their schemes after being successful die with their accomplices, whom they have taught above all things not to fear that Poul-Serrho of the Persians[137] in the next life, raised as an objection by J.J. to those who say that Religion does nothing good. The dogma of the reestablishment of the moral order in the next life used to redress many wrongs in this one, and the final moments of their accomplices were a risk that often served as a brake for the imposters.

---

* Our philosophers never fail to display the word *nature* pompously at the beginning of all their writings. But open the book and you will see the metaphysical jargon they have decorated with this fine name.

But when our philosophy released its preachers from that fear and their disciples from that obligation, it destroyed forever all last-minute repentance. What good are revelations that are no less dangerous than they are useless? If one dies, one has risked nothing according to them by remaining silent, and one risks all by speaking if one survives. Haven't you noticed that for a long time there has been no more talk of restitutions, reparations, reconciliations on the deathbed? That without repentance or remorse, all the dying fearlessly carry away in their conscience the well-being of someone else, the lie and the fraud with which they burdened it during their lifetime? And what good even for J.J. would there be in this supposed repentance of a dying man, whose belated declarations, stifled by those within earshot, even by the priests who would receive them—priests who have become philosophers like the others—would never reach the outside and become known by anyone? Don't you know that the confessors are bribed, that the doctors are accomplices, that all the conspirators spying on one another force others and are themselves forced to remain faithful to the plot, and that surrounded, especially at their death, none of them would find anyone to receive his confession, at least regarding J.J., who was not a false depository taking charge of it only in order to bury it in eternal secrecy. Thus all mouths are open to lying, while among the living and the dead none can be found any longer that opens for the truth. Tell me, therefore, what resource is left for him to triumph, even in time, over the imposture and show himself to the public, when all interests work in concert to keep it hidden and none favors its revelation?

Rousseau

No, it isn't for me to tell you that, you must do it, and my answer is written in your heart. Now it's your turn to tell me what interest, what motive altered your opinions from aversion, from the animosity even that was inspired in you for J.J. to such different feelings. After hating him so cruelly when you thought he was wicked and guilty, why do you pity him so sincerely now that you judge him innocent? Do you really think you are the only man in whose heart justice still speaks independently of all other interest? No, Sir, there are still some, and perhaps more than we think, who are more misled than seduced, who now behave through weakness and imitation as they see everyone else behave, but who—once they have returned to themselves—would act very differently. J.J. himself thinks more favorably than you do about several of those who approach him. He sees them, deceived by his so-called patrons, follow without knowing it the impressions of hatred, believing in good faith that they follow those of pity. There is in the public's attitude a magic illusion maintained by the leaders of the conspiracy. If they relaxed their vigilance for a moment, ideas led astray by their artifices would quickly return to their natural course, and the mob itself, opening its eyes at last and seeing where it had been led, would be amazed at its own aberration. That will happen sooner or later, whatever you may say about it. The question so cavalierly resolved in our century will be better discussed in another, when the hatred in which the public is maintained will no longer be fomented. And when in better generations this one has been valued at its true worth, the judgments they make will form the contrary prejudices: it will be a source of shame to have had its praise and a glory to have been hated. Even in this generation distinctions must still be made between the authors of the plot and its directors of both sexes plus the small number of their confidants initiated perhaps into the secret of the imposture, and the public who—deceived by them and believing him really guilty, yield without a scruple to everything they invent to make him more odious each day. The defunct conscience of the former leaves no room for repentance. But the aberration of the others is the result of a magic illusion that could fade away, and their restored conscience could make them feel this truth so certain and so simple: that the wickedness used to defame a man proves that he is not defamed because of his wickedness. As soon as passion and prejudice cease to be maintained, a thousand things that pass unnoticed now will strike all eyes. Those fraudulent editions of his writings from which your Gentlemen expect such a great effect will then produce the very opposite and serve to denounce them by making the perfidious intentions of the editors manifest even to the most stupid. His life, written during his lifetime by traitors while carefully hiding from him, will bear all the characteristics of the blackest libels. Finally, all the ploys that have him as their object will then appear for what they are. That says it all.

I don't doubt any more than you do that the new philosophers wished to prevent the remorse of the dying with a doctrine that put their conscience at ease, however burdened it might be, noting especially that the impassioned preaching of this doctrine began precisely with the execution of the plot and appears to be related to other plots of which this one is only a piece. But this infatuation with Atheism is an ephemeral fanaticism, a product of fashion that will be destroyed by it too; and the enthusiasm with which the people surrender to it shows it is nothing but a mutiny against its conscience, whose murmur it feels with resentment. This convenient philosophy of the happy and rich who build their paradise in this world cannot long serve as the philosophy of the multitude who are the victims of their passions, and who—for lack of happiness in this life— need to find in it at least the hope and consolations of which that barbarous doctrine deprives them. Men nurtured from childhood by an intolerant impiety pushed to fanaticism, by fearless and shameless libertinage; youth without discipline, women without morals,* peoples without faith, Kings without law, without a Superior whom they fear and free of any kind of limit, all the duties of conscience destroyed, patriotism and attachment to the Prince extinguished in all hearts, and finally no social bond other than strength: it seems to me one can easily foresee what must soon come of all that. Europe prey to masters taught by their own teachers to have no other guide than their interest nor any God besides their passions, at times secretly starved, at times openly devastated, inundated everywhere with soldiers,** Actors, prostitutes, corrupting books and destructive vices, seeing races unworthy to live be born and perish in its bosom, will sooner or later feel that these calamities are the fruit of the new teachings, and judging them by their deadly effects, will view with the same horror the professors, the disciples, and all those cruel doctrines which, conferring absolute empire over man to his senses and limiting everything to the enjoyment of this brief life, make the century in which they reign as despicable as it is unhappy.

Those innate feelings that nature has engraved in all hearts to console man in his misery and encourage him to virtue can easily, by means of art, intrigues, and sophisms, become stifled in individuals; but soon reborn in the generations that follow, they will always bring man back to his primitive dispositions, just as the seed of a grafted tree always reproduces the wild stock. This inner feeling that our philosophers recognize when it suits them and reject when it is inconvenient for them makes its way through the mistakes of reason, and cries out to all hearts that justice has another foundation than this life's interest, and that the moral order, about which nothing here below gives us any idea, has its seat in a different system that is sought in vain on earth but to which everything must someday return.*** The voice of conscience can no more be stifled in the human heart than that of reason can be stifled in the understanding; and moral insensitivity is as unnatural as madness.

* I have just learned that the current generation boasts particularly of its good morals. I should have guessed that. I have no doubt it also boasts of its disinterestedness, rectitude, frankness, and loyalty. Losing all idea of virtues to the point of mistaking the opposite vices for them is as far removed from virtues as it is possible to get. Besides, it is very natural that by dint of secret conspiracies and black plots, by dint of nurturing oneself on bile and gall, one loses the taste for true pleasures in the end. Once that of doing harm has been tasted, it makes one insensitive to all others. This is one of the punishments of the wicked.

** If I am fortunate enough to find at last one reader who is equitable albeit French, I hope he can understand at least this once that *Europe* and *France* are not synonyms for me.

*** *On the Utility of Religion.* Title of a fine book to be written, and a very necessary one. But this title cannot be worthily fulfilled either by a Churchman or a professional Author. It requires a man such as no longer exists in our days and will not be born again for a long while.

Therefore, don't believe that all the accomplices of an execrable scheme can always live and die in peace in their crime. When those who direct them no longer stir up the passion that animated them, when this passion has been sufficiently appeased, when they have caused its object to die in misery, nature will insensibly resume its empire.[138] Those who committed the iniquity will feel its unbearable weight when its memory is no longer accompanied by any pleasure. Those who witnessed it without getting involved but without recognizing it, recovered from the illusion that deceives them, will attest to what they saw, what they heard, and what they know, and pay homage to the truth. Everything has been set to work to anticipate and prevent this return. But that is in vain, the natural order is reestablished sooner or later, and the first to suspect that J.J. may well not have been guilty will be nearly convinced of it and, if he wishes, able to convince his contemporaries who, once the plot and its Authors no longer exist, will have no other interest than to be just and know the truth. It is then that all these monuments will be precious and that a fact that may be only an uncertain indicator now will perhaps lead to the evidence.

It is to that, Sir, that any friend of justice and truth can, without compromising himself, and must consecrate all the care in his power. Transmitting clarifications about this matter to posterity is perhaps preparing and fulfilling the work of providence. Heaven will bless, don't doubt it, such a just undertaking. Two great lessons, badly needed by the public, will result from it. The first is to have confidence that is less reckless, above all at another's expense, in the pride of human knowledge. The other is to learn through such a memorable example to respect natural right always and in all things, and to feel that any virtue founded on a violation of this right is a false virtue that infallibly hides some iniquity. Therefore I will devote myself to this work of justice in every way I can, and I exhort you to collaborate with me on it, since you can do so without risk and you have seen at closer range multitudes of facts that can enlighten those who will someday want to examine this matter. Quietly and at leisure, we can do our research, compile it, add our reflections, and following as much as possible the track of all these maneuvers, the vestiges of which we are already discovering, provide for those who will follow us a thread to guide them in this labyrinth. If we can confer with J.J. about it all, I have no doubt that we would obtain from him much enlightenment that will remain forever extinct, and that we would be surprised ourselves by the ease with which a few words from him would explain enigmas which will otherwise perhaps remain impenetrable through the skillfulness of his enemies. Often in my conversations with him, I have received from his own initiative unexpected clarifications about matters that I had seen very differently, for want of a circumstance I had not been able to guess and which gave them a whole different aspect. But being hobbled by my promises and forced to suppress my objections, in spite of myself I often rejected solutions he seemed to offer me, in order not to appear informed about what I was obligated to keep from saying to him.

If we unite to form a social group with him that is sincere and without fraud, once he is certain of our rectitude and our esteem, he will open his heart to us without difficulty; and receiving from ours the outpourings to which he is naturally so disposed, we will draw out the basis for precious memoirs whose value will be felt by other generations and which at least will enable them to discuss from all sides the questions that are now decided on the basis of his enemies' reports alone. The moment will come, my heart assures me of it, when taking up his defense—which is as perilous as it is useless now—will honor those who wish to undertake it, and cover them at no risk with glory as beautiful and pure as can be obtained by generous virtue here below.

The Frenchman

This proposition is entirely to my taste, and I consent to it with all the more pleasure because it is perhaps the only means in my power to make amends for my wrongs toward a persecuted innocent, without the risk of wronging myself. It isn't that the social group you propose is entirely without peril. The extreme attention paid to all those who talk to him even once will not be overlooked for us. Our Gentlemen have too clearly seen my repugnance to follow their wanderings, and to outwit as they do a man of whom they painted such dreadful portraits, for them not to at least suspect that having changed my language concerning him, I have in all likelihood changed my opinion too. For a long time already, despite your precautions and his, you are inscribed as suspicious on their registers, and I warn you that one way or another it won't be long before you feel that they have been paying attention to you. They are too attentive to everything that comes near J.J. for anyone to escape them. I especially, whom they admitted to their semiconfidence, am certain to be unable to approach the one who was the subject of it without worrying them a great deal. But I will try to behave without falseness, in a manner that will give them the least possible offense. If they have some subject to fear from me, they also have one to treat me with consideration, and I flatter myself that they know I am too honorable for them to fear betrayals from a man who never wanted to become involved in theirs.

So I don't refuse to see him a few times with prudence and precaution. It will be up to him alone to recognize that I share your feelings about him, and if I cannot reveal the mysteries of his enemies to him, he will see at least that being forced to be silent, I don't seek to deceive him. I will gladly cooperate with you to conceal from their vigilance and transmit to better times the facts they work to make disappear, and which will someday furnish powerful indications for obtaining knowledge of the truth. I know that his papers, entrusted at various times with more confidence than selectivity to hands he believed faithful, have all passed into the hands of his persecutors, who didn't fail to destroy those that might not suit them and modify the others at their whim, which they were able to do at will, fearing neither examination nor verification from anyone at all, especially not from people interested in discovering and revealing their fraud. If since that time there are still a few papers remaining with him, they are being watched in order to seize them when he dies at the latest; and given the steps taken, it would be difficult for any of them to escape the hands appointed to seize everything. The only way he has to preserve them is to entrust them secretly, if possible, into truly faithful and secure hands. I offer to share with you the risks of this trust, and I promise to spare no effort in order to have it appear someday for public viewing just as I received it, enlarged by all the observations I have been able to amass that tend to unveil the truth. That is all that prudence allows me to do for the sake of my conscience, for the interest of justice, and for the service of truth.

Rousseau

And that is also all he himself desires. The hope that his memory be restored someday to the honor it deserves, and that his books become useful through the esteem owed to their Author is henceforth the only hope that can please him in this world. Add to that the sweetness of seeing two decent and true hearts once again open themselves to his own. Let's temper in this way the horror of that solitude in which he is forced to live in the midst of the human race. Finally, without making useless efforts on his behalf which could cause great disorders and whose very success would no longer touch him, let's arrange for him the consolation for his final hour that his eyes will be closed by the hands of friends.

HISTORY OF
THE PRECEDING WRITING

I will not speak about the subject, object, or form of this Writing here. I did so in the introduction that precedes it. But I will say what it was intended for, what its destiny was, and why this copy is found here.

I spent four years on these dialogues, despite the heartache that never left me while I worked on them, and I was close to the end of that sorrowful task without knowing or imagining how to make use of it, and without resolving what I would at least try to do for that purpose. Twenty years of experience had taught me what rectitude and fidelity I could expect from those who surrounded me under the name of friends. Struck above all by the glaring duplicity of Duclos,[139] whom I had esteemed to the extent of entrusting my *Confessions* to him and who had used the most sacred trust of friendship only as an instrument of imposture and betrayal, what could I expect from the people placed around me since that time, all of whose maneuvers so clearly announced their intentions. Entrusting my manuscript to them was nothing other than wishing to hand it to my persecutors myself, and the way in which I was entangled left me no other means to approach anyone else.

In this situation, mistaken in all my choices and finding only perfidy and falseness among men, my soul—exalted by the feeling of its innocence and by that of their iniquity—rose up impulsively to the seat of all order and all truth, to seek there the resources I no longer had here below. No longer able to trust any man not to betray me, I resolved to trust uniquely in providence and to give to it alone the complete disposition of the deposit which I wanted to place in safe hands.

In order to do that, I imagined making a fresh copy of this writing and placing it in a Church on an altar; and to make this gesture as solemn as possible, I chose the high Altar of the Cathedral of Notre Dame, judging that everywhere else my deposit would more easily be hidden and misappropriated by the Curés or Monks, and would inevitably fall into the hands of my enemies; whereas it could happen that the noise of this action would bring my manuscript to the eyes of the King, which was the most favorable thing I could desire and which could never happen if I proceeded in any other way.

While I was working on the clean copy of my writing, I was meditating about the means for executing my project, which wasn't very easy, especially for a man as timid as I am. I thought that a Saturday, the day of each week when a motet is sung before the altar of Notre Dame leaving the Choir empty, would be the day when I would have the easiest time entering, reaching the Altar, and placing my deposit there. To plan my move more surely, I went several times at long intervals to examine the state of things and the disposition of the Choir and its accesses. For what I had to fear was to be detained in the passage, feeling certain that if I were, my project was ruined. Finally, with my Manuscript ready, I wrapped it and placed the following inscription on it.

DEPOSIT HANDED OVER
TO PROVIDENCE

"Protector of the oppressed, God of justice and truth, receive this deposit placed on your Altar and entrusted to your providence by an unfortunate stranger, alone, without support, without a defender on earth, insulted, mocked, defamed, betrayed by a whole generation, burdened for more than fifteen years at whim by treatment worse than death and by indignities unheard of until now among men, without ever having been able at least to learn the cause. All explanation is refused me, all communication is taken away, I no longer expect anything from men embittered by their own injustice except affronts, lies, and betrayals. Eternal Providence, my only hope lies in you. Deign to take my deposit into your care and place it in hands that are young and faithful, who will transmit it exempt from fraud to a better generation. Let it learn by deploring my lot how this generation treated a man without rancor and without disguise, the enemy of injustice but patient in enduring it, and who never did, nor wished, nor returned harm to anyone. No one has a right, I know, to hope for a miracle, not even oppressed and misunderstood innocence. Since everything must someday return to order, it suffices to wait. Therefore if my work is lost, if it must be given to my enemies and destroyed or disfigured by them, as seems inevitable, I will not count any less on your work, although I am ignorant of its time and its means; and having tried, as I must, my efforts to cooperate with it, I wait with confidence, I rely on your justice, and I resign myself to your will."

On the back of the title page and before the first page was written the following.

"Whoever you are whom Heaven has made the arbiter of this writing, whatever use you have resolved to make of it, and whatever opinion you have of the Author, this unfortunate Author implores you by your human pity and by the agonies he suffered in writing it, not to dispose of it until you have read the entire thing. Consider that this favor asked of you by a heart broken by sadness is a duty of equity that Heaven imposes on you."

With all that done, I took my package and went to Notre Dame on Saturday, February 24, 1776 at two o'clock, with the intention of presenting my offering there that same day.

I wanted to enter by one of the side doors through which I counted on going into the choir. Surprised to find it closed, I was going to enter further down through the other side door that leads into the nave. When I entered, my eyes were struck by a grill I had never noticed and which separated from the nave the part of the side aisles that surround the Choir. The doors of this grill were closed, so that the part of the side aisles I have just spoken of was empty and it was impossible for me to enter it. At the moment I perceived that grill, I was overcome by a dizziness like a man with apoplexy, and this dizziness was followed by an upheaval of my whole being such that I cannot recall suffering anything like it. The Church seemed to me to be so changed in appearance that doubting whether I was really in Notre Dame, I tried with difficulty to situate myself and better discern what I was seeing. In the course of my thirty-six years in Paris, I had come very often and at various times to Notre Dame. I had always seen the passage around the Choir open and free, and I hadn't even ever noticed a grill or a door, as far as I could recall. All the more struck by this unforeseen obstacle because I hadn't told anyone of my project, I believed in my initial transport that I was seeing Heaven itself collaborate in the iniquitous work of men, and the murmur of indignation that escaped me can only be conceived by a person who can put himself in my place, or excused by one who can read what is at the bottom of hearts.

I left this Church rapidly, resolved never to go back in my life, and surrendering completely to my agitation, I ran about for the entire remainder of the day, wandering everywhere without any idea where I was or where I was going until, unable to do more, weariness and night forced me to return home, dead tired and almost dazed with sadness.

Recovering little by little from this initial shock, I began to reflect more composedly about what had happened to me; and by that turn of mind that is peculiar to me—as quick to console myself about some misfortune that has occurred as to become fearful about a misfortune that is threatening—it was not long before I saw the lack of success of my attempt in a different light. I had said in my inscription that I was not expecting a miracle, and it was clear nevertheless that one would be necessary for my project to succeed. For the idea that my manuscript would reach the King directly and that this young Prince would take the trouble to read this long writing was, I said, so crazy* that I myself was amazed I had deluded myself with it even for a moment. Did I have any doubt that if even the uproar of my step had led to my deposit reaching the Court, it would only have been to fall not into the hands of the King but into those of my most malicious persecutors or their friends, and consequently to be either completely suppressed or disfigured according to their wishes in order to make it fatal for my memory? Finally, the ill success of my project—which had affected me so strongly—seemed to me on reflection a benefice from Heaven, which had prevented me from accomplishing a plan so contrary to my interests. I found it was a great advantage that my manuscript remained with me to be more wisely handled; and here is the use I resolved to make of it.

I had just learned that a man of letters with whom I had been acquainted for years, with whom I had had some connection, whom I had not ceased to esteem, and who spent much of the year living in the Country, had recently come to Paris. I considered the news of his return to be a direction from providence, which was showing me the true trustee for my Manuscript.[140] This man was, it's true, a philosopher, Author, Academician, and from a province whose inhabitants don't enjoy a great reputation for rectitude. But what did all those prejudices matter compared to a point so well established in my mind as his probity? The exception, all the more honorable for its rarity, only increased my confidence in him, and what more worthy instrument could Heaven choose for its work than the hand of a virtuous man?

I am resolved, then. I look for his residence. I finally find it but not without difficulty. I bring him my manuscript and hand it to him in a transport of joy, with a beating heart that was perhaps the most worthy homage a mortal can pay to virtue. Without knowing yet what it was about, he tells me on receiving it that he would make only good and honest use of my deposit. The opinion I had of him made this reassurance very superfluous.

Two weeks later, I return to his house, strongly persuaded that the moment had come when the veil of shadows kept over my eyes for twenty years was going to fall away, and that in one way or another, my trustee would give me the clarifications that seemed to me to follow of necessity from the reading of my manuscript. Nothing of what I foresaw happened. He talked to me about this writing as he would have talked about a literary work that I had asked him to examine in order to tell me his feeling about it. He spoke of transpositions to make to improve the order

* This idea and that of the deposit on the altar had occurred to me during the life of Louis XV, at which time it was a bit less ridiculous.

of my material. But he said nothing of the effect my writing had on him, nor of what he thought of the author. He proposed only to make a correct edition of my works, asking for my directions about that. This same proposition which had been made to me even with perseverance by all those around me made me think that their dispositions and his were the same. Seeing next that his proposition didn't appeal to me at all, he offered to return my deposit. Without accepting the offer, I asked him only to give it to someone younger than he, who might outlive me and my persecutors sufficiently to be able to publish it someday without fear of offending anyone. He particularly liked this last idea, and it seemed to me from the inscription he wrote for the outside of the package and which he shared with me that he took every care to see to it, as I had requested, that the manuscript would not be printed or known of before the end of the current century. As for the other part of my intention, which was that after that the writing was to be accurately printed and published, I don't know what he did to fulfill it.

Since then, I stopped going to his house. He has visited me two or three times which we have had trouble filling with a few indifferent words, since I have nothing more to say to him and he doesn't wish to say anything at all to me.

Without making a definitive judgment about my trustee, I felt I had missed my goal and that probably I had wasted my efforts and my packet. But I didn't lose courage yet. I told myself that my lack of success was due to my poor choice, that I had to be really blind and biased to place my trust in a Frenchman who was too jealous of his nation's honor to demonstrate its iniquity, in a man of letters, a philosopher, an Academician too jealous of that body's interest to unveil its turpitude; in an elderly man too prudent and too circumspect to become excited about justice and about the defense of an oppressed man. Had I looked purposely for the trustee least suited to fulfill my intentions, I couldn't have made a better choice. It's my fault, then, if I have succeeded so badly; my success is dependent only on a better choice.

Deluded by this new hope, I returned to transcribing and making a fair copy with renewed ardor. While I was attending to this work, a young Englishman who had been my neighbor at Wootton came through Paris on the way back from Italy, and came to see me.[141] I did what all unfortunates do who believe they see an explicit directive of fate in everything that happens to them. I said to myself: here is the trustee that providence has chosen for me. It is providence that sends him to me; it rejected my choice only to lead me to its own. How could I not have seen that it was a young man, a foreigner I needed, outside the shady dealings of Authors, far from the schemers in this country, without any interest in harming me and without passion against me? All that seemed so clear to me that, believing I saw the finger of God in this chance opportunity, I hastened to grasp it. Unfortunately, my new copy was not very far along, but I hastened to give him what was done, waiting for the following year to give him the rest if, as I had no doubt, the love of truth gave him the zeal to come back for it.

Since his departure, new reflections have cast doubts in my mind on the wisdom of this new choice. Neither in the manner in which this young man received my packet nor in everything he said when he left me did I find the tone of a man who felt the value of my confidence and who was touched by it. I knew he had connections with the conspiracy of which I am the object, I saw more cajolery than true feeling in the way in which he had behaved with me, and I accused myself of madness for having put my trust in an Englishman, a nation personally aroused against me and which has never been cited for any act of justice going contrary to its own interest. Besides, why had he come to see me? Why his mincing little attentions? Shouldn't that alone have made him suspect to me, and could I be unaware that for a long time no one approached me who wasn't sent expressly, and that putting my trust in the people around me is throwing myself to my enemies? In order to find a faithful confidant, I would have had to seek him far away among those I could not approach. My hope was therefore in vain, all my steps were false, all my troubles useless, and I could be sure that the least criminal use to which those to whom I had entrusted my deposit would put it was to destroy it.

This idea suggested to me a new attempt that I expected to have more impact. It was to write a kind of circular letter addressed to the French nation, make several copies of it and distribute them in parks and on the streets to those strangers whose faces most appealed to me. I didn't fail to argue in my usual manner in favor of this new resolution. I am allowed to communicate, I said to myself, only with people selected by my persecutors. Putting my trust in someone who approaches me is nothing but putting my trust in them. At least among the unknowns, there may be some who are of good faith, whereas whoever comes to my house comes only with bad intentions. I can be sure of that.

So I wrote my little writing in the form of a letter, and I had the patience to make a large number of copies. But in distributing it, I encountered an obstacle I had not foreseen in the refusal to receive it of those to whom I presented it. The address was: *To all Frenchmen who still love justice and truth.* I hadn't imagined that with this address anyone would dare refuse it. Almost no one accepted it. After reading the address, all of them declared with an ingenuity that made me laugh in the midst of my sadness that it was not addressed to them. You're right, I told them, taking it back, I see very well that I was mistaken. That was the only frank statement I have obtained from any French mouth in fifteen years.

Rejected from this side too, I still didn't become discouraged. I sent copies of this note in reply to a few letters from strangers who wanted at all costs to come to my home, and I believed I was doing something marvelous by making my acquiescence to their whim contingent on a decisive reply to this same note. I gave two or three others to people who accosted me or came to see me. But all that produced only rigmarole and evasive replies, which showed me that their Authors were of a falseness that would pass all tests.

This final ill success, which ought to have added the finishing touch to my despair, did not affect me like the prior ones. By teaching me that there was no help for my lot, it taught me not to fight necessity any longer. A passage of *Emile* that I recalled made me return within myself and find what I had vainly sought outside.[142] What harm has this plot done to you? What of yourself has it taken away? What limb has it mutilated? What crime has it made you commit? So long as men don't extract from my breast the heart it contains in order to replace it while I am alive with that of an dishonest man, in what way can they alter, change, deteriorate my being? They make a J.J. that suits them in vain; Rousseau will remain the same always despite them.

Did I know the vanity of opinion only to place myself under its yoke at the expense of my peace of soul and my heart's repose? What does it matter to me if men want to see me other than as I am? Is the essence of my being in their looks? If they mislead and deceive the following generations concerning me, why should that, too, matter to me? I won't be there to be the victim of their mistake. If they poison and change into evil everything useful that the desire for their happiness made me say and do, the damnation is theirs, not mine. Taking with me the witness of my conscience, I will find consolation for all their indignities despite them. If theirs was an error of good faith, I could still pity them while pitying myself, and lament about them and myself. But what mistake can excuse a system as execrable as the one they follow toward me with indescribable zeal. What mistake can allow the same man to be publicly treated as a convicted scoundrel who is prevented with such care from learning at least what he is accused of? In the refinement of their barbarity, they have found the art of making me suffer a prolonged death while keeping me buried alive. If they find this treatment gentle, they must have souls of mire. If they find it as cruel as it is, Phalaris and Agathocles were more affable than they.[143] I was wrong, then, to hope to change them by showing them they are mistaken. That isn't the issue, and even if they are mistaken concerning me, they can't be unaware of their own iniquity. They aren't unjust and wicked toward me by mistake, but by will: they are like that because they want to be, and it isn't to their reason that one must speak, but to their hearts depraved by hatred. All the proofs of their injustice will only augment it. It is an additional grievance for which they will never forgive me.

But I was even more wrong to be affected by their insults to the point of falling into depression and almost into despair. As if it were in the power of men to change the nature of things and take away from me consolations of which nothing can divest an innocent man. And why then is it necessary to my eternal happiness for them to know me and do me justice? Doesn't Heaven have any other way to make my soul happy and compensate it for the ills they have made me suffer unjustly? When death has taken me out of their hands, will I know or worry about knowing what is still happening on earth concerning me? The moment the gate to eternity opens before me, everything on this side of it will disappear forever, and if I then remember the existence of the human race, from that very moment it will be for me only as though it already no longer exists.

So I've finally made up my mind completely. Detached from everything pertaining to the earth and the senseless judgments of men, I am resigned to being disfigured among them forever, without counting any less on the value of my innocence and suffering. My felicity must be of another order. It is no longer among them that I must seek it, and it is no more in their power to prevent it than to know it. Destined to be the prey of error and lies in this life, I await the hour of my deliverance and and the triumph of truth without seeking them any longer among mortals. Detached from all worldly affection and released even from the anxiety of hope here below, I see no hold by which they can still disturb my heart's repose. I will never repress the first impulse of indignation, transport, anger, and I no longer even try to do so. But the calm that follows this passing agitation is a permanent state out of which nothing can pull me anymore.

Extinguished hope stifles desire well, but it doesn't abolish duty, and I want to fulfill mine in my conduct with men until the end. I am excused henceforth from vain efforts to let them know the truth they are determined always to reject, but I am not from leaving them the means by which to return to it insofar as I am able; and this is the final use that remains for me to make of this writing. Ceaselessly multiplying the number of copies in order to place them in this way here and there in the hands of people who approach me would be a useless waste of my strength, and I cannot reasonably hope that of all the copies thus spread around there would be even one that would arrive in one piece at its destination. I will therefore limit myself to a single copy, which I will offer for reading to those of my acquaintances who I believe are the least unjust, the least biased, or who, although connected with my persecutors, seem to me nonetheless still to have some strength in their souls and to be able to be something on their own. All of them, I don't doubt it, will remain deaf to my reasons, insensitive to my destiny, as hidden and false as before. It is a fixed prejudice adopted universally and permanently, especially by those who approach me. I know all about this already, yet I still persist in this final resolve, because it is the sole means remaining in my power to collaborate in the work of providence, and to contribute to whatever I can. No one will lisen to me, experience has warned me of that, but it isn't impossible that there will be found someone who listens to me, and it is henceforth impossible for the eyes of men to be opened by themselves to the truth. That is enough to impose on me the obligation of trying, without hoping that it will succeed. If I am content to leave this writing after me, this prey will not escape the plundering hands that only await my last hour to seize everything and burn or falsify it. But if among those who have read me there were a single human heart or even one truly sensible mind, my persecutors would have labored in vain and soon the truth would shine through to the eyes of the public. The certainty that if this unhoped for happiness occurs, I will not be mistaken about it for a moment encourages me in this new attempt. I know in advance what tone everyone will adopt after reading me. This tone will be the same as before, ingenuous, wheedling, benevolent. They will pity me a great deal for seeing as so black what is so white, for they are all as innocent as Swans. But they will understand nothing of what I have just said. All those have judged in an instant, will not surprise me at all, and will annoy me very little. But if, contrary to all expectations, there is one who is struck by my reasons and who begins to suspect the truth, I will not remain in doubt for an instant about this effect, and I know the sure sign to distinguish him from the others even if he doesn't want to open himself to me. That is the one I will make my trustee, without even examining whether I should rely on his probity, for I need only his judgment to interest him in being faithful to me. He will feel that there is no advantage to himself in suppressing my deposit, that in giving it to my enemies he is only giving them what they already have, that he cannot, consequently, place great value on this betrayal not avoid sooner or later, because of it, the just reproach of having committed a vile act. Whereas in keeping my deposit, he always retains the option of suppressing it whenever he wants, and can one day, if rather natural revolutions change the dispositions of the public, do himself infinite honor and derive from this same desposit a great advantage of which he deprives himself by sacrificing it. If he has foresight and if he can wait, he must by reasoning well be faithful to me. I can go further. Even if the public persists in the same dispositions it has now concerning me, a very natural movement will still bring it sooner or later to want to know at least what J.J. would have said if he had been given the freedom to speak. Showing himself, my trustee would then say to them: so you want to know what he would have said. Well, here it is. Without taking my side, without wanting to defend my cause or my memory, by making himself simply my reporter, and moreover, remaining, if he can, of the same opinion everyone holds, he can still shed new light on the character of the judged man. For it is always a stroke added to his portrait to know how such a man dared speak of himself.

If among my readers I find this sensible man, disposed for his own advantage to be faithful to me, I am determined to give him not only this writing but also my *Confessions* and all the papers that remain in my hands, from which much enlightenment about my destiny can someday be drawn, since they contain anecdotes, explanations, and facts that no one other than myself can give, and which are the only keys to many enigmas which, without them, would forever remain inexplicable.

If this man cannot be found, it is at least possible that the memory of this reading, remaining in the minds of those who have done it, will rewaken in one of them someday some feeling of justice and commiseration, when, long after my death, the public delirium will begin to weaken. This memory can then produce in his soul some happy effect, which the passion that animates them prevents while I am alive. And nothing more is needed for the work of providence to begin. I will take advantage, therefore, of occasions to make this writing known, if I find any, without expecting any success from it. If I find a trustee whom I can reasonably ask to take it, I will do so, considering nonetheless my deposit as lost and consoling myself about it in advance. If I don't find any, as I expect, I will continue to keep what I would have given him, until at my death, if not earlier, my persecutors seize it. This destiny of my papers, which I see as inevitable, no longer alarms me. Whatever men do, Heaven will do its work in due time. I do not know when, by what means, or how. What I do know is that the Supreme Arbiter is powerful and just, that my soul is innocent, and that I didn't deserve my lot. That's all I need. Yielding henceforth to my destiny, no longer persisting in fighting against it, letting my persecutors dispose of their prey as they will, remaining their plaything without offering any resistance during the remainder of my aged and said days; abandoning to them even the honor of my name and my reputation in the future—if it pleases Heaven that they should dispose of it—without any longer being affected by anything regardless of what happens: this is my final resolution. Let men henceforth do everything they wish; after I have done what I must, they will torment my life in vain; they will not prevent me from dying in peace.

COPY
OF THE CIRCULAR NOTE WHICH IS SPOKEN OF IN THE PRECEDING WRITING

To all Frenchmen who still love justice and truth

Frenchmen! A nation that used to be loveable and gentle, what have you become? How you have changed for a wretched stranger, alone, at your mercy, without support, without defender, but who would not need one among a just people. For a man without [disguise] and without rancor, an enemy of injustice but patient in enduring it, who never did, or wished, or returned harm to anyone, and who has been for fifteen years thrown down and dragged by you in the mire of opprobrium and defamation, sees and feels himself burdened at whim with indignities unheard of until now among humans, without ever having been able at least to learn the cause. Is this, then, your frankness, your gentleness, your hospitality? Abandon the old name of *Franks*; it must make you blush too much. The persecutor of Job could have learned much from those who guide you in the art of making a mortal unhappy. They persuaded you, I don't doubt it, they even proved to you—as is always easily done by hiding from the accused—that I deserved these unworthy treatments, a hundred times worse than death. In that case, I must resign myself, because I don't expect or want any favor either from them or from you. But what I want and what I am owed at the very least, after such a cruel and infamous condemnation, is finally to be told what my crimes are, and how and by whom I have been judged.

Why must such a public scandal be an impenetrable mystery for me alone? What good are so many machines, ruses, betrayals, lies to hide from the guilty person his crimes, which he must know better than anyone if it is true that he committed them? And if, for reasons that are beyond me, continuing to deprive me of a right* of which no crminal has ever

---

* What man of good sense will ever believe that such a blatant violation of natural law and the right of nations[144] could ever have a virtue as its principle? If it is permissible to divest a mortal of his human status, it can only be after judging him, but not in order to judge him. I see many ardent executioners, but I have not glimpsed a judge. If these are the percepts of equity of modern philosophy, woe be under its auspices to the innocent and simple weak person, honor and glory to the cruel and cunning conspirators.

been deprived, you have resolved to flood the rest of my sad days with anguish, derision, and opprobrium, without wanting me to know why, without deigning to listen to my grievances, my reasons, my complaints, without even allowing me to speak,* I shall raise to Heaven, as my entire defense, a heart without fraud and hands pure of all evil, asking not, cruel people, that it seek my revenge and punish you (Ah, may it keep all unhappiness and error far from you!) but that it soon provide for my old age a better haven where your insults will no longer reach me.

J.J.R.

P.S. Frenchmen, you are being kept in a delirium that will not cease while I live. But when I am no longer here, when the paroxysm is past and your animosity, no longer stirred up, will allow natural equity to speak to your hearts, you will take a better look, I hope, at all the facts, statements, and writings people attribute to me while staying carefully hidden from me; at everything you have been led to believe about my character; at everything they make you do out of kindness for me. You will then be very surprised! And, less pleased with yourselves than you are now, I dare predict that you will find the reading of this note more interesting than it can appear to you today. When these Gentlemen, crowning all their good deeds have finally published the life of the unfortunate man whom they will cause to die of sadness, this impartial and faithful life they have been preparing for so long with such secrecy and care, before giving credence to their statements and their proofs, you will seek out, I assure myself, the source of so much zeal, the motive for so much care, the behavior above all that they maintained toward me while I lived. With this research done well, I declare my consent, since you wish to judge me without hearing me, to have you judge between them and me from their own production.

---

* Good reasons should always be heeded especially coming from an accused man who defends himself or an oppressed man who complains. And if I have nothing solid to say, why aren't I allowed to speak in freedom! It is the surest way to discredit my cause completely and justify my accusers fully. But as long as I am prevented from speaking or everyone refuses to listen to me, who can ever state without temerity that I had nothing to say?

NOTES

Pléiade	Jean-Jacques Rousseau. *Oeuvres complètes,* vols. 1–5. Paris: NRF-Editions de la Pléiade, 1959ff.
Bloom, I	Jean-Jacques Rousseau. *Politics and the Arts—Letter to M. d'Alembert on the Theatre.* Edited by Allan Bloom. Ithaca, NY: Cornell University Press, 1960.
Bloom, II	Jean-Jacques Rousseau. *Emile.* Edited by Allan Bloom. New York: Basic Books, 1979.
Butterworth	Jean-Jacques Rousseau. *Reveries of the Solitary Walker.* Edited by Charles E. Butterworth. New York: Harper & Row, 1979.
Masters, I	Jean-Jacques Rousseau. *The First and Second Discourses.* Edited by Roger D. Masters. New York: St. Martin's, 1964.
Masters, II	Jean-Jacques Rousseau. *The Social Contract, with Geneva Manuscript and Political Economy.* Edited by Roger D. Masters. New York: St. Martin's, 1978.

NOTES TO INTRODUCTION

1. Edmund Burke, "Letter to a Member of the National Assembly," in *Works,* vol. 3 (London: Henry G. Bohn, 1835), 306.

2. For an exception, see Ann Hartle, *The Modern Self in Rousseau's Confessions: A Reply to St. Augustine* (Notre Dame, Ind.: University of Notre Dame Press, 1983).

3. Ronald Grimsley, *Jean-Jacques Rousseau: A Study in Self-Awareness* (Cardiff: University of Wales Press, 1969), 233.

4. See Roger D. Masters, *The Political Philosophy of Rousseau,* (Princeton, N.J.: Princeton University Press, 1968), 208.

5. Parts of this discussion of the relationship between the *Confessions* and the *Dialogues* are from Christopher Kelly, *Rousseau's Exemplary Life: The "Confessions" As Political Philosophy* (Ithaca, N.Y.: Cornell University Press, 1987).

6. Michel Foucault, Introduction to *Rousseau Juge de Jean-Jaques*: Dialogues (Paris: Librairie Armand Colin, 1962).

7. He did know, or thought he knew, that the books were written by the same author. One of the major topics of the *Dialogues* is how to distinguish books written by Jean-Jacques from books falsely attributed to him or from books he might have plagiarized.

8. See Christopher Kelly, " 'To Persuade without Convincing': The Language of Rousseau's Legislator," *American Journal of Political Science,* May 1987, 321–335.

9. Burke, op. cit., 306.

10. See the *Letter to Beaumont* for Rousseau's comical defense against the charge that he disagrees with the doctrine of original sin.

11. The reference is to the Sermon on the Mount.

12. See Introduction to the Pléiade edition of the *Dialogues* (Pléiade, I, l–lv).

13. "The philosophes . . . thought of themselves as a *petite troupe*, with common loyalties and a comon world view. This sense survived all their high-spirited quarrels: the philosophes did not have a party line, but they were a party" (Peter Gay, *The Enlightenment: An Interpretation. The Rise of Modern Paganism* [New York: Knopf, 1966], 6). Among many other possible sources, see Arthur M. Wilson, *Diderot* (New York: Oxford University Press, 1972); Jean Starobinski, *The Transparence and the Obstacle* (Chicago: University of Chicago Press, 1988); and for England, Joseph Hamburger, *James Mill and the Art of Revolution* (New Haven, Conn.: Yale University Press, 1963).

NOTES TO NOTE ON THE TEXT AND ITS TITLE

1. For this and additional information on the manuscripts see *Oeuvres complètes*, vol. 1 (Paris: Bibliothèque de la Pléiade, 1958), 657, 1901–1905; and Hermine de Saussure, *Etude sur le sort des manuscrits de J.-J. Rousseau* (Neuchâtel: Editions H. Messeiller, 1974).

2. For examples of the alternative translations, see Charles W. Hendel, *Jean-Jacques Rousseau: Moralist*, vol. 2 (New York: Bobbs-Merrill, 1934), 313; and Peter France, *Rousseau "Confessions"* (Cambridge: Cambridge University Press, 1987), 17.

EDITORIAL NOTES TO *DIALOGUES*

1. "Here I am the barbarian because no one understands me." (Ovid, *Tristia*, verse 10). This verse served as the epigraph of Rousseau's *First Discourse*. Hence, its use here identifies the author with both his own earlier work and the Roman poet. The title page of the London manuscript also included the following "Table of Contents":

1. On the Subject and Form of this Writing.
2. Of the System of Conduct toward J.J. adopted by the administration with public approval—First Dialogue.
3. Of J.J.'s character and his habits—Second Dialogue.
4. Of the Spirit of his Books and Conclusions—Third Dialogue. (Pléiade, I, 1615)

2. This Prefatory Notice was written toward the end of 1775, i.e., about three years after Rousseau started to work on the *Dialogues* (Pléiade, I, 1616).

3. Rousseau here uses, for the first time, the word *sensible*, which usually means "sensitive," or moved by feeling and emotion. It is one of a group of words derived from *sens* (sense, sensation, or meaning). Later, Rousseau uses the word *sentiment*, which can mean either an emotion or an opinion held with passion. Throughout this translation, *sentiment* is rendered by "feeling" and *sensibilité* by "sensitivity." Other words derived from *sens* and the translations used are *sensible*

(palpable); *sensiblement* (palpably); *sentir* (the verb, to feel), and *sensitive* (which does not occur in the body of the *Dialogues* although it is used elsewhere by Rousseau).

4. Rousseau's state of mind obviously reflects the persecution and flight that followed his condemnation by the Parlement of Paris in 1762. Given his sensitive personality, such experiences as the stoning of his house at Môtiers, the break with Hume, and the implacable hostility of philosophes like Voltaire and Grimm, combined with the burning of his books in both Paris and Geneva, might well have appeared to be a general conspiracy. On some days, Rousseau was clearly at or over the limit today defined as paranoia. But it is also possible to see, in Rousseau's stance here, a key to his thought. See Jean Starobinski, "The Accuser and the Accused," *Daedalus* 107 (Summer 1978): 41–58.

5. Rousseau's fears of a universal plot against him led to frantic attempts to transmit the manuscript of the *Dialogues* to future generations. On February 24, 1776, his desperation was such that he tried to leave a copy on the altar of the Cathedral of Notre Dame in Paris, only to find the wrought-iron gate to the choir locked. He then gave a copy to the French philosopher Condillac, and—when panic convinced him that this was unlikely to succeed—Rousseau gave another manuscript to an English acquaintance, Brooke Boothby. These tormented efforts are described in detail in the "History of the Preceding Writing" (pp. 246–257). As Rousseau later put it in the *Reveries,* "I wrote my first *Confessions* and my *Dialogues* in a constant anxiety about ways to keep them from the rapacious hands of my persecutors in order to transmit them, if it were possible, to other generations" (First Promenade [Pléiade, I, 1001; Butterworth, p. 7]).

6. The following description of Rousseau's "ideal world" is of great importance. It presents his profound longing for direct or "transparent" human relationships, free from the "obstacles" imposed by civilized life. In the *First Discourse*, this longing was implicit in the praise of earlier times: "Human nature, basically, was no better, but men found their security in the ease of seeing through each other, and that advantage, which we no longer appreciate, spared them many vices" (ed. Masters, p. 37). For a fuller treatment of this theme in Rousseau's life and work, see Jean Starobinski, *The Transparence and the Obstacle* (Chicago: University of Chicago Press, 1988).

7. Rousseau's use of physics to illustrate human passions reflects the importance of Newtonian mechanics as a scientific foundation of his thought. Cf. Roger D. Masters, *The Political Philosophy of Rousseau* (Princeton, N.J.: Princeton University Press, 1968), 285–293.

8. On the difference between "love of self" (*amour de soi*) and "amour propre" (pride or vanity), see *Second Discourse*, note o (Pléiade, III, 219–220; Masters, I, 221–222); and *Emile*, Book IV (Pléiade, IV, 491–493; Bloom, II, 214–215).

9. Rousseau's description of the inhabitants of his "ideal world" corresponds closely to his image of his own character and personality. See *Reveries*, especially Promenade Five (Pléiade, I, 1040–1041; Butterworth, pp. 62–71), in which Rousseau describes his happiness on the Isle of Saint-Pierre in Lake Bienne.

10. It is instructive to compare this "sign" with that of Socrates: Plato, *Apology*, 38d–41a.

11. In the *Confessions,* Rousseau describes the period beginning with his authorship of the *First Discourse* as a period of "effervescence" (Pléiade, I, 351).

12. *Le Devin du village*, Rousseau's opera, was written and performed before the king at Fontainebleau in 1752.

13. Elsewhere, Rousseau remarked that his personality was transformed during the period of composing his major writings: *Confessions*, IX (Pléiade, I, 416–417).

14. On Rousseau's claim that his works could contribute to the "happiness of the human race," see *First Discourse*, Preface (Pléiade, III, 3; Masters, I, 33), and *Second Discourse*, Preface (Pléiade, III, 127; Masters, I, 97).

15. When Rousseau first came to Paris as a young man, he brought with him a system of musical notation that he thought would make his fame; for an account of the examination of the proposal by the Academy of Science, see *Confessions*, VII (Pléiade, I, 282–286).

16. Rousseau here provides evidence of his professional expertise in both poetry and music. The *Allée de Sylvie*, a play in verse, was composed at the Chateau of Chenonceau in 1746; the *Letter on French Music* caused a storm of protest when it was published in 1753 (because Rousseau's praise of Italian music was combined with a denunciation of French musical styles); the *Dictionary of Music*, begun in 1755, was published in 1767.

17. The musician was Gluck, who is generally considered to have created the modern opera as an artistic form after coming to Paris in 1774. Gluck was an admirer of Rousseau's—and especially of *Le Devin du village* (*The Village Soothsayer*) as a musical model for portraying the "natural accent" of human emotion (see Pléiade, I, 1626).

18. Rousseau here uses the word *moeurs*, which is notoriously difficult to translate. Derived from the Latin *mores*, the French word means both "morals" (in the sense of ethical standards) and "customs" (in the anthropologist's sense of a society's practices and habits). Throughout this translation, the word *moeurs* will always be rendered "morals" to preserve the element of evaluation implied in Rousseau's usage. The word *morale* will be translated as "morality."

19. The work to which this refers is probably *The Year Two Thousand Four Hundred and Forty* by Sebastien Mercier, who later wrote a defense of Rousseau, *De J. J. Rousseau considéré comme l'un des premiers auteurs de la révolution*. In the earlier work, Mercier predicts that posterity will revere all of Rousseau's works but only some of Voltaire's.

20. Guillaume Joly de Fleury was the Procureur Général, or attorney general, responsible for executing the writ against Rousseau after the publication of *Emile*.

21. The note to which Rousseau refers is in Book IV of *Emile* (Pléiade, IV, 544–545; Bloom, II, 250–51). In this note Rousseau attacks dueling as he had done at length in the *Letter to d'Alembert on the Theatre*. The supposed defense of murder consists of his claim that there are situations in which the laws are insufficient protection for life and honor. In such situations, a citizen "is the only interpreter and minister of the natural law."

22. On the "interior doctrine," see *Confessions*, Book IX (Pléiade, I, 468). Rousseau's treatment of this doctrine is analyzed in Leo Strauss, "On the Intention of Rousseau," in *Hobbes and Rousseau*, edited by Maurice Cranston and Richard S. Peters (Garden City, N.Y.: Anchor Books, 1972), 254–290.

23. The grave fault referred to is Rousseau's abandonment of his illegitimate children. For his account of this abandonment and its consequences, see *Confessions*, Book VIII (Pléiade, I, 356–359).

24. On Rousseau's attempt to bring his conduct into line with his principles and to act as an exemplary figure, see *Confessions,* Book VIII (Pléiade, I, 368). On the general importance of exemplary figures in Rousseau's thought, see Christopher Kelly, *Rousseau's Exemplary Life: The "Confessions" as Political Philosophy* (Ithaca, N.Y.: Cornell University Press, 1987).

25. The admission occurs in *Emile,* Book I (Pléiade, IV, 262; Bloom, I, 49): "He who cannot fulfill the duties of a father has no right to become one. Neither poverty nor labors nor concern for public opinion exempts him from feeding his children and from raising them himself. Readers, you can believe me. I predict to whoever has vitals and neglected such holy duties that he will long shed bitter tears for his offense and will never find consolation for it."

26. There is a surprising amount of truth to this claim. For an account of inquiries made by d'Holbach and Voltaire, see Pléiade, I, 1639–1640.

27. Elaboration on these events is given in the *Confessions,* Book XII.

28. The Spaniard asked to be permitted to set the castle on fire until the constable left. The constable was Charles, duke of Bourbon (1490–1527), who was conspiring against the French with Emperor Charles V.

29. Xenocrates was a follower of Plato who was famous for his austerity. His continence is referred to in the Profession of Faith of the Savoyard vicar. See *Emile,* Book IV (Pléiade, IV, 598; Bloom, II, 228). Xenocrates is also one of the people Rousseau claims would be an appropriate judge of the *Second Discourse* (Pléiade, III, 133; Masters, I, 103).

30. The reference is to *Don Quixote,* Part 2. Sancho Panza joined Don Quixote on his travels because he was promised rule over an island. Near the end of the novel some nobles pretend to make Pancho a governor as a joke. Sancho abandons his desires to rule but only after being an excellent governor in many respects.

31. Rousseau refers to the story of a servant who was condemned to death because of thefts that had in fact been committed by a magpie. Rousseau refers to the *Messe des Pies* (Mass of the Magpies); see Pléiade, I, 1652.

32. The cases of Grandier, Calas, and Langlade were well-known miscarriages of justice in 18th century France: each was wrongly put to death or tortured for a crime he did not commit.

33. In the Neuchâtel preface to the *Confessions,* Rousseau elaborates on amour-propre as a source of misunderstanding others and ourselves. We mistakenly attribute our own feeling to others and even misunderstand our own feelings (Pléiade, I, 1148). It is this error, characteristic of civilized humans, that the *Confessions* is meant to overcome. Cf. note 8.

34. The line is from Rousseau's play *L'engagement téméraire* (The Reckless Engagement), act 2, sc. 3. The play was written for the entertainment of Rousseau's employers, the Dupin family, and was neither published nor publicly performed during Rousseau's lifetime. Cf. Pléiade, I, 1655–1656.

35. In the *Confessions,* Rousseau says that he wished he could have been imprisoned on St. Peter's Island in Lake Bienne, rather than being driven from place to place. For the details of his stay on the island, see *Confessions,* Book XII (Pléiade, I, 637–646) and *Reveries,* Fifth Promenade (Pléiade, I, 1040–1049; Butterworth, pp. 62–71).

36. The two quotations, which Rousseau translates in the text, are from Menochius, *De praesumptionibus.*

37. Le Blond was the French consul in Venice when Rousseau was secretary to the ambassador. De Bernis was the ambassador to Venice in 1756. Choiseul became prime minister of France in 1758. In the *Social Contract*, Rousseau included a paragraph indirectly praising Choiseul, who unfortunately took the remark as criticism (see Masters, II, 147). Rousseau presents him as one of the chiefs of the conspiracy.

38. Lazarillo de Tormes is the hero of a picaresque novel by Hurtado de Mendoza (Pléiade, I, 768). Actually, the story is in the *Continuation of Lazarillo* (1620) by Jean de Luna; selections from the two works have frequently been published together.

39. The tutor in *Emile* is named Jean-Jacques. On Rousseau's tentative identification of himself with the tutor, see *Emile*, Book I (Pléiade, IV, 263–264; Bloom, II, 50–51). On Rousseau's identification with St. Preux, see *Confessions*, Book IX (Pléiade, I, 430).

40. During Rousseau's stay in England, his portrait was painted by Allan Ramsay. An engraving was made from it by Daniel Martin.

41. Rousseau regarded the portrait by Maurice Quentin de la Tour as the most accurate portrait of him. Ficquet made his engraving from this portrait. Lemoyne sculpted a bust of Rousseau in 1765. Rousseau's spelling of the artists' names is inexact (cf. Pléiade, I, 1663–1665).

42. The story of Panurge buying the sheep is from Rabelais.

43. It is thought that Rousseau is referring to a Doctor Tissot from Vaud (see Pléiade, I, 1666).

44. This discussion should be compared with the treatment of misanthropy in the *Letter to d'Alembert* (Bloom, I, 36–47).

45. When Diderot used the phrase "*Il n'y a que le méchant qui soit seul*" (Only the wicked man is alone) in his work *Le fils naturel*, Rousseau interpreted it as a direct criticism of his move from Paris (see *Confessions*, II; Pléiade, I, 455). This interpretation was all the more plausible because, at one level, *Le fils naturel* can be read as a roman à clef in which the character Clairville is Diderot, and Dorval is Rousseau; if so, Rousseau would have had every reason to be enraged by a work in which he had the role of the *fils naturel* (bastard son).

46. This passage shows some of the complexity of Rousseau's view of the relationship between naturalness and spontaneity. Here he indicates that only reflection allows for an accurate representation of the passions.

47. On the "new English book" and English materialism, see Pléiade, I, 1672. For Rousseau's response to materialism, see *Second Discourse*, Part I (Pléiade, III, 141–143; Masters, I, 113–116); *Emile*, IV, "Profession of Faith" (Pléiade, IV, 570–591; Bloom, II, 270–284).

48. The following discussion is one of Rousseau's most explicit accounts of moral and physical sensitivity. He at one time planned to write a work called *La morale sensitive ou le matérialisme du sage*. From this title it would seem that Rousseau rejected a simple materialism but also that he considered his own doctrine to be a refinement of materialism. For a description of the theme of this work, see *Confessions*, Book IX (Pléiade, I, 409–410).

49. *Robinson Crusoe* is the first book read by Emile. See *Emile*, Book III (Pléiade, IV, 455–458; Bloom, II, 184–188). Rousseau also cites the novel elsewhere in

connection with his own love of solitude and independence. See *Confessions,* Books VII and XII (Pléiade, I, 296, 644).

50. The argument of the *Second Discourse* or *Emile* implies that Rousseau is here discussing what is "natural" to humans who have left the state of nature. In *Emile,* Book I, he argues: "Natural man is entirely for himself. He is numerical unity, the absolute whole which is in relation only to itself or its kind" (Pléiade, I, 249; Bloom, II, 39). It is true, however, that Rousseau consistently argues that the sweetest human existence does take place in some sort of social condition like the "golden mean" between the state of nature and civil society described in the *Second Discourse* (Pléiade, III, 170–171; Masters, I, 150–151). In sum, as Rousseau says in *Emile,* "One must not confound what is natural in the savage state with what is natural in the civil state" (Pléiade, IV, 763–764; Bloom, II, 406).

51. The Fort of Kehl, on the Rhine opposite Strasbourg, was occupied several times by the French during the 18th century.

52. The Baron de Foeneste is a character in a dialogue by Agrippa d'Aubigné, *Les aventures du baron de Foeneste.* The baron, whose name means "appearance," is a pompous member of the court.

53. The "people in the Gospel" refers to Jesus, who says in the Sermon on the Mount, "Do not store up for yourselves treasure on earth, where it grows rusty and moth-eaten, and thieves break in to steal it. Store up treasure in heaven, where there is no moth and no rust to spoil it, no thieves to break in and steal. For where your treasure is, there will be your heart also" Matt: 6:19–21). Rousseau here links Christian concern for salvation with the more general corrupt civilized concern with the future.

54. For Rousseau's account of his childhood reading, see *Confessions,* Book I (Pléiade, I, 8–9).

55. The remark "set aside the facts" echoes the *Second Discourse,* in which Rousseau uses the same phrase to excuse the divergence between his account of the state of nature and the account of the first humans in the Bible (Pléiade, III, 152; Masters, I, p. 103).

56. This maxim should be compared with the maxim that summarizes the morality of the state of nature: "Do what is good for you with the least possible harm to others" (Pléiade, III, 157; Masters, I, 133).

57. This is a description of the inspiration that led to the composition of the *First Discourse.* The "unfortunate question" asked by the Academy of Dijon was "Has the restoration of the sciences and arts tended to purify morals?"

58. Rousseau chose the profession of music copyist when he withdrew from Parisian society after writing the *Second Discourse.* See *Confessions,* Book IX (Pléiade, I, 401–403). The rate of 10 sols a page was about 50 centimes, or half a franc.

59. Rousseau worked on *Daphnis and Chloe* in the mid-1770s (see Pléiade, II, 1165–1166).

60. Rousseau refers to the Reverend Daniel Malthus, father of the well-known economist, David Malthus.

61. On the importance of botany for Rousseau, see *Confessions,* Book XII (Pléiade, I, 641–642); *Reveries,* Promenade VII (Pléiade, I, 1060–1073; Butterworth, pp. 89–103), "Letters on Botany" (Pléiade, IV, 1151–1195); and the introduction to the *Botanical Dictionary* (Pléiade, IV, 1201–1210). In each case, Rousseau

insists that botany has nothing in common with medicine or other practical applications. For a useful discussion of the treatment in the *Reveries*, see Paul A. Cantor, "The Metaphysics of Botany: Rousseau and the New Criticism of Plants," *Southwest Review* 70 (Summer 1985): 362–380.

62. In 1747, while employed by the Dupin family, Rousseau took a chemistry course. He then compiled a set of notes called *Institutions chymiques* (Chemical Institutions).

63. On Mignot, a cook, see the note in Pléiade, I, 1687.

64. Rousseau is referring to his *Considerations on the Government of Poland*.

65. "Friends, keep yourselves from laughing" is from the beginning of *Ars Poetica* by Horace. Horace assumes that one cannot refrain from laughing when presented with monstrous, unnatural images. Rousseau took one of the epigraphs of the *First Discourse*—*"Decipimur specie recti"* (We are deceived by the appearance of right)—from the same work of Horace.

66. Rousseau refers to a concert at the Academy of Beaux Arts in Lyons on May 9, 1770, at which his music was performed without success. (Pléiade, I, 1691).

67. On the difference between submission to necessity and submission to the will of other people, see *Emile*, Book II (Pléiade, IV, 320–321; Bloom, II, 91–92).

68. After inserting this note in the manuscript, Rousseau apparently had second thoughts about it and wrote a new one (below), with the notation "note to substitute for the preceding one" (Pléiade, I, 1693–1694).

69. On Rousseau's object in writing *La Nouvelle Héloïse*, see *Confessions*, Book IX (Pléiade, I, 434–436).

70. On the natural tendency to flee rather than fight, see *Second Discourse* (Pléiade, III, 136, 166–171, 203; Masters, I, 107–108, 146–151, 195); *Confessions* (Pléiade, I, 401–403).

71. The *Confessions* stops with Rousseau's departure from Bienne in October 1765 (Pléiade, I, 656).

72. The modern examples of virtue are Archbishop Fénelon (1651–1715), the author of *The Adventures of Telemachus*, which plays an important part in Sophie's education in *Emile* (Pléiade, IV, 762; Bloom, II, 404), and Nicholas de Catinat, marshal of France (1637–1712). On Lord Marshal George Keith, see *Confessions*, Book XII (Pléiade, I, 595–605).

73. The Hippocrene is the fountain of the Muses, struck out of Mount Helicon by the winged horse, Pegasus.

74. Rousseau's claim about the destruction of his reputation from one generation to the next should be compared with the claim made by Socrates in Plato's *Apology*, 18a–e.

75. Both *The System of Nature* and *The Philosophy of Nature* were published anonymously in 1770. The former was written by the Baron d'Holbach and the latter by Delisle de Sales. The novel by Mme d'Ormoy is *The Misfortunes of Young Emily*.

76. The reference is to Jean-Joseph Dusaulx, a well-known Latinist, who published his correspondence with Rousseau in 1798. The manuscripts show, however, that Rousseau's fears were not justified (Pléiade, I, 1708).

77. Rousseau's term *(droit de la nature et des gens)* refers to the technical legal terminology of the 18th century. What we today call international law was then often called *droit des gens*; because such norms were related to the *consensus mundi*,

they were associated with natural law or natural right. On the use of this term, see Robert Derathé, *Jean-Jacques Rousseau et la science politique de son temps* (Paris: Presses Universitaires de France, 1950).

78. The two men are certainly Diderot and Grimm. For the beginning of Rousseau's quarrel with them, see *Confessions*, Books IX and X.

79. For Rousseau's account of his struggles with shame, see *Confessions,* Book II (Pléiade, I, 86–87).

80. The young woman who visited Rousseau was Charlotte Gussing, daughter of Sir Robert Gussing, the English ambassador to Petersburg. The French ambassador was the Marquis de Juigne.

81. "Inside and under the skin" is from Persius (*Satires*, III, 30). It is the epigraph of the *Confessions*. In Persius, the expression is applied to a man who regrets his departure from virtue.

82. On Rousseau's stay at Montmorency as the guest of the duc de Luxembourg, see *Confessions,* Book X. He wrote the first part of the *Confessions* in Wootton in 1766.

83. The Oratorians were an order founded in Italy and then established in Paris in 1611. They were allied with the Jansenists against the Jesuits. For the individuals Rousseau has in mind, see Pléiade, I, 1713–1714.

84. Bicêtre and les Petites Maisons were hospitals for the insane. The *Gazette* (or *Gazette de France*) was a weekly newspaper originally founded in 1631 under Richelieu's patronage, that provided quasi-official foreign and domestic political information.

85. The magistrate is Antoine-Raymond-Jean-Gaulbert-Gabriel de Sartine, Count d'Alby, who was Lieutenant-General of Police from 1759 to 1774 and Director of Publishing after 1763.

86. For the translation, see *Emile*, III (Pléiade, IV, 483; Bloom, II, 20).

87. *First Discourse* (Pléiade, III, 3; Masters, I, 33). The league (or Holy League) was the name of the Catholic party during the French Wars of Religion.

88. *Letter to Beaumont* (Pléiade, IV, 968). Rousseau has modified the text slightly. There is also a slight variation among the manuscripts of the *Dialogues*.

89. *Emile*, IV (Pléiade, IV, 676; Bloom, II, 343).

90. There are some manuscript variations in the numbering of the quotations from this point on; where differences between Rousseau's citations and the published text may be important, the variants are noted. The Paris manuscript numbers paragraphs separately even within a single quotation.

91. The editions of *Emile* also list "credulity."

92. The editions of *Emile* add "without occupation."

93. The editions of *Emile* read "threaten" instead of "frighten."

94. The editions of *Emile* read "in treating a sick person, one cures him."

95. The editions of *Emile* read "which become current" instead of "which are established."

96. The editions of *Emile* read "dispute" instead of "deny."

97. The editions of *Emile* read "fatal" instead of "harmful."

98. The editions of *Emile* read "help" instead of "helps." For the entire passage, see *Emile*, I (Pléiade, IV, 269–270; Bloom, II, 54).

99. The editions of *Emile* read "millions" instead of "thousands."

100. Pléiade, IV, 306; Bloom, II, 82. The passage is from Book II of *Emile*, not

Book I as the Frenchman claims here. It has some minor changes from the editions of *Emile*.

101. The passage is from Book II of *Emile*, not Book III as the Frenchman claims (Pléiade, IV, 279; Bloom, II, 131). The first section of the passage is a paraphrase of an earlier remark rather than a direct quotation. In *Emile*, the second sentence reads: "He will be inoculated, or he will not be, according to times, places, and circumstances." It is followed by an additional sentence: "It is almost a matter of indifference in his case."

102. The editions of *Emile* read "consult" instead of "look for."

103. The editions of *Emile* add "perhaps."

104. *Emile*, I (Pléiade, IV, 273; Bloom, I, 56).

105. In the editions of *Emile*, this list is in the reverse order.

106. *Emile*, II (Pléiade, IV, 310–311; Bloom, II, 85).

107. There are some minor differences between this quotation and the passage in the *Second Discourse* (Pléiade, III, 188; Masters, I, 173–174).

108. "Under the lure of freedom" is absent from the *Second Discourse*. (Pléiade, III, 112–113; Masters, I, 173–174).

109. The editions of *Emile* read "empires" instead of "States." See *Emile*, II (Pléiade, IV, 309; Bloom, II, 84).

110. *Emile*, IV (Pléiade, IV, 688; Bloom, II, 352).

111. The editions of *Political Economy* read "affairs" instead of "fleeting rumor."

112. "A hundred times" is absent from the editions of *Political Economy*.

113. The editions of *Political Economy* read "I consider him" instead of "he will be."

114. *Political Economy* (Pléiade, III, 271–272; Masters, I, 231).

115. For the text, see *Emile*, V (Pléiade, IV, 740; Masters, I, 231). The passage is in Book V of *Emile*, not Book IV as the Frenchman claims. In the editions of *Emile*, it reads: "Women of Paris and London, pardon me, I beg you. No locale excludes miracles, but I do not know of any; and if a single one of you has a truly decent soul, I understand nothing of our institutions."

116. *Nouvelle Héloïse* (Pléiade, IV, 633).

117. *Project of Perpetual Peace* (Pléiade, III, 573). The date, 1756, is absent from the *Extract*.

118. The editions of *Emile* read "nation" instead of "people."

119. Pléiade, IV, 411; Bloom, II, 153. Bloom's translation has been slightly altered here. Rousseau wrote the phrase "good natured people" in English.

120. The text of the *Social Contract* adds "than the prince."

121. The text of the *Social Contract* reads "republican government" instead of "republic."

122. *Social Contract*, III, vi (Pléiade, III, 410; Masters, II, 88). In addition to the two differences noted above, this passage has some variations of punctuation and word order from the text of the *Social Contract*.

123. For a list of Rousseau's works in their order of publication, see Roger Masters, *The Political Philosophy of Rousseau*, p. xi. It should be noted that the Frenchman is ignorant about the unpublished works such as the *Essay on the Origin of Languages* and *Confessions* (although he has heard of the latter). He is therefore silent about their place or lack of place in the system.

124. The second edition of *The Philosophy of Nature* (published in 1754) was burned in 1775. See note 75 above.

125. Earlier (p. 22), "Rousseau" referred to "Jean-Jacques" as having published 15 volumes. The Rey editions from 1769 and 1772 consisted of 11 volumes; the Duchesne edition consisted of 14 volumes (see Pléiade, I, 1631–1632).

126. Rousseau's motto—*"Di meliora piis, erroremque hostibus illum"* (Heaven grant a better lot to the pious and such madness to our enemies)—is from Virgil's *Georgics*, III, 513, not from the *Aeneid*.

127. The motto is from La Fontaine's fable "The Scythian Philosopher."

128. In fact, in La Fontaine's fable, the Scythian Philosopher addresses the lines to a Greek.

129. These two references concern actions of the French government that Rousseau believed were directed against him. In 1764, he had been asked to draft a constitution for Corsica. He considered seeking refuge there but then was deterred by (among other things) the French invasion in 1765. The port of Versoix, on Lake Geneva, was constructed by the order of the duc de Choiseul at the suggestion of Voltaire. It was intended to increase French influence over Geneva and was to be populated by refugees from Geneva.

130. This passage should be compared with Plato's *Apology*, 38c–42a.

131. Erostratos burned down the temple to Artemis at Ephesus—one of the Seven Wonders of the ancient world—in order to become famous; he is the classic example of the desire for notoriety.

132. Rousseau translates Tasso's Italian loosely into French. The original verse read:

> —*Gran fabro di calunnie adorne in modi*
> *novi. Che sono accuse, e paien lodi.*

The line is from *Jerusalem Delivered*, Book II, 447–449. Rousseau wrote a prose translation of parts of this book but not these lines.

133. In 1770, Rousseau asked to be among the contributors to a proposed statue of Voltaire.

134. Here Rousseau begins to suggest that the plot imposes on him a quasi-natural condition of inactivity.

135. Count Wielhorski commissioned Rousseau to write *Considerations on the Government of Poland*. For the details of this commission, see Pléiade, III, Introduction to *Poland*.

136. In the Preface to the *First Discourse*, Rousseau also argues that there is little difference between extreme partisans of the Enlightenment and earlier religious fanatics (Pléiade, III, 5; Masters, I, 33).

137. In *Emile*, Book IV (Pléiade, IV, 634–635; Bloom, II, 313–314), Rousseau discusses this bridge, at which Persians believed satisfaction must be given for misdeeds.

138. Compare *Social Contract*, II, xi (Pléiade, III, 391–393; Masters, II, 75–76).

139. Rousseau is referring to Charles Pinot Duclos, his most constant friend among the men of letters. *The Village Soothsayer*, the only one of Rousseau's works to be dedicated to an individual, is dedicated to Duclos.

140. The man referred to is Condillac, who left the manuscript of the *Dialogues* to his niece.

141. The young man was Brooke Boothby, whom Rousseau met during his stay in England.

142. The passage from *Emile* is perhaps the imagined scene in Book II (Pléiade, IV, 307–309; Bloom, II, 82–83).

143. Phalaris was a notoriously cruel tyrant from Agrigentum. Agathocles of Syracuse is one of Machiavelli's examples in his chapter of *The Prince* called "Of Those Who Have Attained a Principality through Crimes" (*Prince*, chap. 8).

144. Rousseau's phrase *droit des gens*—see note 77 above.

INDEX